N. Mac Lam

Seán O P. éocaio

CONSTITUTIONAL LAW

LONGMANS, GREEN AND CO. Ltd.
39 PATERNOSTER ROW, LONDON, E.C. 4
6 OLD COURT HOUSE STREET, CALCUTTA
53 NICOL ROAD, BOMBAY
36A MOUNT ROAD, MADRAS

LONGMANS, GREEN AND CO.
55 FIFTH AVENUE, NEW YORK
221 EAST 20TH STREET, CHICAGO
88 TREMONT STREET, BOSTON
128-132 UNIVERSITY AVENUE, TORONTO

CONSTITUTIONAL LAW

AN OUTLINE OF THE LAW AND PRACTICE OF THE CONSTITU-
TION, INCLUDING ENGLISH LOCAL GOVERNMENT, THE
CONSTITUTIONAL RELATIONS OF THE BRITISH EMPIRE AND
THE CHURCH OF ENGLAND

BY

E. C. S. WADE, M.A., L.L.M.

OF THE INNER TEMPLE, BARRISTER-AT-LAW

FELLOW OF ST. JOHN'S COLLEGE, AND LECTURER IN THE UNIVERSITY OF CAMBRIDGE ;
TUTOR, AND FORMERLY PRINCIPAL, OF THE LAW SOCIETY'S SCHOOL OF LAW

AND

G. GODFREY PHILLIPS, M.A., LL.B.

OF GRAY'S INN, BARRISTER-AT-LAW

SUB-LECTOR, AND SOMETIME SCHOLAR, OF TRINITY COLLEGE, CAMBRIDGE

LONGMANS, GREEN AND CO.

LONDON ◆ NEW YORK ◆ TORONTO

1931

Made in Great Britain

PREFACE.

HAVING regard to the number of existing books on the English Constitution some explanation must be offered to justify the appearance of yet another. Experience gained from teaching and examining both university and professional law students has persuaded the authors that there is a need for a single volume on the legal aspect of English government, containing as brief an account as is compatible with reasonable accuracy both of the organs of government and of the critical aspect of Constitutional Law, without neglecting either side of the subject. Such a book should also be of use to students reading for the Honour Schools of Modern History and Economics in Universities, and it is hoped that the layman who is interested in constitutional problems may find it helpful. It is assumed that the reader has some knowledge of Constitutional History. He should also read Professor A. V. Dicey's *Law of the Constitution* (8th edition). That work stands for all time as the classical work on the Constitution of its period (late Nineteenth Century). An attempt has been made in Part II. of this book to deal with the Supremacy of Parliament and of the Law (Dicey's " Parliamentary Sovereignty and the Rule of Law ") in the light of present-day tendencies.

The reader is advised closely to study the Table of Contents Arrangement so as to acquire at the outset an idea of the arrangement of of Book. the book. It will be seen that the Introduction gives a

v

skeleton of the organs of the Constitution : the Executive, the Legislature, and the Judiciary. Part II. deals with general principles ; a short description of legal powers and duties ; an account of the doctrine of the Separation of Powers ; the Supremacy of Parliament ; Ministerial Responsibility ; the Nature of the Royal Prerogative ; the Conventions of the Constitution ; and the Rule of Law. In connection with the last subject some constitutional aspects of the modern Law of Public Administration are considered.

Detailed discussion of Parliament, the Cabinet, the Government Departments, including their functions of special constitutional interest, and the Judiciary covers the next three Parts. Under the Judiciary remedies against the Crown are discussed. An outline follows of the Law of Local Government with emphasis on the relationship between the Central Government and the Local Authorities. This is followed by a chapter on the Judicial Control of Public Authorities. The position of the citizen in relation to the State in normal times as well as in what may be called civil emergencies comes next ; under this heading will be discussed rights in relation to personal liberty and property. The position of the Armed Forces of the Crown is dealt with under Part VIII., which includes a discussion of the Common Law powers of the Executive in times of insurrection. An attempt is made in Part IX. to describe the constitutional position of the Empire as a whole, and in particular the relationship between Great Britain and the Self-Governing Dominions. The final Part deals with Church and State.

No excuse is needed in 1931 for including Local Government Law in brief outline. It is impossible to describe the government of this country without indicating the large share of the work of internal administration which falls to local authorities, either directly or by way of delegation from the Central Departments. Space has not, however, on this occasion permitted adequate discussion of such organisations as Trade Unions or Professional Societies, like the General Medical Council and the Law Society, which have nevertheless a claim to inclusion in a book on the Constitution of to-day.

The difficulty of the subject of Constitutional Law to the student is enhanced by the lack of familiarity with Forms illustrating the rules of law described, particularly in relation to the Executive. To meet this difficulty Appendices A and C contain reproductions of a selection of official documents, which have purposely not been curtailed. The two lengthy documents in Appendix C relating to the Government of the Colony of Fiji are given verbatim, not only to illustrate the system of colonial government,—a matter of interest to the not inconsiderable number of university students destined for the Colonial Service,—but also to draw attention in those documents to the numerous features which are enacted replicas of rules of the English Constitution, the sources of which are not always readily accessible.

The authors have not attempted a standard work on Constitutional Law. No single volume could hold its contents. This consideration accounts for many intentional omissions, as for example Offences against the State. Other omissions would have been more numerous but for the advice and assistance of colleagues. They are indebted in particular to Mr. P. A. Landon, Fellow of Trinity College, Oxford, who has read and commented upon most of the work while still in manuscript; to Dr. A. D. McNair, C.B.E., Fellow of Gonville and Caius College, Cambridge, who has read the proofs of the more controversial chapters;

and to Mr. F. W. McCombe for his assistance with the compilation of the Appendices and for some helpful criticisms of Parts IV. and IX. Mr. W. Adams, Town Clerk of Saffron Walden, and Captain D. A. L. Wade, M.C., Royal Signals (of the Royal Engineer Board), have assisted with their expert knowledge of the subject-matter respectively of Part VI. (Local Government) and Part VIII. (Armed Forces of the Crown). The learned authors and editors of Keir and Lawson's *Cases in Constitutional Law* have kindly allowed references to that indispensable work. But the sole responsibility for the contents of the book rests with the authors jointly, though they have indicated in the Table of Contents those Parts which each has penned.

E. C. S. W.

G. G. P.

CAMBRIDGE, *February*, 1931.

In the absence abroad of my colleague the task of seeing the volume through the press has fallen to me. I desire to express my gratitude to my former pupil, Mr. P. C. F. Lawton, for his invaluable help in the preparation of the Index and Tables of Statutes and Cases; and also to Miss G. Barrett for her clerical assistance.

E. C. S. W.

TABLE OF CONTENTS.

NOTE.—Parts I., II., IV., VI., VII., and VIII. are contributed by Mr. Wade, who has also compiled the Appendices; Parts III., V., IX., and X. are by Mr. Phillips.

TABLE OF STATUTES.

STATUTES OF OTHER PARLIAMENTS.

TABLE OF CASES.

xvii

ABBREVIATION.

K. & L. = *Cases in Constitutional Law*, by D. L. Keir and F. H.
Lawson. (Clarendon Press, 1928.)

PART I.

INTRODUCTION.

Law of the Constitution, pp. 1-36, by A. V. Dicey (8th edition) (Macmillans).
English Constitutional History, Period V, Section K, by F. W. Maitland (Cambridge University Press).

ERRATA AND ADDENDA.

P. 36, l. 4 from end, *for* "*alterum*," *read* "*alteram*."

P. 66, l. 22, *for* "The King," *read* "The rule that the King."

P. 69, l. 4, *for* "this," *read* "the Prerogative in relation to the Established Church which depends upon the Reformation changes carried through by the King in Parliament."

P. 77, l. 4, *delete* "(2) he is not an alien enemy; and (3)," *read* "and (2)." *Add footnote*: "An alien enemy is not permitted to sue in an English Court; to this rule there are certain exceptions. See *Porter* v. *Freudenberg*, [1915], 1 K.B., at p. 880."

P. 82, l. 32, *for* "the Crown," *read* "Crown servants."

P. 112, line 7, *for* "value," *read* "annual value."

P. 138, l. 6 from end, *for* "has," *read* "may be given by resolution of the House."

P. 138, l. 2 from end, *for* "exercise," *read* "may be given."

P. 157, l. 13, *for* "consists," *read* "consist."

P. 184, ll. 3-4 from end, *for* "the majority of," *read* "some."

P. 267, ll. 21-22, *for* "Contributions," *read* "Grants."

P. 350, l. 4, *for* "the self-governing provinces of Canada," *read* "Canada Nova Scotia, and New Brunswick."

Pp. 354 at foot to 355 at top, *delete and read* "Responsible government was a sequel to the Durham Report of 1839. In 1848 Instructions were first sent to the Governor of Nova Scotia and to Lord Elgin in Canada." . . .

P. 374, l. 16, *for* "agreed," *read* "argued."

P. 384, l. 19, *after* "Bishops," *insert* "and."

P. 400, l. 6 of para. (2), *add* "The Sign Manual is a term applied to the execution by signature of instruments which require the King's own hand."

CHAPTER I.

DEFINITION AND SOURCES OF CONSTITUTIONAL LAW.

A.

What is Constitutional Law ?

THE task of the writer of an elementary book on Constitutional Law, who, as in the present case, assumes that his readers are acquainted with the salient features of Constitutional History, is to give an account of the legal aspects of government. It must be borne in mind that many of the rules and practices under which our system of government is worked are not part of the law of England in the sense that violation of them may lead directly to proceedings in a court of law. Nevertheless, such rules and practices are indispensable parts of the machinery of government.

Maitland postponed his answer to the question—what is Constitutional Law ?—until the end of his lectures, now published under the title of English Constitutional History. His theme was the Government of England from the earliest times until the (then) present day. But in a book which deals primarily with the law and practice of to-day, an attempt must be made at the outset to describe the subject-matter. It falls conveniently into two divisions : (1) the organs of the central and local government (structure), (2) the principal functions of those organs (function). A minute account of functions belongs more properly to a book on public administration. It must be confessed that law and administration cannot be separated by a clear boundary line. An illustration or two may serve to show the student what is meant by the distinction. Constitutional Law is concerned with the organisation of courts as well as with the duties of judges ; but rules of procedure for the conduct of cases in court are no part of Constitutional Law, save in so far as they relate to, *e.g.*, the right to trial by jury. Again the office of Secretary of State must be described and the functions of, *e.g.*, the Home Secretary, such as the preservation· of public order, examined. This introduces the Police Force, but stops short of requiring a knowledge of police regulations for the interrogation of suspected criminals.

Definition.　　Constitutional Law is then that body of rules which prescribes (*a*) the structure and (*b*) the functions of the organs of central and local government. Structure must necessarily be dealt with in full ; but only principal functions can be described in any detail in a work on general principles, lest the principles be lost in the mass of detail which surrounds the manifold activities of Government Departments and Local Authorities.

Sovereignty.　　The majority of writers, and among them are to be found Austin, Holland and Dicey, have stressed the notion of sovereignty in their definition of Constitutional Law. It is possible to appreciate the working of the Constitution without discussing the theory of sovereignty. We need to recognise only that all law is the product of social forces ; as lawyers, we require a sanction for law. We can assume that in all developed legal systems it is part and parcel of law. The sanction behind English Constitutional Law is sometimes supplied by the courts, sometimes less directly, but in all cases obedience is secured by the knowledge that undesired consequences, whether legal or political, will follow from non-compliance. Englishmen are correctly credited with a capacity for self-government, but they are impatient of analysis of their methods. Abstract questions of sovereignty or supremacy are repugnant to them. The State is accepted as a reality.

B.

Sources of Constitutional Law.

Some reference has already been made to those rules of 1. Law.
the Constitution which lack the direct force of law. These
extra-legal rules complicate the task of stating the sources
from which Constitutional Law is drawn. By sources are
meant here—though the term is sometimes used to indicate
the historical origins—the means whereby force and expression are given to law. A sufficient definition of law is
" a rule of civil conduct enforced by the courts." Such
rules fall into two categories :

General rules prescribed by legislation, that is by Acts of A. Legisla-
Parliament, or by the enactments of the many bodies in the tion.
State subordinate to Parliament, to which are entrusted the
task of legislating.

Rules to be deduced from the decisions of courts of B. Case-Law.
authority, *i.e.*, the Superior Courts of Record, with which
decisions the lawyer is acquainted in authoritative form only
through the medium of the Law Reports. These decisions
form the bulk of the Common Law. As legislation increases
in volume, and in the twentieth century the output of
legislation is stupendous, the tendency is to confine the
work of the courts more and more to the interpretation
of statute law.

Here then are the two sources of all law ; and it follows
that they are also the sources, though not exclusively so, of
Constitutional Law. The Bill of Rights, declaring in general
terms several important rules of law, *e.g.*, that taxation
may not be levied without the consent of Parliament, is an
example of Constitutional Law of the enacted type. Equally
so is the Parliament Act, 1911. The code of regulations
made by Order in Council under the powers conferred by
the Emergency Powers Act, 1920, to deal with internal
disturbance, is a good example of the delegated type of
enactment, the Home Office being the Department of State
which in practice draws up these regulations. An example
of a judicial decision is the *Case of Impositions* (1606),

2 St. Tr. 371 ; K. & L. 36, which defined the scope of the arbitrary power of the Crown to impose duties for the regulation of trade, or the modern case which decides how the discretionary powers of the Crown (the Royal Prerogative), are limited by a subsequent statute conferring similar powers ; *Attorney-General* v. *De Keyser's Royal Hotel, Ltd.* [1920], A.C. 508 ; K. & L. 325. Again it is a rule of the Common Law that the King cannot be sued in his own courts, a rule which enables Government Departments to a large extent to escape legal liability for the wrongful acts of their employees. This rule depends for its validity on the decisions of the courts.

2. Conventions. There are many rules and precepts to be mastered by men and women engaged in public life, as well as by students of Constitutional Law, which are not, at all events directly, part of the law of England, as enforced by the courts, Breach of such rules will not result in a civil action or criminal prosecution being directed against the offender. Dicey has named these rules Conventions of the Constitution. Can they properly be called law at all ? If the answer is, yes, he argues that they are a source of Constitutional Law. But it is unnecessary to regard them as more than **Dicey's View.** customary. The reader should refer to Dicey's *Law of the Constitution*, Part III., for the classic discussion on this question. Briefly the argument is as follows : a convention is not law in the sense that to violate it would be a breach of law ; but neglect to observe it must (*sic*) prevent the lawful conduct of the government of the country, and sooner or later involve public servants in breaches of the law proper which will result in legal proceedings being brought against them. These conventions are numerous.[1] To take one illustration—it is said that a Ministry when outvoted on any vital question in the House of Commons may appeal once to the electorate by means of a dissolution of Parliament, granted to the Prime Minister by the King. If the popular verdict is against it, a Ministry must resign, either at once or so soon as the inevitable defeat overtakes it in the newly

[1] Part II., Chap. IV.

elected House of Commons. If a Ministry continued to meet a hostile House of Commons when so defeated, it would sooner or later be refused the supplies of money essential for the maintenance of the public services. It would then be faced with two alternatives, either to do without the public services in question—a choice no Government has hitherto adopted—or to raise the money without the sanction of Parliament, in other words to act illegally. As Cabinet Ministers do not collect taxes in person, the result would be that the subordinate public servants charged with this duty would be required to act illegally, and an action for the recovery of the money paid would be available to the taxpayer against any collector of taxes who obeyed the orders of his superiors. So vital then is the observance of this convention that disregard of it would lead to illegalities, and therefore it is properly included in the sphere of Constitutional Law, though in actual fact the considerations which prompt its observance are much more political than legal. On the other hand there are conventions, the breach of which might pass unnoticed, save perhaps in the political columns of the Press, and would make no conflict with the ordinary law. No legal proceedings would follow the refusal of an individual Minister to retire from office when constitutionally he ought to do so.

Dicey's argument is nowadays regarded as fallacious. The effective sanction behind conventions is the force of public opinion. A Prime Minister resigns because public opinion, or the fear of it, prompts him to do so. He does not seek to avoid the dock or the pains and penalties of civil litigation, either for himself or his subordinates, when he tenders his resignation to the King. Nevertheless, conventions are part of Constitutional Law, which may be frankly admitted to include much that is based on custom alone. *The True Sanction to Conventions.*

This important subject will be discussed hereafter when the scope of the Royal Prerogative has been considered ; for these conventions are in the main rules for determining the exercise of the Prerogative, so as to ensure that in the long run effect shall be given to the will of the electorate which has placed the Government of the day in power. Enough has been said at this stage to justify the inclusion of conventions as a source of Constitutional Law. The epithet "un-constitutional" is applied to breaches of conventions as well as of law, meaning that public opinion condemns (or should condemn) the act.

3. Text-books.

Before leaving the subject of sources, reference must be made to text-book writers. The authority of a legal text-book as a source of law is confined to the extent to which it reproduces the law as enacted by the Legislature or decided by the courts. But the lack of interpretation of legislation and the absence of authoritative pronouncements by the courts on matters not covered by legislation are often remedied by the opinions of text-book writers, provided that their reputation stands high. And while these opinions are not law until accepted as such by the courts, nevertheless in the field of Constitutional Law the scope for pronouncement by text-book writers is larger than in any other branch of law with the exception of International Law. This is due partly to the presence of the conventions mentioned above as essential to the machinery of government, and partly to the fact that many of the problems of Constitutional Law are not in practice the subject-matter of litigation, even though they relate to law proper. Thus the duty of the Speaker of the House of Commons in regard to the certification of Money Bills is defined by the Parliament Act, 1911, but it is probably safe to predict that the courts will never be called upon to interpret these provisions. It is left to text-book writers to pronounce upon their effect. Far more reliance, then, may be placed upon text-books as a quasi-authoritative source than is the case, for example, with the law of contract. It must, however, be borne in mind that unanimity is not to be expected in the views expressed upon controversial topics. Nevertheless, such works as May's *Parliamentary Practice* or Anson's *Law and Custom of the Constitution*, or the critical accounts of the government of the country, such as that given in Bagehot's *The English Constitution*—a masterpiece in its day, and still in many respects not out of date—are consulted with a confidence which the practitioner of law cannot afford to give to text-books on branches of private law, where conclusions must be supported by the authority of a statute or a judicial decision.

Writers of text-books on the Constitution fall into three Historians. classes, namely, historians, political scientists, and lawyers, and a word of advice may usefully be uttered with regard to works by members of each class. In particular the historian is apt to stress the value of past experience. While it is not to be suggested that the past does not contain many lessons for the present, it is equally true that, for example, we can find little that is helpful in understanding the position and working of the present House of Commons in an historical account of the Witanagemot, or of the Commune Concilium Regni. On the other hand a clear appreciation of the seventeenth century constitutional struggle is an indispensable requirement for mastering the subject of the Royal Prerogative as it exists to-day.

The political scientist is naturally attracted by the Political possibility of deducing abstract principles in relation to Scientists. the science of government. But the task of the student of Constitutional Law is to master the nature and operations of the existing organs of government rather than to attempt generalisations.

Lawyers who attempt the task of depicting the law of Lawyers. the Constitution are handicapped by the unreality of many of the legal terms which they must of necessity employ. For example, it is a correct statement of law to say that the King is the fountain of justice, or that the King can do no wrong. Yet everybody knows that the King does not sit as judge in his own courts, and that illegal acts are sometimes done in the name of the King by his servants. But the lawyer may claim to be the safe guide to the student, provided that he gives sufficient prominence to the divergence between law and fact in the working of the Constitution.

The sources then of Constitutional Law are :   Summary of Sources.

(1) *Statutory*, *i.e.*, Acts of Parliament and the enactments of other bodies having power to legislate conferred on them by Parliament.

(2) *Judicial*, *i.e.*, the decisions of the High Court of Justice or of courts of higher authority.

(3) *Conventional, i.e.,* rules not having the force of law, but which can nevertheless not be disregarded since they are sanctioned by public opinion, and perhaps indirectly by law itself.

(4) *Advisory, i.e.,* the opinions of writers upon the Constitution.

CHAPTER II.

THE ORGANS OF THE CONSTITUTION.

THE purpose of this chapter is to introduce the student to the principal organs concerned with the central government of the country before embarking on a study of the general principles of the Constitution. Only the barest outline of the organs is given here ; detailed discussion of the structure of this part of State machinery occupies the three later Parts (III., IV. and V.). It is convenient here to remark that, although Parliament is the Parliament of Great Britain (England, Scotland and Wales), and Northern Ireland, and moreover is the so-called Imperial Parliament, the territorial sphere of government for the purpose of this book (except Part IX. dealing with the Empire as a whole) is more limited. The plan is to exclude all but England and Wales in discussing the functions of central and local government ; any departure from this plan will be indicated at the appropriate passages.

A word will be in place here as to the various functions Functions of of government, which it is usual to separate into three Government. divisions—executive, legislative and judicial. It is not always easy, if indeed possible, to determine under which head an act properly falls, but it is true to say that the organs which perform these functions are clearly distinguishable. This does not, however, mean that they may not in some respects trespass into each other's sphere or overlap.

The executive function includes the exercise of various Executive prerogative powers (of which patronage in relation to the Function. chief public offices, foreign affairs, and the summoning and dissolution of Parliament may be regarded as the most important), and the administration and execution of other powers conferred both by statute and the Common Law.

11

In the discharge of this function statutory powers predominate. The object of executive action is largely the direction of general policy, the maintenance of order and the promotion of social welfare. The initiation of legislation, though not strictly an executive function, is normally performed by the Executive.

Legislative Function. The legislative function requires the enactment, after proper scrutiny, of general rules of conduct, proposed in practice by the Executive ; there are types of legislation which it is difficult to regard as prescribing rules of conduct ; they may be said rather to record executive acts, such as a statute creating an office. In England the Legislature does not devote its whole time to consideration of the legislative programme. It is also the body which controls the exercise of executive power by maintaining the Executive in office through approval of its legislative proposals, endorsement of its policy in general and by criticising its administration ; it also performs certain judicial functions.

Judicial Function. The judicial function must be invoked by the subject or the Executive before it can be operated. It has the advantage of declaring what the law is, even after it has been promulgated by the Legislature and administered by the Executive. It is concerned with the application of the law with a view to its observance. Certain legislative and executive functions may also be performed by the Judiciary, such as the enactment of rules of court and the administration of estates of deceased persons.

Inasmuch as the legislative organ rarely in practice functions without the guiding hand of the executive body, it is better to describe the latter first.

The Executive is composed of :

(1) The King in Council.

The Executive. (2) The King's Ministers who are political officials in the sense that they are appointed by, and tender their resignations to, the King in accordance with the wishes of the electorate as manifested at the polls.

(3) The Civil Service and the Armed Forces of the Crown.

The King is the head of the Executive. His title depends on the Act of Settlement, 1701, as amended by the

Succession to the Crown Acts, 1705 and 1707. These enactments recognise the hereditary principle. The King is advised in all the important executive acts of government, not by his Privy Council in fact, but by his Ministers, the most important of whom as a rule act in a double capacity. They are the advisers of the Crown collectively (the Cabinet), and individually they are also responsible to the King and to Parliament for the conduct of a Department of State. A few Cabinet Ministers hold no office involving departmental duties, *e.g.*, General Smuts was a Minister without portfolio during part of the war periods, 1917-1919, but in practice some particular branch of governmental activity is usually entrusted to these. In the Ministry formed by Mr. Ramsay Macdonald in 1929, the Lord Privy Seal and the Chancellor of the Duchy of Lancaster, neither of whose departmental duties are important or arduous, were entrusted with the superintendence of the means to be devised to meet the unemployment problem. Ministers outside the Cabinet—and in recent times the Cabinet has contained about twenty members out of some sixty holding ministerial office—have their departmental duties to perform, but take no part collectively in the deliberations of the inner body. The Cabinet decides major questions of policy; the Departments carry out that policy by administering the law, superintending its execution or devising measures to be presented to Parliament for sanction as law. In routine matters questions of policy do not come before the Cabinet, but are decided by the Departments which in such matters in practice normally work independently of reference to the Cabinet.

The following was the composition of the Government in 1930 :— The Ministry.

Cabinet Ministers.

Prime Minister and First Lord of the Treasury.
Lord President of the Council.
Lord High Chancellor.
Lord Privy Seal.
Chancellor of the Exchequer.

Secretaries of State :—(1) Home Affairs.
                 (2) Foreign Affairs.
                 (3) Colonies.
                 (4) Dominions.
                 (5) War.
                 (6) India.
                 (7) Scotland.
                 (8) Air.

First Lord of the Admiralty.
President of Board of Trade.
Minister of Health.
President of Board of Education.
Minister of Agriculture and Fisheries.
Minister of Labour.
First Commissioner of Works.

Ministers not in the Cabinet.

Minister of Pensions.
Postmaster-General.
Minister of Transport.
Chancellor of the Duchy of Lancaster.
Attorney-General.
Solicitor-General.
Paymaster-General.
Civil Lord of the Admiralty.

Treasury :—Financial Secretary.
           Parliamentary Secretary.
           Junior Lords (5).

Under-Secretaries of State :—

    Home.
    Foreign.
    Colonial.
    Dominions.
    War (also a Financial Secretary).
    India.
    Air.

Parliamentary Secretaries :—

    Admiralty.
    Trade.
    Mines.
    Overseas Trade.
    Agriculture (and Deputy Minister of Fisheries).
    Transport.
    Labour.
    Pensions.
    Education.
    Health.

Assistant Postmaster-General.
Charity Commissioner.
Church Commissioner.

Scotland.

Parliamentary Under-Secretary of State.
Lord Advocate.
Solicitor-General.

In addition there are a few political appointments to offices connected with the Royal Household, such as the Treasurer, Comptroller and the Vice-Chamberlain.

The King is also an integral part of the Legislature. His assent is required to all Acts of Parliament; as, however, he only acts on the advice of his Cabinet, his assent has been a formality since the days when the principle of ministerial responsibility to Parliament became developed. A Ministry which has successfully piloted a measure through both Houses of Parliament will never, it may be assumed, advise His Majesty to withhold his assent to that measure becoming law. On the other hand the Royal Assent is sometimes withheld from legislation submitted by Colonial Legislatures, though not for many years has such a step been taken in the case of any of the Self-governing Dominions. *The Legislature. The King.*

The House of Lords.

The House of Lords consists of some seven hundred members, the bulk of whom hold their titles as hereditary *Houses of Parliament.*

peers of the United Kingdom. There are, however, about 130 holders of titles who are not members of the Upper House of Parliament, their peerages being those of Scotland or Ireland. The actual composition at the present time is as follows :—Peers of the United Kingdom,[1] Representative Peers of Scotland (16), and Ireland, Spiritual Peers (26), and Lords of Appeal in Ordinary (7).[2]

Powers of Lords.

It is important to notice that the powers of the House of Lords to reject measures which have been passed with the approval of the House of Commons are since 1911 governed by the provisions of the Parliament Act. Briefly, the power to reject Money Bills, as therein defined, is now non-existent. Other Public Bills, with the important exception of a Bill to extend the maximum duration of Parliament beyond five years, can only be delayed for a period of two years. The result of these provisions has been paradoxically to enhance the reputation of the Upper Chamber as a serious debating assembly, despite the reduction of its legislative power. Nevertheless, it is still an active member of the Legislature ; particularly it is adapted to dealing with measures of first-class importance which have no political significance. Only a small proportion of those entitled to take their seats play a regular part in its deliberations, but these, with few exceptions, are men of eminence in some walk of public life.

House of Commons.

The House of Commons consists of 615 Members of Parliament, all of whom are elected by ballot ; with the exception of the twelve University Members, the election is on a universal adult suffrage.

DISTRIBUTION OF MEMBERS.

	Counties.	Boroughs.	Universities.	Total Members.
England . . .	230	255	7	492
Wales and Monmouth	24	11	1	36
Scotland . . .	38	33	3	74
N. Ireland . .	8	4	1	13
Total . .	300	303	12	615

The Seventh Parliament of King George V. and the fourth Parliament of Great Britain and Northern Ireland was

[1] 683 in 1928. The number varies through new creations and extinctions through failure of heirs entitled to succeed.
[2] For fuller details of the House of Lords, see Part III., Chap. I.

elected in May, 1929. The composition of the parties was as follows :—

Labour	-	-	-	287
Conservative	-	-	-	260
Liberal	-	-	-	59
Independent	-	-	-	9

The party having an actual majority is entitled to form a Ministry. In recent years the presence of three distinct political parties seeking the confidence of the electorate at General Elections has resulted in the leaders of a party holding ministerial office without that party obtaining a clear majority of seats, and, therefore, of supporters in the Commons over the other two parties. The great advantage of the two party system is to assure the Government of the vigilant criticism of the Opposition which is waiting to succeed them, and under it minority government is impossible.

The King is in theory the head of the Judiciary. His Courts are as follows :— The Judiciary.

APPELLATE TRIBUNALS.

(1) THE HOUSE OF LORDS.—The Lord High Chancellor, seven Lords of Appeal in Ordinary, together with such Lords of Parliament as are holding, or have held, high judicial office.

The House of Lords in its judicial capacity is the final Court of Appeal from the Court of Appeal in England and Wales, the Inner House of the Court of Session in Scotland and the Court of Appeal in Northern Ireland.

(2) JUDICIAL COMMITTEE OF THE PRIVY COUNCIL.—This consists of the Lord Chancellor, the Lord President of the Council and former holders of these two offices, the seven Lords of Appeal in Ordinary, the Lords Justices of Appeal (the judges of the Court of Appeal) and such other members of the Privy Council as shall from time to time hold, or have held, high judicial office, together with judges from the Dominions and India.

The composition of the Committee is governed by statute. Its jurisdiction is to hear appeals and references by the Crown from the overseas parts of the British Empire, subject

to certain statutory restrictions.   It is also the highest court
in ecclesiastical and prize matters, and the Crown has power
to refer to it general matters by way of special reference.

SUPREME COURT OF JUDICATURE.

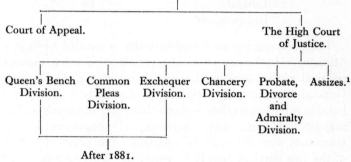

Court of Appeal.

The High Court
of Justice.

Queen's Bench   Common   Exchequer   Chancery   Probate,   Assizes.[1]
Division.   Pleas   Division.   Division.   Divorce
                 Division.   and
                                                     Admiralty
                                                     Division.

After 1881.

Queen's Bench Division (now King's Bench Division).

The above form the Superior Courts of Record.[2]

Civil Courts (before Judicature Act, 1873).

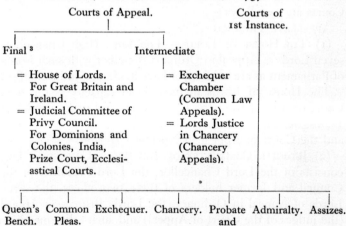

Courts of Appeal.

Courts of
1st Instance.

Final [3]   Intermediate

= House of Lords.   = Exchequer
   For Great Britain and   Chamber
   Ireland.   (Common Law
= Judicial Committee of   Appeals).
   Privy Council.   = Lords Justice
   For Dominions and   in Chancery
   Colonies, India,   (Chancery
   Prize Court, Ecclesi-   Appeals).
   astical Courts.

Queen's   Common   Exchequer.   Chancery.   Probate   Admiralty.   Assizes.
Bench.   Pleas.   and
                                            Divorce.[4]

[1] See Judicature (Consolidation) Act, 1925, S. 70 (4).

[2] For a full account of the Civil and Criminal Courts, see Part V.,
Chap. I.

[3] These courts remain unaltered to-day, except that the House of
Lords no longer hears appeals from that part of Ireland which forms the
Irish Free State.

[4] After 1857.

CHAPTER III.

THE NATURE OF THE CONSTITUTION.

THE brief account of the organs of government which has The Constitution has an existence. been given in the last chapter is only intended to serve as a guide to those who may be unacquainted with the machinery of central government in England, so that in the ensuing discussion of general principles references to those organs may be readily understood. Such an account, which is no more than a catalogue, tells the enquirer nothing as to the law under which the Constitution works. It has been seen that there are four sources of Constitutional Law, of which only two, the Common Law and the Statute Book, are legal in the technical sense. The extent to which custom, or convention, may be regarded as law is debatable, while the fourth source, the opinions of text-book writers, is not binding law at all, though extremely useful in ascertaining what is the state of the law. Just as these four sources supply Constitutional Law, so they give expression to all law, whether it regulates the rights and duties of citizens *inter se* or in relation to the State. This is often regarded as proof that the Constitution has in fact no separate existence, since it is part of the ordinary law of the land. It is true that there is no special source giving expression to the rules of the Constitution in the form of a code which is unalterable save by the act of a special constituent assembly or a reference specifically to popular vote. This does not mean that we have no Constitution but only a mass of miscellaneous rules. Such a view is clearly untenable in a country where constitutional action is respected more than in any other country, and constitutional means are accepted, even by the most ardent reformers, as the only practical way of achieving their aims.

Of what then does the Constitution consist ? When in the late eighteenth century the United States of America framed their constitution, close definition of the powers of government was regarded as all important and was embodied in a formal document, unalterable save by a process which differed entirely from the limited means of enacting ordinary legislation. The provision of a constitutional code is a *sine quâ non* of every new State ; the principal States of the world have adopted constitutions in the form of definite and comprehensive enactments during the last hundred and forty years. Great Britain is still without a constitution in this sense. Those statutes which are properly regarded as part of Constitutional Law are not sections of a code. If a collection were made of all the extant enactments (from the Coronation Charter of Henry I. to the present day), which deal with the form and functions of government, the result would present a most imperfect description of the Constitution. Moreover these enactments can each and all of them be repealed by the simple expedient of an Act of Parliament, unlike formal constitutions, which, expressed to be more or less immutable, contemplate no radical changes, and can only be varied by processes more cumbersome than that of amending ordinary statutes. Such a collection from the English statute-book reveals that in most cases the provisions were declaratory of the existing Common Law. Not even the Bill of Rights, 1689, makes any pretension to enact a Constitution. It was rendered necessary by the fear that future Kings of England might repeat the mistakes of the Stuarts in not recognising that the Common Law was changing. For the Stuarts did not so much act illegally, as fail to realise that the law was gradually developing.

It is the Royal Prerogative which to a large extent supplies the answer to the question. Curtailed though they are by statutes, the prerogative powers of the Crown are to-day the guarantee of the recognition of constitutional principles. The process of evolution, whereby those powers from being the weapon of Kings have become the means of giving effect to the public will, is the important feature of later constitutional history. All this depends upon custom, conventions, understandings, and not on strict law.[1]

The surest evidence that the English Constitution has an existence is to be found in its reproduction in other parts of the Empire in the shape of a formulated code. Early colonial constitutions conferring representative government reproduced only the framework; apart from special requirements of federation, this is mainly true of the Acts of Parliament which establish the form of government for the Federal Dominions. But some conventions are found enacted. The latest important unitary constitution, that of the Irish Free State, has gone much further by making statutory even the doctrine of ministerial responsibility. The English Constitution does exist in the shape of defined principles capable of enactment, but likely to lose much of their utility if reduced to formal rules of law. Only in the sphere of administration of internal services have these principles to any considerable extent already been reduced to statutory form.

It is capable of enactment.

But, although the Constitution depends largely on principles which are definite, these principles are not unalterable. Its strength lies undoubtedly, not in its apparent susceptibility to change, but in its permanence which has resisted, without outward changes of form, such convulsions as were seen in England in the seventeenth century, and even to-day in many of those countries governed by systematic and logical codes. For over two hundred years the Constitution has been adapting itself to new conditions, usually a little behind the trend of informed contemporary opinion, with the result that there has been a complete change almost imperceptible at any given stage so gradual has been the process of evolution from the personal supremacy of the monarch to the collective ascendency of the political executive—a change which has been marked by the retention of existing forms and organs. Much of the structure is now mere form; it is tolerated

It is alterable.

---

[1] Chap. I. (above), and Part II., Chap. IV.

because in practice it functions quite differently. The framework has been empirically constructed, in marked contrast both to the carefully devised machinery of continental governments and to the federal provisions of the constitutions of the United States, Canada and Australia.

Is the Constitution, therefore, flexible?

Many writers, and notably Dicey,[1] speak of the Constitution as flexible, in contrast to the rigidity of a code. The term is not, it is submitted, a happy one. It conveys the idea of instability, whereas what is wanted is a word conveying the idea of evolution and development. Metaphors are unreal when applied to so unique a growth as that of the Constitution, but perhaps grafting on the original trunk conveys the most accurate description. The trunk is of great antiquity. The fruit, which the tree, stimulated by the process of grafting, now produces, has changed and will change, so long as the grafting continues. The serious objection to this metaphor lies in the ominous use to which the term, graft, has been put in modern political life. No such sense is here intended.

[1] *Law of the Constitution*, pp. 122-3.

PART II.

GENERAL PRINCIPLES.

Law of the Constitution, by A. V. Dicey.
 Part I.—The Sovereignty of Parliament.
 Part II.—The Rule of Law, Chaps. IV., XI. and XIII.
 Part III.—The Connection between the Law and the Conventions
  of the Constitution.
Principles of British Constitutional Law, by C. S. Emden (Methuen).
Some Historical Principles of the Constitution, by K. Pickthorn (Philip
 Allan & Co.).
How Britain is Governed, by Ramsay Muir (Constable).

INTRODUCTION.

THIS part of the book is concerned with (1) a statement of orthodox principles, interspersed with (2) some criticism of those principles. Many of the rules of law mentioned in this Part will be discussed in greater detail in succeeding chapters. For example the full treatment of the present law and custom of Parliament is postponed, though some references are here made to parliamentary procedure, especially in Chapter III. (The Legislative Supremacy of Parliament). *Scope of Discussion.*

Under the title, Legal Powers and Duties, it is shown that the duty of the official does not differ in legal character from that of the ordinary individual who holds no office in the public service, though naturally the powers of the former are more extensive. These powers are classified and illustrated, and the extent to which they can be controlled by the courts stated. *(1) Legal Powers and Duties.*

Chapter II. deals with the time-honoured doctrine of the separation of executive, legislative and judicial powers, and the extent of its application to the English Constitution. On this subject there are differences of opinion. There are those who maintain that such separation of functions does exist in England, and ought to be preserved so as to ensure that the executive function may not be swollen by increase of powers from the other two spheres of government. The opposite and newer school of thought denies its application at any time, so far as separation of executive and legislative functions are concerned, except perhaps for a few years at the beginning of the eighteenth century, but on the whole, agrees that the judicial function is, and ought to be, kept separate. The extent to which the complexity of public *(2) Separation of Powers.*

25

administration leads to judicial (as well as legislative) power being vested in the administrative organs has, it is generally admitted, made it increasingly difficult to say with confidence that any rigid line of separation now exists, while it is argued that co-operation more aptly describes the relationship between the Executive and Legislature—co-operation in which the Executive is the predominant partner.

Legislative Power of Parliament.

The position of Parliament as the law-making organ is examined in Chapter III. (1) The history of parliamentary supremacy from the seventeenth century struggle to the Reform Act, 1832, is summarised; (2) the legal supremacy of Parliament in modern times is discussed and attention is drawn to the limitations on this supremacy, which in fact restrict its scope and subordinate it, except on rare occasions, to the dictation of the Government of the day, in which is vested the power of governing.

The Royal Prerogative.

The subject of the Royal Prerogative again involves some consideration of history (Chapter IV.). It is difficult for the student to realise how wide the extent of prerogative power still is, notwithstanding its curtailment in certain all-important directions by the Revolution Settlement of 1689 and succeeding years. In the exercise of prerogative powers conventions or constitutional understandings play their most prominent part. Thus alone is it possible to claim that the real use of the Prerogative is to ensure that the Executive shall act in the long run in accordance more or less with public opinion. It has long been established that the plea, Act of State, cannot succeed under cover of alleged prerogative right to protect officials from the consequences of unlawful action. The chapter closes with a discussion of the cases which establish this check on executive discretion.

Act of State.

Supremacy of Law.

Under the title, Supremacy of Law, the Rule of Law as propounded by Dicey is examined and the principal objections to its acceptance summarised (Chapter V.). Here, too, there is necessarily room for differences of opinion. The legal position should be kept clear. Every act must be authorised by law, whether Common Law or statute. The implication from this, namely that the legality of the act can be

questioned in a court of law, has been weakened by modern
devices for widening the limits of lawful discretion, so as
to exclude the intervention of the courts. The lawyer sees
here obvious dangers of bureaucratic tyranny ; the civil
servant replies that he must have wide discretionary powers
to enable him to execute the policy of the State entrusted to
his administration. It is, therefore, necessary to include
some account of the constitutional aspects of the law of Constitu-
public administration, so that the student may appreciate tional Aspects of Law
how far and by what means legislative and judicial power has of Public
already passed into the hands of the permanent officials of Administration.
the central and local authorities, and what safeguards
exist for checking abuse of power. A note on *Droit
Administratif* and a suggestion for improving the means
of deciding disputes in administrative matters are included.
This part of the book closes with some observations on
recent tendencies of constitutional development (Chapter
VII.).

CHAPTER I.

LEGAL POWERS AND DUTIES.[1]

It is now desirable to discuss the powers and duties alike of citizen and public servant. The powers of the Legislature will be dealt with under the heading of Parliament; members of Parliament, as such, do not individually exercise governmental power. The two Houses of the Legislature possess (*inter alia*) privileges which are recognised by the courts so far as they are confined to enabling each House to control the conduct of its business, including the behaviour of its members, when engaged in their duties in the House to which they belong. For example, a member of the House of Commons was suspended by the House for five days in July, 1930, for the offence of removing the Mace—the emblem of the Speaker's authority—from the table of the House of Commons, and this exercise of judicial power was, of course, perfectly lawful. The members of the Executive and the Judiciary individually wield power, and their duties bring them into direct relation with the law administered in law courts.

Powers and Duties of the Citizen.

It is important for the reader to appreciate that, whether an act be the act of a private individual or of a public servant, its legality will, as a general rule, be tested according to the ordinary principles of the law of contract, tort or crime. It must, however, be realised that public servants exercise a great many powers under statutory authority. Nothing which a statute expressly authorises can be an illegal act.

[1] After reading this chapter, reference should be made to Part VI., Chap. IV. (The Courts and Public Authorities), and to Keir and Lawson, *Cases in Constitutional Law*, pp. 125-44. For a discussion of the Theory of Governmental Powers and Duties, see Stephen's *Commentaries* Vol. IV., pp. 249-60 (19th edition).

It will be well to explain first the position of the ordinary citizen who holds no public office. If A. B. has the power to do an act which is likely to, and actually does, affect the rights of his neighbour, C. D., he must be able to justify his act, if need be, in a court of law. He must exercise his power in the manner prescribed by law, and for the purpose for which the law has sanctioned the power. Suppose that A. B., inconvenienced by a branch of C. D.'s tree, overhanging his garden, wishes to remove the branch, he must first consider his legal position. Having satisfied himself that he is permitted by law to remove the branch, he must then consider whether the law only permits him to do it in a particular way. Can he, if he wishes, enter his neighbour's garden for the purpose ? Again it may be that he is under a duty to exercise his power. This consideration does not arise in this particular example.

The same considerations arise when a person in whose presence a crime is committed arrests the offender. The difference is that in the latter example the power is connected with his duty as a member of the public. It is the duty of every man to assist in quelling a breach of the peace, if called upon to aid a constable. If A. B., instead of being a private citizen, holds a public office, *e.g.*, collector of taxes, or justice of the peace, the same principles apply with regard to his official acts.

Public Duties of Private Citizen.

From what has been said in the first chapter it is clear that to justify the exercise of power in the eyes of the law, the power must be shown to have originated either from statute or from the Common Law. Equally the particular manner in which the power is exercised and the question of the obligatory nature of the power are matters to be referred to the same sources. The tax collector must be able to show, if need be, that Parliament, or a body entrusted by Parliament with the levying of taxation, has conferred the power to collect taxes on holders of his office ; further, he must collect them only in accordance with certain statutory rules ; he is liable for failure to perform his duties, and the courts will enforce that liability. In other words, by accepting office he comes under a duty to collect taxes, exercising his

Justification of Official Acts.

powers in the manner allowed by law. The same is true of
the justice of the peace. He is a member of the Judiciary
with in addition certain executive powers of an administrative nature. He holds a public office empowering him by
virtue of the Summary Jurisdiction Acts, 1848 and 1879, to
deal judicially with certain offences within limits strictly defined by Parliament. He is also under a duty to exercise
those powers if called upon to do so, and the law will
control him, if need be, by removal from office or by process
in the courts compelling him to exercise his powers.

**Royal
Prerogative.** One of the chief Common Law powers which concerns the
student of the Constitution is the Royal Prerogative, whereby
the servants of the Crown are empowered to do certain acts
without parliamentary authority. The courts may enquire
into the scope of the Royal Prerogative, but not into the
discretion exercised under that power.[1]

**Statutory
Powers.** Statutory powers are innumerable ; the examples here
given illustrate administrative, legislative and judicial powers
entrusted to the Executive or separate Government Departments.

1. Special Constables Act, 1914, S. 1 (1).

**Legislative
Power con-
ferred on the
King in
Council.** His Majesty may, by Order in Council, make regulations
with respect to the appointment and position of special
constables . . . and may, by those regulations, provide—
(*a*) that the power to authorise the nomination and
appointment of special constables . . . may be exercised
although a tumult riot or felony has not taken place or is
not immediately apprehended ; and
(*b*), (*c*), (*d*), (other purposes for which the regulations may
be made) ;
and (*e*) for such supplemental and ancillary matters as
may be necessary or expedient for the purpose of giving full
effect to the regulations.

2. Trade Boards Act, 1909, S 11 (1).

**Legislative
Power con-
ferred on a
Department.** The Board of Trade may make regulations with respect to
the constitution of Trade Boards which shall consist of
members representing employers and members representing
workers . . . in equal proportions and of the appointed

---

[1] The term, Royal Prerogative, is used throughout of the Common
Law, as opposed to the statutory, powers of the Crown and its servants.
Some authorities prefer to use the term of all powers of the Crown
which are not possessed by the ordinary citizen.

members. Any such regulations may be made so as to apply generally to the constitution of all Trade Boards, or specially to the constitution of any particular Trade Board or any particular class of Trade Boards.

S. 19. Regulations made under this Act shall be laid as soon as possible before both Houses of Parliament, and if either House within the next forty days after the regulations have been laid before that House resolve that all or any of the regulations ought to be annulled, the regulations shall, after the date of the resolution, be of no effect, without prejudice to the validity of anything done in the meantime thereunder or to the making of any new regulations. If one or more of a set of regulations are annulled, the Board of Trade may, if they think fit, withdraw the whole set. *Parliamentary Control illustrated.*

The difference between legislation by Order in Council and legislation by a Minister is one of form, not of substance. In both cases the content of the legislation is framed by the Department.

3. Diseases of Animals Act, 1894, S. 22.

The Board (now Ministry) of Agriculture may make such orders as they think fit, subject and according to the provisions of this Act, for the following purposes or any of them. *Administrative Powers conferred on a Department.*

[Here follow thirty-seven purposes relating to the prevention or checking of disease. Some of these are in the nature of legislative powers; others relate to administrative acts, pure and simple.]

4. Road Traffic Act, 1930, S. 81 (1).

Any person (here follow five categories of persons who may be aggrieved by the decisions of traffic commissioners or certifying officers) may within the prescribed time and in the prescribed manner appeal to the Minister of Transport. *Judicial Powers conferred on a Minister.*

(2) On any such appeal, the Minister shall have power to make such order as he thinks fit (including an order revoking a licence), and any such order shall be binding upon the commissioners or certifying officer.

In the case of the provision in the Roads Act, 1920, S. 14 (3), which is replaced by the above section, it was further enacted that:

An order made by the Minister . . . shall be final and not subject to appeal to any court, and shall, on the application of the Minister, be enforceable by writ of Mandamus.[1]

The chief feature of statutory powers is that they are governed by the *ultra vires* doctrine. There is more than *Ultra vires doctrine.*

---
[1] Part VI., Chap. IV.

one aspect of this doctrine. For example (1) a person (or body) upon whom the power is conferred acts illegally if he exceeds that power ; *Attorney-General* v. *Fulham Corporation* [1921], 1 Ch. 440. The Borough Council of Fulham arranged to benefit the housewives of the borough by installing a municipal laundry with the latest contrivances worked by corporation officials. Under the Baths and Wash-houses Acts, 1846 and 1847, the Council had power to establish a wash-house, where people could wash their own clothes. A ratepayer tested the question whether the new laundry was *intra vires* this power and sought by an injunction to restrain the Corporation from conducting the laundry as a business. It was held that the statutory power was confined to the establishment of a wash-house and that it was *ultra vires* for the Fulham Corporation to wash the clothes itself, that is, by its servants. Thus were the women of Fulham deprived of the benefit of an up-to-date municipal laundry and restricted to the methods prevailing in the forties.

(2) An authority may be given by Parliament the power to legislate. If it exceeds this power, the statutory regulation will be void. If, for example, the Ministry of Labour under S. 11 (1) of the Trade Boards Act, 1909 (*above*), made regulations in respect of an improperly constituted trade board, those regulations would be *ultra vires*.

If a statutory order or regulation, which is to have effect as if enacted in the Act conferring the power to make regulations, is laid before Parliament before it comes into operation, and Parliament by resolution of both Houses expressly approves the draft regulation, or refrains from annulling it within the time specified, the *ultra vires* rule cannot be invoked ; *Institute of Patent Agents* v. *Lockwood* [1894], A.C. 347 ; K. & L. 10.[1]

The *ultra vires* rule applies both to private and public bodies. In the sphere of public administration it affords a valuable safeguard in enabling the court to put a stop to

---

[1] This case should be distinguished from *The King* v. *Minister of Health, ex parte Yaffé* [1930], 2 K.B. 98 ; [1931], W.N. 90, where the Minister's order did not require approval by Parliament. (See also Part VI., Chap. IV.)

excessive zeal on the part of officials, but its efficiency has been lessened of late by legislative devices.[1]   Section 14 (3) of the Roads Act, 1920 (above), was an example of one of these devices (see italicised portion).

Since the majority of powers are statutory in origin, their validity depends on the construction which the court places upon the particular enactment from which they are derived. In this connection certain presumptions are observed.   In particular it is assumed that, when authority is given to a public body to perform some administrative act, there is no intention to interfere with private rights, unless the power is expressed in such a way as to justify such interference. A case which illustrates this is *Metropolitan Asylums Board* v. *Hill* (1881), 6 App. Cas. 193 ; K. & L. 154.   Parliamentary powers authorising the construction of a smallpox hospital in Hampstead were held not to have sanctioned the erection of the building in such a way as to constitute a nuisance at Common Law in the absence of express words or necessary implication in the statute.   At pp. 212-13 Lord Watson says : *[Interpretation of Statutory Powers.]*

> " I do not think that the Legislature can be held to have sanctioned that which is a nuisance at Common Law, except in the case where it has authorised a certain use of a specific building in a specified position, which cannot be used without occasioning nuisance, . . . Where the terms of the statute are not imperative, but permissive, when it is left to the discretion of the persons empowered to determine whether the general powers committed to them shall be put into execution or not, I think the fair inference is that the Legislature intended that discretion to be exercised in strict conformity with private rights, and did not intend to confer licence to commit nuisance in any place which might be selected for the purpose."

Moreover, if a statute authorises works which cannot be executed without some interference with private rights, due precautions must be taken to prevent the interference being aggravated by negligent execution ; *Mersey Docks Board* v. *Gibbs* (1866), L.R. 1 H.L. 93 ; K. & L. 156.

A further point should be noticed in connection with by-laws made by public authorities.   The courts will not treat these as unreasonable, unless they are manifestly oppressive, *[By-Laws must be reasonable.]*

---

[1] Part II., Chap. VI.

whereas the by-laws of a trading concern, such as a railway company will be rigorously scrutinised, by-laws being assailable on the ground of unreasonableness as well as on the strict *ultra vires* ground.   In *Kruse* v. *Johnson* [1898], 2 Q.B. 91 ; K. & L. 25, a by-law of the Kent County Council punishing the playing of musical instruments or singing in the highway within fifty yards of a dwelling-house to the annoyance of the inmates was held to be good ; the court held that it should be slow to condemn as invalid on the ground of supposed unreasonableness any by-law made by a body legislating under the delegated authority of Parliament within the extent of the authority given to the body to deal with matters which concerned it.

Discretionary Powers.

Whether powers or duties are derived from the Common Law or from legislation by Parliament or by a subordinate legislating body, it is necessary to distinguish discretionary powers and duties, *i.e.*, those which merely enable a man at his discretion to act in a certain manner, or, if he is obliged to act, give him a discretion as to his mode of actions, from ministerial duties, *i.e.*, those which impose upon him a duty to act without any discretion.   Discretionary powers and duties themselves fall into two divisions :

(1) Those which confer absolute power.

(2) Those which do not.

Where Discretion is absolute.

For example, the Secretary of State under the British Nationality and Status of Alien Acts, 1914-1922, may grant a certificate of naturalisation to an alien who satisfies certain conditions.   Even if these conditions are satisfied, his discretion is probably absolute and against his decision there can be no appeal to a court of law.   It appears from the language of the enactment that no process of law could be invoked to compel him to decide or to set aside his decision on the ground of bias.[1]

But many discretionary powers are not absolute.   This

---

[1] It is sometimes the practice to set up an advisory committee to assist a Minister entrusted with an absolute discretion.   During the War of 1914-19 the Home Secretary was advised by a judge of the High Court regarding the internment and treatment of a certain class of aliens.

does not mean that the courts will intervene and substitute How Courts their own discretion for that of the body or person to whom may control
Non-absolute the power has been entrusted. But they will intervene at Discretion-
ary Powers. the instance of the person aggrieved to examine the question whether in fact there has been any exercise of discretion and whether the discretion has been exercised for the purpose for which it was given. Such discretion must be exercised in a judicial manner. The person who decides must not be personally interested in the decision ; he must give the other side an opportunity of being heard ; and he must only exercise the discretion for the particular purpose for which it was conferred. But, provided that these rules are observed, the decision is final. The case of licenses for the sale and consumption of liquor may be taken as an illustration. The licensing law entrusts to benches of magistrates the grant and renewal of these licenses ; they have discretionary power as part of their duty as licensing authorities. A member of a local firm of brewers, who is also a justice of the peace, takes part in a decision affecting one of the firm's licensed premises. This violates the elementary requirements of justice, and the decision of the bench of which he is a member may be quashed. Again a Minister is entrusted with a discretion to confirm a slum clearance scheme of a local authority drawn up in accordance with the statutory rules, which only permit sale of the area for the purpose of rebuilding artisan dwellings. He confirms the scheme for converting the cleared site into a public garden. He has exercised his discretion for a purpose alien to that for which it was created. Unless the Act has expressly made his discretion to confirm absolute, the courts can hold that in fact there is no exercise of the particular discretion entrusted to the Minister, and the confirming order will fail ; *The King* v. *Minister of Health, ex parte Davis* [1929], 1 K.B. 619 ; cf. *The King* v. *Minister of Health, ex parte Yaffé* [1930], 2 K.B. 98 ; [1931], W.N. 90.[1]

The provisions of statutes conferring discretion must be Powers strictly adhered to ; the statute may prescribe a procedure strictly legal.

---

[1] These cases are discussed in Part VI., Chap. IV.

foreign to that adopted in courts of law ; it may even enable an official to decide the issue without that person himself hearing the arguments of the parties, provided that a reasonable opportunity has been given that person to submit those arguments. Nevertheless his discretion is unimpeachable, if Parliament has sanctioned this particular procedure. This is well illustrated by *Local Government Board* v. *Arlidge* [1915], A.C. 120 ; K. & L. 199.

> The Hampstead Borough Council had made a closing order in respect of a house which appeared unfit for human habitation. The owner appealed to the Local Government Board in the manner prescribed by the Public Health Act, 1875, under which the Board might make such order in the matter as might seem equitable and the order so made would be binding and conclusive on all parties. After a public local enquiry the Board dismissed the appeal, and Arlidge applied to the courts to declare the decision to be invalid, mainly on the grounds that the order in which it was embodied did not disclose which of the officials of the Board actually decided the appeal ; that he, the plaintiff, did not have an opportunity of being heard orally by that official ; that he was not permitted to see the report of the Inspector who conducted the public enquiry on behalf of the Board. It was held by the House of Lords, reversing the Court of Appeal, that Arlidge could not object to the order on these grounds, since Parliament had laid down the method of appeal and had entrusted the task to an authority whose function was administrative and not in the ordinary sense judicial.

So long as the officials dealt with the question referred to them without bias, and gave the parties an opportunity of presenting the case in adequate form, the Board could follow its own particular methods of procedure which were necessary, if it were to do its work efficiently, even though that procedure did not follow meticulously that of a court of law.

But it is clear from *Cooper* v. *Wandsworth Board of Works* (1863), 14 C.B. (N.S.) 180 ; K. & L. 194, also a demolition case, that any discretionary power to interfere with the private rights of the subject should be treated as a species of jurisdiction, and as such be exercised judicially. In that case the court applied the rule *audi alterum partem* in a case where the Board proceeded under a statutory (and therefore legal) power to demolish a house without notice to the person who owned it and without giving him an opportunity of showing any reason why the Board should delay. The demolition order was accordingly quashed.

It cannot be too strongly impressed upon students of the Constitution that it is no part of the court's function to exercise a discretionary power expressly conferred upon another body. All the courts can do is to prevent that body exceeding its jurisdiction or acting non-judicially in cases where judicial or quasi-judicial process is prescribed, *i.e.*, where the discretion conferred is not absolute.

Court cannot
exercise a
Discretion-
ary Power.

An example of a ministerial duty is that of a judge to pass sentence of death upon a convicted murderer. The duty is prescribed ; there is no discretion allowed. The majority of powers which are exercised by public officials are of a discretionary nature, though the duty to exercise the discretion one way or another exists.

Ministerial
Powers.

An appreciation of the nature of ministerial and discretionary powers and duties is vital to an understanding of the law of public administration—a term which is preferable to the better known " administrative law," which nowadays bulks so largely in any discussion of the relationship between the State and its citizens.[1]

[1] For the Courts and Public Authorities generally, see Part VI., Chap. IV., where the cases here cited are again referred to.

CHAPTER II.

THE DOCTRINE OF SEPARATION OF POWERS.

Division of
Powers of
Government.

It is at this point appropriate to discuss the doctrine of the separation of powers, which has played so prominent a part in the theory and practice of constitution making, and particularly in the Constitution of the United States of America. A brief comparison between that Constitution and our own is necessary. A summary of the contentions of those who either claim or deny the existence of any real separation in the functions of English Government, save in the independence of the judges, is given and some conclusion attempted. Those who claim that this separation of powers does exist in England generally incline to the view that such a division is desirable and point to inroads upon it, which they are forced to admit, as a menace to liberty. Equally the opposite school, as a rule, sees no particular merit in this eighteenth century doctrine.

It is customary, as has been seen, to divide powers of government into the three-fold classification, legislative, executive and judicial, and for purposes of arrangement this book deals with the organs of State in that order. There is however no dogmatic adherence to a literal interpretation of this division of powers to be found in the working of the Constitution in the twentieth century, except in one important respect, namely, that the Judiciary exercises its functions unimpeded by the influence of the Executive ; even here there must be remarked the growing tendency to remove disputes of an administrative nature from the jurisdiction of the courts.

Montesquieu.

The French jurist, Montesquieu, in formulating the doctrine of the separation of powers drew upon the working of the English Constitution, as he saw it in the first part of the eighteenth century. His statement of the doctrine may be paraphrased as follows :—if the Executive and the Legislature are the same person or body of persons, there must be a danger of the Legislature enacting oppressive laws for the Executive to administer in order to attain its own ends. Particularly is this true of a personal Executive, irresponsible in law to the courts, or politically to a representative assembly. To join the Judiciary to the Legislature is to enable arbitrary law to be enacted, and make the judge the legislator rather than the interpreter of law. Judge and executive officer, if joined in one person, would have arbitrary power, which would amount to complete tyranny, if there were added to the single powers of that person or body legislative capacity.

This doctrine has played an important part in framing constitutional codes in the last one hundred and fifty years. For example, it is rigidly adhered to in the Constitution of the United States of America, the earliest of its type, if we except Switzerland. In this Constitution it was intended that the balance of powers should be attained by mutual control between separate organs of government. Its framers, purporting to imitate our own Constitution,[1] failed to realise that in the eighteenth century the true executive power in England had already passed from the Crown to the Cabinet. In this they were no doubt influenced by George III.'s attempt to restore the personal government of the Sovereign. Like all federal constitutions, that of United States of America differs from our own as being contained in fundamental laws which cannot be altered by a simple parliamentary vote. The executive power is vested in the President. The so-called Cabinet consists of the heads of the chief State Departments (ten in number), each being personally responsible to the President alone for his own department, but not to Congress (Senate and House of Representatives) or to his colleagues. The President holds office for a fixed term ; he is not necessarily of the same political party as the majority in

Separation of Powers in U.S.A.

---

[1] But it should be observed that the Constitutional Convention of 1787 was influenced by the form of colonial charters under which separation of executive and legislative functions was a prominent feature.

either or both Houses of Congress ; he is not removable by an adverse vote ; his powers are defined.

Neither the President nor Members of his Cabinet can sit or vote in Congress ; they have no responsibility for initiating Bills or securing their passage through Congress. The President may recommend legislation in his message to Congress, but he cannot compel it to pay heed to his recommendations. He has a veto which has been frequently exercised. Treaties are negotiated by the Executive, but require the approval of a two-thirds majority of the Senate (Upper House). The Senate and House of Representatives are elected for fixed terms and cannot be dissolved in the interval. The Judiciary (Federal Supreme Court) may declare the actions either of the Executive or the Legislature to be unconstitutional. Despite this rigid demarcation of functions it may be remarked that in practice separation tends to break down.

In England.   But in England the Cabinet system of government is incompatible with a rigid separation of legislative and executive powers. The Cabinet, the centre of executive power, is composed of members of the Legislature, and tends to monopolise the business of that body. It remains in power only so long as it can retain the confidence of Parliament. Not only does the Cabinet to a large extent determine what matters the Legislature should consider and enact, but it is able by use of the party majority it normally commands to obtain the support of the House of Commons in all vital matters. It is true, of course, that the party majority may be small, or power may be secured only by the co-operation for the time being of part of the Opposition. Occasionally it may disappear, and with that event a change of Cabinet follows. The life of a Parliament is apt to coincide with the life of the Government which is responsible to it. The Judiciary has no power to override the will of Parliament expressed in statute form, since no Act of Parliament can be declared inoperative. Inconvenient decisions of the courts can be reversed by retrospective legislation, if need be, whereas in America the Supreme Court's interpretation of the Constitution cannot be altered by an Act of Congress, but only by the special machinery for securing amendments to the Constitution.

Perhaps the most apt description of the difference between the Presidential system and the Cabinet system, which is due to the adherence on the part of the framers of the United States Constitution to the doctrine of separation of powers, is given in the following extract from the pen of the late Lord Balfour in Bagehot's *The English Constitution* (Introduction to 1928 edition) : *Lord Balfour on U.S.A. Constitution.*

> " Under the Presidential system the effective head of the national administration is elected for a fixed term. He is practically irremovable. Even if he is proved to be inefficient, even if he becomes unpopular, even if his policy is unacceptable to his countrymen, he and his methods must be endured until the moment comes for a new election.
>
> " He is aided by Ministers, who, however able and distinguished, have no independent political status, have probably had no congressional (*i.e.*, parliamentary) training, and are by law precluded from obtaining any during their term of office.
>
> " Under the Cabinet system everything is different. The head of the administration, commonly called the Prime Minister (though he has no statutory position), is selected for the place on the ground that he is the statesman best qualified to secure a majority in the House of Commons. He retains it only so long as that support is forthcoming, he is the head of his party. He must be a member of one or other of the two Houses of Parliament ; and he must be competent to lead the House to which he belongs. While the Cabinet Ministers of a President are merely his officials, the Prime Minister is *primus inter pares* in a Cabinet of which (according to peace-time practice) every member must, like himself, have had some parliamentary experience and gained some parliamentary reputation. The President's powers are defined by the Constitution, and for their exercise within the law he is responsible to no man. The Prime Minister and his Cabinet, on the other hand, are restrained by no written Constitution ; but they are faced by critics and rivals whose position, though entirely unofficial, is as constitutional as their own ; they are subject to a perpetual stream of unfriendly questions, to which they must make public response, and they may at any moment be dismissed from power by a hostile vote."

Lord Balfour goes on to emphasise the weakness of the President's position through his narrow prerogatives defined by the Constitution. The President is unable to influence legislation or taxation in face of a hostile Legislature which he cannot dissolve.

Application of Doctrine to Parliamentary Government.

It may be seen then that in a country like our own under parliamentary government the co-operation of Cabinet and Parliament is assured. There seems permissible no clear distinction between the executive and legislative functions of government assigning each function exclusively to its appropriate organ. While it is undoubtedly the law that an Act of the Legislature is supreme in the law-making sphere, that measure must in practice have originated with the approval, and nowadays normally on the initiative, of the Executive alone ; this means the Ministers of the Crown, under the direction of the Cabinet in important matters of policy.[1] Moreover, the Executive, apart from its inter-relation with Parliament under the Cabinet system, is overwhelmed to-day by administrative duties. Most members of the Cabinet and a great many other Ministers are responsible for the exercise of these duties by their subordinates. They have sought and obtained from Parliament extensive legislative and judicial powers to enable their administrative function to operate. There are thus to be found in the working of our Constitution instances of the three-fold tyranny which Montesquieu so greatly feared. Most people are agreed that it is desirable as far as possible to keep executive power under control on account of the efficiency and zeal of officials. It would not be suggested that in modern times the Executive should be denied in administrative matters wide power to make rules or decide disputes. But those powers must be kept under effective control, *e.g.*, the rule-making power should be subject to the effective veto of Parliament. Otherwise there is a danger of undue expansion of bureaucratic power and, in the opinion of most lawyers, a disregard of individual liberty results which is not compensated for by any resultant benefit to the State as a whole. The cost of public administration, both centrally and locally, is very great, and this naturally tends to expand with the relaxation of parliamentary control. An independent Judiciary is the

---

[1] Part III., Chap. IV., A.

surest protection against excess of power by the Executive, and, so far as judicial power is entrusted to that organ alone, this independence has been assured since the Act of Settlement determined that judges could not be removed merely at the Royal pleasure, but should have fixed salaries, and hold office during good behaviour, subject to a power of removal exercisable on an address of both Houses of Parliament.

Those, however, who maintain that the separation of powers applies to the English Constitution of to-day support their contention on the following grounds :—

(1) The Executive's power over the Legislature is limited, as the will of Parliament, and, through Parliament, of the electorate, must in the long run prevail, so far at all events as to be able to dismiss the Ministry and place a new one in power. Under the provisions restricting the life of a Parliament to five years (Parliament Act, 1911) the Government and its majority in the House of Commons are faced with the certainty of an appeal to the electorate at least every five years. Any change in the composition of the majority in Parliament will be forthwith reflected in the Executive. Most adherents of this school maintain that not only does separation exist, but that it is desirable. In favour of this view it may be conceded that the weakening of the party machinery through a permanent third party contending for power has the result of strengthening the control of Parliament, especially when the Government of the day, as with the two Labour Governments of the last decade, has not secured a clear majority over the other parties. Such a situation is not altogether novel, though the cleavage between the three parties is now more clearly marked.[1] In such circumstances the Executive cannot be sure of Parliament falling in with its wishes as to legislation. This does not necessarily mean a frequent recurrence of General Elections, but merely that the Executive for the time being is hampered as to the policy which it can present for the approval of Parliament.

(2) As regards the exercise of judicial functions by the

Does the Separation of Powers exist to-day ? (a) For.

[1] *Cf.* Lord Melbourne's Administration, 1835-41, and Mr. Gladstone's in 1886 and 1893.

Executive, it is maintained that, up to the present day at least, it is only in administrative matters that this inroad upon the doctrine of the separation of powers has been manifested, and not always here.   The independent attitude of the judges during the emergency period of 1914-20 vindicated the rights of the subject at a time when they were most susceptible of invasion by the Executive.   It is remarked with satisfaction that the Judiciary resists the advances of bureaucracy, warns the public of its dangers and is conspicuous in its vindication of the rights of the least meritorious plaintiff who invokes the aid of a legal technicality against the act of the official.   This view accepts separation in all but administrative matters, and regards the inroads made upon the doctrine in this direction as an undesirable tendency.

(*b*) Against.   On the other hand, those who decline to recognise in our Constitution the application of the separation of powers put forward the following arguments :—(1) The political Executive in practice controls in major matters the policy of the Legislature ; but further Parliament cannot function to-day without the guiding hand of Whitehall.   Government has become a business, or rather a number of businesses, requiring the expert guidance of the whole-time official.   He alone is capable of working out the details of a policy, and, when his policy is ready, the parliamentary machine is used to put that policy into the form of law.   It is realised that the public must be educated up to a policy, at all events so far as the main principles are concerned ; and, therefore, the publicity which the measure is ensured in Parliament is utilised to explain both by the lips of Ministers in the House and by memoranda published contemporaneously with the Bill, the way in which it is sought to achieve the object.   An official is never sure that his labours will not be wasted with a change of Government, though the narrowing down of political, as opposed to economic, controversies, has of late given a succession of political administrations pursuing more or less continuity of policy.   At the worst he is in a better position than if his Department were not responsible to the Legislature, since that very responsibility enables his policy, once accepted by the Government of the day, to be brought to fruition by means of the party majority. The inter-connection of Legislature and Executive saves the business of governing from the violent fluctuations that may occur where the Legislature is not working in the same sphere as the Executive. On this view separation of Legislature and Executive is largely non-existent and is not considered desirable.

(2) It is further observed that much legislation is to-day entrusted to the Executive, subject to what in practice is only a nominal veto of Parliament. Sometimes the veto is non-existent, as where a Minister is given power to make regulations, " as if enacted in this Act." It is impossible to deny the accuracy of this observation, and the power may be defended by arguing that if government is the business of the expert, there are many matters of detail where convenience demands that administrative action should not be impeded by the delays of possible opposition inseparable from reference to a non-expert body, such as Parliament. Moreover, by this means is achieved the desideratum of certainty, *e.g.*, of town planning schemes or other dealings with land where titles might be doubtful. No dogma of eighteenth century publicists should be allowed to hold up the execution of a policy which in principle, and to some extent in detail, has already been sanctioned by Parliament in the measure which conferred on the Executive the power to legislate in relation to this subject. Here again separation does not in practice exist, nor is it desired by those who hold this view.

(3) To some extent adherents to this school of thought decline to admit even the manifestation of this doctrine in the independence of the judges. They point to innumerable instances in the past forty years when disputed issues have been referred to special tribunals or ministerial officials rather than to the courts. They note that the volume of litigation (apart from running down cases, matrimonial suits, and disputed revenue claims), has steadily declined, whereas the number of possible conflicting interests has increased in volume. They observe the reluctance of the average citizen

to face the uncertainty of the law courts, if he can possibly avoid it. This has allowed the expert to devise other methods of solving disputed issues unattended by the publicity and perhaps expense which has to be faced by a plaintiff or defendant in a court of law. But it does not necessarily mean that separation of judicial and executive function is not desirable. Dissatisfaction with the existing legal machinery does not imply that the citizen would prefer his disputes to be tried by civil servants.

Historical Aspect.

The historical inaccuracy of the doctrine of the separation of powers may be noted without being stressed over-much. The very form of the Constitution with the King as the head of the Executive and the Judiciary, and yet a part of the Legislature, is a negation of the doctrine even to-day, though every lawyer knows that the forms are more picturesque than essential. The offices of Lord Chancellor and Justice of the Peace both afford interesting obstacles to be surmounted by adherents to the doctrine.

Conclusion.

The truth, as has been submitted, lies somewhere between the two contentions. It cannot be denied that the three-fold division of State organs is attractive in its simplicity ; but at the same time it cannot be overlooked that, while the Judiciary remains alone in its independence, ministerial powers are not the only concern of Ministers. Government Departments, in addition to administration in the strict sense, have legislative as well as judicial or quasi-judicial tasks to perform. Nor is it easy to classify powers under ministerial, judicial and legislative with clear distinctions between each. In the opinion of many it is absolutely essential that the Departments should be entrusted with sufficient powers to perform these tasks. More important still, the Cabinet relies on the assurance of support from the House of Commons to co-operate in its legislative proposals by vesting them with the form of law, and generally supporting its policy. It must not be forgotten that Montesquieu viewed the English Constitution as a foreign observer comparatively soon after the Bill of Rights, which marked the highest level of parliamentary supremacy, and before the growth of a modern parliamentary Executive. He had seen the attempt, in the Act of Settlement, to exclude all servants of the Crown from Parliament, whereas since his day there has been established the responsibility of Ministers to Parliament and their presence there. This responsibility covers acts of officials in each Department. The independence of the judges remains then, in our Constitution, the chief result of the doctrine, and it is entirely desirable that this should be maintained.

On the Continent the doctrine led not to an independent Judiciary, but to an unhampered Executive. That there is some danger of a similar development in England to-day cannot be denied. So long, however, as ministerial powers of a legislative and judicial nature are kept within bounds, the danger, it is submitted, is not so great as many have indicated. The legislation of Government Departments should, however, be limited by the *ultra vires* rule, and their judicial powers should be subject to a right of appeal in matters of strict law, not necessarily to the ordinary courts. Given these safeguards, there is less to fear from the concentration of powers, which approximates, it is submitted, more nearly to the truth than the separation of functions.

Concentration of Powers.

CHAPTER III.

THE LEGISLATIVE POWER OF PARLIAMENT.

FROM the discussion of the doctrine of the separation of powers we turn naturally to examine the position of Parliament as the law-making organ of the State. Dicey discusses the right of the King in Parliament to make or unmake any law whatever within the limits of physical possibility. From the strictly legal point of view it is unquestionable that this power rests with Parliament, and, since the Parliament Act, 1911, this to a greater extent than hitherto means with the House of Commons. So far as Constitutional Law consists of statutes, there is no Act which Parliament could not repeal ; the Bill of Rights could be cast overboard by the same process as the Rats and Mice Destruction Act, namely, by a repealing measure passed in the ordinary form. So far as it is embodied in case law, Parliament can, even with retrospective operation, over-ride the decisions of the courts. It could restore to the Executive unfettered power to legislate as freely as if the *Case of Proclamations* had never been accepted as representing the law. The most firmly established convention could be declared illegal by statute. No one supposes that such an exercise of law-making power is within the realm of probability.

Legal Power unlimited.

A.

History of Parliamentary Supremacy.

It is necessary to give a short historical sketch of the growth of parliamentary supremacy. The following passage gives as

Growth of Parliamentary Supremacy.

48

complete a survey as is possible in a short space [1] :—When modern England began to take shape after the Wars of the Roses, Parliament was already established as the King's highest court. What was declared by Parliament was law, apart from the survival of the doubtful doctrine that the courts might avoid any law if contrary to common right and reason. But in some spheres the scope of the King's absolute power was undefined, as in foreign affairs ; moreover, the King possessed a residue of judicial power exercised by the Council which enabled him to enforce his wishes. One qualification was that in some matters the Church, and not the State, was supreme.

Henry VIII. and Elizabeth made the Crown of England supreme over all persons and all causes. But they used Parliament to achieve this end. Then metaphysical sanction was invoked and national sovereignty was fortified by the Divine Right of Kings. Parliament, however, from being an instrument of the Tudors demanded, first partnership, and then mastery. The doom of the Divine Rights of Kings with the execution of Charles I., and the abolition of the Council's jurisdiction in 1640, so far as it conflicted with the Common Law, prepared the way for the action of Parliament when James II. flouted the will of his people. The Bill of Rights firmly established that, without losing his remaining prerogative rights, the King could not overstep them, nor make decisions in spheres where Parliament had definitely established control. Henceforward the control of the majority in the Commons was to determine supremacy, as George III. realised when he attempted to revive personal government. The methods whereby this control was obtained vary, and it will be seen that over a century was to elapse before parliamentary democracy attained its present form.

The struggle for legislative supremacy between the King and Parliament may be illustrated from the history of the seventeenth century, and is closely connected with the Prerogative to be discussed in the next chapter.

(1) Ordinances and Proclamations.

There was a lack of any clear distinction between the

---

[1] See also Pickthorn's *Some Historical Principles of the Constitution* (Philip Allan & Co.), upon which the survey is largely based.

4

Statutes of Parliament and the Ordinances of the King in Council long after the establishment of the Model Parliament. The Statute of Proclamations, 1539, gave the King very wide, but not exclusive, powers of legislating without reference to Parliament by proclamation which had replaced the ordinance as a form of legislation. Despite the repeal of this Statute in 1547, both Mary and Elizabeth continued to resort to proclamations as a means of governing. This apparently irregular procedure can no doubt be explained by the fact that the judicial powers of the Council, and in particular of the Court of Star Chamber, were available to enforce proclamations. But the fact remains that the scope of the Royal Prerogative was largely undefined. It is a most difficult task for the constitutional historian to say at any given period prior to 1689 exactly what must be enacted by Parliament alone and what could be achieved by prerogative ordinance. Nor is this surprising when it is remembered that legislative power originally lay with the King in Council, and that the influence of the Council varied with the ability of the monarch to choose his counsellors. James I. made full use of this power with the result that in 1611 Coke was consulted by the Council, along with three of his brother judges who were added at his request, for an expression of opinion on the legality of proclamations. The result of their considerations is to be found in the *Case of Proclamations* (1611), 12 Co. Rep. 74 ; K. & L. 63, and may be regarded as final.

" 1. The King by his proclamation cannot create any offence which was not one before ; for then he might alter the law of the land in a high point ; for if he may create an offence where none is, upon that ensues fine and imprisonment.

" 2. The King hath no prerogative but what the law of the land allows him.

" 3. But the King, for the prevention of offences, may by proclamation admonish his subjects that they keep the laws and do not offend them upon punishment to be inflicted by law ; the neglect of such proclamation aggravates the offence.

" 4. If an offence be not punishable in the Star Chamber the prohibition of it by proclamation cannot make it so."

A definite limit is thus put upon the exercise of the Prerogative, the full force of which was only effective when the Court of Star Chamber was abolished in 1640. The scope of the latter's existing jurisdiction was left undefined except that in Coke's opinion proclamations could no longer increase it. The gist of the *Case of Proclamations* is that the King is the Executive ; his business, the enforcement of the existing law ; his Prerogative is under the law, and Parliament can alone alter the law which the King is to administer.[1]

It had been conceded by the time of Edward I. that the (2) Taxation. consent of Parliament was necessary for direct taxation. The history of the struggle over indirect taxation is more complicated, but it was under the control of Parliament before the Wars of the Roses, so far as specific commodities were concerned. Yet the prerogative right to tax was claimed by the Stuart monarchs not as something novel, but on the basis of undoubted prerogative right. The *Case of Impositions* (*Bates' Case*) (1606), 2 St. Tr. 371 ; K. & L. 36., in which the courts upheld the claim of James I. to impose or increase taxes on imported commodities, showed that there was no clear distinction between the right to impose taxes by way of customs duties and the Prerogative in relation to foreign affairs, which included control of foreign trade. Nor does the decision seem to have been regarded as a corrupt one. Neither precedent nor statute were conclusive on either side, which is not surprising since they were mainly drawn from documents two hundred and fifty years old.

Equally startling to modern notions are the admissions in favour of the Crown's executive power in time of emergency made by Hampden's counsel in the *Ship Money Case* (1637), 3 St. Tr. 825 ; K. & L. 39. He conceded everything in favour of the Crown, except the final point that the danger which could alone justify the resort to arbitrary taxation was not imminent. The result of the case was the decision that *Rex* is *Lex*, and that the King was the source of all law. The decision was reversed by the Long Parliament and this aspect of the struggle is concluded by the Bill of Rights.

---

[1] Anson, *Law of the Constitution* (5th edition), Vol. I., p. 343.

That the levying of money for or to the use of the Crown by pretence of Prerogative without grant of Parliament for longer time or in other manner than the same is or shall be granted is illegal.

Not even the extraordinary powers conferred on the Executive by the Defence of the Realm Acts, 1914-15, admitted an interpretation which derogated from the Bill of Rights in this respect; *Attorney-General* v. *Wilts United Dairies* (1922), 91 L.J.K.B. 897; K. & L. 119.

(3) Dispensing and Suspending Powers.
The power of the Crown to dispense with the operation of statutes within certain limits seems to have been a necessary one having regard to the scanty wording of many ancient statutes and the irregular meetings of Parliament. Violations, however, of the Common Law or the statutory enactment of the Common Law were probably not within the scope of the Royal Dispensation. The leading cases of *Thomas* v. *Sorrell* (1674), K. & L. 56, and *Godden* v. *Hales* (1686), K. & L. 55, point to a distinction between the Crown dispensing with a particular, or even continuous, breach of a penal statute passed for the Crown's own benefit, as compared with a continuous breach of a general penal statute passed in the interests of the whole realm. But fortified by a favourable decision in the latter case, James II. proceeded to set aside statutes as he pleased. Hard though it may be to define the dispensing power, there is no doubt that James overstepped all limits of legality in granting a suspension of the penal laws relating to religion in the Declaration of Indulgence. The validity of his act only came before the courts in an indirect way at the trial of the Seven Bishops for seditious libel arising out of their petitions to James against reading the declaration. The Bill of Rights disposed summarily of the claim :

> The pretended power of suspending laws or the execution of laws by regal authority without the consent of Parliament is illegal.

Comparison should be made with the provision relating to the dispensing power :

> (1) That the pretended power of dispensing with laws, or the execution of laws by regal authority, *as it hath been assumed and exercised of late*, is illegal.

(2) That from and after this present session of Parliament, no dispensation by *non obstante* of or to any statute, or any part thereof, shall be allowed, but that the same shall be held void and of no effect, except a dispensation be allowed of in such a statute, and except in such cases as shall be specially provided for by one or more bill or bills to be passed during this present session of Parliament.

It is apparent from these provisions that, while James II.'s dispensations were regarded as illegal, earlier dispensations were not called in question. Further, it was recognised that the power might be required by the Executive in future. For this provision was to be made by Parliament. Actually no such provision was made. In the *Case of Eton College* (1815), there was upheld a dispensation granted by Queen Elizabeth to enable fellows of the College to hold benefices up to a certain value in conjunction with their Fellowships, notwithstanding College statutes forbidding this type of plurality.

Since the tenure of office by the judges came to depend upon the Royal Pleasure, the subservience of the bench seems to have been more or less unquestioned. No doubt some of the decisions such as the *Case of Impositions* and *Thomas* v. *Sorrell* should be accepted without accusing the Judiciary of bias. But it is difficult to absolve the judges who favoured the Crown in *Hampden's Case* or in *Godden* v. *Hales*. It was left to the <u>Act of Settlement</u>, enacting a provision which was originally intended to have taken its place in the Bill of Rights, to ensure the independence of the Bench " <u>that . . . . judges' commissions be made *Quamdiu se bene gesserint*, and their salaries ascertained and established</u> ; but upon the address of both Houses of Parliament it may be lawful to remove them." Henceforward in any case of conflict the bench can be relied upon not to show favour, <u>and of late the judges have shown a marked strictness in handling claims of the Executive to over-ride the law.</u> The supremacy of Parliament has nothing to fear in the attitude of the judges. At an earlier date the executive power had been checked by the abolition of all jurisdiction of the Council in Common Law matters (1640).

Here then is the result of the seventeenth century conflict

(4) The Independence of the Judiciary.

Act of Settlement, 1701.

between the Executive and Parliament.   The Bill of Rights and the Act of Settlement gave to Parliament the supremacy on all points, while preserving the prerogative rights of the Crown in matters which had not been called in question. But as yet there was absent the recognition of the principle that the King's Ministers could best be controlled by their becoming members of Parliament, and so responsible to Parliament, as well as servants of the monarch.   It was at a later date that their presence in Parliament was recognised to be desirable and, indeed, essential, if the will of Parliament was to prevail.   The process of impeachment was too cumbrous and drastic to be used as the everyday method of ensuring that ministers should not disregard the will of Parliament, but the ultimate solution of Cabinet Government was not at first perceived.   The Bill of Rights was the first great victory of Parliament.   The Act of Settlement by attempting to exclude Ministers showed how far from realisation was the solution of the ultimate problem of co-ordination between the Executive and Parliament.

In the eighteenth century the nature of the struggle changes.   The absolute discretion of the Crown, which the events of the closing years of the seventeenth century had still left in many respects unimpaired, could not be left with the Crown and its Ministers in such a way as to enable them to govern without responsibility in those matters which still fell within the Royal Prerogative.   The significance of the period from 1688 until after the Reform Act, 1832, lies in the development of ministerial responsibility to Parliament.

What was wanted was to bring ultimate responsibility in Parliament to individual servants of the Crown for their actions, and, secondly, collective responsibility of those individuals as a body for general policy and for the actions of each other.   This responsibility is political, and not legal, though for his individual acts contrary to law each Minister was, and is, responsible to the Courts.   *Danby's Case* (1679), went a long way towards establishing the principle that a Minister cannot shelter himself from legal responsibility by a plea of obedience to the command of the Sovereign, cf. *Somers' Case* (1701).   But the irresponsibility of the Cabinet, a more or less illusive body at this stage, was apparent. The solution which was reached in the nineteenth century was not realised under Anne. Not merely did she, like her predecessors, retain a personal initiative in the Councils of the Crown, frequently presiding at meetings of the Cabinet, but the consultative body itself was by no means always of the same composition.[1]

As we have seen, the Act of Settlement at the end of the previous reign excluded the Ministers of the Crown, as holders of offices of profit, from membership of the House of Commons. At the same time it attempted to impose personal responsibility for executive acts on Privy Councillors. It is true that neither of these provisions came into operation, as they were repealed before the death of Anne, but they serve to illustrate the lack of appreciation of the modern solution.

The real point of transition to Cabinet Government came with the accession of the House of Hanover. The absence of George I. from meetings of the Cabinet made it essential that another should be selected to preside at these meetings. Here is to be found the beginning of the office of Prime Minister. Henceforth the leaders of the two great parties of State, Whigs and Tories, control the direction of policy by means of maintaining a majority of supporters in the House of Commons. George III. tried through the King's Friends to re-establish personal government, but on parliamentary lines, through the use of methods which both the Whigs and the Tories freely resorted to, namely, pensions, gifts of sinecure offices, Government contracts, not to mention the influence of powerful peers under an unreformed franchise, by means of " pocket boroughs." The long Whig supremacy illustrates the effectiveness of these weapons. Since the Bill of Rights it was impossible for the Executive to govern without the support of Parliament. As long, however, as Parliament was unreformed, that support could be secured by

Transition to Cabinet Government.

---

[1] Anson gives three such bodies under titles of :—(1) The Cabinet, or Lords of the Cabinet Council. (2) The Committee of Council. (3) The Privy Council or Great Council. Anson, *op. cit.* (3rd edition), Vol. II., Pt. I., pp. 93, 94.

the use of bribery and influence, except in times of great
popular feeling, *e.g.*, the loss of the American Colonies and
the fall of Lord North's Ministry. With the coming of
parliamentary reform in 1832 it was no longer possible to
govern by influence. The necessity of parliamentary support,
which had existed since 1689, meant henceforward that the
Executive must hold the same political views as the majority
in Parliament. Gradually there was evolved an Executive
responsive to the will of the people. It is true that at first
" the people " meant property-owners. To-day it means
every adult male and female.

Reform Act, 1832.

Conclusion.   Thus executive power has become impossible without the
support of Parliament, which support is only obtainable by
winning the confidence of a vast electorate. Parliament has
the final voice in legislation, in taxation and in the tenure of
office by the judges. Parliament could not dismiss a King
without a revolution. It can now dismiss a Ministry, which
advises the King. Consequently the political influence of
the King has steadily declined with the growth of responsible government.

B.

Legal Supremacy Illustrated.

The legal supremacy of Parliament, as opposed to its
political supremacy, may be well illustrated by Acts which
from time to time have fixed the duration of Parliament's
own life, the Triennial Act, 1694, the Septennial Act, 1714,
and the Parliament Act, 1911. Immutability is not a mark
of supremacy. One Parliament cannot bind its successors ;
otherwise the succeeding Parliament would not be sovereign
or supreme. The fact that Parliament can extend its own
life emphasises the supremacy of Parliament. The life of
the Parliament which met in January, 1911, was extended for
nearly three years beyond its normal duration of five years
by reason of war, which made it desirable to avoid a General
Election and possible change of Government. A preceding
Act of Parliament cannot be a legal limitation of its supremacy.
Another strong illustration is to be found in the Irish Free

Acts fixing Duration of Parlia- ments.

State (Agreement) Act, 1922. By this measure the Parliament of the day cast off part of its jurisdiction. In strict law its successors could perhaps amend that enactment. But this Act may also be taken as an example of the *de facto* limitation of parliamentary supremacy which may be found in political expediency. The Irish Free State, having been established by Parliament with a Constitution adapted to the requirements of a Self-governing Dominion, cannot be deprived of control of that Constitution, since an absolute convention forbids further interference by Parliament against the wishes of the inhabitants of the Free State.

A further illustration of the supremacy of Parliament may be found in measures which legalise past illegalities, such as the Indemnity Act, 1920, and the War Charges Validity Act, 1925, which made legal many otherwise unlawful acts of servants of the Crown during the Great War. Parliament alone possesses the power to legalise illegalities. The existence of this power denies supremacy to the courts. It can be utilised by an Executive which commands a majority in Parliament to reverse as a matter of policy, or even of politics, inconvenient decisions of an impartial Judiciary.

Negatively the supremacy of Parliament is proved by showing that there is no rival legislative authority. Such Acts as those which prolong the life of Parliament show that the electorate has no say in the matter, since it need not be consulted. But at the same time no Parliament, save in a great emergency, would prolong its own life and, therefore, the electorate can exert its political supremacy at regular intervals. It would, however, be incorrect to describe the twenty-nine and a half million electors as legislators.

It is sometimes argued that Parliament does not attempt to exert its supremacy in many fields and that, therefore, it is idle to speak of its supremacy to this extent. Admittedly there is a large amount of delegation of legislative powers to subordinate law-making bodies. But each and all of these subordinate bodies may have their powers taken away by Parliament. Moreover, the *ultra vires* principle can be an important safeguard in this connection, provided that the

Marginal notes:
Indemnity Acts.

Negative Aspect; no Rival Authority.

Act of Parliament does not make an absolute delegation of legislative power, but enables the courts to hold void the rules and orders made by the delegatee. Again, it has been suggested that resolutions in the House of Commons make law. From time to time the courts have decided against the validity of resolutions passed by the House of Commons.[1]

Electorate; Referendum and Initiative.

It has been said that the electorate cannot claim to be a rival of the Legislature, but recent events have given prominence to two constitutional experiments, neither of which has, as yet, found a place in our constitutional machinery, which aim at securing the direct influence of the electorate on legislation, namely, the referendum and the initiative. The referendum which enables a poll of the electorate to be taken on a particular measure of legislation serves to isolate a particular issue. It may take several forms. It may precede, or come after, discussion of a measure by Parliament. It may be confined to constitutional changes or made applicable to legislation of any type. Preferably the referendum should be applied to a measure which has already passed through Parliament, but has not yet come into operation pending the approval of the electors being obtained. It has been suggested as a solution of deadlocks between the two Houses of Parliament, *i.e.*, on application of either House or of a given number of members of the House of Commons. In its favour may be urged that it assists the principle of an electoral mandate ; against it that it is incompatible with a representative system of government.

If a referendum be incompatible, the initiative is the negation of representation. Both are dangerous weapons in the hands of a huge electorate. The initiative is a device for enabling the electorate to instruct Parliament to proceed with a measure ; it may take the form of a general instruction to the Government to prepare a Bill and submit it to Parliament ; or the completely drafted Bill may be presented to the electorate for approval prior to submission to the Legislature. To set the initiative in motion there must be provisions to ensure that a fairly large section of the electorate

[1] Part III., Chap. III.

support the proposal, *e.g.*, a petition by a due proportion of voters as a whole, including a substantial proportion in a given number of constituencies. Otherwise initiation might become the weapon of fanatics and cranks.

Should either, or both, of these devices ever find a place in our Constitution, it will be necessary to revise our present conception of parliamentary supremacy in face of these experiments in direct democracy. The conclusion which most people incline to is that democracy must work through representation alone. Experience of the referendum, *e.g.*, in constitutional changes in the Commonwealth of Australia, indicates that the voter, when confronted with an isolated issue, is slow to favour any change in the *status quo*.

It cannot then be seriously questioned that Parliament is the supreme law-making organ of the State; but does the interrelation between the Executive and the Legislature, which was discussed under the separation of powers, prevent Parliament from in fact regulating the Executive, or enable the Executive to use the legislative power without restriction? The law cannot be changed, save by an Act of Parliament, but for the time being the Executive is able, as a matter of fact, to secure approval of its policy and legislative effect for measures which it may propose by means of the majority it possesses, or can command by political arrangement, in the House of Commons. The extent to which it can impose its wishes on Parliament, and so on the nation, depends largely on the nature of that majority, and in any event there is the knowledge that at the end of, at most five years, the electorate will have an opportunity of refusing to present the Executive with a majority of supporters in the Commons. Despite, then, the legal supremacy of Parliament, there are limitations as to the way in which this supremacy can be utilised. Considerations of party politics, particularly the fear of a reversal at the next General Election; the very nature of the men who engage in public life; the knowledge that in the last resort even in these days Governments may be overthrown by force; these are all-important limitations which in fact limit the use that can be made of parliamentary supremacy. It does not serve any useful purpose to emphasise the supremacy of Parliament in law without drawing attention to the many limitations by which it is restricted in fact.   While there is no doubt that the form of law-making is preserved as a necessary function of Parliament, it is not unreasonable to assert that this form is utilised almost exclusively by the Government of the day, with which rests the political supremacy to give effect to its own policy.   Thus the co-operation between the Government and Parliament (or rather the House of Commons) involves a partnership in which the former rules and the latter, with occasional protests, confirms the senior partner's decisions by formal approval.

CHAPTER IV.

THE ROYAL PREROGATIVE.

A.

History and Nature of the Prerogative.

DICEY defines the Royal Prerogative as follows: "The Prerogative appears to be historically and, as a matter of actual fact, nothing else than the residue of discretionary or arbitrary authority which at any time is legally left in the hands of the Crown."

Dicey's definition, standing by itself, is wide enough to include the numerous statutory powers conferred on the Crown in modern times. It is convenient to restrict the use of the term Prerogative to the Common Law powers of the Crown. Both Common Law and statutory powers confer discretions upon the Executive. The Prerogative in the strict sense is uncontrolled by the courts. The courts may question whether an act is within the Prerogative or not; but once established as a prerogative act, the legality of the exercise of ministerial discretion cannot be questioned in legal proceedings. The proper place to call it in question is in Parliament.

For example, the resumption of diplomatic relations with Russia, which has troubled Governments in the last few years, is a matter within the scope of the Royal Prerogative. Pressure may be brought to bear upon a Government in Parliament, and, though the question of recognition or non-recognition may easily become relevant in legal proceedings, *e.g.*, if the Russian Government was suing or being sued, no actions could lie to test the legality of the decision of the

British Government to grant or withhold recognition. But the plea of the Prerogative affords no escape from legal liability, if, for example, action is taken by the Government against a British subject, in order to enforce the terms of a law-making treaty which it has concluded with a foreign country. The contents of the treaty cannot be questioned, as these fall within the scope of the Prerogative, but this Prerogative does not extend to enabling the modification of existing rights of British subjects.[1] If the terms of such a treaty require for its execution such modification, only an Act of Parliament can make them enforceable against the subject ; *Walker v. Baird* [1892], A.C. 491 ; K. & L. 310.

King a party to Prerogative Acts.
By virtue of the Royal Prerogative the King summons, prorogues and dissolves Parliament ; to these, and many other important State acts, he is directly a party. Though legally irresponsible, he is not above the law. Except where statutory powers are imposed directly upon Ministers, his act is essential to executive actions and executive action is the action of the Crown. He appoints, on the advice of his Ministers, to the majority of executive, administrative and judicial offices. The more important appointments are made in his name, minor patronage being exercised by his Ministers in their own names. In the name of the King treaties, declarations of war and of peace are made ; honours are conferred, and charters granted. The text of the Letters Patent and the subsequent Order in Council, appointing Counsellors of State during the King's illness, 1928-29, gives some insight, behind legal form, into the many and varied activities of the King of England in the twentieth century.

History of Prerogative.
Before stating in detail the existing powers of the Royal Prerogative, it is necessary to say a word or two about its historical development. It was, of course, an exaggerated view of their prerogative powers which led to the con-

---

[1] But the declaration of war, which is an act of the Prerogative, may have this effect ; *cf.* also *The Fagernes* [1927], P. 311, where the statement of the Home Secretary that the place where a collision at sea had occurred was not claimed to be within His Majesty's jurisdiction was accepted by the Court of Appeal. The effect of this was to non-suit the plaintiff, a British subject, and see Part IV., Chap. VII.

stitutional excesses of the Stuarts. They failed to realise that the law was changing. Some of the powers of the Prerogative may be traced to a feudal origin. The King was, and in strict theory of the law of real property still is, the absolute owner of all land. It is from this feudal origin that his immunity from judicial process sprang. Like other feudal lords, the King could not be sued in his own feudal courts. It is easy to extend this idea of immunity to courts which the King later established outside the feudal system. Many other of his powers are accounted for by the imperative need for the preservation of the State against external foes. These powers are older than Parliament itself and earlier than the establishment of the central courts; they include the Prerogative in foreign affairs, and the headship of the Armed Forces of the State. The need for a strong Executive is always more apparent in time of emergency. Hence the claims of the Crown are extended in such times, which were of frequent occurrence in the Middle Ages.

When, by the fourteenth century, Parliament and the Common Law Courts may be said to have been definitely established, there was necessarily left an undefined residue of power with the King and his Council. The judicial activities of the Council at the time of the Tudors, including the Prerogative Courts, such as the Courts of Star Chamber, of Requests and of High Commission, and indeed the Court of Chancery itself; the frequent use of the ordinance or proclamation where statute law would now be imperative; the exercise, unquestioned at the time, of the dispensing power; the admissions of Hampden's counsel in the *Ship Money Case ;* all these point to an undoubted reserve of power in the Crown, long after Parliament and the Common Law Courts had established their position. On the whole, these powers must be regarded as necessary and in the main exercised in beneficial ways. The crude form of early statutes; the infrequent meetings of Parliament; the need for rapid action against external foes in an unsettled age; all are evidence of the need of executive power which can be exercised without question. Long periods of emergency resulted in the growth of this power, just as to-day the exceptional powers which the Executive obtained from Parliament during the years 1914-20 linger on as part of our law and, in the opinion of some critics, have materially changed the attitude of the higher officials of Whitehall towards the maintenance of the supremacy of Parliament and of the rule of law.

Seventeenth Century Conflicts.
With the Stuarts came the conflict between the Crown and Parliament. In the *Case of Impositions* it was declared that the King's power was ordinary and absolute. The law applicable to the ordinary transactions of life was inapplicable to the conduct of government; the latter required decisions on matters of high policy decided by the Council, with the King's unfettered discretion prevailing, if need be. Convenient though the existence of absolute power may be in emergency, it is in normal times apt to prove an instrument of oppression.

The following is a summary in chronological order of the more important decisions in connection with the Prerogative during the seventeenth century.[1]

(1) *The Case of Monopolies* (1602), 11 Co. Rep. 84.

> The grant of a monopoly by the Crown is bad, being void both against the Common Law and statute. Nor may the Crown dispense for private gain with an Act passed *pro bono publico*.

Later, in 1623, the Statute of Monopolies—a declaratory Act: (i) controlled the Crown's power to grant to first inventors the monopoly of working and making new manufactures; this formed the basis of modern patent law:

(ii) reserved the rights of bodies corporate and companies of merchants; *East India Co.* v. *Sandys* (1684), Skinner 132.

(2) *The Case of Impositions*, or *Bates' Case* (1606), 2 St. Tr. 371; K. &. L. 36.

> The King by virtue of his complete control of foreign affairs may impose a duty on merchandise imported (indirect taxation) as part of the regulation of foreign trade, but not for revenue purposes, because by fourteenth century statutes the King cannot tax without the consent of Parliament.

---

[1] Cases on the Prerogative are collected in Keir and Lawson, *Cases in Constitutional Law*, pp. 31-70, where they should be studied.

The Bill of Rights, 1689, declared illegal the levying of money by pretence of Prerogative and without consent of Parliament. The practice was also declared illegal by the Petition of Rights, 1628, and by the Tonnage and Poundage Act, 1640. (See also the *Ship Money Case* below.)

(3) *Prohibitions del Roy* (1607), 12 Rep. 63 ; K. &. L. 276.[1]

> The King in person cannot sit as a judge to try cases in the courts.

(4) *The Case of Proclamations* (1611), 12 Rep. 74 ; K. & L. 63.[2]

(5) *The Five Knights', or Darnel's Case* (1627), 3 St. Tr. 1 ; K. &. L. 37.

> The King can imprison without cause shown *per speciale mandatum regis*. This was an extension of the power, recognised at this time, of imprisonment in time of emergency to imprisonment to enforce arbitrary taxation.

The Petition of Right, 1628, declared this arbitrary power of committal illegal.

(6) *The Case of Ship Money, or Hampden's Case* (1637), 3 St. Tr. 825 ; K. & L. 39.[3]

> The King may levy direct taxation in time of emergency. He is the sole judge of what constitutes an emergency.

(7) *Godden* v. *Hales* (1686), 11 St. Tr. 1166 ; K. & L. 55.

> The King may dispense with a statute, thereby causing the mischief which the statute aimed at preventing, even though the statute be one passed in the public interest, and not merely for the King's personal advantage ; *cf. Thomas* v. *Sorrell* (1674), Vaughan, 330. This was a power which was undoubted in cases of emergency.

(8) *The Seven Bishops' Case* (1688), 12 St. Tr. 183.

> It is right of the subject to petition the King ; the dispensing and alleged suspending powers of the King were discussed.

---

[1] Part V., Chap. III.
[2] Discussed in Chap. III. above.
[3] Chap. III. above.

5

The Bill of Rights also declared the right to petition a lawful one and commitments or prosecutions for petitioning to be illegal.[1]

By the end of the seventeenth century, as a result of these decisions and the enactment of the Bill of Rights and Act of Settlement, [2] matters of government were subject to the law of the land to a large extent, but there remain untouched a great many discretionary powers of the Crown which may here be detailed :

Existing Prerogative Powers.

(1) Prerogatives relating to the Royal dignity.

1. *Sovereignty.* In practice this means that no court can have jurisdiction over the King, but this must be read subject to Part V., Chap. IV., where remedies against the Crown are discussed.

2. *Perfection.* The King can do no wrong. This maxim has two applications :

(a) Ministers cannot plead the orders of the Crown as a defence for their wrongful acts.

(b) The King cannot be sued or otherwise held responsible for executive actions. He must, therefore, act through Ministers who can be made responsible and, if necessary, sued.

The King must act through a Minister is to ensure that some one is responsible. Seals of Office are entrusted to Ministers and play an important part in securing the responsibility which attaches to their holders. The same is true of Orders in Council. The Councillors present at a formal meeting of the Privy Council are legally responsible for the contents of the documents to which the Council gives its sanction. Politically the responsibility is that of the Departments which draw up the documents laid before the Council. The actions of the Departments are attacked through the Ministers in charge in Parliament.

It will be seen hereafter that even such remedies as are available against the Crown in the courts do not extend to a tortious act committed by, or on behalf of, the Govern-

---

[1] The Dispensing and Suspending Power are discussed in Chap. III. of this Part.

[2] The texts of both these enactments should be familiar to all students of modern Constitutional Law.

ment. This doctrine does not protect the servant of the Crown, who is the actual wrongdoer. Another consequence is embodied in the rule *Nullum tempus occurrit regi ;* this means that, subject to important statutory exceptions, particularly in criminal matters, the right of the Crown to initiate prosecutions and to start civil actions is not barred by lapse of time. This rule applies also to Departments acting as agents for the Crown ; *Public Works Commissioners* v. *Pontypridd Masonic Hall* [1920], 2 K.B. 233.

Other matters relating to this group of prerogative rights, namely, the minority of the King and the attribute of perpetuity will be discussed hereafter.[1]

The collection and expenditure of the public revenue has for long been a matter of statutory regulation, and very little remains of the Prerogative under this heading ; the subject will be dealt with under Parliament (Part III., Chap. IV.) and the Executive (Part IV., Chap. VII., The Treasury). *(2) Prerogatives relating to the Royal Income*

By virtue of these Prerogatives, reinforced by innumerable statutory provisions, the King is the supreme executive authority in the State. They give him in particular the right of making appointments to all the more important offices in State and Church. Even though in many cases his powers are exercised, not merely on the advice of Ministers, but actually by and in the name of Ministers in person, the acts are still the executive acts of the Crown since the Ministers themselves owe their appointment to the Crown. It must be noticed, however, that many of the powers of Ministers derived from statute are not conferred upon them as agents of the Crown. The powers are given to Ministers in charge of Departments as such, and may be enforceable by the writ of Mandamus[2] This process is never available against a Minister acting as agent of the Crown. *(3) Prerogative relating to the Royal Authority.*

The King is the sole representative of the nation in international dealings ; it is his Prerogative to make treaties ; to cede territory ; to make war and peace ; to recognise the status of a foreign country or of its Government (that is, to decide whether or not to recognise a new State as a sovereign *Foreign Affairs.*

---

[1] Part IV., Chap. I.   [2] Part VI., Chap. IV.

5 *

independent State or the persons in control of an old or new State as its official Government); to appoint representatives of his own country abroad and to receive the representatives of other States at his Court.[1]

(4) The King is the Fountain of Justice. Though the judges are no longer subject to the control of the Executive, the appointment of judges is made by the Crown, and their authority is derived from the Crown. It is true that the qualifications for many judicial offices are, nowadays, regulated by statute, and to this extent, of course, the discretion of the Crown is restricted. The courts are the King's Courts, despite the statutory basis of most courts given by the Judicature Act, 1925, and other statutes. The defendant is summoned to the courts by the King's command, though the King can no longer absolve him from the consequences of non-appearance or remit any civil sanction which the courts may impose upon him. In criminal proceedings every prosecution must be in the name of the Crown; it is the Crown alone which can stifle a prosecution, either by declining to offer evidence, or entering a formal *nolle prosequi*. The power of pardon is also the King's Prerogative. It is by virtue of this branch of the Prerogative that appeals lie to the Judicial Committee of the Privy Council from the overseas parts of the Empire. Although the jurisdiction of the Judicial Committee is regulated by statute, the Acts expressly reaffirm the prerogative right to grant leave to appeal.

(5) The King is the Commander-in-Chief of the Armed Forces of the Crown. This Prerogative operates, nowadays, in regard to the Navy more fully than the Army. The Bill of Rights prohibits the keeping of a Standing Army in time of peace, without the consent of Parliament, which prohibition extends to all Forces of the Crown serving on land within the realm. The Army, Air Force, and to some extent the Marines, therefore, require an annual Act of Parliament legalising their existence, but the Navy, although its recruitment and discipline are governed by statute (Naval Enlistment Acts, 1853 to 1884, and Discipline Acts, 1866 and 1884) is still a Prerogative Force.[2] This branch of the Prerogative covers

---

[1] Part IV., Chap. VII.   [2] Part VIII., Chap. I.

the Prerogative in relation to the Established Church, which depends upon the Reformation changes carried through by the King in Parliament

the command of the Forces, and includes an extensive patronage. All officers of the Forces hold their commissions from the King.

The best illustration of this is seen in the appointment of Bishops and other high Church officers. The Convocations of the Church are also convened and dissolved by Royal Writ.[1]

(6) The King is the Governor of the Established Church.

Other Prerogatives may be mentioned briefly : the conferment of honours which includes the creation of hereditary peers and thus, in the last resort, enables the King's Ministers to control the composition of the House of Lords.[2] The creation of corporations by charter ; rights in connection with harbours and the coasts of the realm generally ; the guardianship of infants and lunatics ; franchises, which include the right to wrecks, treasure trove, markets, ferries and fisheries.

(7) Other Prerogatives.

The majority of these miscellaneous prerogative rights have been regulated by statute, chiefly in the last fifty years. For example, the care of lunatics, which as regards their property, is entrusted to the Lord Chancellor and the Lord Justices in Lunacy, *i.e.*, the Lord Justices of the Court of Appeal, and as regards their persons to the supervision of the Board of Control, a branch of the Ministry of Health, is subject to the Lunacy Act, 1890, as amended.

The Crown has never ceased to take its part in legislation. The prerogative rights under this head include the giving of the Royal Assent to Bills which have been passed by both Houses of Parliament, and the formal summons, prorogation and dissolution of Parliament, but these topics can more appropriately be discussed under Parliament.[3]

(8) The King is a Member of the Crown in Parliament.

The limit of these prerogative rights may, as has been seen, be enquired into by the Courts. Acts of Parliament may curtail, and even destroy, the Prerogative. No longer is there a general discretion to over-ride the law in the public

Prerogative and Statutory Limitation.

---

[1] Part X.

[2] It is unlikely that this Prerogative will in the future be utilised to secure the passage of a Bill through the House of Lords, having regard to the Parliament Act, 1911 (see Part III., Chap. IV., and Anson, *op. cit.*, Vol. I., pp. 299-309).

[3] Part III., Chap. II.

interest.   As late as 1920 it was possible for the Crown to argue that, where the Crown originally had a Prerogative and was afterwards given statutory powers by an Act of Parliament covering the sphere of that prerogative right, the Crown might, at its option, elect to proceed either under the Prerogative or under the statutory power.   Had such an argument been upheld, it would have been possible for the Crown to disregard conditions or safeguards which the statute might impose.   The case in which this argument was rejected both by the Court of Appeal and the House of Lords was *Attorney-General* v. *De Keyser's Royal Hotel, Ltd.* [1920], A.C. 508 ; K. & L. 325, which may be regarded as the leading case on the scope of the Prerogative in modern times. The facts and arguments may be summarised as follows :

> The hotel was required for the purpose of housing the administrative staff of the Royal Flying Corps during the War.   The Army Council offered to hire the hotel at a rent, but, negotiations having broken down, the premises were taken possession of under the Defence of the Realm Acts and Regulations made thereunder.   A Petition of Right was brought against the Crown claiming compensation as a matter of right for the use of the hotel by the Army authorities.   (At the time of the Army Council taking possession the Royal Flying Corps had not been superseded by the Royal Air Force, and was under the control of the War Office.)
>
> It was argued for the Crown that there was a Prerogative to take the lands of the subject in time of emergency in time of war, and that no compensation was payable for land so taken.   This argument overlooked the provisions of the Defence Act, 1842, which had been incorporated into the Defence of the Realm Acts.   These provisions imposed conditions upon the compulsory acquisition of land and provided for payment of compensation *as a matter of right* to persons whose land had been taken.
>
> The argument on behalf of the owners of the hotel was that in fact the Crown had taken possession under the statutes and regulations and so could not fall back on the prerogative right, under which no compensation could be claimed, except as a matter of grace.
>
> Both the Court of Appeal and the House of Lords rejected the argument of the Crown, and held that the Prerogative had been superseded for the time being by the statute, and therefore the Crown was not in any event entitled to act under the Prerogative.   It may be noted in passing that the Courts were prepared to hold, had it been necessary, that the alleged Prerogative to requisition land in time of war without paying compensation had not been proved.

It may still be regarded as open to question whether the Crown has not a wide discretion to act in time of grave emergency by virtue of the Prerogative alone. But it is unlikely that the power will again be exercised ; or if it be necessary to exercise it, the matter will be brought immediately to the attention of Parliament and the legality of the action taken confirmed by statute. An example is afforded by the Trading with the Enemy Acts, 1914-16. The Crown had Common Law rights in time of war to seize and forfeit private property belonging to the subjects of an enemy State ; *Daimler Co.* v. *Continental Tyre and Rubber Co.* [1916], 2 A.C. at p. 347 ; *In re Ferdinand, ex-Tsar of Bulgaria* [1921], 1 Ch. 107. It was found more convenient to restrict trading with the enemy in 1914-20 by statutory enactment. The Defence of the Realm Acts, 1914-15, which gave the widest powers to the Executive, probably sanctioned much that in strict law might have been effected by use of the Prerogative alone.

How much remains to-day of the theory of the Prerogative as enunciated by the Royalist lawyers in defending the King's acts at a time when the law was changing, so as to make them unconstitutional ? [1] *Comparison of Seventeenth and Twentieth Century Prerogative.*

(1) The King is still in theory of law the personification of the State.

(2) The old distinction between natural and politic capacities of the King is obsolete, but for some purposes he is regarded as a private individual, *e.g.*, as a landed proprietor of the Sandringham Estate. Even in this capacity he cannot be sued.

(3) There is still a distinction between the ordinary and absolute power of the King, as declared in the *Case of Impositions*. The exercise of the absolute discretion in foreign affairs cannot be questioned in a court of law, but only by attacking the Ministers concerned in Parliament, though legislation is necessary to take away existing rights of British subjects.[2] On the other hand, the ordinary powers of

---

[1] For a full discussion of this question see Keir and Lawson, *op. cit.*, pp. 57-62.

[2] But see as to treaties p. 67 below.

the King and his Ministers are within the law, and to these must be added the innumerable statutory powers conferred in recent years. The development of the Cabinet System was required just because of this distinction between ordinary and absolute powers.

(4) The Crown must make good its claim to the Prerogative. Neither the special plea of an Act of State nor of the Prerogative any longer ousts the jurisdiction of the courts, if invoked to protect the rights of a subject.

The disappearance of the Star Chamber in 1640, and with it the jurisdiction of the Council over that portion of public business, styled public law or matters of State and Government, which was usually transacted in the Privy Council, dealt a final blow at public law in England. Nevertheless, the classification of public and private law is retained for purposes of analysis and classification. The *General Warrant Cases* (1765) show that the idea of special treatment for the Government did not immediately disappear.[1]

(5) The King can do no wrong. This is still law and its consequences have been noted.

(6) The Prerogative and the statutory power to do the same act may overlap. Where Parliament has provided by statute for powers previously exercised by virtue of the Prerogative, they can only be exercised within such limitations as the statute may contain. The position is uncertain where the same power exists by Prerogative and statute, but where the statutory power restricts the prerogative power and does not merely put it into statutory form in identical terms, the Prerogative must be exercised as restricted by the statutory power; *Attorney-General* v. *De Keyser's Royal Hotel* (above).

(7) Since the *Case of Proclamations* (1611), legislation, otherwise than under the authority of Parliament, is against the law.

---

[1] Part VII., Chap. I.

B.

The Prerogative as Limited by Convention.

The intimate connection between the Conventions of the Constitution and the exercise of the Royal Prerogative has been emphasised by Dicey. The nature of these conventions has already been briefly touched on and enough has been said to justify their inclusion as a source of Constitutional Law (see Part I., Chap. I.). Their existence is due to the inadequacy of the legal rules relating to our Constitution. They may be described as forming a code of rules or precepts, outside the pages of the Statute Book or Law Reports, for the guidance of those who govern. Three further examples, in addition to that already discussed, may be taken from Dicey.

1 " The Cabinet is responsible to Parliament as a body for the general conduct of affairs." Dicey's Examples.

2 " The action of any Ministry would be highly unconstitutional, if it proclaimed war or peace in defiance of the wishes of the House of Commons."

3 " If a sudden emergency arises, *e.g.*, from the outbreak of an insurrection, the Ministry ought, if they require additional authority, at once to have Parliament convened and to obtain any powers that they may need for the protection of the country. Meanwhile, Ministers ought to take every step, even at the peril of breaking the law, which is necessary for restoring order or for repelling attack, and, if the law of the land is violated by them, must rely on Parliament passing an Act of Indemnity." [1]

The reader will observe the non-legal phraseology in which these three conventions are expressed. They have one thing in common ; they all relate to the exercise by Ministers of those discretionary powers which are theirs to exercise in the name of the King as part of his Prerogative. Conventions and Exercise of Prerogative.

It is not, of course, true that every so-called convention governs the use of the Prerogative ; others relate to the

[1] Dicey, *op. cit.*, pp. 416-18.

privileges of Parliament, *e.g.*, the convention which must be
regarded as obsolete since the passing of the Parliament Act
that " at some point or other in the event of a deadlock the
Lords ought to give way to the Commons." But there is a
close connection between the Prerogative and privilege, as
Dicey [1] points out : " The result follows that the conventions
of the Constitution looked at as a whole are customs or understandings as to the mode in which the several members of
the legislative body, which it will be remembered is the King
in Parliament, should each exercise their discretionary
powers, be they termed the Prerogative of the Crown or the
privileges of Parliament." The House of Commons in
particular has in the past claimed to exercise a wide discretion under claim of privilege, just as the Crown claimed
to exercise discretion under cover of Prerogative.

Conventions secure that Will of the People prevails. The observance of these conventions in relation to the
Prerogative secures that the will of the representative
assembly shall prevail, and further, if that assembly is out
of harmony with the majority of the electors, that new
representatives shall be elected. The exercise of the Prerogative of dissolution is designed to secure this. The
conventions bring out clearly the distinction between legal
and political control. Legally the Cabinet is responsible to
the Crown whose servants the members are. The declaration
of war or the conclusion of a treaty are matters in which the
Crown is legally competent, so long as there is no interference
with existing rights or imposition of new pecuniary burdens.[2]
At law, even to-day, the Crown has more or less absolute
power to deal with an emergency ; at all events the Crown
seemingly shares with its subjects the right to repel force
by force. But conventions regulate the use of the legal
power, so that it is exercised to give effect to the will of the
people, either through their representatives or directly by
ensuring an appeal to the electors. The Cabinet is dismissible by adverse vote of the Commons on a vital issue.
No Government would declare war or conclude a political
treaty without approval (previous or subsequent) of its action

---

[1] Dicey, *op. cit.*, p. 424.   [2] *Cf.* p. 76 below.

by the House of Commons. No Government would hesitate to call Parliament together in a grave emergency, and, meanwhile, to take steps to carry on orderly government, even if the steps were illegal and had subsequently to be legalised by an Indemnity Act. It is not going too far to say that the efficient working of the Constitution is secured as much by this code of conventions as by those rules which are embodied in law proper.

Perhaps the best example of the importance of convention is the understanding which governs the relations between Great Britain and the Self-governing Dominions in other parts of the British Empire. The status of the Self-governing Dominions has been achieved, not so much by changes of the law, as by mutual recognition that the Dominions are entitled to manage their own affairs.[1] Without altering the legal supremacy of Parliament, the convention, in practice absolute, of non-interference by the Home Government and Parliament, save at the request of the Dominion concerned, has enabled the Dominions to achieve their political independence.

C.

Act of State or State Necessity.

No account of the Prerogative is complete, if we omit to note that in addition (1) to the continued recognition by the courts of the Prerogative in matters where it has not been curtailed, and (2) to the growth of the political responsibility of the King's Ministers, the plea of State necessity, sometimes called " Act of State," will not avail to protect a person accused of an unlawful act. If the Government of the day needs, in order to cope with an emergency, greater powers

---

[1] This is not true of the establishment of the Irish Free State (Part IX., Chap. II.), which, while based on the Agreement of 1921, depends for its actual Constitution on legislation passed the next year, both by the United Kingdom Parliament and the Free State Legislature, set up under the Agreement which was also ratified by Parliament. See Irish Free State (Agreement) Act, 1922, and Irish Free State (Constitution) Act, 1922, in U.K. Statutes.

than the law allows, these powers must be obtained from Parliament, *e.g.*, the Defence of the Realm Acts, 1914-15 ; or, if need be, retrospective legality must be given to measures taken in an emergency, *e.g.*, Indemnity Act, 1920. But no official can be heard to say in a court of law in answer to the claim of a subject, that his act is that of the sovereign power, and, therefore, cannot be questioned, unless, of course, the act can be justified as falling within the Prerogative or statutory powers of the Crown.

Act of State as a Defence. The term, " Act of State," in its wider sense, means an act of the Executive as a matter of policy performed in the course of its relations with another State. Such matters as fall properly to be determined by the Crown as Acts of State in this sense are not subject to the jurisdiction of the municipal courts, and rights alleged to be acquired thereunder, *semble* even by British subjects, cannot be enforced by such courts. Acts resulting from a treaty of cession or by reason of annexation of territory fall into this class ; such acts may confer a title to property on the Crown which must be accepted by municipal law ; *West Rand Central Gold Mining Co.* v. *The King* [1905],[1] 2 K.B. at p. 409 ; *Nabob of the Carnatic* v. *East India Company* (below), and *cf.* the cases cited in Part IX., Chap. IV. (below), dealing with the acts of the Crown in a Protectorate. But it is clear from *The Parlement Belge* (1879), 4 P.D. 129, and *Walker* v. *Baird* (below) that, when the enforcement by the Crown of a treaty with a foreign State would necessitate the deprivation of a British subject of his existing rights, the Crown will be unable, without the sanctioning authority of a statute, to give effect to the treaty. In a narrower sense, the plea, Act of State, can be raised as a defence to an action brought against a

---

[1] In this case a British corporation failed to establish by petition of right the right to enforce against the Crown a claim for a wrong inflicted upon it by the Government of a State (the former South African Republic) which had been extinguished by acts upon the part of the Crown which were " Acts of State," namely, conquest and annexation. No interference with the rights of British subjects enforceable in British courts was thereby involved, and it lay within the discretion of the Crown to determine which, if any, of the liabilities of the extinguished State it was prepared to assume.

servant of the Crown by a subject of a foreign State for injury done to him or his property, provided that (1) the act of which the foreign plaintiff complains was committed on foreign territory ; (2) he is not an alien enemy ; and (3) the act was authorised or subsequently ratified by the Crown. The use of the term in such a case is in the nature of a special defence qualifying the rule of municipal law which normally prevents a wrongdoer setting up that his tortious act was done by command of the Crown.

The following cases serve to illustrate these two uses of the term, Act of State :—[1]

(1) In the wider sense, *Nabob of the Carnatic* v. *East India Company* (1792), 2 Ves. Jun. 56 ; 4 Bro. C.C. 180.

> A Bill in equity founded upon treaties between the Nabob and the Company was dismissed ; the treaties were political by nature, made between a foreign ruler and subjects of the Crown acting as an independent State under charter and statutory powers, and therefore were not subject to the jurisdiction of the English Courts.

(2) An act may become an Act of State in the narrower sense of a special defence to an action in an English court by subsequent ratification by the defendant's Government.

Buron v. *Denman* (1848), 2 Ex. 167 ; K. & L. 295.

> A Naval commander stationed on the coast of Africa was ordered by the Governor of a British Colony to secure the release of British subjects detained as slaves on foreign territory. He exceeded his instructions, since, in addition to releasing the slaves, he set fire to a barracoon belonging to a Spaniard who was trading in slaves at the place. The Spaniard brought an action in the English courts against the officer, but, the proceedings having been reported to the Home Government, the Crown adopted the act of the officer. The court held that the subsequent ratification by the Crown was equivalent to prior authorisation.

But such a defence is not available against (1) a British subject.

Walker v. *Baird* [1892], A.C. 491 ; K. & L. 310.

> An action for trespass was brought against a Naval captain who had seized the respondent's lobster factory under Admiralty orders with the object of enforcing the terms of a

[1] See also *Commercial and Estates Co. of Egypt* v. *Board of Trade* [1925], 1 K.B. 271, at pp. 290, 297, and Part IX., Chap. IV., below.

treaty with France. The lobster factory was situated on British territory. Held that the defence of Act of State was untenable and that legislation would have been required to legalise such action. The Crown tried unsuccessfully to establish the right, as an incident of its treaty-making power, to compel its subjects to recognise the provisions of a treaty having for its object the preservation of peace. The Privy Council, however, decided that the question was not properly raised and refused to decide it.

(2) Nor against an alien, the subject of a friendly State resident on British territory.

Johnstone v. *Pedlar* [1921], 2 A.C. 262 ; K. & L. 312.

An American subject was arrested by the Dublin police (before the establishment of the Irish Free State) and subsequently sentenced to a term of imprisonment for illegal drilling. At the time of his arrest a considerable sum of money was found on his person. Having served his sentence, the prisoner sued the police for the return of his money. The police put in at the trial a certificate by the Chief Secretary for Ireland confirming the seizure of the money. Held that the alien had a legal remedy for the recovery of the money, his status being as regards civil rights assimilated, with minor exceptions, to that of a subject ; *per contra* if the alien had been residing abroad, the only remedy would have been by diplomatic methods.

It is probable, in the case last cited, that the defence of Act of State might have prevailed, had the Crown formally withdrawn its protection owing to the alien's treasonable acts.

Any person, then, whether he be a private individual or a public officer, who interferes with rights of the subject renders himself liable to an action in tort. He can only plead the defences which the law allows, and State necessity is no defence to the servants of the Crown, despite the immunity which the Crown itself enjoys and such statutory protections as an official may often find in the Public Authorities Protection Act, 1893, and kindred Acts.

It has been clearly established since the eighteenth century group of cases known as the *General Warrant Cases* [1] that the Crown has no arbitrary power to arrest, but as the above cases indicate, the doctrine of State necessity lingered on until the twentieth century. ✓

[1] See Part VII., Chap. I.

CHAPTER V.

THE SUPREMACY OF LAW, OR THE RULE OF LAW.

THE portion of Dicey's Law of the Constitution which has been most subjected to criticism in recent years is that which deals with his conception of the Rule of Law, its nature and general application. Under this term, Dicey sees three distinct aspects. It is the purpose of this chapter to examine these aspects in the light of present-day conditions. Dicey's Rule of Law.

One aspect is that "the general principles of the Constitution result from judicial decisions determining the rights of private persons brought before the courts ; or, that with us the Law of the Constitution, the rules which elsewhere naturally form part of a constitutional code, are not the source but the consequence of the rights of individuals as defined and enforced by the courts." By this is meant that the legal position of the subject, *e.g.*, his freedom of action, of speech, is not secured by a guaranteed right in a formal code, but by the operation of the ordinary remedies available to a litigant against any, and all, who unlawfully interfere with his liberty of action. A person libelled can sue his defamer ; free access to courts of justice capable of affording any remedy to which he may be entitled is an efficient guarantee to the plaintiff against all wrongdoers. Provided that we except the immunity which the Crown enjoys as a litigant, this conception is in the main true. Such exemptions from liability from wrongful acts as the law recognises, *e.g.*, privilege in defamation, which allows what would otherwise be defamation to go unpunished, are available equally whether the person claiming the exemption be an ordinary citizen General Principles of Constitution deducible from Judicial Decisions.

or a State servant; to this the privileges attaching to parliamentary and judicial proceedings may seem to form an exception. But such immunities are recognised by the courts as part of the law of the land and therefore may be properly included in the conception—the Rule of Law. It does, however, overlook the fact that constitutional principles established in the past by the courts may be sacrificed by decisions of administrative officials under statutory powers enabling them to decide questions affecting the rights of the subject.

Other Meanings. In the second place, to Dicey the Rule of Law conveyed the meaning that no man is punishable, or can be lawfully made to suffer in body or goods, except for a distinct breach of law established in ordinary legal manner before the ordinary courts of the land. In this sense the Rule of Law is contrasted with every system of government based on the exercise by persons in authority of wide arbitrary or discretionary powers of constraint.

This may be regarded as the negative aspect of the Rule of Law and may conveniently be discussed with the positive meaning given by Dicey that " no man is above the law, but that every man, whatever be his rank or condition, is subject to the ordinary law of the realm and amenable to the jurisdiction of the ordinary tribunals." It has been seen that the courts of this country will not accept the plea of State necessity as a defence to an allegation of a wrongful act. Two things must be conceded, if we are to accept Dicey's propositions :—

(1) " The ordinary courts of the land " are not confined to a single system of judicature.

(2) Persons in authority are, in fact, clothed with many of those " wide arbitrary or discretionary powers," the absence of which Dicey regards as distinguishing our Constitution from the continental systems, greatly to the advantage of ourselves.

It is not suggested that, if these powers exist, they are unlawful, but that their existence deprives the citizen of the benefits of the Rule of Law, unless the Rule of Law means simply that the acts of all must be tested by law, and not that the legal test is uniform.

The following are some of the important criticisms which Criticisms have been used to question the existence of the Rule of Law :—

(1) *The Immunities of the Crown in Litigation.*[1] In practice this means the immunity of State Departments, but not the immunity of individual Crown servants, from process of law, and, in particular, immunity from tortious liability. This immunity is available against both the private citizen and the State servant who seek redress. Though the special process of Petition of Right is provided to remedy a breach of contract or detention of property by the Crown, not even this remedy is always available to the Crown's servants (*Leaman v. The King* [1920], 3 K.B. 663, where a soldier failed to recover arrears of pay at the rate agreed upon at the time of enlistment) ; nor possibly to others, if the defence is put forward that the agreement which has been broken tends to fetter the future executive action of the Crown. In *Rederiaktiebolaget Amphitrite* v. *The King* [1921], 3 K.B. 500 ; K. & L. 242, a Swedish shipping company sought, unsuccessfully, to establish liability for the breach of an agreement to release a ship of the company on completion of a voyage, the Ministry of Shipping having given an undertaking to that effect. This bears a close resemblance to the doctrine of State necessity.

(2) *Personal and Proprietary Immunities of Foreign States, their Rulers and Diplomatic Agents.*[2] These immunities do not free those who enjoy them from legal liability as such, but exempt them from process in English courts as a matter of international comity ; *Dickinson* v. *Del Solar* [1930], 1 K.B. 376. So long as the immunities were only claimed by foreign monarchs and their diplomatic representatives in respect of their personal misconduct, they could hardly be regarded as sufficiently important to form a serious exception to the Rule of Law ; but modern States engage in trade ; their vessels are State property, which, as such, is exempt from process ; *The Parlement Belge* (1880), 5 P.D. 197 ; *The Porto Alexandre* [1920], P. 30.

(3) *Trade Unions.* Section 4 (1) of the Trade Disputes Act,

[1] See Part V., Chap. IV.   [2] See Part IV., Chap. VII.

6

1906, prohibits the bringing of any action against a trade union, as such, in respect of tort.[1] This applies equally, whether the trade union is sued in its own name, or whether the action is brought against it through its officers. A trade union can, to a limited extent, sue and be sued on its contracts. This is not the place to discuss the merits or demerits of the immunity enjoyed by trade unions. To put the funds of powerful organisations outside the scope of legal liability, has the effect of depriving the citizen of his remedy, though he can still sue the actual individual who committed wrongful acts, unless acts normally wrongful are protected by some other statutory provision, *e.g.*, s. 3 of the Trade Disputes Act, 1906, which removes liability for inducing breach of contract, if the act is done in contemplation or furtherance of a trade dispute. It is to be noted that the immunity in tort is not confined to acts done in contemplation or furtherance of a trade dispute. This immunity seems also to be enjoyed at Common Law by a large number of unincorporated societies, such as social and games clubs, the Free Churches, and many charitable institutions ; *Brown* v. *Lewis* (1896), 12 T.L.R. 455 ; *Hardie and Lane Ltd.* v. *Chiltern* [1928], 1 K.B. 663 ; but it was held (prior to the Trade Disputes Act, 1906) that it did not extend to trade unions which, though recognised by statute, are also unincorporated bodies and cannot be incorporated ; *Taff Vale Railway* v. *Amalgamated Societies of Railway Servants* [1901], A.C. 426.

(4) *The Public Authorities Protection Act,*[2] *1893, and similar enactments.* This Act deprives a subject of a remedy by process in the courts, unless proceedings are started within six months after the act, neglect or default of the public authority (which includes the Crown and individuals executing public duties). Further, in the event of the defendant being

---

[1] But the trustees of a trade union may be sued in relation to the property of the union, which is by law necessarily vested in them, provided the action does not relate to a tortious act committed by or on behalf of the union in contemplation or furtherance of a trade dispute S. 4 (2). *Vacher* v. *London Society of Compositors* [1913], A.C. 107, only establishes the immunity of the trade union as such.

[2] The provisions of the Act are summarised in Keir and Lawson, *op. cit.*, at pp. 213 ff.

successful, there are penal provisions as to costs, the effect of which has been to render litigation with a public authority hazardous and expensive. The Act, which replaced a number of statutory provisions imposing shortened time limits to actions brought against various public bodies, serves to check both belated and unfounded actions against public authorities ; *Bradford Corporation* v. *Myers* [1916], 1 A.C. 242. The statute extends to lawful and unlawful acts, provided the latter are committed *bonâ fide* in the course of duty. It does not make an unlawful act lawful, since, apart from the time limit for suing, the courts have full jurisdiction. The protection ceases, however, if the default is from motives other than a desire and intention to perform a statutory or other public duty. The performance of a specific contract, *e.g.*, to supply coke to a consumer, made in pursuance of a statutory duty, such as maintaining a gas works, is not the performance of a public duty within the Act, even though the defendant body is a public authority and such contract would have been *ultra vires*, save for the statutory power. Further, the protection does not extend to actions for the recovery of land, since it is merely a private duty to respect the proprietary rights of others ; *Bradford Corporation* v. *Myers* (above) ; *Scammell* v. *Hurley* [1929], 1 K.B. 419. The Act has been held to apply to actions for threatened injury ; *Graigola Merthyr Co.* v. *Swansea Corporation* [1929], A.C. 344. The Constables Protection Act, 1751, protects constables who act in obedience to the warrant of a magistrate, even though the magistrate has acted without jurisdiction. The Customs Consolidation Act, 1876, s. 269, and the Inland Revenue Act, 1890, s. 29, afford Customs and Excise Officers a considerable measure of statutory protection. This principle is carried even further than the protection of officials in the strict sense, *e.g.*, the Lunacy Act, 1890, s. 330, protects, in the absence of proved negligence, doctors who have mistakenly branded a sane person with the stigma of insanity.

(5) *The Immunity of Judges.* This extends even to magistrates sitting in Courts of Petty Sessions.[1]

---

[1] Part V., Chap. II., where the subject is fully discussed.

6 *

(6) *Arbitration*. The growing practice of settling disputes without recourse to the courts must be noticed. By arbitration is meant an undertaking by the parties to submit the issues in dispute to the decision of a third party. Commercial contracts, insurance policies, and leases habitually contain a clause by which the parties agree to submit their differences to arbitration. In some cases Parliament has prescribed arbitration as a matter of law, *e.g.*, Agricultural Holdings Act, 1923. This is not a true exception to the Rule of Law, though subject to the provisions of Arbitration Act, 1889, the practice has the effect of ousting the trial of the issues in dispute from the adjudication of the courts. The Act applies when the submission to arbitration is expressed in writing, unless there is a contrary intention in the instrument. Under s.19, the arbitrator may state a question of law in the form of a special (consultative) case for the opinion of the court (a Divisional Court of the King's Bench Division), or under s. 7, he may state his award for the opinion of the court on questions of law. In the latter case he becomes *functus officio*, unless the case is remitted to him by the court (a single judge of the King's Bench Division). Moreover, an award may be set aside by the court if the arbitrator has been guilty of misconduct, or the award is bad in point of law, or has been improperly procured.

(7) *The Legislative and Judicial Powers of Officials*. Dicey emphasised the freedom enjoyed in this country from the effects of the continental system of *Droit Administratif*. He was at pains to contrast the disadvantages involved by a system of administrative law and administrative courts to judge disputes between officials and citizens with the advantages enjoyed by Englishmen through the absence of such a system. He seems to have lacked an appreciation of the working of administrative law in France, and, moreover, to have paid too little attention to the volume of administrative powers which had begun to spring up in this country, even in his day.[1] Although it is perhaps hardly correct to speak of the miscellaneous body of powers which officials

---

[1] But see Introduction to 8th edition.

exercise in this country as a system of administrative law, nevertheless their presence is regarded by many as a direct negation of the Sovereignty of Parliament and the Rule of Law. This is because these powers sometimes enable administrative officials to make rules and regulations having the force of law, without reference to, or adequate supervision by, Parliament and to decide disputes without possibility of appeal to courts of law.

The purport of these criticisms, then, is to emphasise two points : Summary of Criticisms of Rule of Law.

(1) That the Rule of Law is the rule of more tribunals than those which form the courts of the judiciary in the hitherto accepted sense.

(2) That there are privileged persons (and bodies) to whom are given by law immunities from the operation of the rules of law applicable to subjects in general, and who are entrusted with wide powers beyond the control of any court.

(1) There is no inherent reason why " the ordinary courts " should mean a single system of judicature. It is judicial method that matters rather than that the tribunal should be one of the regular courts. A judge requires the training of practice at the Bar ; the expert, be he civil servant or not, is, as such, a bad judge, and apt to prejudge the issue. It is suggested with some force that there are grave dangers in allowing the Executive to attain to judicial powers, since the official may have a double interest in the dispute he is called upon to decide. He is there not merely to see justice done, but to achieve a comprehensive working of the administrative policy out of which the dispute may have arisen. But a great many administrative disputes do not lend themselves to apt decision by a strictly judicial process, either on account of their nature, or even their multiplicity of numbers. On the other hand, there is less objection to taking a matter out of the hands of the ordinary courts, if for the great variety of tribunals which to-day exist, mainly as the result of modern administrative legislation, there could be substituted a system of administrative courts, where judicial procedure could be ensured for the settlement of those disputes which are capable of adjudication

after forensic argument. An even greater need is for a properly constituted tribunal to which appeals on points of law could be brought.

(2) The immunities which the Crown enjoys as litigant, and perhaps the legal position of trade unions are anomalies due to historical causes. So long as the former endure in their present form, it is difficult to accept the Rule of Law without important qualifications which may seem to negative its existence. The helplessness of the tens of thousands of Crown servants who are liable to dismissal at will without hope of legal redress ;[1] the absence of any remedy in tort against the Crown ; the protection afforded to public authorities, including individuals, by the Public Authorities Protection Act, 1893 ; all make it difficult to accept the proposition that every man is subject to the ordinary law administered by ordinary tribunals. Yet it must be remembered that these immunities are part of the law and are recognised as such by the ordinary courts. The immunities enjoyed by the judges, may be regarded as indispensable for the administration of justice. Moreover, they are shared to a large extent with the parties, their legal advisers and witnesses.

Origin of
Rule of Law.
Before forming any definite conclusion on the Rule of Law, as a feature of the English Constitution, it will be well to remember whence it came. For long the struggle for supremacy was between the personal monarch and the representative assembly, in practice, the landowners. Magna Charta, Habeas Corpus, the *General Warrant Cases*, have all helped to secure the liberty of the subject from the arbitrary conduct of the Executive. No personal tyranny is any longer to be feared. While it provides safeguards for rights, the State, nowadays, demands in return many duties from its subjects beyond allegiance and the payment of taxes. It is in imposing these duties, particularly the obligations involved by the vast schemes of social services, that the State dispenses with those very safeguards which

---

[1] It is not suggested that in practice the Crown arbitrarily dismisses its servants.

have long ensured freedom from interference. Few will
question the necessity for these services, but it is open to
dispute whether the absence of evil intention makes the
interference with liberty less objectionable. A cast-iron
system of bureaucracy may hold as many dangers to the
well-being of the subject as the rule of the autocratic monarch.

But our task is to observe the legal position. Whatever Conclusions.
demerits (and these are apt to be viewed from one side
only) there may be in the rule of Government Departments and public authorities in general, it is to be observed
that this rule is strictly legal, though the test of legality
may not be uniform. The control of Parliament may be
relaxed to allow other bodies to legislate ; the checks
obtainable through supervision by the courts may be taken
away by express enactment in particular cases ; but what is
sanctioned is lawful. To the student of the Constitution the
real question is whether the law should be moulded in the
direction of tightening up the Rule of Law, which Dicey saw
as safeguarded by parliamentary control and the submission
of all judicial issues to courts of law. To this subject we
will revert in the next two chapters.

To sum up : (1) The subject has legal remedies by
judicial process against his fellow-subject to protect his
liberty of action. These legal remedies are of two kinds :
(a) the ordinary remedies of the courts by way of money
damages, injunctions, decrees of specific performance, declarations, and in addition (b) the extraordinary remedies
by way of prerogative writs. The best known of these is
the writ of Habeas Corpus, but the writs of Prohibition and
Certiorari [1] are nowadays far more important in practice,
since they can be used to challenge the validity of powers
of a judicial or quasi-judicial nature which now frequently
affect the free enjoyment by the subject of his property and
freedom of action in general.

(2) The subject has limited legal remedies against the
Crown and the other public bodies which perform the
functions of government. In this respect the law gives

---

[1] Part VII., Chap. I. ; Part VI., Chap. IV.

immunities which correspondingly detract from the remedies available to the person aggrieved, and in some cases leave the subject without legal redress. Redress by political means is always open to him. So far as these immunities enable a person in authority to be a law unto himself, the Rule of Law as seen by Dicey may be said to be negatived, except in the sense that every act must have the authority of law behind it.

CHAPTER VI.

CONSTITUTIONAL ASPECTS OF THE LAW OF PUBLIC ADMINISTRATION.[1]

WE have preferred the term—Law of Public Administra- Definition. tion to Administrative Law. One authority has defined the latter as " law covering fields of legal control exercised by law-administering agencies other than courts and the field of control exercised by courts over such agencies." Public administration in England is mainly based on law adminis- tered by agencies other than courts of justice. In some matters the courts have control; in others such control is expressly excluded. There is no doubt that in this branch of governmental activity are to be found the chief developments of our Constitution, since Dicey and Maitland first pub- lished their views on Constitutional Law. The latter almost anticipated some of these developments.[2]

It is not difficult to explain the growth of this branch of Growth of law. So long as the State existed mainly for the purpose of Law of Public Ad- keeping order by repelling external enemies and by adminis- ministration. tering justice to its subjects, the safeguarding of rights was its paramount concern, though it may be observed that in backward societies the conception of law is almost exclusively concerned with duty to the ruler ; the ruler is not regarded as a power to enforce rights, except so far as he is the pro- tector of his people against their external foes. Nowadays, social welfare and economic problems generally play at least as important a part in the work of government as the older

---

[1] The most complete work on the subject is *Administrative Law*, by F. J. Port (Longmans, 1929), but *Justice and Administrative Law*, by W. A. Robson (Macmillan, 1928), is an equally important book on one aspect of the problems here discussed.

[2] *English Constitutional History*, pp. 405 ff.

and no less indispensable functions. State regulation involves the imposition of a variety of duties upon the subject to achieve the common purpose. But it has yet to be decided whether the methods adapted to the fulfilment of these older functions of government are equally efficient for achieving the social inter-dependence of modern times. The object of this chapter and the next is to state the principal forms of the law of public administration which encroach upon the Sovereignty of Parliament and the Rule of Law, and to attempt some conclusion.

It has always been recognised that in extreme emergency legislative and judicial safeguards may have to be ignored. The wide extension of governmental activity of recent years in the field of internal administration has produced legislation which confers upon the Executive powers uncontrolled, to a greater or less degree, by these safeguards. That these powers assist the task of the administrator in working out the details of a complex scheme of social amelioration is not denied. But doubts have arisen in the minds of lawyers in particular, and to a less degree of historians, lest the increased powers of the Executive should impose upon the subject a recrudescence of Stuart absolutism in the form of undisguised bureaucratic control.

A.

Legislation by Executive and Administrative Bodies.[1]

Parliament has never exercised its undoubted power to acquire the whole realm of original legislation. Prerogative legislation, by Order in Council or Letters Patent, is still employed by the Colonial Office as the principal mode of enactment for Colonies which have no representative government. The Annexation of the Colony of Kenya was so provided in 1920.[2] Orders in Council and Regulations made by Departments are recognised modes of exercising delegated legislative authority in time of emergency. The

---

[1] *Delegated Legislation*, by C. T. Carr (Cambridge University Press), contains a full and authoritative account of this subject.

[2] See Appendix C, pp. 404-5.

Defence of the Realm Acts, 1914-15, and the Emergency Powers Act, 1920, confer such power on the Executive. Administrative legislation has since the Reform Act been entrusted by Parliament to Government Departments in normal times to such an extent that it has now become an almost invariable practice. Statutory Rules and Orders of a legislative nature are published annually on the authority of the Rules Publication Act, 1893.

In 1920 there were enacted 82 Acts of Parliament and 2473 Statutory Rules and Orders. In 1925 the number of Public General Acts was 94, of which those (7) relating to the law of property produced 26 codes of rules, *i.e.*, detailed rules required by the Acts to complete the machinery for their operation. Of the remaining 84 Acts, 44 delegated powers of legislation to various authorities, among which may be mentioned the Privy Council, 5 Ministers in charge of Government Departments, 5 Government Departments proper, 7 bodies of Commissioners, the Lord Chancellor, the Lord Chief Justice, the Rules Committee of the Supreme Court, and local authorities. The activities of these and other authorities produced 1700 pages of Rules and Orders. But even this immense bulk excluded temporary rules, local rules, rules merely confirmed by Order in Council or Government Departments (*e.g.*, University Statutes confirmed by the Privy Council), any rules which are considered to be confidential and rules which are repeated annually. In addition to prerogative orders there are four classes of administrative legislation which are not included in the annual volumes.[1] The volume of this legislation has decreased somewhat in the last few years, but Statutory Rules and Orders still approach about 1200 in number each year, and this may be regarded as the normal post-war figure.

It is necessary to examine the reasons for the delegation of legislative power by Parliament. Lack of parliamentary time is usually urged in mitigation of Parliament's inability

Bulk of Delegated Legislation.

Reasons for Delegation.

---

[1] The figures given here have been taken from Allen, *Law in the Making*, Chap. VII. ; Port, *op. cit.*, 127.

to perform the whole task, or even the greater part of the task, of legislation.   There is undoubtedly some force in this argument, but on the other hand there is much to be said for a thorough revision of parliamentary procedure.   This is particularly so in the sphere of finance.   Urgency is another reason.   Parliament is not always in session, and its procedure is unnecessarily slow.   In the third place it is quite impossible at the time of the initial legislation in Parliament to foresee all the conditions that may arise out of the measure which is being considered.   It is, therefore, necessary to give to an administrative authority power to deal with the situation by means of rules and regulations. Finally, subordinate legislation is far more elastic than the parliamentary method and can, therefore, be utilised experimentally, should it appear that the original Act requires modification.

Types of Delegated Legislation

The following are types of delegated legislation :   Orders made by the King in Council ;   Rules and Orders made by Ministers ;   Provisional Orders ;   By-laws and Regulations of local authorities.   The first type is usually issued without further reference to Parliament.   Rules and Orders made by Ministers have normally to be submitted to Parliament, either before or after they have come into force, and Provisional Orders require statutory confirmation ; in the case of by-laws confirmation by a Central Department is generally required.[1]

Checks on Delegated Legislation.

What safeguards are available against the abuse of the legislative powers conferred on administrative bodies ?

(1). In the first place, Parliament retains the power to revoke or vary the delegated power.   Sometimes it requires that the Rules or Orders should be submitted to it, either in advance, or within a short while after taking effect.   The most stringent form of supervision is when an Order has to be approved by resolution of both Houses before it takes effect.   In other cases a draft of the Order must lie before Parliament for a specified number of days.   It must not, however, be supposed that these means afford an effective

---

[1] Specimen forms of Orders in Council and Ministerial Rules and Orders are given in Appendix C.

supervision over the exercise of powers. In practice they amount to little else than mere formality.

(2) The principal judicial safeguard is that rules and regulations made by administrative bodies under statutory authority are liable to be subjected to examination by an action raising the question of *ultra vires*. But various devices have restricted the application of this doctrine. In particular, the delegating Act sometimes contains such words as " general rules may be made under this section and shall be of the same effect as if they were contained in this Act, and shall be judicially noticed." The effect of this is to exclude the *ultra vires* doctrine and give the rules the force of an Act of Parliament ; *Institute of Patent Agents* v. *Lockwood* [1894], A.C. 347 ; K. & L. 10.[1]

(3) The principal administrative safeguards are that the powers should be defined as closely as possible, and only entrusted to suitable authorities. Even so, the supremacy of Parliament would appear to be imperilled by the delegation of powers in the following form which is taken from the Rating and Valuation Act, 1925, s. 67 (1) : " To do any other thing which appears to him (the Minister) necessary or expedient . . . for bringing the said provisions into operation, and any such order may modify the provisions of this Act so far as may appear to the Minister necessary or expedient for carrying the order into effect." This is known as the Statute of Proclamations, or Henry VIII., clause and occurs about ten times in modern statutes, usually, if not invariably, being restricted in its operation to a limited period of time deemed necessary to bring a new scheme into effective operation. It is imperative to have some such power where far-reaching schemes of social legislation are being created.

(4) Another administrative safeguard is to prescribe a

---

[1] But *cf. The King* v. *Minister of Health, ex parte Yaffé* [1930], 2 K.B. 98, where the Court of Appeal declined to take judicial notice of a Departmental Order expressed to have statutory effect on the ground that the procedure prescribed by the statute had not been followed. The decision of the Court of Appeal was reversed by the House of Lords [1931], W.N. 90, but the House was of the same opinion as the Court of Appeal that, if the Order did not comply with the statutory conditions, it was open to question.

public enquiry before an order can be made, *e.g.*, Shops Act, 1912, s. 7, under which a public enquiry can be held to ascertain the demand for early-closing in any district. A further safeguard lies in public notice of intention to exercise legislative powers, such as publication in the London Gazette, giving to public bodies interested an opportunity to make representations or suggestions regarding proposed rules. This in practice is usually done.

(5) Finally, and this is particularly important with regard to the by-laws of local authorities, supervision by a Government Department is able to ensure some sort of uniformity and to give the local authority the advantage of the experience of the Department.

Suggested Check.

A suggestion which has been made in relation to parliamentary control over delegated legislation is that there should be set up Standing Committees of both Houses of Parliament to scrutinise all Statutory Rules and Orders before they come into force, and to refer for the consideration of Parliament in the shape of an enabling or disabling resolution such of the Rules and Orders as appeared to the Standing Committees not to comply with the requirements of the Act by which they are authorised to be made.[1] The volume of work which would fall to these Committees would necessarily be large, but this difficulty could be overcome by the employment of a rota system. The functions of the Committees would be to censor delegated legislation and thus restore the parliamentary veto.

B.

Administrative Bodies in relation to Judicial Action.

Illustrations.

Numerous examples may be given of the growing tendency to transfer the decision of judicial disputes to non-judicial tribunals. There has already been noticed the growth of arbitration, whether by agreement between the parties or as the result of special statutory provision as under the Workmen's Compensation Act, 1925. Sometimes expert assistance is provided for the court without withdrawing from the court

[1] *The Times* Newspaper, 18 Feb., 1929.

the duty of decision. The Landlord and Tenant Act, 1927, s. 21, constitutes the County Court the tribunal for deciding claims by outgoing tenants in respect of improvements and loss of goodwill, but enacts that claims shall be referred for enquiry and report to one of a panel of referees appointed by four *ex-officio* nominators, two of whom are Supreme Court judges and two presidents of professional institutions.

Of greater constitutional importance is the multiplicity of permanent tribunals which are independent of the ordinary courts. Of these the Railway Rates Tribunal is a good example on account of its strictly judicial procedure. The General Commissioners for Income Tax, who form the initial appeal tribunal against ordinary assessments to tax and the Umpire under the Unemployment Insurance Acts exercise judicial duties in pursuance of statutory provisions. Many disputes are settled by purely administrative officers, *cf. Local Government Board* v. *Arlidge* [1915], A.C. 120 ; K. & L. 199 ; and *Board of Education* v. *Rice* [1911], A.C. 179, in which the House of Lords held that an administrative department had both the power and the duty to determine questions referred to it by statute, whether these questions involved law or fact.

Finally, there may be noticed the judicial powers conferred on private or semi-private corporations. The General Medical Council and the Law Society afford illustrations. Under the Solicitors' Acts, 1888 and 1919, a statutory committee, known as the Discipline Committee of The Law Society, was established for the purpose of hearing applications against solicitors, either to strike them off the Roll, or to compel them to answer allegations made against them by clients. This Committee is appointed by the Master of the Rolls. For the hearing of applications there sits a board of at least three members. Formerly only an advisory body, it now has power to order the solicitor to be struck off the Roll, to suspend him from practice or to order him to pay costs. It acts as a judicial body, hearing formally applications by complainants, administering oaths and generally conducting its procedure as a court of law. An appeal from an order of the Discipline Committee lies to the

Discipline Committee of Law Society.

High Court of Justice. A description of this tribunal has been given, because it affords a good example of what is meant when it is said that the Rule of Law can exist without a single system of judicature.

Absence of Right of Appeal. But where Parliament sanctions judicial or quasi-judicial powers being exercised by a single official, from whose decision no appeal is allowed, and who is given complete discretion as to the mode of procedure, including orders as to costs, then it may be argued that the Rule of Law has disappeared from the English Constitution. The Roads Act, 1920, s. 14 (3) [1] afforded an excellent illustration of this complete bestowal of judicial power on an administrative authority. In defence of this apparent departure from the Rule of Law it is urged that to delegate judicial power to an administrative body is an obvious means of determining the rights of individuals under some far-reaching measure of social reform, the carrying-out of which is entrusted to a Government Department. Prompt decisions of disputes are essential. Technical rules of evidence and procedure, not to mention the high cost of ordinary litigation, tend to make this difficult, if not impossible, to achieve through the ordinary judicial process. The very large number of disputes for adjudication, running into thousands in the case of insurance or pension claims, makes ordinary judicial proceedings impracticable. At all events the system seems to have come to stay, but certain difficulties which make their appearance from time to time in specific instances might well be removed. The secrecy of administrative methods, as illustrated by *Arlidge's Case*, might in some cases be abandoned. The provision of a final right of appeal to the courts on questions of law is another desideratum. Some would prefer administrative tribunals, both as courts of first instance and appeal. These should conform both as to their personnel and procedure to the normal judicial standards.[1]

Proposed Reforms. The reforms advocated in this connection are :

(*a*) Greater uniformity of procedure.

(*b*) Appeals on questions of law, whether to an adminis-

---

[1] Part II., Chap. I.

trative court of appeal or to a judge or judges of the High Court.

(c) The placing of administrative tribunals under the Lord Chancellor, and not under Government Departments.[1]

C.

Administrative Law and Administrative Lawlessness.

Dicey's views on the *Droit Administratif*[2] emphasise the disadvantages with which the French citizen is faced, when seeking a remedy against an official on account of the system prevailing in France (and elsewhere) of administrative courts with jurisdiction in administrative law. While it would be incorrect to consider administrative law as discussed by Dicey as completely equivalent to the law of public administration of to-day, his views on the subject of *Droit Administratif* are generally regarded as based upon a misconception of the position in France, as it was in his own day.

Our law of public administration is not an isolated body of law complete in itself. Much less has its development been on any scientific lines. No special system of courts exists to enforce its provisions which consist of an infinite variety of powers exercisable by a confusing number and variety of authorities, sometimes responsible to nobody but themselves. In France[3] *Droit Administratif* " consists of all the legal rules governing the relation of public administrative bodies to one another or to individuals." In its method the French system differs from our own in that the execution of an administrative decree is left to the discretion of the authority charged with its observance. For example, a decree takes this form : " All dogs shall be muzzled. Prefects of Departments are charged with the execution of

---

[1] For these and other proposals see Port, *op. cit.*, p. 358.

[2] Dicey, *op. cit.*, Part II., Chap. XII.

[3] See *Droit Administratif*, by Professeur Achille Mestre, in *Cambridge Law Journal*, 1929, pp. 355 ff., for a short account of the subject. M. Mestre claims that *Droit Administratif* no longer has any enemies in France to decry its arbitrary character.

7

this law." In England such an order would be enforced by an elaborate code of regulations issued by a Government Department to local authorities concerned. In contrast with the French Civil Law *Droit Administratif* is not codified. Its leading principles involve the responsibility of public administrative officers and the avoidance of irregular administrative acts (*faute de service* as compared with *faute personelle*) committed by officials. The *Conseil d'État* is the general court of law for administrative matters, organised as a court and distinct from the *Conseil* as an administrative body.

Dicey rightly points out that responsibility for irregular administrative acts has not always prevailed in this system, but he does not seem to appreciate to the full the influence of the *Conseil d'État* in replacing irresponsibility by the doctrine of *faute de service*. The *Conseil d'État* is certainly an administrative organ, and has repeatedly declared that there is a difference between the responsibility of the State and its agents and that of private individuals. *Actes de gouvernement* are not amenable to the jurisdiction of any court, any more than Acts of State under our law. Such *actes* can be definitely ascertained by means of the reported cases of the *Conseil's* decisions. On the other hand the liability of the Executive is increased, rather than reduced, in the administration of some public services. Further, to cite M. Mestre, " a method of redress is open free of charge to all who consider themselves aggrieved by any act of the public authority," where it takes certain forms tending to interfere with the subject's liberty, such as decrees in connection with the police. " This redress, modified by remedies for excess of powers, enables everyone subject to the administration who has been prejudiced in his lawful interests by reason of such act to demand annulment of the measure by the *Conseil d'État*." It is claimed for the *Conseil* that it represses the improper direction of administrative energies, such as " police measures applied in the financial interests of the administration or for the purpose of unjust discrimination against special classes of citizens." Conflicts of competence between the administration and the judicial authority are determined by a Tribunal of Conflicts.

The increased legislative and judicial powers of the Executive in this country are not subject to review by any tribunal corresponding to the *Conseil d'État*. Suggestions have been made that, in addition to the tightening of parliamentary control over delegated legislation, the establishment of a system of appeals in administrative cases is desirable. But the problem is a complex one, not rendered any more easy of solution by the presence of the Royal Prerogative in our Constitutional Law. Enough perhaps has been said to justify the application of rationalisation, to use a current term, to our law of public administration.[1]

D.

Consultation of the Judiciary by the Executive.[2]

An attempt was made in 1928 to secure the interpretation of administrative legislation by the High Court in the form of answers to hypothetical cases propounded by a Government Department. Under pressure from the judicial element in the House of Lords,[3] the device was withdrawn from the Bill in Parliament. Few lawyers will be found to commend this form of co-operation between the Executive and the Judiciary, because decisions on points of law which may subsequently arise in actual cases before the courts embarrass the judge and prejudge the issue of litigation. But it is submitted with some confidence that one solution of our administrative ills would be the adoption of a procedure whereby both Ministers in charge of Departments and other parties actually affected by the operation of the law could refer the legal issues raised for final adjudication by a single High Court judge. Such a procedure, avoiding the cumulative stages of ordinary appellate jurisdiction, would be well

---

[1] See Allen, *op. cit.*, pp. 347-8 ; for a short account of Administrative Law in Germany, see J. H. Morgan's Introduction to *Public Authorities and Legal Liability*, by G. E. Robinson (University of London Press).

[2] See Article by E. C. S. Wade, *L.Q.R.*, Vol. XLVI., pp. 169 ff. ; C. K. Allen's criticism in *L.Q.R.*, Vol. XLVII., pp. 43 ff. ; with Mr. Wade's reply, pp. 58 ff.

[3] Rating and Valuation Bill, 1928, Cl. 4 ; *Hansard : Lords Debates,* 1928, Vol. LXX.

adapted to the determination of doubtful points of the law of public administration, and is not without precedent.[1]   It is not only the Executive which chafes under the law's cumbrous machinery.   That the Executive has acquired its present degree of power is in some part due to the average citizen's desire to avoid the law courts.   It is in any event unjust that the citizen should have to face as at present three or four stages of appeal before his dispute with a Department can be settled, and in some cases not even this doubtful advantage is open to him, but his dispute is decided by the Department itself.

[1] Unemployment Insurance Act, 1920, s. 10.

CHAPTER VII.

CONCLUSION.

BEFORE closing the examination of general principles it will be well to state some tentative conclusions on the problem of constitutional development. Lawyers are by training, and usually by temperament, conservative in their outlook. Some generations have now been nurtured on the doctrines of Parliamentary Sovereignty and the Rule of Law. It would accordingly have been heretical to have approached a discussion of principles without examining these topics and their present-day implications. But it cannot be pretended that the result is satisfying. Lawyers are not concerned with sovereignty in the abstract. They are interested only in ascertaining where lies the supreme power to decide rules of conduct in any particular sphere of human activity. Can it be said with any approach to accuracy in 1931 that the supreme power is vested in the Central Government, secured by the harmonious co-operation of the Executive and a majority of the Legislature ? Or are we deceiving ourselves by paying too much attention to the unchanged form of law-making, neglecting the under-currents, which beneath the surface of artificial legalism have disintegrated the supreme law-making power within the State ?

The local authorities starting from the Reform Act era have acted as a check on the legislative organ. The policy of placing these institutions on a democratic footing was intensified and consummated by the end of the last century. The process of decentralisation was deliberately encouraged and with it the internal force of central government weakened. It is of little use for Parliament to be persuaded by the Executive that a new development in internal government

Checks and Balances of Legislative Power. (1) Local Authorities.

is desirable, if the co-operation of the local authority which has to administer the new public service, when constituted by statute, cannot be secured. Examples of Acts of Parliament which have proved to be " dead letter law " are not unknown. Consequently local authorities may operate as a powerful check on the exercise of legislative powers by the Central Government in imposing fresh duties upon them.[1] That the Central Executive is alive to this may be observed from the Local Government Act, 1929, and other measures of recent years, the indirect effect of which has been to re-impose central control, chiefly through finance. But local government, strengthened by the elimination of various *ad hoc* bodies, and with its chief powers concentrated upon larger units than in the past, may well in the future achieve equal partnership in legislative supremacy with the Central Executive and Legislature.

(2) Trade Unions. Nor can the influence of Trade Unions and kindred bodies be overlooked. Powerful combinations, such as Chambers of Commerce, Federations of Industries, Associations of Manufacturers and Unions of employed workers, professional, technical and manual, cannot in the long run be disregarded by Governments. The play and interplay of conflicting forces is the determining factor in all modern legislation. It is in the sphere of the interests of these organisations that the bulk of law-making takes place. Recent Acts relating to the mining industry and the railways afford illustrations of this check. The Coal Mines Act, 1930, Part III., is a good example.

(3) Advisory Committees. In this connection rule by advisory committees is becoming a feature. The Ministry of Transport, for example,[2] is required by law to consult a Rates Advisory Committee before revising charges or special transport services. The composition of the Committee is interesting ; it consists of a lawyer nominated by the Lord Chancellor, of two representatives of trading and agricultural interests, appointed by the Board of Trade after consultation with trading and agricultural organisations, of one representative of transport

[1] *Cf.* Part VI., Chap. I.
[2] Ministry of Transport Act, 1919, ss. 21, 22, 23.

interests, and of one of labour interests, appointed after consultation with the Parliamentary Committee of the Trade
Union Congress, and, at the discretion of the Minister of
Transport, of one additional member. This is an admirable
illustration of the checks and balances afforded by interested
parties. In addition the same Minister is to be advised by
a Roads Advisory Committee, and apart from these two
appointed bodies, the Act requires the Minister to set up a
panel of experts and of impartial persons of wide commercial
and trading experience appointed from nominees after consultation with interests concerned. The Minister cannot
exercise his powers of controlling transport undertakings
under s. 3 (1) *b* of the Act until he has consulted an advisory
committee so composed and the committee has reported.
The Police Council [1] is another interesting example of government by checks and balances.

Further evidence of the disintegration of legislative power (4) Semi-
may be found in the setting up of *ad hoc* bodies, which can- Govern-
not be regarded as Departments of State directly responsible Bodies.
to the Legislature, to control the internal development of the
country in a particular sphere, or manage the affairs of a
public or semi-public service, in whole or in part. Under
the Electricity Act, 1926, the Central Electricity Board was
set up to buy current from selected generating stations and
to sell it to authorised undertakings, as well as to construct
main electrification lines. The Board has power to enforce
its objects, *i.e.*, to legislate by schemes and otherwise impose
regulations which affect all electricity undertakings. The
National Wages Board, to settle in the last instance disputes
concerning the wages of railway employees, may be noticed
under this head.

Of particular interest are the legislative powers of the (5) Devolu-
National Assembly of the Church of England. The Assembly tion of
is constituted a legislative body ; after consultation between Governing
a committee of its own and a joint committee of both Powers.
Houses of Parliament, its legislation comes before Parliament
to be approved or vetoed by a simple resolution. There is
no power to amend.[2]

[1] Part IV., Chap. V.   [2] Part X., Chap. II.

Conclusion.

The conclusion is that the power to legislate is being disseminated. There is no longer, if indeed ever there was, one body of persons in the State with power to enforce its wishes by means of a parliamentary majority in disregard, or in opposition to, special or local interests concerned. Legislation is a compromise of conflicting issues ; Parliament can no longer compel, save in outward form.

Administration.

Turning to the second doctrine—the Rule of Law [1]—the conclusions advanced earlier in this Part have endeavoured to fit the facts of 1931 to Dicey's theory of 1885 by straining his meaning of ordinary courts and justifying and explaining the inroads of executive power. But it may be that Dicey's contentions are ill-founded ; that administration of internal government as understood to-day cannot be conducted on purely legal lines, leaving disputes and doubtful points to be determined judicially by organs independent of the administration. An " order " of a Government Department may be executive in form, legislative in effect, yet based upon a discretion judicially exercised. Orders confirming slum clearance schemes under the Housing Act, 1925 (now Housing Act, 1930), are of this nature. Where is the Rule of Law here, unless it means merely that there must be legal authority for all acts, and does not imply a uniform test of legality ? Where stands the separation of powers ? The solution may be, not in restoring the rule of the courts to a sphere where it is doubtful if it can function, but in augmenting the control exercised over the expert administrator by the lay members of elected bodies, whose servant the expert in fact is, be the elected body Parliament or a local authority. Such control could avoid the defects of bureaucracy—a stereotyped service and arbitrary rule, neither of which defects is it suggested is as yet characteristic of the Central Government of England.

---

[1] In 1929 the Lord Chancellor (Lord Sankey) appointed a Committee, under the chairmanship of the Earl of Donoughmore, representative of all interests concerned to examine and report on the present position of the Sovereignty of Parliament and the Rule of Law. The Report of this Committee has not yet been published (Feb. 1931).

PART III.

PARLIAMENT.

Law and Custom of the Constitution, by Sir Wm. Anson, Vol. I., 5th edition (Clarendon Press).

This book should be read for further information on all topics relating to the Law and Custom of Parliament.

Parliamentary Practice, by Sir T. Erskine May, 13th edition (Sweet & Maxwell).

The standard work for reference.

How Britain is Governed, by Ramsay Muir (Constable).

A recent criticism of the working of Parliamentary Government.

Governance of England, by Sir Sidney Low (T. Fisher Unwin).

A first-rate account of the practical working of the English Constitution.

Daily Life in Parliament, by H. Snell (Routledge).

An entertaining and readable little paper of the work of a member of Parliament.

CHAPTER I.

THE COMPOSITION OF PARLIAMENT.

A.

The House of Lords.

PARLIAMENT consists of two Houses, the House of Lords and The Two the House of Commons. These two Houses sit separately Houses. and are constituted on entirely different principles. The two Houses and the relations between them must be considered together in order to understand the process of legislation, but in considering their composition it is simpler to consider them separately.

The House of Lords consists of (i) about seven hundred The House of temporal and (ii) twenty-six spiritual peers. The Lords. temporal peers are :

(a) Princes of the Blood Royal.

(b) All hereditary peers of England and the United Kingdom ; these numbered 683 in 1928.

(c) Sixteen representative peers of Scotland elected from their own number for each Parliament by the hereditary peers of Scotland in accordance with the provisions of the Act of Union of 1707.

(d) Representative peers of Ireland elected for life. Until the Irish Free State Agreement of 1921 there were twenty-eight representative peers of Ireland, but there have been no elections since the foundation of the Free State.

(e) Seven Lords of Appeal in Ordinary appointed to perform the judicial duties of the House of Lords and holding their seats in the House for life.

107

The spiritual peers consist of twenty-six Bishops of the Church of England.

The Hereditary Peers of England and the United Kingdom.

The English House of Lords before the Act of Union with Scotland consisted of all the hereditary peers of England, and the Lords Spiritual. After the Act of Union all new peerages created were peerages of Great Britain, and similarly, after the Act of Union with Ireland, peerages of the United Kingdom. Peers of Great Britain and the United Kingdom have, like peers of England before the Union, the right to sit in the House of Lords.

Creation of Peers.

Peerages are created by the King. They are, except the judicial peerages, hereditary and, except in the case of Scottish and Irish peerages, carry with them the right to a seat in the House of Lords. A hereditary peerage can be created either by the issue of a Writ of Summons to the House of Lords, followed by the taking of his seat by the recipient of the Writ, or by Letters Patent, the method invariably adopted since very early times.[1] A peerage created

Descent.

by Letters Patent descends according to the limitation expressed in the Letters Patent, which is almost always to the heirs male of the body of the grantee, *i.e.*, to and through the male line in direct lineal descent from the grantee. A peerage created by Writ of Summons descends to the heirs general of the grantee, *i.e.*, to his heirs male or female, lineal or collateral. Thus in the absence of a special limitation in the Letters Patent, it is only a peerage created by Writ of Summons which ever devolves upon a female. Where there is only one female heir, she becomes a peeress in her own right. Where, however, there are two or more female descendants of equal degree, the elder is not preferred to the younger, and both or all inherit as co-parceners. In such cases a peerage falls into abeyance. Such an abeyance may on the advice of the Committee of Privileges of the House of Lords, which on reference from the Crown decides claims to existing peerages,[2] be terminated by the Crown in favour of one co-heir, or in process of time may become vested in

[1] See specimen Letters Patent in Appendix C.

[2] The validity of new creations is determined by the House itself, acting through the Committee.

one descendant of the last holder of the peerage. The House of Lords has recently resolved to restrict drastically the practice of terminating abeyances.

Where a grantee has no direct male heir, the Letters Patent in order to preserve a peerage from extinction often limit the peerage to the daughter of the grantee and her heirs male of the body, in default of heirs male of the body of the grantee, *e.g.*, the Roberts, Wolseley, and Strathcona peerages of late years. Special Remainders.

A peerage cannot be alienated nor surrendered, nor has a peerage any connection with the tenure of land. This last point was finally decided by the *Berkeley Peerage Case* (1861), 8 H.L.C. 21. A peerage cannot be created with a limitation of descent which is unknown to the law relating to real property; *Wiltes Peerage Case* (1869), 4 H.L. 126. It was decided by the *Wensleydale Peerage Case* (1856), 5 H.L.C. 958, that the Crown, although able to create a life peerage, cannot create such a peerage carrying with it the right to a seat in the House of Lords. This case illustrates the importance of the distinction between a peerage and lordship of Parliament. It was perhaps unfortunate that the decision in this case shut the door on any attempt to strengthen the House of Lords without the need of legislation and without increasing the number of the hereditary peerage. The decision was given in spite of weighty arguments to the contrary. The view which prevailed was that, as the issue of a Writ of Summons followed by the taking of his seat by the recipient created a hereditary peerage, it was therefore impossible to allow to take his seat one whose peerage was by Letters Patent limited to his life. An alien cannot receive a Writ of Summons to the House of Lords, nor may a Writ of Summons be issued to a bankrupt peer. Neither an infant nor a woman may sit in the House of Lords. It was decided in the case of *Viscountess Rhondda's Claim* [1922], 2 A.C. 339, that the Sex Disqualification (Removal) Act, 1919, gave no right to a peeress in her own right to receive a Writ of Summons to Parliament. Felony followed by penal servitude or imprisonment with hard labour or for twelve months disqualifies from sitting or voting until after pardon or Restrictions and Disqualifications.

completion of the term of punishment. The House itself when sitting to try one of its own members [1] can impose any sentence of disqualification.

The right of the Crown to create new peers was, until the passing of the Parliament Act, 1911, an important weapon to enable the Crown on the advice of the Prime Minister of the day to compel the House of Lords to give way to the House of Commons in cases of conflict. The Peerage Bill of 1719 attempted to limit the power of the Crown to create new peers, but the proposal was rejected.

The Peers of Scotland. No new Scottish peerages can be created since the Act of Union of 1707. When a new Parliament is summoned, the Scottish peers elect sixteen of their number to represent them in the House of Lords. Scottish peerages in respect of which no vote has been given since 1800 have been struck off the electoral roll. It was at one time thought that the Crown could not confer upon a peer of Scotland a peerage of the United Kingdom entitling him to a hereditary place in the House of Lords, but this view was rejected by the judges in 1782 in advising the House upon the claim of the Duke of Hamilton and Brandon.

The Peers of Ireland. The Act of Union with Ireland provided that the Irish Peerage might be maintained to the number of a hundred. During the Union there were twenty-eight representative life peers of Ireland, and elections took place as and when vacancies occurred.

The Lords of Appeal in Ordinary. The Lords of Appeal in Ordinary are the seven judicial peers appointed by virtue of the provisions of the Appellate Jurisdiction Acts, 1876-1929, to perform the judicial functions of the House of Lords. They have the right to sit and vote for life. They are entitled to a salary of £6000 per annum, and must have held for two years high judicial office,[2] or have practised at the Bar for fifteen years.

The Lords Spiritual. The Lords Spiritual are twenty-six Bishops of the Church of England holding their seats in the House of Lords until they resign from their episcopal office. The Archbishops of Canterbury and York and the Bishops of London, Durham

---

[1] Part. V., Chap. I.   [2] *Ibid.*

and Winchester have the right to a seat in the House of Lords. The remaining twenty-one spiritual peers are the twenty-one diocesan Bishops having seniority of date of appointment. When a Bishop dies or resigns, his place in the House of Lords is taken not by his successor, but by the next senior diocesan Bishop.

A summons to Parliament cannot be withheld from a peer who is entitled to it, and individual Writs of Summons are sent to both the temporal and spiritual peers. Although peerages are now invariably created by Letters Patent, a Writ of Summons must be received for each Parliament before a peer is entitled to take his seat. The Writ addressed to a Bishop contains the *præmunientes* clause which instructs the Bishop to warn the clergy of his diocese to be present and consent to whatever Parliament ordains. This clause is a reminder of the time when the clergy attended Parliament as a separate estate. The clergy always attended reluctantly and preferred to grant taxes in Convocation. Since the fourteenth century they have not, except for the spiritual peers, attended Parliament, and since the seventeenth century they have ceased to tax themselves. Writs of attendance are also issued to the High Court judges and the Attorney-General and Solicitor-General. It is in fulfilment of this summons that the judges have, in the past, performed the duty of advising the House of Lords on points of law in particularly difficult cases.[1]

The Summoning of Peers.

B.

The House of Commons.

The House of Commons consists of 615 members, representing 595 constituencies in England, Wales and Northern Ireland. Of these constituencies eighteen return two members each and one (the Scottish Universities) returns three members. The remainder are single member constituencies, each with an approximately equal number of electors.

The Constituencies.

[1] Part V., Chap. I.

History of the Franchise —the County Franchise. Since 1929 every adult person has, apart from certain disqualifications, possessed the franchise, or the right to vote. Before 1832 the franchise in county constituencies was exercised only by those males possessing freehold property worth 40/- a year. In 1832 the county franchise was extended to long leaseholders and copyholders of property of the value of 40/-, and to all male leaseholders for terms of not less than twenty years of property of £50 annual value. Various minor changes were made in the county franchise by the Representation of the People Act, 1867, and the Representation of the People Act, 1884, enfranchised all male householders and lodgers occupying rooms of the annual value of £10 unfurnished. This Act enfranchised the agricultural labourer.

The Borough Franchise. The borough franchise before 1832 varied from borough to borough. The most common qualifications were : tenure of land, membership of a corporate body, tenure of particular tenements, and in certain cases merely residence. The Act of 1832 established for the boroughs a uniform occupation franchise for any male who occupied as owner or tenant any house, shop or other building of the annual value of £10. The Act of 1867 extended the franchise to any male householder occupying a separate dwelling house, and to lodgers occupying lodgings of the annual value, unfurnished, of £10. The borough franchise was substantially unaffected by the Act of 1884. The Act of 1867 may be said to have enfranchised the skilled artisan.

Representation of the People Act, 1918. The Representation of the People Act, 1918, established a uniform franchise for county and borough constituencies. The franchise was given to all adult males possessing the qualifications either of residence in the constituency or of the occupation of business premises in the constituency. The franchise was also given to women of thirty years of age who, or whose husbands, occupied, in accordance with the requirements as to occupation for local government elections, a dwelling house or land or premises of the annual value of not less than £5. In the university constituencies, which were created by the Act of 1867, and subsequently increased in number, all male graduates were entitled to vote, and all women of the age of thirty who were either graduates, or would have been graduates if their university had admitted women to degrees.

The present qualification for the franchise depends upon the Representation of the People Acts of 1918 and 1928. The requirements for men and women are the same. The franchise can be exercised by all adults possessing any of the following qualifications :— *The present Franchise.*

(*a*) Residence.

(*b*) Occupation of business premises of annual value of £10.

(*c*) Being the husband or wife of any occupier of such business premises.[1]

(*d*) In the case of the universities, being a graduate.

It is a condition precedent to exercising the vote that the elector should be placed upon the register of electors. The register is prepared once a year by the registration officer of each parliamentary borough and county. To be registered in respect of either the residence or occupation of business premises qualification the elector must have resided or occupied business premises in the constituency, or in another constituency in the same parliamentary borough or county, or in any adjoining parliamentary borough or county, for a period of three months ending in the June before the annual preparation of the register which comes into force on October 15. An elector may record not more than two votes.[1] If two votes are given, one of them must be given in virtue of a residence qualification ; nor may an elector vote more than once in respect of the same qualification or in the same constituency. The register is prepared by the registration officer, who is either the clerk of a county council or the town clerk of a borough. Any person may claim to be placed upon the register, and anyone may object to such claims. An appeal lies from the decision of a registration officer to the County Court, and on a point of *The Register of Electors.*

---

[1] The Representation of the People Bill, 1931, proposes to abolish, except in the case of the City of London, (*b*) and (*c*), leaving residence as the sole qualification, apart from the university franchise. The Bill removes the last traces of plural voting.

law from the County Court to the Court of Appeal. Once placed upon the register any person not suffering from any legal incapacity, such as infancy or insanity, is entitled to vote. The refusal by a returning officer at an election to accept the vote of any person of capacity upon the register is an infringement of a right of property, and renders the returning officer liable to an action for damages ; *Ashby* v. *White* (1704), 2 Lord Raymond, 938 ; K. & L. 72.

Disqualifications for the Franchise. The following are the various disqualifications for the franchise. The franchise may not be exercised by :

(*a*) Infants.

(*b*) Peers, other than peers of Ireland who are members of the House of Commons.

(*c*) Returning officers,[1] *i.e.* Sheriffs of counties, or Mayors of parliamentary boroughs.

(*d*) Aliens.

(*e*) Idiots.

(*f*) Persons convicted of treason or felony who have not completed their punishment or been pardoned.

(*g*) Persons convicted of certain offences under the Corrupt and Illegal Practices Act, 1883.

Disqualifications for Membership. There are also disqualifications which prevent a person from being elected as a member of the House of Commons. The following persons may not be elected :

(*a*) Aliens who have not become naturalised.

(*b*) Infants.

(*c*) Lunatics. By the provisions of the Lunacy (Vacating of Seats) Act, 1886, the committal or reception of a member must be reported to the Speaker. The Speaker obtains a report from the Lunacy Commissioners, followed by another report after an interval of six months, and, if the member is still of unsound mind, his seat is vacated.[2]

(*d*) Peers, other than Irish peers, who have not been elected as one of the twenty-eight representative peers.

(*e*) Clergy of the Church of England, the Church of Scotland and the Roman Catholic Church.

---

[1] A returning officer, if registered as an elector, may give a casting vote in the event of a tie.

[2] For other methods see Anson, *op. cit.*, Vol. I., pp. 81 and 82.

(*f*) Persons holding pensions at the pleasure of the Crown, other than holders of civil and military service and diplomatic pensions.

(*g*) Bankrupts.[1]

(*h*) Persons guilty of corrupt practices, contrary to the Corrupt and Illegal Practices Act, 1883.

(*i*) Persons convicted of treason or felony who have not completed their term of punishment or been pardoned, provided that they were sentenced to penal servitude or imprisonment with hard labour or for more than twelve months. A member convicted of a misdemeanour may be expelled by the House of Commons, but such expulsion does not amount to a disqualification.[2]

(*j*) Persons holding or undertaking any contract or commission for, or on account of, the Public Service. Any person so disqualified is subject to a penalty of £500 for every day on which he sits and votes.[3] In the case of *Sir Stuart Samuel* [1913], A.C. 514, it was held by the Judicial Committee of the Privy Council, to which the question was referred, that this disqualification applied to a member of a firm employed by the Secretary of State for India in Council to purchase silver for the purpose of the Indian currency. An Act of Indemnity may be passed to relieve a member from the penal consequences of sitting or voting during the existence of such a disqualification, *e.g.*, The William Preston Indemnity Act, 1925, which was passed to relieve a member from the consequences of sitting as a member of the House of Commons, while holding a contract with the Postmaster-General.

(*k*) The holding of certain offices under the Crown. Disqualification by Office. This disqualification requires a more detailed discussion. Many office-holders are expressly excluded from membership of the House of Commons by various statutes.[4] No

---

[1] The disqualification lasts until five years after discharge, unless the discharge is accompanied by a certificate that the bankruptcy was not caused by the bankrupt's misconduct. [2] Chap. III.

[3] The House of Commons (Disqualification) Act, 1931, removes the disqualification on this ground in the case of certain contracts, such as a lease to the Post Office of a site for premises or a telephone agreement.

[4] For a full list see Anson, *op. cit.*, Vol. I., pp. 101 ff.

statutory disqualification applies to civil servants in general, but it has been provided by Order in Council that any civil servant seeking election to the House of Commons must resign office on announcing his candidature. Officers in the Navy, Army, and Air Force (other than officers in the Reserve, and Army and Air Force officers on the Retired List), are forbidden by King's Regulations to seek election to the House of Commons. The House of Commons has determined that the acceptance of a commission by a member vacates his seat. Returning officers are excluded from sitting for the constituency in which they act as returning officer, unless they have delegated their duties to the registration officer as deputy returning officer. Judges of the High Court of Justice and the Court of Appeal are excluded by the provisions of the Supreme Court of Judicature (Consolidation) Act, 1925, which embodies the effect of a long standing disqualification.

History of Statutory Disqualification of Office Holders.   By the Act of Settlement of 1701 it was enacted that no person holding any office of profit under the Crown should be capable of being elected as a member of the House of Commons. This provision, which would have prevented the development of the Cabinet system, as we understand it, by excluding Ministers from the House of Commons, was repealed before it took effect. The basis of the present law on this subject is an Act passed in 1707 in the reign of Queen Anne. This Act disqualified from election persons accepting any " new " office created since 1705. The acceptance of any " old " office, *i.e.* pre-1705 office, unless disqualification was expressly attached to such office by statute, though annulling the election of the person accepting it, left him eligible for re-election. Many " new " offices have been expressly excepted from this statute by the statutes creating them, and correspondingly certain " old " offices have had attached to them total disqualification. Other " old " offices received complete exemption from disqualification, *e.g.*, Secretaryships and Under-Secretaryships of State and the Chancellorship of the Exchequer. But no more than six Secretaries of State and six Under-Secretaries of State may sit in the House of Commons at

the same time. In 1929 it was necessary to pass an Indemnity Act to relieve from penalties Under-Secretaries
who had broken this rule, through too many members of
the Commons being appointed to these offices ; Under-
Secretaries of State Act, 1929.

A reference to the full list of special statutes imposing dis- Ministerial
qualification will show that in the twentieth century the Act Office.
of Anne was very far from being of general application, but
it applied to some important ministerial offices. The Re-
election of Ministers Act of 1919 exempted from the necessity
of re-election any member accepting an " old " office within
nine months after the summoning of a new Parliament,
and the Re-election of Ministers Act, 1926, abolished
altogether the necessity for re-election, provided, of course,
that the office accepted was one not involving total disqualification from membership of the House of Commons.
This Act thus abolishes those of the provisions of the Act of
Anne which relate to the necessity for re-election on acceptance of an " old " office.[1]

From early times a member has been unable to resign Cessation of
his seat, and the acceptance of an office disqualifying for Membership.
membership is the only method of cessation. The offices
commonly used for this purpose are the Stewardship of
the Chiltern Hundreds and the Stewardship of the Manor
of Northstead. The Re-election of Ministers Acts do not
apply to these offices.

Voting Methods.

In the single member constituencies each elector can
vote for only one candidate. When, as at the present
day, there are more than two political parties seeking the
votes of the electorate, this system of election makes little
provision for the representation of minorities, and can lead
to strangely anomalous results.

It is mathematically possible for one party to obtain the
largest aggregate of votes in the country and yet not win a

---

[1] For discussion of reasons for retaining up to 1926 ministerial offices
as " old " offices, see Anson, *op. cit.*, Vol. I., pp. 88-90.

single seat in the House of Commons. In 1922 the Conservative Party polled 38 per cent. of the votes cast in the election and obtained 347 seats in Parliament. In 1929 the Conservative Party again polled 38 per cent. of the votes cast, but obtained only 253 seats.

Alternative Vote.

Various systems of voting have been suggested with a view to securing a better representation of minorities and a distribution of seats corresponding more nearly to opinion in the country. The most notable of these are the alternative vote and proportional representation. If the alternative vote was adopted,[1] single member constituencies would be retained, but the elector would be allowed to express his choice of candidates in order of preference. If no candidate obtained a clear majority, the lowest on the list would be eliminated, his votes being distributed according to the second preferences shown on the voting papers. While making it more probable that in each particular constituency the final choice would be the real choice of the electors, the alternative vote would not provide adequately for the representation of minorities in the country. Under proportional representation, which is used in the university constituencies returning more than one member, the country would be divided into large constituencies, each returning several members. The elector would vote for the candidates in order of preference, and any candidate obtaining a certain quota of first preferences would be immediately elected. His surplus votes would be distributed to other candidates according to the second preferences expressed, and again any candidate then obtaining the quota would be returned and a similar distribution of his surplus would take place. This system would undoubtedly provide adequate representation of minorities, but the drawback to any such system is that the more variety of opinion is represented, the more difficult it becomes to secure a Government of any one party with a reasonable working majority in the House of Commons.

Proportional Representation.

---

[1] The Representation of the People Bill, 1931, proposes to adopt this method.

CHAPTER II.

THE SUMMONING, OPENING, PROROGATION AND DISSOLUTION OF PARLIAMENT.

PARLIAMENT is summoned by the King by Royal Proclama- The Crown tion,[1] and it is by the King that it is prorogued and dissolved. and Parliament. The modern practice is that one Proclamation both dissolves Parliament and summons a new one. Parliament cannot meet without a summons from the Crown. There is no express rule of law requiring an annual meeting of Parliament.[2] But in practice legislation relating to the essential business of governing the country, including taxation and the expenditure of public funds, is only passed for one year and must be renewed annually, thereby ensuring that Parliament meets at least annually.

After the summoning of Parliament by Royal Proclama- Elections to tion, individual writs are issued to the members of the House of Commons. House of Lords, and writs are issued to returning officers commanding them to cause an election of members of the House of Commons to be held. The returning officer gives notice of the date and place of election, now the same day for every constituency, namely, the eighth day after the Proclamation summoning a new Parliament. On this day, which is known as Nomination Day, candidates must be proposed. Every candidate must be proposed and seconded by an elector, and eight other electors must sign his nomination paper. If there are more candidates than vacancies, a poll is ordered and is held nine days after Nomination Day. Voting is by secret ballot, and each elector indicates his choice by placing a mark against the name of the candidate

[1] See Form of Proclamation in Appendix C.
[2] The Triennial Act, 1694, requires Parliament to meet every three years.

whom he favours.   There are provisions enabling soldiers
and sailors and others who have been placed upon the absent
voters' list to vote by post or in certain circumstances by
proxy.   University electors send voting papers by post to
the returning officer.

By-elections.   When a vacancy occurs in the House of Commons during
the course of a Parliament, the Speaker issues a warrant for
the issue of a writ for the holding of a by-election.

Dissolution.   Parliament endures for five years, unless it is sooner dissolved by the King.   It has for long been a convention of
the Constitution that the King will dissolve Parliament at
the request of the Prime Minister of the day, and similarly
will not dissolve Parliament unless so requested.   The right
to request a dissolution is a powerful weapon in the hands
of a Prime Minister, who may use it to threaten recalcitrant
supporters with the expenses of an election, and to compel
the House of Lords to give way to the House of Commons,
unless they are prepared to face the unfavourable result
of an appeal to the country.   A Prime Minister, whose
Government is defeated in the House of Commons on a
major issue, is expected either to resign, or to request
a dissolution.   This convention might be enforced, if the
majority of the House of Commons was prepared to
paralyse the government of the country by refusing to pass
essential Acts, *e.g.*, Finance Act or the Army and Air Force
(Annual) Act.[1]   Whether the convention as to the right to
a dissolution will survive the growth of three parties it is
difficult to determine.   It may be that the King would
refuse, should the occasion arise, to grant a dissolution at
the request of a Prime Minister who had never had a clear
majority in the House of Commons.   If, for instance, a
Labour Government without a clear majority took office
with the support of the Liberals, and that support was
withdrawn, there is no over-riding constitutional objection
which would prevent the King from sending for the leader
of either the Conservative Party or the Liberal Party before
granting a dissolution at the request of the defeated Labour

[1] Part VIII., Chap. I.

Prime Minister, though a dissolution was granted in such circumstances in 1924.

Until 1867 the death of the King affected the duration of Parliament. Since the Representation of the People Act, 1867, the duration of a Parliament has been independent of the life of the King. Should the King die after a dissolution, but before the day fixed for the meeting of the new Parliament, the old Parliament assembles and sits for six months or until sooner dissolved. Should Parliament be prorogued or adjourned at the time of the death of the King, it meets at once without summons. *Demise of the Crown.*

Prorogation brings to an end, not the existence, but a session of Parliament. Prorogation is effected either by the King in person or by a Royal Commission. It terminates all business, and any Bills not having reached their final stages must be begun again when the new session of Parliament is opened. *Prorogation.*

An adjournment of Parliament is affected by either House of Parliament for such time as it pleases, but does not put an end to any uncompleted business. The King may call upon Parliament to meet before the conclusion of an adjournment intended to last for more than fourteen days. *Adjournment.*

Parliament, after a dissolution or a prorogation, is opened either by the King himself or by Royal Commissioners. As soon as the Houses have assembled, the Commons are summoned to the House of Lords and, at the opening of a new Parliament, are bidden to choose a Speaker. After choosing the Speaker the House adjourns until the following day, when the election of the Speaker is announced to the Lord Chancellor in the House of Lords. When a new Parliament meets, the Lords take the oath of allegiance as soon as. Parliament has been opened, and the Commons as soon as the Speaker has been approved by the King and has himself taken the oath. *Opening of Parliament.*

The first business of a new session of Parliament is the reading and discussion of a Speech from the Throne. The Speech, which is prepared by the Cabinet, and announces in outline the Government's plans for the session, is delivered in the House of Lords either by the King himself or, when *The Speech from the Throne.*

Parliament is opened by Commission, by the Lord Chancellor. In each House an address is moved in answer to the Speech, and the debate on this address provides an opportunity for a general discussion of the political situation. Before the address is moved the ancient right of Parliament to deal with matters not brought before it by the Crown is asserted by the formal first reading of an obsolete bill ; in the Lords usually a Bill for the better regulation of " Select Vestries " ; in the Commons a Bill for the better preventing of " Clandestine Outlawries."

CHAPTER III.

PRIVILEGES OF PARLIAMENT.

A.

House of Commons.

In order that neither the House collectively, nor members The Speaker. of the House, may be obstructed in the performance of their high and important duties, there have from earliest times been attached both to the House itself and to members thereof certain privileges and immunities. It is convenient before discussing these privileges to say something of the Officers of the House through whom those privileges are claimed and enforced. The Chief Officer of the House of Commons is the Speaker. It is through the Speaker that the House communicates with the Sovereign. He, too, issues writs for the filling of vacancies, and the warrants of the House for the commitment of offenders, and the summoning of offenders to the Bar of the House. He has the important duty of determining whether or not a Bill is a Money Bill within the meaning of the Parliament Act, 1911.[1] Except when the House is sitting in Committee he is its Chairman and is responsible for the orderly conduct of debates. The Speaker is appointed at the commencement of each Parliament. The party with a majority in the House selects a candidate for the Speakership. Such selection is usually made after consultation with the other parties, in order that the selection may be the unanimous choice of the House. It is customary for the previous holder of the office to be re-elected, if he is again willing to serve.

[1] Chap. IV.

123

Chairman of Ways and Means.   When the House is in Committee the chair is taken by the Chairman, or Deputy Chairman, of Ways and Means, or one of a panel of five chosen by the Speaker. These officers preside over Committees of Supply and Ways and Means, and over other Committees of the Whole House. They preside also over the House as Deputy Speaker in the unavoidable absence of the Speaker. They are party appointments, and are made afresh with every change of Government.

Permanent Officers.   The permanent Officers of the House are the Clerk of the House of Commons and his assistants who prepare the journals of the House, and the Sergeant at Arms and his assistants who attend the Speaker and enforce the orders of the House.

Demand of Privileges.   At the commencement of each Parliament the Speaker formally claims from the Crown for the Commons " their ancient and undoubted rights and privileges." Those particularly mentioned are " that their persons may be free from arrests and molestations ; that they may enjoy liberty of speech in all their debates and may have access to His Majesty's Royal person whenever occasion shall require ; and that all their proceedings shall receive from His Majesty the most favourable construction." The right of access is a collective privilege of the House exercised through the Speaker. These privileges are formally granted through the Lord Chancellor.

Freedom from Arrest.   The privilege of freedom from arrest is to-day of little importance. It extends only to civil arrest, other than arrest for contempt of court. Since the abolition of imprisonment for civil debt (except where it is shown that a debtor has means to satisfy a judgment, but has neglected to do so), civil arrest is of rare occurrence. Since the reign of George III. this privilege has not extended to members' servants. It extends to members for a period of forty days before and after a meeting of Parliament. This privilege does not protect a member from proceedings under the Bankruptcy Acts.

Freedom of Speech.   The privilege of freedom of speech, though so well established as to be unquestioned, is manifestly of the first importance. In 1397 one Haxey questioned the expenses of *Haxey's* the King's household. The King rebuked the Commons *case.* and Haxey was condemned in Parliament as a traitor, but this judgment was reversed after the accession of Henry IV., and the privilege of freedom of speech was judicially recognised by the Crown and the House of Lords. In Henry VIII.'s reign one Strode was imprisoned by the Stannary *Strode's case.* Court of Devon for invading the province of that Court by introducing a Bill in Parliament to regulate the tin mines of that county which were within that court's jurisdiction. He was fined and imprisoned, but an Act[1] was passed declaring that any legal proceedings " for any bill, speaking, reasoning, or declaring of any matter or matters concerning the Parliament should be utterly void and of none effect." In 1629 Eliot, Hollis and Valentine were convicted for *Sir John* seditious speeches in Parliament. The judgment was *Eliot's case.* subsequently reversed in the House of Lords on the ground that words spoken in Parliament could only be judged in Parliament. Finally it was enacted by the Bill of Rights, Bill of 1689, " that the freedom of speech or debates or proceedings Rights. in Parliament ought not to be impeached or questioned in any court or place out of Parliament." No action will lie against a member of Parliament for words spoken by him in the course of parliamentary proceedings, and similarly no action will lie for any publication among members of Parliament by order of the House, or in the ordinary course of parliamentary business. It was held in *Lake* v. *King* (1667), 1 Saunders 131, that an action would not lie for defamatory matter contained in a petition printed and delivered to members.

In connection with the privilege of freedom of speech it is Privacy of convenient to consider also the right of the House to secure Debate. privacy of debate, and also to publish its debates and proceedings outside Parliament. The House has always enjoyed the right to exclude strangers. Until the eighteenth century the House resented and prevented any publication of accounts of its proceedings, but since the famous conflict

[1] 4 Hen. VIII. c. 8 ; *Statutes of the Realm*, iii. 53.

between the House of Commons and Alderman John Wilkes in 1771 this privilege has not been insisted upon. The House, however, may at any time resolve that publication is a breach of privilege.

Publication of Debates and Speeches.
The right of the House to publish its proceedings otherwise than among its own members was at Common Law restricted by the ordinary law of defamation (libel and slander). In the case of *Stockdale v. Hansard* (1839), 9 A. & E. 1 ; K. & L. 78, Stockdale sued the publisher of certain reports, which were published by order of the House of Commons and were available for sale to the public. The defendant contended that he had acted under an order of the House of Commons, a court superior to any court of law, whose orders could not be questioned ; and further that the House of Commons had declared that the case was a case of privilege ; that each House of Parliament was the sole judge of its own privileges ; and that a resolution of the House declaratory of its privileges could not be questioned in any court of law. The Court of Queen's Bench rejected the defence, holding that only the King and both Houses of Parliament could make or unmake laws ; that no resolution of any one House of Parliament could place anyone beyond the control of the law ; and that, when it was necessary in order to decide the rights of private individuals in matters arising outside Parliament, courts of law should determine the nature and existence of privileges of the House of Commons. They held further that there was no privilege of the House of Commons which permitted of the publication outside the House of defamatory matter. Similarly, although a member of Parliament might speak freely within Parliament, if he published his speech outside Parliament, he was liable to proceedings for defamation ; *Rex v. Creevey* (1813), 1 M. & S. 278.

The case of *Stockdale v. Hansard* was followed by the Parliamentary Papers Act, 1840, which enacted that any proceedings in respect of defamatory matter contained in a publication made by authority of the House of Lords or the House of Commons would be stayed on the production of a certificate from an Officer of the House. This Act also protects in the absence of malice the publication of fair and accurate extracts from papers published under the authority of Parliament. Although not strictly connected with parliamentary privilege, it may be added for the sake of completeness that, unless a plaintiff can prove malice, a fair and accurate unofficial report of proceedings in Parliament is privileged. This was decided in *Wason v. Walter* (1868), L.R., 4 Q.B. 73 ; K. & L. 105. The interest of the public in the publication of parliamentary proceedings is of more importance than occasional inconvenience to individuals. This decision does not protect reports of detached parts of proceedings published with intent to injure individuals, nor does it protect the publication of a single speech for the purpose of injuring an individual. It was decided in *Davison* v. *Duncan* (1857), 7 E. & B., 229, that privilege attaches to the *bonâ fide* publication of a speech by a member for the information of his constituents.

The House of Commons has the right to control its own proceedings and to provide for its own proper constitution. Except in cases of ordinary crimes committed within the precincts of Parliament, the courts will not interfere with what takes place inside Parliament. The House lays down its own rules for the regulation of its own internal concerns and has the power to enforce those rules. This question will be discussed more fully in considering the relations between the House of Commons and the courts. *Right to control Internal Proceedings.*

It was for long doubtful as to whether or not the House had the right to determine questions of disputed elections. A dispute arose upon this question between James I. and the House of Commons in 1604, when one Goodwin, an outlaw, was elected for Buckinghamshire. A compromise was effected, but the Commons exercised the right to determine such questions from 1604 to 1868. They were first determined by Committees, but since 1672 were determined by the whole House. The growth of party government resulted in disputed election returns being settled purely by party votes. In 1770 Grenville's Act transferred the decision of these questions to a committee chosen by lot. In 1868 the House handed over the duty of deciding disputed *Disputed Elections* *Goodwin's Case.* *Grenville's Act.*

elections to the courts. The procedure is regulated by the Parliamentary Elections Act, 1868. A petition against an election is presented to the High Court of Justice, and the trial of such petition is conducted by two judges of the High Court sitting in the borough or county in which the election took place. The determination of the court is notified to the Speaker, and is entered upon the journals of the House.

Expulsion.

The House of Commons still retains the right to pronounce upon legal disqualifications for membership, and to declare a seat vacant on such ground. The House may, however, as in the case of Mitchel, in 1875 (I.R. 9 C.L. 217), refer such a question to the courts. The House of Commons cannot, of course, create disqualifications unrecognised by law, but it may expel any member who conducts himself in a manner unfit for membership. A constituency may re-elect a member so expelled, and there might, as in the case of John Wilkes, take place a series of expulsions and re-elections. Expulsion is the only method open to the House of dealing with a member convicted of a misdemeanour.

Committal for Contempt.

The House of Commons has the right to enforce its privileges and regulate its proceedings by punishing those who offend against the House. Punishment may take the form of an admonition by the Speaker, or in more serious cases of a reprimand by the Speaker, or of commitment to prison by order of the House. The House of Commons may, in virtue of its inherent and essential right to control its own proceedings and maintain its dignity, commit any person for contempt, but such commitment cannot be for a fixed term, as a prisoner is automatically entitled to release when the House is prorogued.

Quasi-Privileges.

The right of the House of Commons to the exclusive control of financial measures,[1] and the right of impeachment [2] cannot strictly be described as privileges, and are more conveniently discussed when considering the financial and judicial functions of Parliament. It is convenient to consider

---

[1] Chap. IV. and pp. 190-1. [2] Part V., Chap. I.

here the question of the payment of members of Parliament. Since 1911 every member not in receipt of an official salary has received a salary of £400 a year. Members, too, are sometimes paid by private bodies, *e.g.*, trade unions. Lord Shaw has expressed the view that a contract to pay a man in return for his support in Parliament of the views of a particular person or party would be unenforceable as contrary to public policy; *Osborne* v. *A.S.R.S.* [1910], A.C. at p. 110 *et seq.*

Questions of privilege have been a source of conflict between the House of Commons and the courts. As has been seen the court, in the case of *Stockdale* v. *Hansard*,[1] maintained the right to determine the nature and limit of parliamentary privileges, should it be necessary to determine such questions in adjudicating upon disputes between individuals. The courts will not, however, except in the case of crimes, take notice of matters arising within the precincts of Parliament. In *Eliot's case* the question as to whether or not the court could deal with an assault committed in the House of Commons was expressly left open when the judgment was reversed upon another ground, but it seems clear that there is no authority showing that crimes committed in the precincts of Parliament cannot be punished by the ordinary courts. The present relationship between the courts and Parliament is made clear by the cases centring round Mr. Bradlaugh. In *Bradlaugh* v. *Gossett* (1884), 12 Q.B.D. 271 ; K. & L. 96 the Queen's Bench refused to declare void an order of the House of Commons preventing Mr. Bradlaugh, who had been duly elected member for Northampton, from taking the oath. It was held that the House of Commons had the exclusive right to regulate its own proceedings, and that no court could interfere with the exercise of such right. The Parliamentary Oaths Act, 1866, permitted certain persons to make a declaration or affirmation instead of taking an oath. It was disputed whether or not Mr. Bradlaugh was a person entitled to make such a declaration. Any person making

The Courts and Parliamentary Privilege.

---

[1] P. 126 (above).

the declaration, otherwise than as authorised by the Act, could be sued for certain penalties. The House of Commons permitted Mr. Bradlaugh to make the declaration. In a subsequent action against Mr. Bradlaugh for penalties— *Clarke* v. *Bradlaugh* (1881), 7 Q.B.D. 38 ; *Bradlaugh* v. *Clarke* (1883), 8 A.C. 354—it was established that the Parliamentary Oaths Act, 1866, and the Promissory Oaths Act, 1868, did not authorise Mr. Bradlaugh to make the declaration.   It is pointed out in the judgment of Stephen J. in *Bradlaugh* v. *Gossett* that, should the House of Commons have attempted by resolution to state that Mr. Bradlaugh was entitled to make the statutory declaration, such a resolution would not have protected Mr. Bradlaugh against an action for penalties :

> " We should have said that for the purpose of determining on a right to be exercised within the House itself, the House, and the House only, could interpret the statute ; but that as regarded rights to be exercised out of, and independently of, the House, such as the right of suing for a penalty for having sat and voted, the statute must be interpreted by this court independently of the House." [1]

In *Paty's Case* (1704), 2 Lord Raymond 1105, Chief Justice Holt, in a minority judgment, held that a writ of Habeas Corpus would go to release anyone committed for contempt by the House of Commons, where the cause of committal stated in the return to the writ was insufficient in law.   If, however, no cause for committal is shown in the return, other than contempt of the House, the Court of King's Bench is powerless.   As it is put by Lord Ellenborough in *Burdett* v. *Abbot* (1811), 14 East 1 : " If a commitment appeared to be for a contempt of the House of Commons generally, I would neither in the case of that court nor of any other of the superior courts enquire further." This view prevailed in *The Sheriff of Middlesex's Case* (1840), 11 A. & E. 809 ; K. & L. 92. It appears, therefore, that there may be two views laid down as to the privileges of the House of Commons. The House may act upon one

---

[1] Oaths Act, 1888, now permits an affirmation in lieu of an oath in all places and for all purposes where an oath is required by law.

view when regulating its own proceedings and committing for contempt, while the court may act upon another view when privileges arise in civil disputes. As has, however, been pointed out many times in the decided cases, the court will naturally pay the greatest attention to the views and customs of the House of Commons in deciding what are the privileges of that House.

B.

House of Lords.

The privileges of the House of Lords are :

(*a*) Freedom from civil arrest for themselves and their servants for a period of forty days before and after a meeting of Parliament.

(*b*) Freedom of speech.

(*c*) Freedom of access to the Sovereign for each peer individually.

(*d*) The right to commit for contempt. The House of Lords can commit a person for contempt for a definite term, and the imprisonment is not terminated by prorogation of Parliament.

(*e*) The right to try and be tried by their fellow peers for treason or felony or misprison of either.[1] This privilege should more properly be described as a privilege of the peerage rather than of the House of Lords and extends to peeresses.

(*f*) The right to exclude disqualified persons from taking part in the proceedings of the House. The House itself exercises, through the Committee of Privileges, the right of determining the validity of new creations to the peerage. Claims to old peerages are referred by the Crown to the House of Lords, and are also decided by the Committee of Privileges of the House. This body is not bound by its own previous decisions.

Privileges of the House of Lords.

---

[1] Part V., Chap. I.

9 *

Officers of
the House.

The House of Lords is presided over by the Lord Chancellor. This office may be, but in practice is not, held by a commoner, and the Woolsack on which the Lord Chancellor sits as Speaker of the House is technically outside the precincts of the House. Permanent Officers of the House are the Clerk of Parliaments, the Gentleman Usher of the Black Rod and the Sergeant-at-Arms.

CHAPTER IV.

THE FUNCTIONS OF PARLIAMENT.

A.

Legislation.[1]

THE function of legislation is the most important function of Parliament, and when we speak of parliamentary supremacy,[2] or rather of the supremacy of the King in Parliament, we mean that Parliament has in co-operation with the Crown the right to legislate on every topic, and that no other body may legislate, except with the permission of Parliament. *Legislative Sovereignty.*

Parliament cannot legislate without the concurrence of all its parts, and therefore the assent of the King is required. The King, not only summons Parliament and can dissolve Parliament, but the assent of the King is necessary before any legislation can take effect. After a Bill has passed through all its stages in Parliament it is sent to the King for the Royal Assent, which is given either by the King in person or by Commission. In giving the Royal Assent ancient forms are used. A Public Bill is accepted by the words " Le roy le veult." The formula for the veto was " Le roy s'avisera." A Bill of a personal nature is assented to by the words " Soit fait comme il est désiré." A Money Bill is assented to with the words " Le roy remercie ses bons sujets, accepte leur benevolence et ainsi le veult." The right of veto has not been exercised since the reign of Queen Anne, and may be said to have fallen into disuse.[3] *The Royal Assent.*

---

[1] Appendix A. contains specimen legislative forms.
[2] Part II., Chap. III. [3] Part I., Chap. II.

Parliament
Act, 1911.

Except as provided by the Parliament Act of 1911, all legislation needs the assent of both the House of Lords and the House of Commons. A Bill may be introduced in either House, but it must pass through all its stages in both Houses. It was for long part of the unwritten law that the House of Lords might reject, but might not amend a Money Bill—a Bill dealing only with national taxation or finance.[1] To have amended a Money Bill would have been a trespass upon the exclusive right of the Commons to grant or refuse supplies to the Crown. The rejection by the House of Lords in 1909 of the annual Finance Bill, led to the passing of the Parliament Act of 1911. By the provisions of that Act legislation may in exceptional circumstances be effected by the King and Commons alone. A Bill may be presented for the Royal Assent without the concurrence of the Lords,

(1) If the Lords fail to pass a Bill certified by the Speaker to be a Money Bill, *e.g.*, the annual Finance Bill,[2] within one month after it has been sent up to them by the House of Commons ; or,

(2) If they refuse in three successive sessions to pass a Public Bill—a Bill affecting the community generally—other than a Money Bill, and if two years have passed between the dates when it was read a second time in the first and a third time in the last of those sessions. A Bill to extend the duration of Parliament is excepted from the provisions of the Parliament Act. In view of the increased power given by this Act to the House of Commons, a provision was embodied into it limiting the duration of Parliament to five, instead of seven, years.

There have been many proposals for the amendment of the Parliament Act. Those most commonly advocated are the transferring the duty of certifying a Bill as a Money Bill from the Speaker to some impartial committee, and the exception from the provisions of the Parliament Act of any Bill to alter

---

[1] See definition in Parliament Act, 1911, S. 1 (2).

[2] It is curious that the Finance Bill is not always endorsed with the Speaker's Certificate, nor are many Bills which are unquestionably Money Bills.

the constitution of the House of Lords itself. Those who believe in the necessity of a second chamber with power to revise and insist on its revisions, and with power to compel the democratically chosen first chamber to appeal to the electors who appointed it before introducing any drastic changes in the law, would welcome the repeal of the Parliament Act, but any such proposal involves the reform of the House of Lords.

It would be impossible to give new powers or restore its old powers to the House of Lords as at present constituted on the hereditary principle. Many proposals have been brought forward for a reformed House of Lords, *e.g.*, the nomination of life peers by the Crown on the advice of the Government of the day, election by large constituencies, and combinations of those and other methods. It has at present been found impossible to secure agreement upon any proposal for House of Lords reform. Reform without an increase of powers would be useless. The House of Lords as at present constituted performs competently the duty of revising legislation which is not regarded as sacrosanct by the Government of the day, and of debating matters of public importance. A reformed House of Lords, if based upon the elective principle, would inevitably come into conflict with the House of Commons, while, if based on any other principle, its composition would almost inevitably be predominatingly conservative. It is noticeable that in all countries where the second chamber is of most value and authority the constitution is federal. The lower house is elected by constituencies composed of an approximately equal number of electors, while the upper house is elected [1] by the component parts of the federation, *e.g.*, the States, regardless of their population, and safeguards state rights against the claims of the Federal Government.

Before discussing the process of legislation it is convenient to notice other practical qualifications of the statement that Parliament alone possesses legislative power. The growth of delegated legislation is discussed elsewhere in this book.[2]

House of Lords Reform.

Delegated Legislation.

---

[1] Not in Canada, see p. 352.
[2] Part II., Chap. VI.

The increasing complication of the business of governing
the country has led to ever-growing readiness to delegate
legislative powers. Power is given to Government Departments to draw up Provisional Orders which achieve the same
object as Private Acts of Parliament. Acts of Parliament
frequently contain provisions giving power to Departments
to draw up regulations which will come into force either
after approval by Parliament, or immediately, subject to
annulment by Parliament within a certain time. It is, of
course, true that these powers of legislation are conferred by
Parliament, and can be annulled or restricted by Parliament,
but in fact the real power of legislation in such cases rests
with Government Departments.[1]

Legislation and the Executive.

It must further be remembered that, even in the case of
ordinary Public Bills, the legislation which is given legal
form by Parliament is in practice legislation by the Cabinet,
or more often legislation by individual Ministers. The
increasing rigidity of the party system, due largely to
the increase in the number of electors and the fact that only
a large and powerful party can afford the expense and
provide the machinery necessary for reaching the present
day electorate, has made it possible for the Cabinet of the
day, at least where that Cabinet has a clear party majority
in the House of Commons, to force through Parliament any
legislation which it proposes. In old days Ministries were
frequently defeated in the House of Commons, and still
more frequently were forced to withdraw measures by
threats of revolt among their followers. To-day members
are returned by the assistance of their party; without the
assistance of their party they cannot hold their seats; the
threat of a dissolution involving the expense of an election,
and still more the threat of the withdrawal of the support of
the party organisation will, except in rare cases, enable a
Government to force its legislation through Parliament.
Almost all Acts of Parliament are brought forward by the
Government of the day. Really important measures are
the result of decisions of policy taken in the Cabinet, but the

[1] Part II., Chap. VI.

bulk of such legislation is initiated by Government Departments,[1] is drafted by the legal staff of Departments and the Parliamentary Counsel to the Treasury, who are responsible for drafting Government Bills,[2] and is subsequently administered by Government Departments. Measures which are really proposed by the Cabinet may be said to have been proposed by Parliament, inasmuch as the Cabinet represents that party which has a majority in the House of Commons.

Private members of Parliament have the opportunity, if they are successful in a ballot, of introducing Public Bills on Fridays, and on certain other days, unless, owing to pressure of business, these times are annexed by the Government. A Private Member's Bill has no opportunity of becoming law, unless the Government will allot sufficient time to it later in the session, or adopt the measure as its own after the second reading.

Private Members' Bills.

The process of legislation is complicated. A distinction must be drawn between Public and Private Bills. A Public Bill is a Bill which effects the community generally. A Private Bill is a Bill relating to some matter of individual, corporate or local interest. A Private Bill must not be confused with a Public Bill introduced by a Private Member. It will be convenient first to state in outline the process by which a Public Bill, other than a Money Bill, becomes an Act of Parliament, reserving for later discussion Money Bills and Private Bills. A Public Bill is presented and receives a formal First Reading. It is then printed. Then follows a Second Reading. The debate on the Second Reading is a debate on the general merits of the Bill. When a Bill has received a Second Reading, it is referred either to one of the six Standing Committees of between forty and sixty members appointed

The Process of Legislation.

Public Bills.

[1] As part of the policy approved by the Ministers in charge of the Departments.

[2] In spite of the efforts of Parliamentary Counsel modern legislation becomes increasingly obscure and ill-drafted. Pressure of parliamentary time necessitates legislation by reference to other statutes, and amendments are hastily inserted in Parliament at the last moment in order to secure the passage of a Bill.

by the Committee of Selection, or in the case of more important measures to the whole House sitting in Committee, if the House so decides on motion. In Committee members may move relevant amendments, and may speak any number of times in support or opposition to such amendments. When a Bill is committed to a Committee of the whole House, the Speaker leaves the chair, and his place is taken by the Chairman of Committees.[1] The Committee of Selection appoints a panel of Chairmen, who choose from among themselves the Chairmen of the Standing Committees. After the Committee stage, which is necessarily lengthy, the Bill as amended is reported to the House, and is again discussed. Further amendments and alterations may be made on the Report stage, and, if necessary, the Bill may be recommitted to Committee. Finally the Bill is submitted to a Third Reading. During the Third Reading debate only verbal alterations may be made.

Closure. The complicated stages which a Bill must go through and the amount of time involved have led, with the increase of the amount of business to which Parliament must attend, to the adoption of various methods of curtailing debates. The simplest method is that known as the "Closure." Any Member may, either in the House or in Committee, move "that the question be now put." The Chairman may refuse to put the motion on the ground that it is an infringement of the rights of the minority, but, if the motion is put and carried, it brings to an end the debate which is pending. The motion "that the question be now put" is voted upon without debate. It can only be carried in the House itself, if the number voting in the majority is not less than 100. Another method is known as the "Kangaroo" closure. The Speaker has the power, when a Bill is being discussed on the Report stage, to select from among the various amendments and additions proposed those which shall be discussed. The Chairman of a Committee of the whole House may exercise similar power. In 1930 this procedure was adopted in the case of a Bill under consideration by

---

[1] The Chairman of Ways and Means or his Deputy.

one of the Standing Committees. More drastic still is the
" Guillotine." By resolution of the House (which means in
practice the determination of the Government), various
periods of time are allotted to each stage of a Bill. At the
end of each period the portion of the Bill in question is
carried without discussion.

After passing through the House of Commons a Bill is Conflict
sent up to the House of Lords,[1] where it must pass through between
Lords and
the same stages as in the House of Commons. If the Lords Commons.
accept a Bill without amendment, they announce to the
Commons that they have agreed to the Bill. If they amend
the Bill, they return it with a message that they agree to the
Bill with amendments to which they desire the consent of the
House of Commons. In the past if the Commons disagreed
with the amendments made by the Lords, there were two
methods for attempting to effect an agreement. A conference
could be held. A conference was a formal meeting of
members appointed by each House and known as
" Managers." The Managers of one House drafted reasons
for their disagreement, and delivered these reasons to the
Managers of the other House. If the conference was what
was known as a " free " conference, the Managers
endeavoured to convince the Managers of the other House
and to effect an agreement. Conferences were not, in
practice, often held and may be regarded as obsolete. It was
more usual for a Committee of the House which was disagree-
ing with amendments to send to the other House a statement
of their reasons together with the amended Bill. In practice
a settlement is reached, if at all, by informal conferences
between the party leaders.

The passing of a Money Bill differs from the passing of Money Bills.
an ordinary Public Bill. A Money Bill can only be introduced
in the House of Commons. Apart from the provisions of the
Parliament Act, custom forbids that a Money Bill (whether
or not certified as such under the Parliament Act) should
be amended by the Lords. This rule is, however, often

---

[1] It must be remembered that a Bill may be introduced in either House.
Important Bills which do not raise acute political controversy are frequently introduced in the House of Lords.

waived owing to the fact that so many Money Bills raise issues of general political, as much as financial, importance. The passing of the Parliament Act made this rule less important to the Commons. If the Lords amend a Money Bill, the question of privilege is raised when the Bill is returned to the House of Commons, but the House may waive privilege and consider the amendments made by the Lords on their merits. Legislation involving the expenditure of money can be initiated only by a Minister of the Crown.[1] The House of Commons may reduce the proposed expenditure, but may not increase it. Finally, Bills involving the raising or spending of money must commence in a Committee of the whole House.

Committee of Supply. The Speech from the Throne always contains a request for Supply, and at the commencement of each Parliament the House of Commons fixes days on which it will resolve itself into Committee of Supply. The Committee of Supply decides what money shall be spent. The Financial Year begins April 1. By December the estimates of the different Departments are prepared. They are revised by the Treasury and are in the hands of Parliament by March. Ministers present the estimates of their Departments to the Committee of Supply, which discusses them and passes resolutions (votes of supply), authorising the expenditure demanded. These resolutions are reported to the House, which invariably agrees with them. By August, which usually means at the end of the session, the resolutions are embodied in the annual Appropriation Act.[2] The Appropriation Act deals with the financial year in which it is passed, and at the end of each financial year steps are taken to provide for the expenditure of the next financial year in anticipation of the coming Appropriation Act. Votes on Account are obtained in Committee of Supply, and a Consolidated Fund Act is passed before March 31, authorising the drawing out of the Consolidated Fund of the monies so voted. This Consolidated Fund Act also authorises expenditure on supplementary estimates of the year about to end. These are estimates presented during

Appropriation Act.

Consolidated Fund Acts.

[1] The same rule prevails regarding a Bill to impose taxation.
[2] See specimen Vote of Supply scheduled to Act in Appendix A.

the financial year by Departments which find that they have under-estimated their needs in their original estimates. Another Consolidated Fund Act is passed, if needed, during the year in anticipation of the Appropriation Act in which ultimately the Consolidated Fund Acts are embodied. In times of emergency, when it is impossible to bring forward estimates, the Crown asks for a Vote of Credit by which Parliament places a sum of money at the disposal of the Executive without specifying how it should be spent. Except where expenditure is authorised by statutes which hold good until repealed (Consolidated Fund Services),[1] no revenue can be expended without annual parliamentary authority, which is given by the Appropriation Act authorising expenditure on the Supply Services.

The discussion of the estimates in Committee of Supply provides an opportunity for a general discussion on the administrative work of the Department, the estimates of which are under discussion, but it provides no opportunity for any detailed examination of the departmental expenditure or for discussing policy. The accounts are not presented in a form which can be easily understood by members ; nor is there time for any detailed criticism ; nor is the House as a whole a suitable body to provide such criticism. Motions may be brought forward to reduce the salary of the Minister responsible for the estimates, but such motions are treated as votes of confidence in the Government, and are invariably withdrawn or rejected. The procedure is designed mainly to secure that all expenditure shall be appropriated by Parliament to specific items. *Examination of Estimates.*

In the Committee of Ways and Means it is decided how the money needed for supply is to be raised. Part of the National Revenue is raised under statutes which endure until repealed, but a large part of the revenue depends upon taxes, *e.g.*, Income Tax, which are imposed annually. The Committee of Ways and Means has two duties. It passes resolutions for the raising of taxes, and it passes *Committee of Ways and Means.*

---

[1] See Part IV., Chap. VI. Under this head comes the service of the National Debt which accounts for at least three-eighths of the total expenditure in recent years.

resolutions authorising the drawing of monies which stand in the Consolidated Fund as the result of the proceeds of taxation, whether levied under statutes valid until repealed or annual statutes. The resolutions of the Committee are reported to the House at the conclusion of each sitting. They are finally embodied in two annual measures—the Finance Act, which authorises the annual taxation and amends existing taxes ; and the Appropriation Act, which authorises the employment of the Consolidated Fund.

Although it may be said to ensure full discussion, the procedure of the Committee of Ways and Means interposed between the Committee of Supply and the subsequent Finance Bill seems an unnecessary expenditure of parliamentary time.

The Budget.   It will be convenient at this stage to explain the annual Budget Speech of the Chancellor of the Exchequer, which has purposely been postponed until after the examination of the control of expenditure and taxation by the House of Commons. Shortly after the opening of the Financial Year in April the Chancellor " opens his Budget " in Committee of Ways and Means. The Speech falls into two parts. The first is a retrospect of the past year, comparing yield of revenue with estimated yield, and actual with estimated expenditure. The second part deals with the estimated expenditure of the new year and the Chancellor's proposals for meeting this out of taxation on the existing basis, coupled with his intentions as to the imposition of new taxation or the remission of existing taxes. Subject to the sentences following, statutory effect is not given to the Budget proposals until the passing of the Finance Act, which cannot usually take place before July or August.

Budget Resolutions.   Resolutions of the Committee of Ways and Means agreeing to certain of the taxes proposed in the Budget are passed immediately after the annual Budget statement. These include income tax and sur-tax, customs and excise duties. Other taxes, such as death duties, which endure until varied or repealed by a Finance Act, are unaffected by the Budget resolutions. But the effect of any changes may by the Finance Act be made retrospective to the date of the Budget, or any selected date. It was for long the practice to begin at once to collect the taxes under the authority of these resolutions. This practice was challenged in *Bowles* v. *The Bank of England* [1913], 1 Ch. 57; K. & L. at p. 117, in which Mr. Gibson Bowles sued the Bank of England for a declaration that it was not entitled to deduct any sum by way of income tax from dividends, until such tax was imposed by Act of Parliament. The decision given in favour of the plaintiff illustrates the fundamental principle maintained in *Stockdale* v. *Hansard*, that no resolution of the House of Commons can alter the law of the land. In 1913, however, there was passed the Provisional Collection of Taxes Act, which gives statutory force for a limited period to a resolution of the Committee of Ways and Means varying an existing tax or renewing a tax imposed during the preceding year. An Act, however, confirming such resolution must become law within four months from the date of the resolution. The Act only applies to customs and excise duties and to income tax and sur-tax.

The financial procedure of the House of Commons is adequate for the purposes for which it came into being, namely, ensuring that no taxes should be imposed without the authority of Parliament, and that money should only be spent with the authority of Parliament and for the purposes authorised by Parliament, but it provides no opportunity for real control of expenditure and insistence upon departmental economy. It is difficult to see how economy of public expenditure can be achieved. The expenses of administration forms a comparatively small fraction of the total expenditure, the bulk of which has been imposed upon the Departments by Parliament itself in legislating for schemes of state services, all of which involve an outlay of the public funds.

The process of passing a Private Bill is partly legislative, Private Bills. partly judicial. A Private Bill is commenced by a petition. The promoters of a Private Bill must give notice of their intention to all bodies and persons whose interests may be affected by their proposals. Provided that the formalities required by the Standing Orders of the House in which the

Bill is introduced are complied with, the Bill receives a first reading. On the Second Reading the general principle of the Bill may be discussed. If read a second time, the Bill is committed to a Committee of four members in the Commons ; in the Lords a Private Bill Committee consists of five members. The Committee stage is a quasi-judicial proceeding, at which the opponents of the Bill are permitted, after certain formalities, to appear. The supporters and opposers of a Bill are heard, usually by counsel, in support or opposition. It is first decided whether or not to pass the preamble, or introductory paragraph, setting out the expediency of the proposed measure. If the preamble is rejected, the Bill is dead. If the preamble is accepted, the clauses are then taken in order. After the Committee stage the Bill is reported to the House, and its subsequent stages are similar to those of a Public Bill. A Private Bill may be opposed in Committee in both Houses. With a view to expediting local legislation by Private Bill many of the formalities have been recently dispensed with by empowering the Lord Privy Seal to certify such Bills as being designed to relieve unemployment. In view of the very expensive and dilatory nature of Private Bill procedure, this change may be a forerunner of a complete overhaul of the Standing Orders concerned.

B.

OTHER FUNCTIONS OF PARLIAMENT.

Judicial Functions. — The judicial functions of Parliament—the appellate jurisdiction of the House of Lords and the process of impeachment—are discussed elsewhere.[1]

Petitions. — Another function of Parliament is the receiving of Petitions. Any subject may petition Parliament and Parliament decides whether or not to receive such petitions. Petitions must be presented by a member. They are referred to a Select Committee, which may direct their circulation among members. They may be debated.

[1] Part V., Chap. I.

Either House may set up a Committee of Inquiry into any matter of public importance, and a resolution to set up such an Inquiry may be an expression of no confidence in the Government of the day. Such Committees may be composed solely of members of Parliament or may have a wider composition. Parliamentary Committees may examine witnesses upon oath and by the Tribunals of Inquiry (Evidence) Act, 1921, a Tribunal appointed by both Houses to inquire into a matter of urgent public importance may be given all the powers of the High Court with regard to the examination of witnesses and production of documents. *Committees of Inquiry.*

Certain officers, such as judges, are removable upon the presentation of an address to the Crown by both Houses of Parliament. The proceedings in relation to such an address are of a judicial character. *Addresses of Removal.*

It has been stated that the control of expenditure by Parliament is of little value as a means of guiding and restraining departmental expenditure. It has been shown, too, that the real power to legislate rests with the Cabinet and the individual Ministers. It remains to consider how far Parliament can exercise any general control over the Executive. The daily Question Hour, during which questions are addressed to Ministers, provides an opportunity for focussing public attention on inconvenient topics. Important debates arise on the Address in reply to the Speech from the Throne at the opening of a Session ; on the Budget Speech of the Chancellor of the Exchequer ; on a formal motion of censure and on other occasions apart from legislative procedure. Debates unconnected with the process of legislation are particularly useful in the House of Lords for the discussion of foreign affairs and non-party matters of national concern. Forty members may at any time move the adjournment at a fixed time of the House of Commons in order to discuss a matter accepted by the Speaker as of urgent importance. Any matter may be raised on the adjournment of either House each day. Motions criticising the Government or individual Ministers may be moved, but the difficulty under a rigid party system of any effective opposition to the Cabinet has already been explained. *Control of Ministers.*

10

Ministers, of course, will pay attention to general feeling in Parliament as being some indication of feeling in the country, but the weakness of parliamentary control lies in the fact that there is no time or opportunity for real control over the work of Government Departments. Mr. Ramsay Muir [1] suggests that the Departments should have attached to them Committees of Parliament chosen for their special knowledge of the work of a Department or group of Departments. These Committees might really examine and revise the estimates of their Department or group. They would be smaller than the existing Standing Committees, and to them there would be committed Bills brought forward by their Departments. The present Committee on Estimates fails as being expected to deal with the estimates of all departments. Unless there is either some such reform of procedure, or some measure of devolution and the setting up of subordinate legislatures for, *e.g.*, Scotland, Wales, the North of England, it will be impossible to restore parliamentary control of the Executive.

---

[1] *How Britain is Governed*, pp. 231 ff.

PART IV.

THE EXECUTIVE.

Law of the Constitution, by A. V. Dicey.   Part II. (The Rule of Law),
   Chapters X. and XI.
The Whitehall Series (Putnams).
How Britain is Governed, by Ramsay Muir (Constable).
The Governance of England, by Sir Sidney Low (Fisher Unwin).

CHAPTER I.

THE KING.

To write of the organs of State which exercise the executive Introductory. functions is the most difficult task that a writer on Constitutional Law has to perform.   He is of necessity without that acquaintance with what takes place in Cabinet meetings or within State Departments which could alone give him an intimate knowledge of the machine in operation.   When dealing with the Legislature and the Judiciary he is writing of organs which work in the public eye.   The proceedings of both Parliament and the Law Courts can be followed with fair accuracy by anyone with sufficient leisure and inclination to peruse the columns of *The Times* from day to day. But the Departments pursue the even tenor of their ways free from the glare of publicity.   True that from time to time questions in Parliament or strictures from the bench remind the public that Whitehall is encroaching on their liberty.   Occasionally a retired civil servant gives the world a glimpse behind the scenes, but strict convention forbids any active member of that great service from writing of his work.[1]   Even for the average lawyer acquaintance with Whitehall is limited to interviews with subordinate officials, while the layman perhaps gets no further than an occasional interview with the local inspector of taxes.

For the student there is another barrier.   He has to face Termin-ology. a branch of law where the terminology is of a non-legal description.   Executive acts are done in the name of the

---

[1] Attention is drawn to the Whitehall Series, edited by Sir James Marchant, K.B.E., LL.D.   In this Series, retired permanent officials of the Civil Service have written of the Departments in which most of their experience has lain.   Volumes of the Series are published by Putnams at a price of 7s. 6d. each.

King, the King in Council, the Ministers, the Departments, or Commissioners. The King and the King in Council are known to the law. The law recognises State Departments and the offices held by their presiding political chiefs. The Crown represents a legal idea, the sum total of prerogatives, other powers and rights of government, but it is not a term of art. The terms, Cabinet, Ministry, Administration, Government, are extra-legal, as to all intents is the office of Prime Minister. Yet some appreciation of their meaning is essential to an understanding of the constitutional machine. These terms are used haphazard to describe the political Executive of the day, the body of Crown servants who control policy. The Cabinet is the term applied to the inner body of Ministers, with whom rests the real direction of policy. We must needs often speak of ministerial responsibility, while the Ministry or Administration of a particular Prime Minister are the accepted terms of reference to the body of men who from time to time hold the reins of government. The fact that these terms are outside the law makes the duplication of terminology less objectionable. They will not be found in the Law Reports; nor, with two isolated exceptions, in the Statute Book.[1]

Acts of Parliament do not bind the Crown, unless the particular statute expressly so enacts; *Cooper* v. *Hawkins* [1904], 2 K.B. 164. On the other hand the Crown is bound by judicial decisions, *e.g.*, defining the limits of prerogative power, though, since the property of the Crown cannot be taken to satisfy a judgment, enforcement even of these limited remedies which are available against the Crown can only be effected at the Crown's pleasure; in practice effect is given by the Treasury to adverse judgments; and no Government Department can question a decision of a final appellate court which has been established against it.

Title to the Crown.   The King's title to the Crown is derived from the Act of Settlement, 1701, " The Crown . . . shall remain and continue to the said most excellent Princess Sophia " (the Electress of Hanover, grand-daughter of James I.) " and the

---

[1] The word, Government, appears in the Nauru Island Agreement Act, 1920, and the Trade Disputes and Trade Unions Act, 1927, S. 1.

heirs of her body being Protestants." The title to the Crown recognises the hereditary principle, but the King in Parliament may alter the succession. This provision involves the Crown descending, with certain exceptions, as if it were real property under the law of inheritance in force before 1926, when this branch of property law was altered. The rules of descent may be briefly illustrated from the present Royal Family. The heir-apparent, the eldest male lineal descendant of King George V., is the Prince of Wales, a bachelor ; next in succession is the King's second son, the Duke of York ; then comes the Princess Elizabeth, as the elder child of the Duke of York. In spite of her sex the Princess Elizabeth would take priority over her uncles, the King's younger sons, and her aunt, Princess Mary, and her issue. She is also preferred to her younger sister. The Royal Marriages Act, 1772, by placing certain restrictions upon the right of a descendant of George II. to contract a marriage without the consent of the Sovereign, guards against undesirable marriages which might affect the succession to the throne.

These are two ceremonies which mark the accession of the Accession new Sovereign. Immediately on the death of his predecessor and Coronation. the Sovereign is proclaimed, not by the Privy Council as such, but by the Lords Spiritual and Temporal and other leading citizens, a body which is a survival of an old assemblage meeting to choose and proclaim the King. The Proclamation is afterwards approved at the first meeting of the new King's Privy Council. After an interval of time, on the last occasion over a year, follows the Coronation, the ancient ceremony which gave religious sanction to title by election of the Witanagemot or the Commune Concilium, and brought to a close the interregnum, when no King reigned, between the death of one King and the election of his successor. Anson remarks that, as the recognition of hereditary rights strengthened, the importance of the election and coronation dwindled, while the great practical inconvenience of the interregnum, the abeyance of the King's Peace, was curtailed.

The modern coronation ceremony is full of historical interest. There are three stages : (1) The acceptance of their King by the people and the taking of the oath of royal duties by the King.

(2) The purely religious ceremony, which includes the anointing and crowning.

(3) The rendering of homage in person by the Lords Spiritual and Temporal.

It should be noted that the oath illustrates the contractual nature of the sovereign power, and has survived both the extravagant prerogative claims of the Stuarts and the revolution of 1688.

Incapacity of the King.

The principal modern case of incapacity occurred during the serious illness of King George V. in 1928-29. On that occasion the King was able on his sick bed to put his signature to Letters Patent delegating by Commission under the Great Seal the bulk of his power, but not all, to Counsellors of State, who consisted of the Queen, the Prince of Wales, the Duke of York, the Archbishop of Canterbury, the Lord Chancellor, and the Prime Minister then in office. When the King became convalescent, an Order in Council was issued, curtailing the powers exercisable by the Counsellors to the less important duties. Earlier examples of incapacity may be found during the period of insanity of George III.

The circumstances which render the King incapable of performing his duties are not, however, confined to illness, and include absence from the kingdom, lack of age and moral incapacity. The last ground may be dismissed with the mere mention of James II. Absence from the Kingdom does not present serious difficulties in these days of rapid communication, and many of the powers can be delegated to a Council of State. Provision was made in 1837 by the Lord Justices Act for Vice-Regents in case of the successor to Queen Victoria being out of the realm at her death. Infancy, however, raises several questions. By a fiction of law the King is immune from the ordinary incapacities of infants. The last case was that of Edward VI., in whose predecessor's reign was enacted the only Regency Act which has so far taken effect by reason of infancy. The Act gave Henry VIII. the power of nominating the Council of Regency either in his lifetime or by his will. Provision was made in 1910 for the event of minority, but this provision is now spent.

Formerly the death of the Sovereign involved the disso- Demise of
lution of Parliament and the termination of the tenure of all the King.
Duration
Crown offices, since Parliament meets on the personal sum- of Parlia-
mons of the King, and all offices are in theory held at his will ment.
and pleasure. By an Act passed in the reign of William and
Mary it was enacted that a Parliament in existence at the
time of the King's death should continue, if not sooner dissolved, for six months. By the Representation of the People
Act, 1867, the duration of Parliament was made independent
of the demise of the Sovereign.

The question of tenure of office is somewhat more difficult. Tenure of
Whatever may be said for the dissolution of Parliament, Offices.
the inconvenience of the vacation of all executive offices on
the death of the King was clearly intolerable and in the past
might have endangered the succession of the heir to the
throne. But the Succession to the Crown Act, 1707, continued for six months from the demise of the Sovereign the
Privy Council and the tenure of State offices. In the reign
of William IV. there was a further increase to eighteen months
in the case of office held overseas. Such was the state of the
law at the death of Queen Victoria. The position was complicated by other provisions of the same Act (since repealed),
which involved the re-election of Ministers on the acceptance of office. The continuing of each office holder in
his existing office had to be confirmed by King Edward VII.
Legislation was clearly desirable, and it was enacted by
the Demise of the Crown Act, 1901, that the holding of
any office whether within or without His Majesty's dominions should not be affected by the demise of the Crown,
nor should any fresh appointment be necessary. The Act
was made retrospective to the death of Queen Victoria.

The duties of the King of England closely relate to the Duties of
prerogative rights already discussed in Part II., Chapter IV. the King.
He holds formal meetings of his Council, gives audiences to
his Ministers, and other holders of offices at home and overseas, such as Colonial Governors on appointment, receives
accounts of Cabinet decisions, receives the credentials of

foreign diplomatic representatives, is the Commander-in-Chief of the Royal Forces, and confers honours. Innumerable State papers require his signature, and he has to acquaint himself with contents of despatches and similar documents. Apart from his duties as a constitutional monarch, the King and his Consort, and indeed the whole of the adult members of the Royal Family, are the servants of the public, in that they take a most active part in the ceremonial affairs of public life.[1]

[1] Appendix C. contains specimens of a few documents which require the Royal signature.

CHAPTER II.

THE KING IN COUNCIL.[1]

THE King in Council, or the Privy Council, was until recently the sole repository, in theory of law, of executive power. Despite the many powers conferred by statute on individual Ministers during the last fifty years, the Order in Council remains one of the chief methods of giving the force of law to executive acts. It has been seen above that the King executes a large number of documents, under his own hand or a facsimile thereof. But the Order in Council is the document in general use for giving effect to the more important orders of the Executive, though a Royal Proclamation is used, when it is desired to give wide publicity to the action of the Council, as for the purpose of summoning, proroguing, or dissolving Parliament. Technically the members of the Council present are liable for the Orders they enact. Nowadays Orders in Council are authenticated by the signature of the Clerk of the Council. Constitutional history makes us familiar with the decline in both the advisory and judicial functions of the Council and its supersession in the former capacity by the Cabinet. To-day the acts of the Privy Council are purely formal and give effect to orders drawn up by Government Departments. These orders are made either by virtue of the Common Law prerogative, *e.g.*, legislation for a Colony with a non-representative assembly, or under the authority of an Act of Parliament. The Council having ceased to be an advisory Council of the Crown, meets for the purpose of making orders, issuing proclamations or performing formal

[1] See Dicey, *The Privy Council* (Arnold Prize Essay) (Macmillans), for an historical account of the Privy Council.

155

State acts, such as admission to ministerial office. A few traces remain of its former advisory functions; the Committee for Channel Island business is the sole survivor of the old Standing Committees appointed by the King at the beginning or in the course of his reign. Apart from the Judicial Committee [1]—also a Standing Committee—which exercises its appellate and other judicial functions by advising His Majesty, Committees of the Council are appointed from time to time for various purposes, *e.g.*, to consider applications for incorporation by Royal Charter. The Judicial Committee has a statutory duty of answering references apart from purely judicial appeals. A good example of this is to be found in the submission of the long-standing Labrador Boundary dispute in 1927 to the reference of the Judicial Committee by the Governments of the Dominion of Canada and Newfoundland. Still more recently a point of dispute over the payment of compensation to civil servants formerly employed in the area of the Irish Free State was referred in the unusual circumstance of having already been decided in the course of its appellate jurisdiction by the Committee; *Wigg and Cochrane* v. *Attorney-General for Irish Free State* [1927], A.C. 674; and *Re Transferred Civil Servants' (Ireland) Compensation* [1929], A.C. 242.

The office of Privy Councillor is to-day an office of honour. Appointments are made by the King on ministerial advice. There are three classes of members. By convention all Cabinet Ministers become Privy Councillors, since the oath (or affirmation in lieu of oath) binds to secrecy. Holders of other high offices of a non-political character, such as Archbishops, Lords Justice of Appeal, are usually sworn members of the Council. In addition the office is a recognised reward for faithful public and political service and appointments of this nature usually figure in the New Year and Birthday Honours Lists. The Council numbers about 320 members at the present day. Members are entitled to the prefix, " Right Honourable." Alienage is a disqualification, but on naturalisation an alien

[1] See Part IX., Chap. V., and the Judicial Committee Acts, 1833 and 1844.

becomes qualified for membership ; *The King* v. *Speyer*, *The King* v. *Cassel* [1916], 1 K.B. 595 ; [1916], 2 K.B. 858.

The functions of the Council are distinct from those of the Cabinet. The former is an executive body, the latter deliberative. Although all members of the Cabinet are Privy Councillors, it is not as a Committee of the Council that they meet, but as " His Majesty's Servants." The Cabinet is summoned by the Prime Minister, who has no place in the legal theory of the Constitution. The Council is convened by the Clerk of the Council, whose office dates back to the sixteenth century. Meetings of the Council at the present day to give formal effect to executive orders consists of only four or five members. The only connecting link between the modern Cabinet and the Council is the oath and obligation of secrecy which binds Cabinet Ministers as members of the Council ; but it will be remembered that the first use of the term, Cabinet, was to describe inner bodies of the Privy Council. *Relation of Cabinet to Council.*

The House of Lords is still in theory a Council of the Crown. It has not been summoned, as such, since 1688, but traces of its former function are preserved in the writ of summons. Moreover, it is the privilege of a peer to seek individual access to the Sovereign, though the privilege may not be used by peers in these days of ministerial responsibility for the purpose of tendering advice on matters of government. *House of Lords as Council of the Crown.*

CHAPTER III.

THE CABINET.

THE Cabinet system rests upon principles which are partly legal, partly political or conventional. The Cabinet (for composition, see Part I., Chap. II.) is the motive power of executive government. The changes brought about by the Revolution of 1688 led the Legislature to take to itself many of the powers of government which are properly the function of the directing organ. The modern system began with the development of a political Executive deriving its authority from the people. To-day Parliament does not in practice so much govern as regulate the Executive. The Executive, through the Cabinet, is the directing power. Legislation is initiated by the Cabinet, or by individual Ministers. Bills are usually the work of the Departments and the Parliamentary Draftsmen. To the Executive is entrusted the conduct of external relations. All public expenditure must be proposed by its Ministers. Usually the Executive secures discretionary powers in the administration of Acts of Parliament. It is, however, in the long run, dismissible at rare intervals by Parliament, should it cease to command a majority of supporters in the House of Commons. The Cabinet in practice exercises important rights of patronage. Practically all important appointments in State and Church are in the gift of the Government of the day, *e.g.*, governor-generalships, judgeships of all degrees, bishoprics and even a few university chairs. These, being in the gift of the Crown, are filled on the recommendation of the Prime Minister and his colleagues.

The King, as the head of the Executive, acts in political matters almost exclusively on the advice of a small number of his servants, his Cabinet Ministers. In recent times they have numbered about twenty. They have no formal status, except that by convention they hold the office of Privy Councillor. The members of the Cabinet are drawn almost exclusively from men (and women) who hold the headship of the Departments of State entrusted with the executive and administrative acts of government, though a few officers of State, who are free from arduous departmental responsibilities, are usually included.

The principles of Cabinet government can be summarised as follows :

(1) The King is bound in political matters to follow the advice of his Cabinet. This is the result of the Prerogative of Perfection, namely, that the King can do no wrong. *King acts on advice of Cabinet.*

(2) Secondly, the political responsibility of the Cabinet is collective. It tenders unanimous advice to His Majesty, even when it is a commonplace that the members do not hold identical opinions on a given issue. The difference between the responsibility of a Cabinet Minister (and indeed of Ministers in general) and the responsibility of civil servants is that the former are liable to lose office on political grounds as well as legal, whereas the latter are in no way dependent for their tenure of office upon party politics. Civil servants, though legally dismissible at pleasure without notice and without compensation, in practice hold office during good behaviour. *Collective Responsibility.*

(3) Thirdly, the Cabinet must command a majority in the House of Commons. It is by the party system, weakened by the presence of a third permanent party in the House of Commons, that Cabinet Government functions. The Executive must command a majority in the House of Commons. To achieve office a political party must first gain the confidence of the electorate. This means under the present system of representation a majority of seats in the Commons, but not necessarily of votes cast at a General Election. Once in office an Executive is practically sure of retaining its majority more or less intact. This is due to party discipline, not altogether unaffected by future expectation of office among its supporters in Parliament and by the reluctance of *Party System.*

members of all parties to face a General Election with its attendant expense and possible loss of seat and salary.

Cabinet Ministers sit in Parliament.

(4) Fourthly, the Cabinet and other Ministers should be members of one or other House of Parliament. This is only a convention, but it is an important one. Until the realisation that some such rule was desirable, ministerial responsibility was difficult to achieve. Once Ministers are in Parliament, they may be kept in check by a vigilant Opposition, and indeed by a fire of questions emanating both from the Opposition and the more independent members of their own party. Questions in the House, particularly the House of Commons, play a very important part in testing the feeling of the country towards the policy of the Cabinet.

Composition of Cabinet.

Invitations to sit in the Cabinet are given at the discretion of the Prime Minister who in this matter is entitled to make his own choice of personnel and of numbers. The Prime Minister himself is selected by the King, who is understood to choose, whether of his own initiative, or on the advice of the out-going Prime Minister, the leader of the party which is sure of the support of a majority in the House of Commons. The answer to the agitation recently conducted by two newspaper proprietors, urging that leaders of political parties should before a General Election indicate those of their supporters destined for Cabinet office, is that, until the Prime Minister himself is appointed by the King, he cannot advise His Majesty, much less the public through the medium of the press, of his choice of Ministers. It seems unlikely that a peer will again hold the office of Prime Minister, at all events in an unreformed Upper House, on account of the curtailment of its powers since 1911 and of the overwhelming preponderance of Conservative peers in the present House of Lords. The effect of this preponderance is to deprive the Labour party, when in office, of any adequate support in controversial matters from their own party in the Upper House. The Marquis of Salisbury, 1895 to 1902, was the last Prime Minister who sat in the Lords.

The Ministers are appointed to their office by the King. No Minister can claim by virtue of office to be included in the Cabinet, but there may be said to be a convention that

certain offices carry with them Cabinet rank. The Lord
Chancellor, the Chancellor of the Exchequer, the eight
Secretaries of State, the Ministers in charge of Departments
supervising the more important social services, such as the
Ministers of Health, Education and Labour, may be taken by
way of illustration. The chief Law Officer of the Crown,
the Attorney-General, is sometimes included, but this is
undesirable. The Attorney-General is the executive officer, Attorney-
who authorises prosecutions, including prosecutions for General
offences of a political nature, such as sedition. He would, and Cabinet.
if a Cabinet Minister, also be a member of the political body
which might be called upon to decide whether or not to
proceed with a prosecution. An Attorney-General in the
Cabinet is likely to find sooner or later that his political and
legal opinions may be in conflict. It is better to keep him
independent, as the legal adviser of the Cabinet, and so free
him as far as possible from the political responsibility en-
tailed by actual membership of that body. Nevertheless
there have been occasions in the last ten years when the
Attorney-General has been included in the Cabinet, and in
1924 this factor was in part responsible for the downfall of
Mr. Ramsay MacDonald's first Government as a result of a
decision to drop a political prosecution.

The Cabinet usually includes two or three members who Non-
have few, if any, departmental duties attaching to their par-Depart-
ticular offices. The Lord Privy Seal, the Lord President of Ministers.
the Council, and the Chancellor of the Duchy of Lancaster
are Ministers who may be included in the Cabinet. Their
executive duties leave them free to assist the Prime Minister
in special matters, such as acting as delegates at meetings
of the Council of the League of Nations, or co-ordinating
the work of different Departments concerned with a single
problem, such as unemployment. During the War of 1914-19
as many as three Ministers without portfolio were appointed
at one and the same time.

The mechanism of Cabinet government is completed by Cabinet
the Committee of Imperial Defence, the Economic Advisory Committees.
Council, which has recently taken the place of the Committee
of Scientific and Civil Research, and *ad hoc* Committees

Committee of Imperial Defence.

within the Cabinet itself. The Committee of Imperial Defence is not strictly a committee of the Cabinet, and has no executive power. Its deliberations are confidential and secret, and its functions purely advisory. It owes its existence in its present form to the late Lord Balfour, when Prime Minister. It exists for the purpose of co-ordinating the best advice obtainable on questions of Imperial Defence for the benefit of the Cabinet and the Departments concerned with defence. The Prime Minister is always a member and acts as chairman. The Heads of the Defence Departments, both political and expert, normally assist in its deliberations.

Economic Advisory Council.

The Economic Advisory Council was set up by decision of Mr. Ramsay Macdonald's second Government early in 1930. It is a standing body reporting to the Cabinet, and its purpose is to advise the Government in economic matters. It has to make continuous study of development in trade and industry, and of the use of national and imperial resources, of the effect of fiscal legislation at home and abroad, and of all aspects of international, imperial and national economics with a bearing on the prosperity of the country. While it keeps in close touch with Departments affected by its work, it interferes in no way with the functions or responsibilities of Ministers, and has no administrative or executive power. The Chairman of the Council is the Prime Minister, and the other members fall into three classes :

(*a*) The Chancellor of the Exchequer, the Lord Privy Seal (as at present employed),[1] the President of the Board of Trade and the Minister of Agriculture and Fisheries.

(*b*) Such other Ministers as the Prime Minister may from time to time summon.

(*c*) Such other persons as are chosen by the Prime Minister in virtue of their special knowledge of and experience in industry and economics. The first panel of members of this class was of a representative nature.

The Council is entitled to initiate, subject to the approval of the Prime Minister, enquiries into, and to advise upon, any subject falling within its scope, including proposals for

[1] Part I., Chap. II.

legislation. One of its duties is to prepare a list of expert advisers who may from time to time be required to assist in its deliberations.

The *ad hoc* Committees are composed only of Members of the Cabinet itself.

The Cabinet Secretariat, introduced as a measure of emergency during the War of 1914-19, may be regarded as an innovation of some significance. Proceedings of the Cabinet have always been communicated to the Sovereign ; they are otherwise secret deliberations of Ministers. It was feared that with the establishment of a Secretariat the informal nature of the deliberations might be imperilled. Sir John Marriott [1] suggests that it has been responsible for a diminution of departmental responsibility, especially in the case of the Foreign Office, and has exalted the power of a Prime Minister. It may be regarded as a recording department, and as a means of transmitting to Departments decisions, not merely of the Cabinet, but of the large number of Cabinet Committees which have been set up in every modern administration. In 1925 there were sixty-two meetings of the Cabinet ; nearly one hundred meetings of Committees, exclusive of one hundred and fifty-four meetings of the Committee of Imperial Defence and its sub-Committees. In 1924 the personnel of the Secretariat consisted of a Secretary and thirty-seven others.

Cabinet Secretariat.

The result of the Cabinet system has been a virtual monopoly of parliamentary time for Government business. More and more the time available for private members' business is curtailed, and no measure introduced by a private member succeeds in progressing further than a second reading in the House of Commons, unless it is adopted by the Government, or time is allowed for its further progress in fixing the parliamentary time-table, which is a matter for the Prime Minister and his Cabinet. Nevertheless a powerful Opposition has many devices open to it, apart from the initiation of legislation, by which it can exercise an important influence over the time-table.[2]

Cabinet monopolises Legislative Work of Parliament.

[1] See Sir John Marriott, *Mechanism of Modern State*, II., 83.
[2] Part III., Chap. IV.

11 *

CHAPTER IV.

THE CENTRAL GOVERNMENT DEPARTMENTS.

A.

Introductory. THE executive government of the country is carried out almost exclusively by Departments, together with a few high officials, such as the Lord Chancellor, who perform somewhat similar functions to those of the Departments. A list of the Cabinet and other Ministerial offices has been given in Part I., Chap II. above. A list of the Departments follows; there will be discussed in detail later under the appropriate Departments some functions of government which raise important points of Constitutional Law. A few lines are given here to indicate the functions of those Departments which will not again be mentioned. No attempt has been made to cover in detail the vast field of activity of the Central Government.

Personnel of a Department. Generally speaking, a Department consists of (1) a Minister, who, in the case of all the more important Departments, is a member of the Cabinet;

(2) his Assistant in Parliament, designated Under-Secretary of State or Parliamentary Secretary;

(3) a Permanent Under-Secretary of State, and a staff of administrative, executive, and clerical officers, all of whom are members of the Civil Service.[1] The Civil Service, strictly, includes all the civilian servants of the Crown and numbers about 350,000. The Post Office is by far the largest

[1] There are various grades of the Civil Service. Not all the employees of the Crown are in the " established " service; some appointments are temporary; others non-established and, therefore, non-pensionable.

Department from the point of view of the number of its employees. The salaries of civil servants, if not expressly provided by statute, as in the case of a few of the higher appointments, are regulated by the Crown in exercise of its discretionary authority. The salary rates may be allowed by the Treasury or appointed by Order in Council. The total sums required figure in the annual estimates laid before Parliament.

(*a*) **The Treasury.**[1]

(*b*) **Departments presided over by Secretaries of State.**

Government Departments.

The Home Office.[2]

The Foreign Office.[3]

The Dominions Office. This Department was organised as a separate office in 1925. Until 1930 it remained under the same Secretary of State as the Colonial Office. It is concerned with the relations between the Mother Country and the Self-governing Dominions and Southern Rhodesia.[4]

The Colonial Office. The work of this Department deals with all the Colonies and some other dependencies of the Crown, exclusive of the Self-Governing Dominions and India. It is responsible for a large measure of colonial legislation by Orders in Council, and exercises a wide patronage over appointments in the Colonial Service.[5]

The War Office.[6]

The India Office. The Secretary of State for India, assisted by the Council of India, a salaried body of prominent men experienced in Indian affairs is responsible for such portions of the government of British India as are dealt with in this country, as well as for the relationship between the King-Emperor and the Indian Native States.[7]

The Scottish Office. This Office, together with the Scottish Board of Health and the Scottish Education Department, is responsible for the internal government of Scotland.

[1] Chap. VI. below.
[2] Chap. V. below.
[3] Chap. VII. below.
[4] See also Part IX.
[5] See also Part IX.
[6] Part VIII., Chap. I.
[7] See also Part IX.

The Air Ministry.[1]

(*c*) **Departments presided over by other Ministers, usually of Cabinet rank.**

The Admiralty.[2]

The Board of Trade. The Board, which, as the successor of the Committee of the Privy Council for Trade and the Plantations, includes the Archbishop of Canterbury, consists nominally of a body of permanent commissioners, who never meet. The President is the ministerial head. Its functions are mainly regulative and statistical, and relate to industrial matters, including mines (separate Under-Secretary), mercantile marine, the coastguards, and administrative matters relating to bankruptcy, company law, and patents.

The Ministry of Health. This is the Department which supervises or controls local government services. It superintends the work of local authorities in relation to health and housing. It absorbed the old Local Government Board. Health and civil pension services under the national insurance schemes against sickness, old age, widowhood, and orphanage, are centrally administered by this Department.[3]

The Board of Education. This is a statutory body, which, like the Board of Trade, never meets, but exercises its administration of the national scheme of state-provided or state-aided education under its President in collaboration with the local education authorities.

The Ministry of Agriculture and Fisheries. Except that the Minister is also responsible for the Ordnance Survey and answers in Parliament for the Commissioner of Crown Lands, the name sufficiently explains the functions of the Department.

The Ministry of Labour. The Unemployment Insurance Acts and the chain of Employment Exchanges, together with legislation relating to industrial disputes, are administered by this Ministry.

The Post Office. To this Department is entrusted a State monopoly of the postal, telegraphic, and telephonic communications of the country. The British Broadcasting

---

[1] Part VIII., Chap. I.   [2] *Ibid.*   [3] See also Part VI.

Corporation is in the nature of a special Department of the Post Office. Inasmuch as there are post offices throughout the country, the Post Office is utilised by many Government services which involve local dealings with the public, but yet remain under central control. Among these may be mentioned the issue of licences, the collection of certain taxes, the payment of old age, widows', orphans' and some other civil pensions, the sale of insurance stamps, the issue of savings certificates and the conduct of a savings bank business.

The Ministry of Transport. It is the work of this Department to regulate and improve the means of locomotion and transport. On its creation in 1919 there were transferred from the Board of Trade the regulative powers relating to railways, canals, roads and harbours. Its exercise of powers under the Road Traffic Act, 1930, is among its more important functions.

The Ministry of Pensions. This Ministry administers a scheme of disablement and dependents' pensions arising out of the casualties of the War, 1914-19. Though it is still responsible for the disbursement of many millions of pounds of public money annually, the amount tends to diminish somewhat rapidly, and with it the work of the Department.

The Office of Works. The Commissioners of Works and Public Buildings provide buildings throughout the country to house Government Departments and are responsible for repair and maintenance. They are also entrusted with the care of royal palaces and royal parks. The First Commissioner is sometimes a member of the Cabinet.

The Lord Chancellor's Office. The Chancellorship is a legislative, judicial, and executive office, always carrying Cabinet rank. In addition to his Speakership of the House of Lords, and his Presidency of the House, and the custody of the Great Seal, the Lord High Chancellor in practice controls the machinery of the courts, both through his patronage and administrative powers conferred by the Judicature Act, 1925, and other Acts. He is also a member of the Judicial Committee of the Privy Council. He can dismiss County Court judges and remove justices of the peace. He also exercises an extensive ecclesiastical patronage. His office is not a Department, but he has certain departmental functions attached to him. Despite its judicial nature the office has remained political, in the sense that it is held by an eminent ex-member of the Bench or Bar adhering to the party in office.[1]

The Law Officers' Department. Although all Government Departments have departmental solicitors, either in the person of the Treasury Solicitor [2] or the solicitor for the Department, the Law Officers of the Crown, the Attorney-General and Solicitor-General represent the Crown in courts of justice, act as legal advisers to Government Departments on more important matters and represent them in court. They are assisted by Junior Counsel to the Treasury. As representing the Crown, the Attorney-General and Solicitor-General take part in many judicial or quasi-judicial proceedings relating to the public interest, such as the administration of charities and patent law. The appointments are political, and are conferred on successful barristers who are supporters of the party in power. The remuneration and fees attached to their offices are far higher than other ministerial salaries, and advancement to judicial or political office is more or less assured to the holders of either appointment.

Minor Departments.

There are in addition a number of minor Departments, mainly of the non-political type, *e.g.*, the Public Trustee, the Land Registry, the Stationery Office, the Charity Commissioners and the Public Record Office. Offices of State connected with the Royal Household, such as the Lord Chamberlain, the Keeper of the Privy Purse and the Master of the Horse are in part under the patronage of the Government, and partly personal appointments by the Sovereign.

Co-ordination of work of Government.

It has been a source of criticism by many that the Departments of Central Government are so organised that no one Department may be entirely responsible for the administrative action required by a pressing problem calling for the

---

[1] See also Part V., Chap. I.   [2] See p. 190.

intervention of the Government. Moreover, the efficiency of ordinary routine administration suffers from divided control or, may be, overlapping. An industrial dispute may very well be found to affect several of the Departments, *e.g.*, the Home Office, Board of Trade, Ministries of Health, Labour and Transport, and perhaps the Treasury and Service Departments. To counteract this difficulty it has been the practice in recent years for a Home Affairs Committee to meet at frequent and regular intervals. The Committee is composed of ministerial and civil service representatives of the principal Departments concerned with internal government. Its purpose is to co-ordinate governmental action in a common sphere where administrative overlapping or division of control is possible. It also reports to the Cabinet on the scope and policy underlying Private Bills of local authorities.

B.
Secretaries of State.

Something must be said about the Office of Secretary of State. There are now eight Secretaries of State, who preside over some of the more important Departments. For all but Peers and Privy Councillors the Secretary of State is the only avenue of approach for the subject to the Sovereign, save by petition. Whereas Departments may be approached by direct communication, this is not so in the case of approach to the Sovereign. Similarly, authentic communications by the Sovereign to his people are normally countersigned by a Secretary of State. It is interesting to notice that the duties of Secretaries of State are legally interchangeable and independent of any distinction on account of the Departments over which they preside, apart from any powers which may be conferred by statute on a particular Secretary of State, *e.g.*, on the Secretary of State for War by the Defence Act, 1842.[1] During the absence abroad, or through ill-health, of the Foreign Secretary, it would be usual to ask one of his brother Secretaries to act in his place. In practice, documents signed by these officers do not

---

[1] The Act speaks of the "principal officers of the Ordnance," whose powers and duties have been vested in the War Secretary by subsequent enactments.

indicate that they are signed by the head of any particular Department, the signature being followed by the words " One of His Majesty's Principal Secretaries of State." In this respect the position of a Secretary may be compared with that of a High Court judge, who, although attached to a particular Division, is liable to be called upon to adjudicate in any Division of the High Court.

History of
Secretary-
ships of
State.

The Office of Secretary of State springs from a humble origin, and it is not easy to say at what precise moment in history the King's Secretary became a definite office. In the Tudor period the Secretary became a channel of communication for home and foreign affairs, and the office seems to have grown in importance, largely perhaps on account of the personal rule of the Tudors. From about 1540 two Secretaries of State were appointed, but not at first as an invariable practice. It was when the Privy Council sought to combine deliberative and executive functions that the office assumed its present importance. The Secretaries of State ceased in fact, though not in law, to be servants of the King and his Council and became one of the motive forces in the Cabinet. On two occasions before 1782 a third Secretaryship was added for the time being. It was in that year that the Home Office and the Foreign Office came into existence as separate Departments. For some 150 years there had been a Secretary of State for the Northern Department, in charge of business relating to the Northern Powers of Europe, and another for the Southern Department, which embraced France and the Southern Countries. Ireland fell to the senior Secretary, while the Colonies and Home Affairs came under either.[1] On March 27th, 1782, the Foreign Office came into existence as a result of a circular letter addressed by Fox to the representatives of Foreign Powers in London, to the effect that he had been entrusted with the sole direction of foreign affairs, while his colleague, the Earl of Shelburne, had been appointed Principal Secretary of State for Domestic Affairs and the Colonies. The Home Secretary from that date took

[1] But compare the account in Anson, *op. cit.*, Vol. II., Part I., pp. 157 ff.

precedence of all other Secretaries. At that time he had very few of the statutory powers and duties which subsequent legislation has conferred upon him. The other Secretary-ships of State may be said to have been created out of this Secretaryship. In 1794 a Secretary of State for War was appointed, who in 1801 also took over the Colonies. In 1854 a Secretary of State for the Colonies was appointed on account of the Crimean War. In 1858 as the result of the Indian Mutiny, Indian affairs were entrusted to a Secretary of State for India. It was not until 1918 that another Secretaryship was created, namely, that for Air. In 1925 the Secretary of State for the Colonies was appointed to a separate Secretaryship for Dominion Affairs, the Colonial Office and the Dominions Office being henceforth organised in separate Departments, though the offices were, until 1930, held by the same holder. In 1926 the Secretary for Scotland, who, as head of the Scottish Office, controls the greater part of the internal government of Scotland, assisted by subordinate Departments, was given the status of Secre-tary of State. In 1930 Lord Passfield relinquished the office of Secretary of State for the Dominions, while retain-ing the Colonial Secretaryship.

C.

Qualifications of Ministers.

This is a convenient place to discuss the advantages accruing from the practice of appointing political chiefs to State Departments, and in particular the Departments charged with technical services. Nowhere is the practice so open at first sight to criticism as in the case of the three Service Departments, the War Office, the Admiralty and the Air Ministry. The positions of a solicitor-politician or a trade union leader in control of army affairs and a co-operative expert in charge of the Admiralty present more apparent anomalies that those of a university don at the Board of Education, or a financial expert as Chancellor of the Exchequer—to illustrate from office-holders of the last few years. There is little doubt that the technical work of government can only be carried on by a permanent Civil Service (assisted by other expert Crown servants, in the case of the Service Departments), enjoying security of tenure, so far as political fluctuations are concerned. But at the same time the traditions of such service incline to routine methods. The higher officials may lack the incentive to adopt progressive methods. They have not the business man's expectation of pecuniary gain, or even the professional man's hope for fame and fortune. For the Parliamentary Head of a Department there is the political stimulus, the hope of public advancement, and the publicity afforded by criticism in Parliament, which he must answer, and from the press, which may, sooner or later, drive him and his colleagues from office.

In the case of the Service Departments in particular, both the Cabinet and Parliament are more likely to acquiesce in the financial demands of a Department, if they are presented by a civilian or non-expert who has no particular temptation towards excessive expenditure. Secretaries of State for War do not become famous on account of the amount of public money they cause to be expended, but a professional soldier, if put in a similar position at the head of the War Office in peace time, might be prejudiced from the outset by a desire to maintain his personnel and equipment at the highest margin of security. It is better that the technical advisers of these Departments should not come direct to Parliament as the heads of the Service in which they have spent their professional lives, but should voice their demands through the political Chief of the Department, and by him through the Cabinet. What may be lost in departmental efficiency will be gained by the introduction of outside opinion and incentive. On the other hand, it must be admitted that the position of the higher civil servant, or Chief of Staff of one of the Services, whose life-work may be terminated, or indefinitely postponed, by a change of government, and, in consequence, change of political chief, is not an enviable one. This is perhaps one of the facts which induces many to leave the higher ranks of the Civil Service for the field of commerce and finance, where individual ability has greater scope.

CHAPTER V.

INTERNAL GOVERNMENT : DUTIES OF HOME OFFICE.

ALL matters not specifically allotted to other Departments fall to the province of the Home Secretary. In this chapter it is only proposed to discuss those of his duties which are concerned with the maintenance of public order (excepting his powers in time of emergency, which will be dealt with in Part VII.). The King's Peace is the peculiar concern of the Home Secretary. While every citizen has a legal duty to aid in keeping the peace, it is clear that this object cannot be achieved without some organisation for which the Executive is naturally responsible. The duties of the Home Secretary in this respect include police administration, appointments in connection with the administration of justice, the control of aliens and naturalisation, and certain duties in connection with public morals. *Mainten-ance of Public Order.*

A.

The Police.

The Metropolitan Police are under the control of the Home Secretary.[1] Elsewhere in the country the Police are organised as county or borough forces. The local police authority for a county is the Standing Joint Committee. In those boroughs [2] which have a separate police force, the authority is the Borough Council acting through its Watch Committee. The Standing Joint Committee is so called *Local Police Authorities.*

---

[1] The City of London Police are an independent force, but the appointment of the Commissioner (Chief Officer) must be approved by the Home Secretary.

[2] Less than half the boroughs maintain their own police force.

173

because its members are drawn, half from the County Council and half from the Justices of Peace in Quarter Sessions. The local authority has the following powers :

(a) The power of appointment.[1]

(b) The duty to pay salary or wages.

(c) The power to make regulations.

(d) The power to dismiss.

Home Secretary and Local Police Forces.

Nevertheless the central administrative control of the Home Secretary is important. The Police Act, 1919, s. 4, provides that " it shall be lawful for the Secretary of State to make regulations as to the government, mutual aid, pay, allowances, pensions, clothing expenses and conditions of service of all members of all police forces within England and Wales, and every police authority shall comply with the regulations so made." These regulations can only be made after consultation with the Police Council, a body constituted by the Act, on which representatives of police authorities and of all ranks of the police force sit. There is a uniform system of police pensions throughout the country (Police Pensions Act, 1921). Any member of the police force who feels aggrieved by the decision of the local police authority to dismiss him may appeal to the Home Secretary against such dismissal (Police (Appeals) Act, 1927). In addition to regulation under the Police Act, 1919, which constitutes a system of legislation on all points of police administration, the Secretary of State exercises considerable control through the purse. Since 1856 a grant has been made out of the funds of the Exchequer towards the police expenses of local authorities, but the payment of this grant is by statute made conditional on the Home Secretary's certificate that the force is efficient in numbers and discipline. Inspectors of Constabulary have proved powerful instruments in main-

---

[1] The authorities charged with the preservation of the peace have always had power to appoint special constables to supplement the salaried police force in an emergency. Nowadays this power is exercised by two or more Justices of the Peace. Able-bodied male residents between the ages of twenty-five and fifty-five may be enrolled, notice of appointment being given to the Home Secretary and the Lord Lieutenant of the County. Special constables may be appointed apart from an actual or apprehended emergency.

taining efficiency. As the amount of the grant is now one-half of the whole expenses, it is clear that no local authority can afford to forgo its certificate of efficiency. The appointment of Chief Constables, apart from the Metropolitan Police, is subject to the veto of the Home Secretary.

In the Metropolitan area, which for police purposes extends, roughly, to a fifteen miles radius from Charing Cross, the Home Secretary is the police authority and, as such, responsible for the executive acts of the Commissioner of Police at Scotland Yard and the Force under his command. Not even in detective matters is there a National Force, although for the purpose of unravelling complicated crimes the Criminal Investigation Department of the Metropolitan Police has a great advantage over local forces. The assistance of this Department of the Metropolitan Police is always available to the local forces, but so far the difficulties which arise in securing co-ordination between the Department and the independent local forces seem to be insuperable, and it rests with the local authorities to decide whether or not Scotland Yard's assistance shall be invoked in any particular case. *{Metropolitan Police.}*

A policeman is subject to the jurisdiction of the courts, like any other citizen. He is not *primâ facie* a servant of the local authority which appoints and dismisses him, but a servant of the State, a ministerial officer of the central power, though subject in many respects to local supervision and regulation. The local authority cannot, therefore, be sued for the wrongful acts of members of its police force ; *Fisher* v. *Oldham Corporation* [1930], 2 K.B. 364. An action for damages lies against a constable who exceeds his powers and thereby does damage to a private citizen. His powers of arrest are somewhat wider than those of the ordinary citizen ; he is, moreover, protected if, in the course of acting, as he is bound to do in obedience to a justice's warrant, he commits an illegality due to the fact that the warrant has been issued in excess of the justice's jurisdiction ; Constables Protection Act, 1751. *{Legal position of a Police Officer.}*

Prisons, Borstal Institutions and the Criminal Lunatic Asylum at Broadmoor are administered by the Home *{Prisons.}*

Office, while Industrial and Reformatory Schools, though still mainly private establishments, are largely financed by the Central Government and as a result come under Home Office inspection.

B.

The Administration of Justice.

Patronage.   The Home Secretary has by custom or statute certain functions with regard to the holding of local courts, other than the Assize Courts, and the appointment of certain judges and magistrates. He has the power to grant separate Courts of Quarter Sessions to boroughs, the appropriate Order in Council being made on his advice, and he makes recommendations for appointments to the Recordership of boroughs possessing such courts. The Metropolitan Police Magistrates, who are paid officials, and their equivalent in the larger provincial towns, Stipendary Magistrates, are appointed by the King on the recommendation of the Secretary of State. All the arrangements for the Metropolitan Police Courts are made under his control, and he confirms appointments of Clerks to Justices elsewhere. His functions do not extend to Courts of Assize which are presided over by judges of the High Court. The arrangements for these are in the hands of the Lord Chancellor.

Director of Public Prosecutions.   The Director of Public Prosecutions is appointed by the Home Secretary and, he, jointly with the Lord Chancellor, approves the rules made by the Attorney-General as to the Director's duties. Nevertheless, the Director acts on his own responsibility under the direction of the Attorney-General.

C.

The Prerogative of Pardon.

Until 1908 English Law provided no adequate means of reviewing judicially the judgment of a criminal court,[1]

---

[1] By Crown Cases Act, 1848, the practice of the judges to hold informal meetings from time to time to discuss difficult questions arising

and accordingly the way of rectifying any injustice was by the grant of a Pardon. The Prerogative of Mercy is exercised by the King on the advice of the Home Secretary. Thus the Home Office was forced into the position of a final court of appeal in criminal cases, without possessing any of the ordinary powers of a court of law, such as taking evidence on oath. The Criminal Appeal Act, 1907, established the Court of Criminal Appeal—a similar Court was established for Scotland in 1928—and thus relieved the Home Secretary and the Secretary for Scotland of responsibilities which ought not to have been placed upon them. But the King's Prerogative still remains and is in particular exercised by the Home Secretary in relation to death sentences. By s. 19 of the Criminal Appeal Act, 1907, the Secretary of State, on the consideration of any petition for the exercise of the Prerogative, may (*a*) refer the whole case to the Court of Criminal Appeal, and the case shall then be heard and determined by the Court, as in the case of an appeal by the person convicted, or (*b*) if he desires the assistance of the Court on any point arising in the case refer that point for their opinion thereon. Pardons under the Prerogative are of three sorts :

Court of Criminal Appeal.

(1) A Free Pardon rescinds both the sentence and the conviction.[1]

Types of Pardon.

(2) A Commutation, or Conditional Pardon, substitutes one form of punishment for another. A capital sentence is usually commuted to penal servitude for life, if the Home Secretary advises an exercise of the Prerogative.

(3) Remission reduces the amount of a sentence without changing its character, *e.g.*, reduces a sentence of imprisonment from six months to two months, or remits part of a fine.

In addition to the above three modes of pardoning, a reprieve or respite should be noticed. This postpones the carrying out of a sentence, and is largely resorted to in

at criminal trials was regularised by the institution of the Court for Crown Cases Reserved. This court had power to determine points of law reserved by the trial judge solely at his own discretion.

[1] For specimen see Appendix C.

capital cases pending the formal grant of a commutation, or conditional pardon ; the Secretary of State can signify the King's pleasure in this way by an order under his own hand, whereas the more formal modes, which formerly to have full legal effect had to be passed under the Great Seal, still require a warrant under the Royal Sign Manual, countersigned by the Secretary of State.

Limitations on Prerogative.

The Prerogative of Pardon closely resembles the dispensing power, but it can only be exercised subject to the following limitations :

(1) The offence must be of a public character, and the Crown has no power to remit judgment in suits between subject and subject.

(2) The pardon cannot be used as a licence to commit crimes. It can, however, be pleaded in bar to the indictment, or, after verdict, in arrest of judgment, but, under the Act of Settlement, 1701, a pardon may not be pleaded in bar of an impeachment by the Commons in Parliament. Nor can the King pardon the unlawful committing of any man to prison out of the realm (Habeas Corpus Act, 1679). Occasionally, however, the Crown withdraws a prosecution with leave of the court, or alternatively declines to offer the further evidence, without which a conviction cannot be secured. Moreover, the Attorney-General, as representing the Crown, can at his absolute discretion, enter a *Nolle prosequi*, which effectually stops all further proceedings. A private prosecutor has no absolute right to withdraw a charge.

(3) A pardon only relieves from the penalty resulting from criminal proceedings, but not the conviction, unless a free pardon is granted.

D.

Aliens, Admission, Supervision and Deportation of Aliens.

The policy of admitting or excluding aliens is not, of course, solely governed by the desire to check elements of possible disorder. For example, the admission of large numbers of aliens from countries where low wages prevail may have the effect of lowering wages to starvation point in unorganised trades in this country. Moreover, the habits of such people may have a demoralising effect in the crowded areas where they settle. The Aliens Act, 1905, threw a burden on the Home Office of a difficult character on account of the imperfect provisions of the Act. The present law is governed by the Aliens Acts, 1914 and 1919, and regulations made thereunder by Order in Council on the advice of the Home Secretary. The regulations fall under three heads [1] :

1. *Admission.*

Under the control of immigration an alien has to satisfy the Immigration Officer that he is qualified for admission under the regulations. The regulations are strictly enforced in the case of persons coming with a view to permanent residence. The requirements deal with health, a good character and sufficiency of means, and moreover, permission may be refused if an alien seeks admission with a view to taking employment which is likely to displace British workers. This permission is obtained from the Ministry of Labour.

2. *Supervision.*

The registration and supervision of registered aliens is carried out by the police under Home Office instructions and is compulsory after two months' residence.

3. *Deportation.*

The Home Secretary has an unrestricted power to order the deportation of any undesirable alien. In the case of an alien convicted of a criminal offence, this power is usually exercised on a recommendation which the court can make under the regulation for the expulsion of any convicted alien.

The Home Secretary's duties and powers in connection with aliens afford a good example of the interconnection between the functions of various Government Departments. Interconnection of Government Departments.

---

[1] These regulations afford an excellent example of subordinate legislation and of the complexity which may result from what is virtually subdelegation of legislative powers. See Allen, *Law in the Making*, p. 309.

The Foreign Office, the Dominions and Colonial Offices, the Board of Trade and the Ministry of Labour are all concerned in matters relating to aliens. In this connection it is interesting to note that there is an inter-departmental committee consisting of representatives of these offices and of the police, which meets to settle questions in which more than one of these Departments are concerned.

E.

Nationality and Naturalisation.

While the Home Secretary has no power to deprive a natural-born British subject of his nationality, he has important powers in connection with acquired nationality. Before detailing these powers it may be convenient here to state in summary form the existing law of British nationality as regards natural-born subjects as contained in the British Nationality and Status of Aliens Acts, 1914 to 1922. These Acts apply only to persons born on or after the 1st January, 1915, but they recognise the two principal criteria adopted by a previous Act of 1870.[1] These are the place of birth and the nationality of the father.

British Nationality. (i) Any person born within His Majesty's dominions and allegiance is a British subject whether his parents are British subjects or aliens. For this purpose His Majesty's dominions include the Self-governing Dominions, and the Colonies, but not Protectorates. British ships all over the world are regarded as being within the dominions of the Crown, but a foreign ship, even in British waters, is not.

(ii) British nationality is also acquired at birth by any person born out of His Majesty's dominions whose father was at the time of that person's birth a British subject, and who fulfils any of the following conditions :

(*a*) The father was born within His Majesty's allegiance.

(*b*) The father had been naturalised.

(*c*) The father had become a British subject through annexation of territory.

---

[1] Naturalisation Act, 1870.

(*d*) The father was at the time of the child's birth in the service of the Crown.

(*e*) The birth was registered at a British Consulate, normally within one year of its occurrence, subject in this case to a formal declaration of retention of British nationality, coupled with the divesting of any foreign nationality which the person may also have acquired, so far as the law of the foreign country permits. This declaration must be made within a year after the person so claiming British nationality attains the age of twenty-one.

The status of a wife depends on that of her husband. Thus an alien-born woman obtains British nationality by the fact of marrying a British husband. Correspondingly British status is lost by a woman who marries an alien, but a wife who is a British national can retain her British nationality by express declaration if, during the continuance of the marriage, the husband loses his British nationality. Widows and divorced women retain the status of their former husbands. Infants take the status of their parents, save that if a widow of a British subject marries an alien her children by her first marriage do not lose their nationality.

Nationality acquired by birth, as well as that acquired by naturalisation, may be divested. This was not so at Common Law, but by the Acts a British subject who becomes naturalised when in a foreign State ceases automatically to be a British subject, and, moreover, in certain circumstances a declaration of alienage may be made without formal naturalisation in a foreign state. In one circumstance a British subject cannot divest himself of his nationality. In time of war, neither by naturalisation in an enemy nor (possibly) in a neutral State,[1] nor by a declaration of alienage, can a British subject revoke his nationality. The leading case is *Rex* v. *Lynch* [1903], 1 K.B. 444; K. & L. 289. Lynch (who subsequently sat in the House of Commons as a Nationalist member for an Irish constituency) was accused of high treason. One of the overt acts alleged was that he had taken the oath of allegiance to the enemy during the Boer War.

[1] See *Vecht* v. *Taylor* (1917), 116 L.T. 446, which leaves the point open.

He was convicted, but subsequently pardoned. A resident alien's duty of allegiance does not cease when the King's protection is temporarily withdrawn, owing to the occupation of the British territory where he is residing by enemy forces in time of war. In *De Jager* v. *A.-G. of Natal* [1907], A.C. 326 ; K. & L. 291, a resident alien was held guilty of treason, who, in such circumstances, joined an invading force, although that force was composed of nationals of his own country.

Acquired Nationality.   With regard to acquired nationality (Part II. of 1914 Act), the Home Secretary exercises an absolute discretion to refuse a certificate of naturalisation to an alien who desires to become a British subject. He is precluded by the Act from granting a certificate unless the alien satisfies the following conditions:

(*a*) That he has resided in His Majesty's dominions for five out of the preceding eight years, of which the year immediately antecedent to the application must have been spent in the United Kingdom. This qualification need not be shown by a widow or divorced wife of an alien who was herself a British subject before marriage, nor by an alien who has served under the Crown for five, out of the last eight, years.

(*b*) That he is of good character and has adequate knowledge of the English language.

(*c*) That he intends to reside in the dominions of the Crown, or to enter into, or continue in, the service of the Crown.

But the alien has no right to the certificate if, in spite of his being qualified under these conditions, the Home Secretary declines to exercise his discretion in his favour. Minors may be naturalised without fulfilling the above qualifications. The effect of naturalisation is that the alien, on taking the oath of allegiance, becomes entitled to all political and other rights, powers and privileges, and subject to all obligations and duties to which a natural-born British subject is entitled or subject. But the Home Secretary also has a discretion to revoke a certificate of naturalisation, whereas he has no power to deprive a natural-born British subject of nationality. The discretion is exercisable if the Secretary of State is satisfied that the person to whom the certificate has been granted has shown himself by act or speech to be disaffected or disloyal. Such act may be indicated by the naturalised person being convicted of a serious criminal offence.

Disaffection and disloyalty are sufficiently vague terms to enable the discretion to be regarded as virtually absolute. And indeed " good character " is so vague as to be capable of causing injustice to the naturalised alien whose certificate is revoked, should political considerations ever be allowed to influence the exercise of the discretion. Revocation of a certificate does not affect the status of the wife or children, unless the Secretary of State expressly so directs, and if the wife be a natural-born British subject, the Secretary of State cannot, of course, order the revocation of her status.

Although the Dominions (other than the Irish Free State, where the Act applies, since it was passed before the establishment of that Dominion and no steps have been taken since to amend it) have now adopted Part II. (Imperial Naturalisation) of the British Nationality and Status of Aliens Act of 1914, the law on this topic in the past has not been uniform throughout the Empire. This is well illustrated by a naturalisation case arising under the Act of 1870, which still remains the chief Act governing British nationality for persons born before January 1st, 1915. *Uniform Acquired. British Nationality.*

> A man, who was born in Germany in 1859 and who went to Australia at the age of nineteen, became naturalised under the Commonwealth law in 1908. He afterwards came to reside in London, where he was charged with, and convicted of, an offence under the Aliens' Restriction Order then in force. The Court held that taking the oath of allegiance to the King after the grant of a certificate of naturalisation under the Commonwealth Act did not make him a British subject in the United Kingdom; *The King v. Francis, ex parte Markwald* [1918], 1 K.B. 617; *Markwald v. Attorney-General* [1920], 1 Ch. 348.

The Dominions are all agreed that a common status is desirable, but it is within the legislative competence of any Dominion to define its own nationals. As the law stands in 1930, the Dominions, having adopted Part II. of the Act of the United Kingdom Parliament of their own free will, are bound by its terms and cannot, in law, repeal it. But the proposed repeal of the Colonial Laws Validity Act, 1865, as to future legislation by Dominion legislatures, coupled with the contemplated removal of the ban on extra-territorial legislation, will enable each Dominion to repeal that part of the Act which they have adopted.   The Imperial Conference, 1930, agreed that no change should be made apart from reciprocal action by all members of the British Commonwealth, so as to preserve the common status of a British national under the Act of 1914.   In this connection it may be observed that the Acts of 1914-22 define the circumstances which go to make up a *natural-born* British subject throughout the Empire,[1] but local nationality may still be conferred by both Dominion and Colonial legislatures.   This power was reserved by s. 26 of the 1914 Act.

F.

Extradition.

Extradition relates to the surrender of fugitive criminals, whether accused or convicted.   The Home Office is concerned in all extradition proceedings, whether the claim is for the surrender of persons who have committed crimes in foreign States and then sought refuge in this country, or for the surrender of accused persons who have escaped from the jurisdiction of our courts.   No proceedings can be taken unless an extradition treaty has been concluded with the foreign Power which seeks the surrender of the fugitive, or into whose territory the fugitive has escaped from British justice.   The Extradition Acts of 1870, 1873, 1895 and 1906, require that the terms of a treaty be brought into force by means of an Order in Council. About forty such treaties have been concluded.   In the majority of cases there is no provision for the extradition of nationals of the contracting parties, *e.g.*, an Italian, who is wanted on a criminal charge in this country cannot be

---

[1] In the opinion of an authority this definition is of Imperial validity, and without any saving for the Dominions; Keith, *Responsible Government in the Dominions* (2nd edition), II., 1043.

extradited from Italy, if he has succeeded in escaping thither. This restriction does not, of course, affect any remedy which his home State may have against a national in respect of his crimes committed in this country. There is one universal exception to the category of crimes in respect of which extradition proceedings may be brought under the treaties. No person accused of a political offence can be extradited.

The process for securing the extradition of an offender Procedure. who has escaped to this country is as follows: The diplomatic representative of the country desiring extradition of a fugitive offender makes a request to the Foreign Office for his arrest, sending at the same time evidence on which the charge is based, or, if the person has already been convicted in the country where he committed the crime, evidence of his conviction and sentence. The Foreign Office forwards the request to the Home Office, whereupon the Home Secretary, unless he considers the offence to be a political one, issues an order to the Chief Metropolitan Magistrate at Bow Street, who, in turn, issues his warrant for the criminal's arrest to the Metropolitan Police. This process may be curtailed, as the Extradition Acts provide for a warrant being issued on sworn information prior to the order for proceedings by the Home Secretary; but the order must be made later, if proceedings are continued. All cases have to be investigated before the Chief Magistrate. In the event of the Magistrate deciding that the offender should be committed to prison to await his surrender, fifteen days must elapse, during which the offender may apply to the High Court of Justice for his release by means of a writ of Habeas Corpus. The surrender will not be ordered, unless the offence alleged is one which substantially coincides with an indictable offence under English criminal law and may be refused on the following grounds:

(1) Insufficient evidence of identity.

(2) That the offence is not within the treaty.

(3) That no *primâ facie* case has been made out.

(4) That the offence is political, or that the surrender is sought for a political object.

Rex v. Corrigan (1930), 47 T.L.R. 27 affords an interesting case on this subject, involving a discussion of the whole process of surrender.

The surrender of fugitive criminals to, or by, British Dominions and Colonies is dealt with by the Fugitive Offenders Act, 1881. The procedure thereby authorised is similar to that for extradition, but is simpler. Political offences are not excluded, and there is, of course, no diplomatic application, the case going direct to the Chief Magistrate.

G.

Miscellaneous.

Church of England.

It also falls to the Home Secretary, from time to time, to consider whether the law, as it stands, is adequate to deal with the elements of possible disorder in the widest sense, including public morals. A reference to this topic will be found under Freedom of Speech, Part VII., Chap. II.

The Home Office is concerned with many other duties besides the maintenance of order. Some of these lie within the sphere of the Prerogative. The Home Secretary, for example, is the proper medium of communication between the King, who is by law its Governor, and the Church of England ; communications between the King to Convocation are made through the Home Secretary, but in the matter of the appointment of Archbishops and Bishops, and in some cases Deans and Canons, the King's adviser is now the Prime Minister, and the Home Secretary's functions are purely ministerial. A large number of appointments under the Prerogative to high office pass through the Home Office, to which is entrusted the preparation of warrants under the Sign Manual or Letters Patent. The warrants

Royal Commissions.

authorising appointments of Royal Commissions are submitted to the King through this channel, and the Commission submits its report, when completed, to the Home Secretary, who, in turn, submits it to the King and afterwards presents it to Parliament. The Home Office is frequently consulted by Royal Commissions on questions as to their powers and procedure.

By statute wide and important regulative duties are entrusted to the Home Office in connection with the administration of the Factory Acts, the Shops Acts, employment of children, workmen's compensation, the sale of intoxicating liquors and dangerous drugs, explosive firearms, picture-houses and theatres. The Home Office has also recently become the central authority under the Acts relating to parliamentary and municipal elections.

CHAPTER VI.

PUBLIC FINANCE: THE TREASURY.[1]

Treasury Board.

THE office of Treasurer was first put into commission in 1616. Since 1714 it has always been in commission. The Treasury Board, as are the Commissioners for executing the office of the Lord High Admiral, *i.e.*, the Admiralty, is a body of Commissioners. The Board is created by Letters Patent under the Great Seal and is composed as follows:

(1) First Lord of the Treasury (which office is almost invariably held by the Prime Minister).

(2) Chancellor of the Exchequer.

(3) Financial Secretary (who is the Chancellor's deputy in the House of Commons).

(4) Parliamentary Secretary (sometimes called the Patronage Secretary, who, by custom, is the Chief Government Whip).

(5) Junior Lords of the Treasury (Assistant Government Whips).

The Board never meets, individual members being responsible for the business transacted. Treasury Warrants are generally signed by two of the Junior Lords. The Chancellor of the Exchequer is the Finance Minister, not by virtue of his membership of the Board, but by separate patents of office. He is invariably a Member of the House of Commons.

Sub-Departments.

Before discussing the part played by the Treasury in revenue matters, it is necessary to give a brief account of the Sub-Departments which work in connection with the Treasury.

---

[1] For the history of the Exchequer and the Office of Treasurer, see Anson, *op. cit.* (3rd edition), Vol. II., Part II., pp. 138 ff.

(1) These Boards are the Departments of the Civil Service The Board of Customs charged with responsibility for the collection of Customs and Excise and Excise Duties and direct taxation such as Income Tax, and the Sur-Tax, Death Duties and Stamp Duties respectively. Board of Inland To some. extent the Post Office must be regarded as an Revenue. adjunct of the Treasury for the collection of many duties and taxes, *e.g.*, Wireless Receiving Licences.

(2) In addition to the important function of auditing Comptroller State accounts, this official can alone authorise the Bank of and Auditor- England to give credit to the Treasury for payments out of General. the Consolidated Fund, which is the account at the Bank of England through which all the public revenue passes. He will only give this authority when satisfied that the requirements of the Treasury have been sanctioned by Parliament. As Auditor of the public accounts, this officer examines the accounts of Departments annually and reports to a Standing Committee of the House of Commons, called the Public Accounts Committee, which, in turn, makes its report to the House. The Controller draws attention to any excess of authorised expenditure, as well as to unnecessarily extravagant or irregular items in the accounts of a Department. The importance of this office is such that the salary attached to it is not subject to the annual vote of Parliament, but is charged on the Consolidated Fund by an Act which does not require annual renewal. In this respect the Controller and Auditor-General is in the same position as the judges, and, like the judges, he holds his office during good behaviour, but can be dismissed by the King upon an address presented by both Houses of Parliament.

(3) This office is a political one, but it is unpaid. Its Paymaster- function is ministerial. Payments on account of the public General. services are made to the Paymaster-General by the Bank of England, and he pays out the money to the Departments and other persons authorised by the Treasury.

Other Departments which may be mentioned briefly are Other De- the Mint, through which money is coined; the Public partments. Works Loan Board, which advances money to local authorities for the purpose of public utility undertakings; the Civil Service Commission, which controls the entrance of candidates into the Civil Service ; the Parliamentary Counsel, who perform the actual drafting of Government Bills. The Treasury Solicitor, in addition to being legal adviser to the Treasury and Defence Departments, acts as Solicitor for these and other Departments, as well as for the Crown directly and the Attorney-General in certain matters, *e.g.*, charities. By custom and Royal Warrant the holder of the office is also Procurator-General, or King's Proctor, to appear for His Majesty in civil, maritime and ecclesiastical matters, *e.g.*, in prize or divorce. Many Departments, however, have solicitors of their own, *e.g.*, the Ministry of Health, Ministry of Labour, Post Office.

Functions of Treasury.
The main functions of the Treasury are twofold :

(1) To ensure that no more money is asked for by the spending Departments than is required for their annual needs.

(2) To check the expenditure of the Departments, so that no more money is spent than is authorised by Parliament.

The whole of the National Revenue is the King's Revenue. The raising and spending of the King's Revenue is subject to the control of the House of Commons. This, in the first place, means that, with unimportant exceptions, the Crown cannot raise any money except by the authority of an Act of Parliament. Secondly, public money cannot be expended without the consent of Parliament and it is the practice of the House of Commons to appropriate every item of national revenue to specific purposes. The procedure in relation to Supply Bills has already been dealt with under Parliament, where some comment will be found on the ineffectiveness of parliamentary control so far as securing economy of expenditure is concerned.[1]

It has long been provided by Standing Orders of the House of Commons that no charge can be placed upon the public revenue except on the recommendation of a Minister of the Crown. The same rule prevails with regard to taxation. A private member may move to reduce a tax, but not to increase it. Thus the Government of the day is responsible

---

[1] Part III., Chap. IV., A.

for all taxation and expenditure, and no private member can propose that the public funds be utilised for any public purpose that is not approved by the Government.

All the revenue collected for the National Exchequer is paid into the nation's account at the Bank of England, which is known as the Consolidated Fund. The solitary exception is where a Department, having received money in the course of performing its functions, uses it to defray its own expenses. Such items are known as " appropriations in aid " and are under strict parliamentary control. While this expenditure does not require prior parliamentary authorisation, it is dealt with in the departmental estimates presented to Parliament. *Consolidated Fund.*

The expenditure of the country is grouped under two heads, namely, Consolidated Fund Services and Supply Services. The Consolidated Fund Services are payments under statutes which make a permanent grant, either for a fixed number of years or without limitation of time. Payments on account of the Supply Services have to be voted each year by the House of Commons. The principal item of expenditure under the heading, Consolidated Fund Services, is the interest upon, and management of, the National Debt. This accounts for at least three-eighths of the annual expenditure of the country in recent years. It is obvious that credit which depended for its security on annual review by Parliament would not prove attractive to lenders. Accordingly Government Loans are charged under statutes which give permanent authority for meeting the obligations incurred to lenders. The sum of £305,000,000 is now set aside to meet the annual interest and management of the National Debt as a Consolidated Fund Service. A further £50,000,000 is provided by a fund (the New Sinking Fund), whereby it is anticipated that the National Debt will be liquidated in the course of fifty years. This Sinking Fund is not now included in the Consolidated Fund Services. Further, any surplus in the national income at the end of the financial year is applied in reduction of the Debt. The sum so allocated is called the Old Sinking Fund. *Expenditure; Consolidated Fund Services.*

Payments to the Exchequer of Northern Ireland on account

of the revenues collected within its boundaries by the Treasury Sub-Departments, are made in the form of a grant charged on the Consolidated Fund Services. The King's Civil List was granted to the King by the Civil List Act, 1910, for his reign and six months after and accordingly forms one of these Services.[1] The Civil List is the annual income granted to the Sovereign to meet certain charges. It is granted at the beginning of each reign in lieu of the ancient hereditary revenues of the Crown, including the income from Crown lands. At one time the pay of public servants was one of these charges, but the present Civil List is appropriated exclusively to the Privy Purse and the expenses, including salaries of the Royal Household. The small sum of £1200 per annum is allowed each year for pensions awarded to distinguished persons or their dependents who are in poor financial circumstances. The salaries of those officials whom it is desired to make more independent of parliamentary control than the ordinary departmental officials are also made Consolidated Fund payments. Whereas the salaries of the Government Departments, as a whole, come under annual review by Parliament, the salaries of the Lord Chancellor (as Speaker of the House of Lords),[2] the Speaker of the House of Commons, the Comptroller and Auditor-General, the Lords of Appeal in Ordinary, the judges of the Court of Appeal and the High Court of Justice and subordinate judges (County Court and Recorders) are charged on the Consolidated Fund Services. There is thus no special opportunity of criticising in Parliament each year the work of these officials, as in the case of servants who are paid from the Supply Services.

Supply Services. These fall under three main heads, the Armed Forces of the Crown, the Civil Services and the Revenue Services. The financial year of the country runs from April 1st to March 31st, except for the purposes of income tax and sur-tax, when the period is April 6th to April 5th. Each

---

[1] For History of Civil List, see Anson, *op. cit.*, Vol. II., Part II., pp. 163 ff.

[2] Part of the salary is charged to the Supply Votes.

year in the autumn the Government Departments submit to the Treasury an estimate of their expenditure for the ensuing year. The estimate is closely scrutinised by the Treasury and cannot be submitted to the House of Commons until it has received Treasury approval. In this way to a limited extent the Treasury is able to check a tendency to extravagance on the part of the spending Departments. No doubt a strong Chancellor of the Exchequer can make administration as economical as possible. But it must be remembered that the Treasury itself must assist in carrying out the policy of the Cabinet. It is the Cabinet, by forcing legislation involving expansive expenditure through Parliament, which really increases expenditure, and, if Parliament saddles a Department with an item of expenditure, the Chancellor of the Exchequer must submit or resign. In these days policy is apt to be synonymous with expenditure, and therefore the opportunities for the Treasury to curtail expenditure are largely confined to curtailing the expenses of management. If, for example, the Cabinet as a whole decides to increase the unemployment benefit by statutory amendment, the estimates of the Ministry of Labour, when submitted to the Treasury, must show the increase on account of the extended benefit. The Treasury may insist that the administration expenses be restricted, but they have no control whatever over the statutory rate of benefit, once it is approved by Parliament. A strong Chancellor of the Exchequer may, however, as a member of the Cabinet, use his influence with his colleagues by indicating that he is unable to find the money to carry their proposed policy into effect.

No proposal involving the expenditure of public funds is nowadays presented to the Cabinet by the Head of a Department until it has been examined both by the Treasury and any other Department which may be concerned with the proposal. Thus the financial implication of any policy which it is proposed to put into effect is ensured full examination.

Another reason why an annual examination of the estimates by the Treasury is necessary is to enable the Chancellor of the Exchequer and his Staff at the Treasury to prepare the annual Budget statement in time for presentation to the House of Commons early in the new financial year.[1] An examination of the estimates can alone enable the Chancellor of the Exchequer to determine whether or not additional taxation will have to be imposed, or again, whether the requirements of the ensuing year will enable him to remit some portion of the existing taxation.

The Treasury is responsible for the rates of pay of civil servants. The Civil Service Commission controls the entry of candidates into the competitive appointments of the Service.

Revenue. Ordinary Revenue.

The revenue of the Crown is divided into ordinary and extraordinary, the latter being derived mainly from taxation. The principal item of " ordinary " revenue, the total of which is nowadays negligible, is the income derived from Crown lands, which in the main have long since been surrendered to the public. The rents and profits so derived are paid into the Consolidated Fund. The Crown is also, as part of its " ordinary " revenue, entitled to property found without any apparent owner. The most important illustration of this is the property of an intestate who dies without a spouse or blood-relations entitled to take under the Administration of Estates Act, 1925, ss. 46 & 47.

Extraordinary Revenue.

The " extraordinary " revenue derived from taxation falls under several heads. Taxes are levied either by the Finance Acts of each year or under specific Acts which contain a code governing the particular tax in question and either fix the rate of tax or leave it to be fixed by subsequent Finance Acts. The Income Tax Act, 1918, as amended by subsequent Finance Acts, is a good illustration of a taxing code, whereas the rate of income tax is fixed each year through the Finance Act.

Indirect Taxation.

The following are the most important items of indirect taxation, *i.e.*, taxation which is, generally speaking, capable of being passed on to the consumer by the taxpayer.

[1] Part III., Chap. IV., A.

(1) These consist of duties imposed upon commodities Customs imported into this country from foreign countries. Some of Duties. the duties are imposed by the Finance Act of each year. Others are collected under the authority of permanent Acts. Customs duties are not levied on all imported goods and form the subject-matter of much political controversy.

The Customs Consolidation Act, 1876, contains a code of regulations and imposes penalties upon those who attempt to evade the duties. Goods may only be imported free of duty if they are deposited in a warehouse, the owner of which has entered into a bond with the Crown that the proper duties will be paid if, and when, the goods are released for sale at home. The provision of bonded warehouses is particularly useful for enabling goods intended for re-exportation to other countries to escape duty.

(2) These, like the customs duties, are controlled by the Excise Commissioners of Customs and Excise. They are imposed Duties. upon commodities produced for consumption in this country. The revenue officials have important powers of entry and search to check evasion of the tax, which largely consists of duties on alcoholic liquors. The term, excise duty, is not used strictly in the sense of a tax on commodities, but also covers a number of taxes in the form of licences to manufacture certain articles, *e.g.*, beer and spirits, licences to carry on certain occupations, *e.g.*, pawnbroker, money-lender, auctioneer and retailer of beer, spirits, wine and tobacco ; and licences to use certain articles which are deemed luxuries such as keeping a dog, driving a motor-car, employing a male servant. Another excise duty is the duty on entertainments.

As an equivalent to the bonded warehouse in the case of imported goods, excise duties in the strict sense are generally subject to drawback, *i.e.*, repayment of the duty if the goods are exported to a foreign country. The exporter of beer is allowed a drawback on the excise duties paid on the manufacture. The object is to enable British manufacturers to compete in foreign markets with foreigners who may not have had to pay duties on the same commodities. In the case of a customs duty on an article in the raw state, which

13 *

is imported into this country for manufacture and then re-exported in the finished form, the manufacturer can claim repayment of the customs duties paid on importation. Tobacco to be manufactured into cigarettes for exportation is an example of this.

Direct Taxation. A direct tax is one which falls on the actual person who pays the tax.

Death Duties. (3) Certain duties become payable to the Crown on the death of an individual leaving property, the value of which exceeds £100. The duties are paid either upon the property which the deceased enjoyed or upon the interests to which others succeed on account of his death. The duties are known as Estate Duty, Succession Duty, and Legacy Duty. Estate Duty is levied on all the property of the deceased whether land, money or goods, while Succession Duty is payable in respect of succession by others to the land of the deceased or to investments previously settled. Legacy Duty is payable by the successor on account of personal property accruing to him by will or intestacy or a gift made in contemplation of death. It is unnecessary in a work of this description to give an account of this extremely complicated branch of law.

Stamp Duties. (4) This is a method of collecting duties upon certain legal instruments, notably instruments of transfer.

Income Tax and Sur-Tax. (5) This tax treats a man's income as falling under five possible heads, called schedules, by the Income Tax Act, 1918. Income Tax is a tax on a flat rate; for 1930-31 it was at 4s. 6d. in the £, subject to certain deductions and allowances from the income which is liable to assessment. As with Death Duties, it is not proposed to give an account of this important, but highly specialised branch of law.

The five schedules are as follows:

Schedule A imposes a tax on the annual value of land and buildings, subject to certain deductions on account of repairs. This is not a tax upon income, but on ownership of land and buildings, and is usually known as Landlord's Property Tax.

Schedule B is a tax on the occupation of land and is chargeable in addition to the tax under Schedule A. It has come to be a tax upon agricultural land and is essentially the farmers' Income Tax, unless he elects to be assessed under Schedule D on actual profits.

Schedule C taxes income derived from public revenue, *i.e.*, interest on British, colonial and foreign securities payable in the United Kingdom.

Schedule D taxes the annual profits and gains from any kind of property, from any trade or profession, or from any other source not specifically charged under other schedules. The assessment is made on the amount of profits or gains of the previous year.

Schedule E is a tax on salaries and other perquisites of office.

Sur-Tax is a graduated tax on income above a certain figure. At present the tax is levied on the excess of income over £2,000, the rates rising with the amount of such excess.

There are important allowances and deductions which have the effect of making the tax a graduated one. The effect is that no one with an income of less than £3,000 per annum pays the full rate of tax. These allowances are only applied to the income of individuals, and not of societies.

From a constitutional point of view something must be said about the administration of these taxes. The Commissioners of Inland Revenue are charged with the general management of the tax, representing the interests of the Crown on behalf of the general body of taxpayers. The duties of the Commissioners in each district (the civil parish is the normal unit) are carried out by Inspectors, whose work covers a number of adjoining districts. In each district there is a body, known as the General Commissioners (Commissioners of the General Purposes of the Income Tax) ; this body, which contains no official element, holds office independently of the Inland Revenue Commissioners, and is a quasi-judicial tribunal interposed between the Crown and the individual taxpayer, from whose ranks its members are drawn. It is the duty of the General Commissioners, subject to certain important exceptions, which include assessments to sur-tax,[1] to confirm assessments of taxation, and to hear appeals by the taxpayer and the Revenue authorities on

Administration of Income Tax.

[1] Made by the Commissioners of Inland Revenue acting as Special Commissioners.

questions of law and fact. From their decision, which will not, as a rule, be questioned on a matter of fact as opposed to law, appeals lie to the King's Bench Division, thence to the Court of Appeal and House of Lords. There is a tendency for the work of actual assessment and collection of the tax to fall more and more into the hands of the Inland Revenue officials. There is much to be said for this in the interests of uniformity and economy of administration, but against this must be set the direct relationship between the taxpayer and the State, which the General Commissioners, their Assessors and Collectors, were intended to reduce to a minimum. Moreover, the methods of the Revenue officials are subjected to severe criticism from time to time, mainly on the grounds that they are apt to interpret the law too strictly in favour of the Crown. But it must be remembered that it is in the interests of the general body of taxpayers that the administration of taxation should be strictly conducted.

ESTIMATED REVENUE AND EXPENDITURE, 1929-1930.

REVENUE.		EXPENDITURE.	
Customs	£119,850,000	National Debt	£304,600,000
Excise	130,330,000	New Sinking Fund	50,400,000
Motor Vehicle Duties		Northern Ireland	5,400,000
(Exchequer share)	4,680,000	Local Taxation	15,000,000
Estate Duties	81,000,000	Local Revenues	15,560,000
Stamps	31,000,000	Other Consolidated	
Land Tax, House Duty,		Fund Services	3,500,000
and Mineral Rights		Navy	47,312,000
Duty	800,000	Pensions	8,533,000
Income Tax	239,500,000	Army	32,280,000
Super-Tax	58,000,000	Pensions	8,265,000
Excess Profits Duty ⎫		Air Force	15,983,000
Corporation Profits ⎬	1,700,000	Pensions	217,000
Tax ⎭		Civil Services [1]	223,325,000
Post Office Services		Tax Collection (Cus-	
(Net)	8,900,000	toms, Excise and	
Crown Lands (Net)	1,250,000	Inland Revenue)	11,569,000
From Sundry Loans,			
etc.,	30,550,000	Total	£741,964,000
Miscellaneous Receipts :—		Surplus	4,096,000
Ordinary	12,500,000		
Special	26,000,000		
Total	£746,060,000	Total	£746,060,000

[1] Both nationally and locally administered, so far as paid out of national revenue as opposed to local rates or loans.

CHAPTER VII.

FOREIGN AFFAIRS : THE FOREIGN OFFICE.[1]

A.

THE powers of the Crown in foreign affairs are exercised, Prerogative. like all prerogative powers, subject to the collective responsibility of the Cabinet. The Secretary of State for Foreign Affairs presides over the Department designated the Foreign Office. It is in this sphere that the Prerogative remains supreme.[2] Although the Foreign Secretary, like all Ministers, is responsible for the conduct of his office to the House of Commons, the necessity for secrecy, which attaches diplomacy, renders parliamentary control less effective than in other branches of Government. The House of Commons, with its strong partisan conflicts, is not the best assembly in which to debate foreign affairs. On the other hand, the House of Lords, containing as it does, men eminent in all branches of the public service at home and abroad, is singularly fitted to discuss foreign policy. In Parliament, the Foreign Secretary is assisted by two Under-Secretaries, one, the Under-Secretary of State for Foreign Affairs, the other, who is also Parliamentary Secretary to the Board of Trade, represents the Department of Overseas Trade.

The conduct of foreign relations involves the collection Functions of information and correspondence on an extensive scale. of the It also involves the exchange of diplomatic representatives Office.

[1] Acts of State have been discussed in Part II., Chap. IV. ; they are part of the topic of the Crown and Foreign Affairs.

[2] Some authorities do not regard the Crown's powers in relation to Foreign Affairs as part of the Prerogative, arguing that what the Crown does is an Act of State, which cannot be challenged, controlled or interfered with by municipal Courts ; that it is not sanctioned by the law, but the sovereign power itself. Per Warrington, L.J., *In re Ferdinand, ex-Tsar of Bulgaria* [1921], 1 Ch. at p. 139.

and other agents (consular officers). The former represent the State in its external relations with other States ; the latter (consuls) are chiefly concerned with British subjects resident or travelling abroad ; matters of commerce, industry and navigation fall within their scope.[1]

Constitu-
tional
Topics.

There are three topics of importance in Constitutional Law which should be discussed under the duties of the Foreign Office :—

(1) The Immunity from Processes of Law enjoyed by Heads of States and other Representatives, including the Immunity which attaches to the Property of Foreign States.

(2) The Treaty-making Powers of the Crown.

(3) Declarations by Government Departments relating to Foreign States.[2]

The Immunity of Heads of State and State Property. This subject may be classified under three heads :—

(a) Immunity of Heads of States.

(b) Diplomatic and Consular Immunity.

(c) Immunity in respect of Public Property of a Foreign State.

Nature of
Immunity
illustrated.

The immunity is one from legal process, and its nature may be illustrated by the following cases :—

(1) *Mighell* v. *Sultan of Johore* [1894], 1 Q.B. 149.

> The Sultan, while visiting this country, became engaged to a young woman to whom he disclosed his identity as being that of Mr. Albert Baker. The Sultan having failed to fulfil his promise of marriage, the lady attempted to serve a writ on him for breach of promise of marriage.
>
> Held that as a ruler of an independent foreign State, Johore, being so regarded for this purpose, the Sultan was immune from process, unless he submitted to the jurisdiction.

(2) *The Parlement Belge* (1880), 5 P.D. 197, laid down the important principle, that as a consequence of the independence of every sovereign authority, each State declines to exercise any of its territorial jurisdiction through its courts

---

[1] For functions, see Oppenheim, *International Law* (Longmans), 4th edition, by A. D. McNair, Vol. I., pp. 661 ff.

[2] These topics bear equally on the sphere of International Law, and the reader is referred to Oppenheim, *op. cit.*, 4th edition, Vol. I., Parts III. and IV. for further information.

over the person of any sovereign or ambassador, or over the public property of any State destined for the public use, or over the property of any ambassador, even though the sovereign, ambassador, or property be within its territory.

This statement was occasioned by the seizure, under process of the Admiralty Division (to secure redress for collision damage), of a packet steamer which had collided with a ship of a British subject. The vessel was the property of the King of the Belgians, and carried mails for his Government, as well as private passengers and merchandise.

The immunity may be waived by an unequivocal act of submission; *Duff Development Co.* v. *Government of Kelantan* [1924], A.C. 797; K. & L. 316. It is an immunity, not from liability, but from local jurisdiction. Accordingly, a motor-car insurance policy indemnifying a person who enjoys immunity against legal liability is enforceable, if the insured submits to being sued, even though he could not have been sued in respect of his liability, except on his own voluntary submission; *Dickinson* v. *Del Solar* [1930], 1 K.B. 376.

Heads of States consist of Monarchs and Presidents. *(a)* Immunity of Head of State. A Monarch of a foreign State visiting this country with the knowledge of the Government is afforded certain honours and enjoys certain protection and immunities. In particular, he cannot be subjected to the criminal jurisdiction of the courts, nor compelled against his will to plead in a civil court. He may, of course, himself be a plaintiff. Under the so-called doctrine of extra-territoriality he is immune from all taxation and his residence is inviolable. The position of a President is less certain, but it may be predicted that, having regard to the number of important States having this type of ruler, the practice for the future will not differ substantially from that adopted in the case of visiting monarchs.

The immunity of diplomatic representatives is part and *(b)* Immunity of Diplomatic Representatives. parcel of that enjoyed by the heads of the States which they represent, though some writers attribute it to the necessity of such persons being free from the local jurisdiction, in order the better to perform the duties they owe to the

accrediting country. We are not concerned with this branch
of International Law as such, for in English Law immunity
is founded on statute.

The Diplomatic Privileges Act, 1708, enacts that

> " all writs and processes that shall at any time hereafter be
> sued forth or prosecuted whereby the person of any ambas-
> sador or other publick minister of any foreign prince or state
> authorised and received as such by Her Majesty her heirs or
> successors, or the domestick or domestick servant of any
> such ambassador or other publick minister may be arrested
> or imprisoned or his or their goods or chattels may be dis-
> trained or seized or attached shall be deemed and adjudged
> to be utterly null and void to all intents constructions and
> purposes whatever."

This Act is declaratory of the Common Law and international practice, and behind it lies the principle accepted by
the courts in *The Parlement Belge*. The person of a diplomatic envoy is inviolable and is protected by the criminal
law, which makes interference with State envoys a misdemeanour. The protection is extended to their families,
suites, official residence, papers and mails. No diplomatic
envoy may be punished for any criminal offence by the
courts, but this does not mean that he may misconduct
himself with impunity. He is expected to conform to the
law of the land, unless it is likely to interfere with his free
conduct of his duties. He is liable to be recalled on representation made to his home government by the Foreign
Office. Oppenheim puts the consequences of the extra-
territoriality granted to diplomatic envoys by municipal law
under five principal heads.[1] These may be taken to be the
law of England.

(*a*) Immunity of domicile, so far as is necessary for the
independence and inviolability of envoys.

(*b*) Exemption from civil and criminal jurisdiction ; even
the issue of a writ of summons is void ; *Musurus Bey* v.
Gadban [1894], 2 Q.B. 352. There are some minor exceptions from the immunity from civil process, and the immunity may be waived.

(*c*) Exemption from being subpœna-ed as a witness.

---

[1] Oppenheim, *op. cit.*, Vol. I., pp. 629 ff.

(*d*) Exemption from police orders and regulations.

(*e*) Exemption from taxation and local rates.

Consular immunities are not of great importance, and their extent is inconsiderable.

It was in connection with this head of immunity that *The Parlement Belge* (above) was decided. It will suffice to reproduce Oppenheim's statement of the law relating to ships (other than men-of-war) which in International Law enjoy immunities.[1]

(*c*) Immunity in respect of Public Property of a Foreign State.

> (i) A British Court of Law will not exercise jurisdiction over a ship which is the property of a foreign State, whether she is actually engaged in the public service or is being used in the ordinary way of a shipowner's business, as, for instance, being let out under a charter-party ; nor can any maritime lien attach, even in suspense, to such a ship, so as to be enforceable against it, if and when it is transferred into private ownership.

> (ii) Ships which are not the property of a foreign State, but are chartered or requisitioned by it or otherwise in its possession and control, may not be arrested by process of the Admiralty Court while subject to such possession and control, nor will any action lie against the foreign State ; . . . but when the governmental possession and control cease to operate and she is redelivered to her owner, an action *in personam* will lie against him in respect of salvage services rendered to her while in governmental possession and control, when he has derived a benefit from those services.

From the case of *The Porto Alexandre* [1920], P. 30—a case of salvage—it appears that this immunity extends to the freight earned by such ships, and presumably to the cargo itself, if publicly owned. On the other hand, a mere declaration by a foreign State which is not a party to the proceedings that the property concerning which the litigation is proceeding is its state property is not conclusive. Nor is a declaration by a Government Department in this country as to a right of property binding on the courts ; *The Jupiter*, No. 3 [1927], P. 250 (below).

The subject of immunity, while part of International Law, is of constitutional importance, because, as has been remarked earlier, the immunities enjoyed constitute a class of persons outside the ordinary law of the land. So long as the

Importance of Immunity in respect of Property.

---

[1] Oppenheim, *op. cit.*, p. 678.

immunities were confined to the persons of sovereigns or other rulers and their representatives, they were comparatively unimportant. The same cannot be said of their extension to property. As Scrutton, L.J., remarks in *The Porto Alexandre* (above) :—

> "No one can shut his eyes . . . to the fact that many States are trading, or are about to trade, with ships belonging to themselves ; and if these national ships wander about without liabilities, many trading affairs will become difficult ; but it seems to me the remedy is not in these courts. *The Parlement Belge* excludes remedies in these courts. But there are practical commercial remedies. If ships of the State find themselves on the mud because no one will salve them when the State refuses any legal remedy for salvage, their owners will be apt to change their views. If the owners of cargoes on national ships find that the ship runs away and leaves them to bear all the expenses of salvage, as has been done in this case, there may be found a difficulty in getting cargoes for national ships. These are matters to be dealt with by negotiations between Governments, . . ."

A convention entered into by Great Britain and other maritime States in 1926 embodied the general principle that ships (and cargoes) operated and owned by States for commercial purposes shall be subject to ordinary maritime law. The convention has not yet been ratified and will probably be modified before ratification takes place. It will, of course, call for legislation before any change in the existing law can be effected.

B.

Treaties.

Closely allied to the executive power of making war and declaring peace is the Prerogative of treaty-making. No one but the King can bind the community by treaty. But the contents of the treaty may involve an alteration in the rights of British subjects in respect of their nationality or their property, or may lay a pecuniary burden on the State. The term, treaty, is unfortunately used very loosely of all international engagements in written form, but it must be remembered that such engagements are as capable of classification as documents in municipal law, *e.g.*, it would be incorrect to describe the effects of a simple contract in writing and a conveyance as identical, so a commercial agreement with another State differs from a treaty of cession, or from a law-making treaty. At first sight the treaty-making power appears to conflict with the constitutional principle that the King by Prerogative cannot alter the law. In practice it must be remembered that treaties are concluded on the advice of Ministers, and that those Ministers will normally be in a position to command a majority in Parliament. There is then no difficulty in obtaining from Parliament itself any consequential amendment of the law which the treaty may involve. Treaties involving the cession of territory were at one time thought to be exempt from this necessity of obtaining Parliament's consent, just as are declarations of war and treaties of peace, as such. But nowadays treaties of cession are either made conditional on confirmation by Parliament (see Anglo-Italian (East African Territories) Act, 1925), or are subsequently submitted to Parliament for express approval. It is easy to see that such treaties may sometimes involve an alteration in the substantive rights of subjects, particularly those who live in the ceded territory, in respect of their nationality. Moreover, the assumption of part of the national debt appropriate to the ceded territory will normally involve a charge on the public funds of the State to which the territory is ceded.

The question—When do British treaties involve legislation ?—has recently been answered by a leading authority [1] in the following summary :—

(1) Treaties which, for their enforcement by British courts of law, require some addition to, or alteration of, the existing law, cannot be carried into effect without legislation. Therefore the King will not be advised to ratify them, unless and until such legislation has been passed, or Parliament has given necessary assurance that it will be passed. A treaty imposing upon Great Britain a liability to pay money either actually or contingently, usually falls within this category, because, as a rule, money cannot be raised or expended without legislation.

[1] See article by Dr. A. D. McNair, in *British Year Book of International Law*, 1928,

(2) Treaties, *e.g.*, some of the Hague Conventions which modify the rights of the Crown when engaged in maritime warfare, and thus the law administered in British Prize Courts, will be recognised by the courts without legislation, but not treaties or other prerogative orders which attempt to increase the rights of the Crown ; *The Zamora* [1916], 2 A.C. 77 ; K. & L. 66.

(3) Treaties made expressly subject to the approval of Parliament require its approval, which is usually given in the form of a statute.

(4) It is the practice, and probably by now may be regarded as a binding constitutional convention, that treaties involving the cession of British territory (apart from the Indian Empire) require the approval of Parliament given by a statute.

C.

Declarations by the Executive relating to Foreign States.

It rests with the Executive to decide whether or not recognition shall be accorded to a foreign government or State. The subject of recognition is one for International Law, but the fact of recognition may have an important bearing on the result of litigation in which a British subject is engaged. In *Duff Development Co.* v. *Government of Kelantan* (above) the House of Lords recognised that it had

> for some time been the practice of the courts to take judicial notice of the sovereignty of a State and for that purpose (in any case of uncertainty) to seek information from a Secretary of State ; and when such information is so obtained the court does not permit it to be questioned by the parties. See *A. M. Luther* v. *J. Sagor & Co.* [1921], 3 K.B. 532.

Still more recently in *Engelke* v. *Musmann* [1928], A.C. 433, a statement made to the court by the Attorney-General on the instruction of the Foreign Office as to the status of a person claiming immunity from judicial process by reason of diplomatic privilege was accepted. The Foreign Office did not attempt here to interfere in the litigation ; it merely furnished a record of what had been done by virtue of the Prerogative in recognising the diplomatic status of one of the parties. The fact of recognition is peculiarly within the knowledge of the Department and is regarded by the courts as conclusive.

But neither the Executive of this country nor a foreign government can furnish the court with a statement which will be regarded as conclusive on the question of issues affecting the rights of the subject. In *The Jupiter*, No. 3 [1927], P. 250, the court refused to accept a declaration as to past ownership of a ship by a foreign government, not the owner of the ship at the time of the action, and, therefore, not claiming immunity from jurisdiction. In a question between the Crown and a private person as to property a Minister of State cannot conclude the issue in favour of the Crown by a sworn declaration. Nor can the declaration of a foreign government be accepted as conclusive when a question as to property is litigated between private persons in the courts.

The Crown can claim no Prerogative, save such as the law allows; the courts, therefore, have jurisdiction to enquire into the existence and scope of any alleged Prerogative. Accordingly, statements on behalf of the Crown are not conclusive as to the existence or extent of alleged prerogative power, so as to prejudice the rights of subjects. But where an act has been done by virtue of an undoubted Prerogative, such as the recognition of a foreign State, the statement made by the Government Department concerned as to the exercise of the Prerogative will be accepted as conclusive. That this is true of declarations by the Executive as to the beginning and end of a state of war is clear from *Janson* v. *Driefontein Consolidated Mines* [1902], A.C. (at p. 500). In *The Fagernes* [1927], P. 311, the Court of Appeal accepted the Attorney-General's statement, made on the instructions of the Home Secretary, that a place where a collision at sea had occurred was not claimed to be within the limits to which His Majesty's jurisdiction extended. The collision occurred in the Bristol Channel several miles from the nearest land.

PART V.

THE JUDICIARY.

History of English Law, especially Vol. 1., by Sir W. S. Holdsworth (Methuen)—for reference.

CHAPTER I.

THE COURTS.

THE most important of the inferior courts are the County Inferior Courts. Courts for the settlement of small civil disputes, and the Petty Sessional Courts presided over by magistrates for the trial of innumerable minor offences. Such crimes range from summary offences, such as bicycling without a light to offences, such as simple larceny, which are indictable and can be tried by Quarter Sessions or Assizes. They are, however, triable at Petty Sessions without a jury, should the accused desire it and the magistrates consider it expedient.

Magistrates, or Justices of the Peace, are appointed in Justices of the Peace. each county, and for each borough, which has its own commission of the peace, by the Lord Chancellor on the recommendation in counties of the Lord Lieutenant who acts on the advice of an advisory committee, and in boroughs on the recommendation of separate advisory committees. Men and women are eligible. They are not paid for their services. They perform many judicial and a few administrative duties entrusted to them by various statutes. In the Metropolitan Police District of London the police courts are presided over by paid Metropolitan Police Magistrates, and many of the larger towns in the provinces have paid Stipendiary Magistrates. These are appointed by the Crown on the recommendation of the Home Secretary. Any court of summary jurisdiction consisting of two or more justices sitting in a petty sessional court house forms a Court of Petty Sessions.

From the local justices sitting in Petty Sessions an appeal Appeals from Magistrates. lies to the justices of the whole county sitting in Quarter

Sessions.[1] Such an appeal is a re-hearing of the case. The expense of such appeals is usually prohibitive. This is a real hardship to the poor, as a very large proportion of the appeals which are made at Quarter Sessions, limited in number though they are, are successful. From Quarter Sessions a further appeal lies on a point of law by means of a case stated for the opinion of the King's Bench Division of the High Court, or a case may be stated by the justices in Petty Sessions without any preliminary appeal to Quarter Sessions. Such appeals are heard by a Divisional Court of three judges of the King's Bench Division.

Suggested Reforms.

The value of associating laymen with the administration of justice and the resulting economy to the State is obvious. It is, however, by no means certain that these considerations outweigh the defects of justices' justice. Many benches of magistrates are efficient and fair, but many are rightly criticised. There is too great a readiness to accept police evidence, and decisions of the bench are often the decisions of the clerk, who, though sometimes a whole-time official, is often a solicitor in private practice and sometimes has but small qualifications for his post. It is true that the majority of persons elect to be tried summarily rather than to await trial at Quarter Sessions by a jury, but this can be chiefly attributed to the natural desire to avoid delay. Suggested reforms are the appointment of whole-time clerks serving two or more Petty Sessional Divisions; the provision of a cheaper form of appeal, perhaps to the County Court; and possibly the substitution of paid stipendiary magistrates for unpaid justices. This last proposal would, however, involve great expense in addition to losing the value of the association of laymen with the administration of law.

County Courts.

The County Courts are presided over by a paid judge appointed by the Lord Chancellor, sitting usually alone, but sometimes with a jury. An appeal lies from them to the King's Bench Division of the High Court or in certain special cases, *e.g.*, under the Agricultural Holdings Act, direct to the Court of Appeal. These appeals to the King's Bench Division are tried by a Divisional Court of two

---

[1] Or from Borough Petty Sessions to Borough Quarter Sessions sitting with the Recorder as sole judge.

judges. County Court jurisdiction, confined to civil matters,[1] is local and limited. In general only those cases can be tried in the County Court in which the amount involved does not exceed £100, but there are many exceptions to this rule. Where cases are brought in the High Court which could have been brought in the County Court, there are penal provisions as to costs.

The Court of Aldermen [2] appoints the Recorder of London who acts as a judge both of the Central Criminal Court and the Mayor's and City of London Court. The appointment of the Recorder must be approved by the Crown before he can exercise his judicial functions. The Mayor's and City of London Court is the County Court for the City. It is an amalgamation of two courts, the Mayor's Court with a jurisdiction unlimited as to amount and the City of London Court, a court for small causes. There sit as judges, in addition to the Recorder, the Common Sergeant and two judges of the City of London Court, one of whom is also a judge of the Central Criminal Court. *City of London Courts.*

Certain boroughs have ancient courts which exercise civil jurisdiction. Their jurisdiction is usually limited as to area, but, unlike that of the County Court, is unlimited as to amount. The most important is the Liverpool Court of Passage. Appeals from the Court of Passage lie direct to the Court of Appeal; for other borough courts appeals lie to the King's Bench Division. *Borough Courts.*

The more serious, or indictable, crimes are tried either at Quarter Sessions, or at Assizes, or at the Central Criminal Court. The jurisdiction of Quarter Sessions is not so wide as that of Assizes, but the tendency of recent legislation has been to increase it extensively. It is doubtful how far this is a wise course. There is power to transmit to Assizes any case which the Court of Quarter Sessions considers should be more properly tried at Assizes owing to the gravity of the charge, or the difficulty of any point of law involved. This power is not freely used, and many cases are tried before magistrates in Quarter Sessions, often presided over by a lay *Criminal Courts. Quarter Sessions.*

---

[1] Including bankruptcy, outside the London area.
[2] Part VI., Chap. II.

chairman, that need the careful direction to a jury, which only a trained lawyer can give. It is difficult to take away a jurisdiction recently given, but the danger indicated might be avoided by providing for County Quarter Sessions a paid chairman with legal qualifications. The problem does not arise in boroughs which have their own Quarter Sessions, for these are presided over by a Recorder, a salaried barrister [1] as sole judge.

Assizes.

Criminal cases committed to Assizes are tried before judges of the King's Bench Division travelling the seven circuits into which England and Wales are divided. These Courts of Assize are branches of the High Court of Justice. The judges trying criminal cases on circuit derive their authority from Commissions of Oyer and Terminer and General Gaol Delivery. The former give power to try all prisoners against whom a grand jury finds a true bill; the latter give power to try all prisoners in gaol or who have been released on bail. These Commissions are sometimes issued to King's Counsel and other Special Commissioners who are not judges of the High Court. Assizes are held three times a year in each county and in the few large towns which, being themselves counties, have their own Assizes. In Manchester, Leeds and Liverpool, the Assizes are held four times a year. At the Winter and Summer Assizes civil business is taken as well as criminal, but except in a few large towns the Autumn Assize is confined to criminal business. Judges taking civil business at Assizes derive their authority from Commissions of Assize and have the unlimited jurisdiction of the High Court. The Central Criminal Court at the Old Bailey acts as the Court of Assize for criminal business for London, Middlesex and part of the Home Counties. The judges are the Recorder of London, the Common Sergeant, a judge of the City of London Court and the judges of the King's Bench Division, one of whom in rotation attends each of the monthly sessions of the Court.

Criminal Jurisdiction of King's Bench Division.

The King's Bench Division of the High Court of Justice also possesses criminal jurisdiction. This jurisdiction is

[1] Part IV., Chap. V., B.

mainly supervisory and derived from the ancient Curia Regis. The King's Bench Division can try certain offences of a special nature, *e.g.*, crimes committed abroad by public officials. It can try also any indictable offence committed in London or Middlesex and any misdemeanour in respect of which an information has been filed by one of the Law Officers.[1] It can further remove into the King's Bench Division by Certiorari,[2] or an order in the nature of Certiorari, an indictment found in any court of Assize or Quarter Sessions. The writ of Certiorari is used to remove cases to the Central Criminal Court from counties in which, owing to local prejudice, it is impossible to ensure a fair trial. It is used also to quash for an error of law the proceedings of Quarter Sessions or any inferior tribunal. Cases of grave importance are sometimes removed into the King's Bench Division in order to secure a trial at bar before three judges, as when Sir Roger Casement was tried for treason in 1916,[3] or in order to enable a prisoner charged with a misdemeanour to be tried by a special jury on the civil side of a Court of Assize, a special jury not being obtainable in a criminal court. The original, as opposed to the supervisory, criminal jurisdiction of the King's Bench Division is rarely exercised.

With the exception of summary offences tried at Petty Sessions all criminal cases are tried by a jury. Such juries are known as petty juries and consist of twelve persons. They must be distinguished from grand juries by whom a true bill must be found before any charge of an indictable offence proceeds to trial at all. The grand jury consists of not less than twelve and not more than twenty-three persons. Twelve must agree before a true bill is proved, but, unlike a petty jury, a grand jury need not come to a unanimous decision. The original function of the grand jury was to present to the court any criminals in their own neighbourhood of whom they were aware. Their main duty to-day is to decide, after a short preliminary enquiry, whether there is any case which ought to be answered by the various prisoners committed for trial by magistrates, or in the case only of murder or manslaughter, also by Coroners' Courts.[4]

Grand and Petty Juries. Preliminary Enquiries.

---

[1] Part IV., Chap. IV.
[3] Rex v. Casement [1917], 1 K.B. 98.
[2] Part VI., Chap. IV.
[4] Part VI., Chap. II.

There are presented to them bills of indictments stating the charges against the prisoners. If, on any such bill, the grand jury consider that there is a *primâ facie* case to answer, they find a true bill, and an indictment is presented to the petty jury. It is still possible for a grand jury to present a voluntary bill of their own volition or at the instance of a private prosecutor. In practice almost all criminal proceedings in respect of indictable crimes (other than those tried by consent at Petty Sessions) begin with a preliminary enquiry by a magistrate, before whom an information is laid either by the police or a private prosecutor. It is the duty of the magistrates holding the preliminary enquiry to decide whether or not there is a case to go to trial. It is also for the magistrates to decide whether to commit the accused to Assizes or Quarter Sessions where both have jurisdiction. The power to present voluntary bills has been drastically limited by the Vexatious Indictments Act, 1859.

Court of Criminal Appeal. From both Assizes and Quarter Sessions an appeal lies against conviction or sentence (but not against acquittal), to the Court of Criminal Appeal. This court, which consists of the Lord Chief Justice and the judges of the King's Bench Division, is usually constituted by three judges, the minimum number required by statute. A single judgment of the court is delivered. Appeal lies to it as of right on a question of law, and by leave of the court itself or of the trial judge on a mixed question of law and fact or against sentence. From the Court of Criminal Appeal an appeal lies, either by the Crown or by the accused, to the House of Lords on a point of law certified by the Attorney-General to be of special public importance. Very few criminal appeals have been heard by the House of Lords since this jurisdiction was instituted by the Criminal Appeal Act, 1907.

Superior Civil Courts before 1875. Civil cases outside the jurisdiction of the County Courts are tried in the High Court of Justice. There were, before 1875, several superior Courts each with its own special province, though between the three Common Law Courts there was much overlapping. The Common Law Courts were the Court of King's Bench, originally concerned with offences against the King's Peace, the Court of Common Pleas for the trial of cases between subjects and the Court of Exchequer for the trial of matters touching the revenues of the Crown. Both the Court of King's Bench and the Court of Exchequer had invaded the original province of the Court of Common Pleas. There were also the Court of Chancery, exercising the equitable jurisdiction of the Chancellor, the Admiralty Court, the Court of Probate and the Court for Divorce and Matrimonial Cases, and the Chancery Courts of the Counties Palatine of Lancaster and Durham. The Court of Appeal from the three Common Law Courts was the Court of Exchequer Chamber.[1] Chancery Appeals immediately prior to the Judicature Act went to two Lords Justices in Chancery, sitting with or without the Lord Chancellor.

By the Judicature Act, 1873, all these Courts (except the two Palatine Courts) and the Courts of Assize were amalgamated into the Supreme Court of Judicature, consisting of the Court of Appeal and the High Court of Justice. The Act was chiefly directed to the reorganisation of court machinery. So far as the law of the land was concerned it made, with a few exceptions, no change. The High Court of Justice was divided into five divisions: Queen's Bench; Common Pleas; Exchequer; Chancery; Probate, Divorce and Admiralty. These divisions have now been reduced to three: King's Bench; Chancery; Probate, Divorce and Admiralty. The jurisdiction of the High Court is unlimited as to amount. Judges of the High Court are appointed by the Crown, on the recommendation of the Lord Chancellor.[2]

The King's Bench Division is concerned with every class of common law action, in addition to its criminal and appellate jurisdiction and its power to supervise inferior courts and judicial bodies by means of the prerogative

Judicature Act, 1873.

King's Bench Division.

---

[1] The judges of the two Common Law Courts other than the Court from which the appeal came, *e.g.*, King's Bench appeals came before the judges of the Common Pleas and Exchequer.

[2] For a table of the Courts before and under the Judicature Act, 1873, see Part I., Chap. II.

writs which will be discussed in later chapters.[1]   It exercises
the jurisdiction of the three former Common Law Courts.
It acts as the Assizes for London and Middlesex, so far as
civil business is concerned, and countless cases are tried in
London in the King's Bench Division which might equally
be tried on circuit at Assizes.   It is for a Master [2] or District
Registrar [3] of the High Court to decide whether an action
shall be tried in London or at Assizes.   Cases inviting long
legal arguments or the citation of authorities are more
suitably tried in London or the largest assize towns, while
cases in which many country witnesses are concerned are
best tried in the county in which the dispute arose.   The
judges of the King's Bench Division are the Lord Chief
Justice and fifteen puisne judges.[4]   Trials in this Division
take place both before judges and juries, and before judges
alone.   There is a right to a jury in purely common law
actions ; in other cases a jury may be granted at the discretion
of the court.   Juries in civil cases are either special juries
or common juries.   Special jurors have a higher property
qualification.   In cases with a jury matters of law are for the
judge, matters of fact are for the jury.

Chancery Division.   The old Court of Chancery exercised the equitable
jurisdiction of the King's Chancellor, delegated to him by the
King in Council, supplementing the Common Law by the
granting of new remedies and dealing also with matters of
which the Common Law courts took no cognisance.   Equity,
originally an elastic system for meeting hard cases, had
developed an important body of law, almost as fixed as the
Common Law courts.

As a result of the Judicature Act any judge of the High
Court may sit in any Division, and any Division may give any
remedies available, whether they are based on the Common
Law or on Equity.   Each Division, however, has in practice
its own particular business, and to the Chancery Division

---

[1] Part VI., Chap. IV., and Part VII., Chap. I.

[2] Masters are officers of the court who deal with the preliminary
stages of an action.

[3] These carry out the duties of Masters in certain provincial towns.

[4] There are now 16, but the increase is not permanent.

there are specifically assigned those matters formerly dealt with by the courts of Equity. They include partnerships, mortgages, trusts, the specific performance of contracts and the administration of the estates of deceased persons. Company business also is administered by the Chancery Division. There is also assigned to this Division the bankruptcy business of the High Court. There are six judges of the Chancery Division. The Lord Chancellor, though still nominally president of this Division, has long ceased to sit. A Divisional Court of two judges of this Division hears appeals from County Courts in matters of equity and bankruptcy. The Chancery Courts of Lancaster and Durham have a jurisdiction over Chancery suits, which is limited as to area, but unlimited as to amount. An appeal lies from them direct to the Court of Appeal.

The business of the Probate, Divorce and Admiralty Probate, Division is apparent from its name. It is manned by the Divorce and President and two judges. On the Admiralty side it exercises Division. the jurisdiction of the old Court of Admiralty, and is concerned with maritime matters [1] and particularly collisions at sea. On the Probate side it takes the place of the Court of Probate, which in 1857 took over from the ecclesiastical courts the granting of probate of wills and letters of administration. On the divorce side it grants the matrimonial remedies formerly granted by the Court for Divorce and Matrimonial Causes. Until 1857 the ecclesiastical courts could grant decrees of judicial separation, but could not dissolve marriages. The matrimonial business of those courts was transferred in that year to the newly constituted Court for Divorce and Matrimonial Causes, which was also given the new power of decreeing a dissolution of marriage. There is little in common between the three sides of this Division save that both probate and divorce business were originally exercised by the ecclesiastical courts, and that the law administered by all three

---

[1] Actions relating to the Carriage of Goods by Sea are usually tried in the King's Bench Division in what is known as " The Commercial Court," *i.e.*, before a judge appointed at the beginning of the sittings to try commercial cases. The procedure is simple and speedier than that ordinarily employed in the King's Bench Division.

sides of the Division is more influenced by Roman Law than are either Common Law or Equity. The combination of probate and divorce with admiralty in one Division is due, not to logic, but expediency. When the new High Court was formed, this Division was the residuary legatee of the old Courts. A Divisional Court of two judges of this Division hears appeals from the justices in matrimonial matters, and from County Courts in admiralty matters.

Court of Appeal.

Except where it is limited by statute, there is a right of appeal from any Division of the High Court to the Court of Appeal. An example of such limitation is the making final the decision of a Divisional Court on an appeal from a County Court, except where the Divisional Court or the Court of Appeal itself gives leave to appeal. In certain matters, *e.g.*, those arising under the Workmen's Compensation Act, 1925, and the Agricultural Holdings Act, 1923, an appeal lies direct to the Court of Appeal from the County Courts. The judges of the Court of Appeal are the Lord Chancellor,[1] the Lord Chief Justice,[1] the Master of the Rolls,[1] the President of the Probate, Divorce and Admiralty Division,[1] the Lords of Appeal in Ordinary,[1] Ex-Lords Chancellors and five Lords Justices of Appeal.[1] There usually sit the Master of the Rolls and the five Lords Justices assisted, if need be, by judges of the High Court. The Court sits in two divisions of three judges.

House of Lords.

From the Court of Appeal an appeal lies to the House of Lords, the supreme tribunal of England and Wales, Scotland and Northern Ireland, in which is vested the ancient jurisdiction of the High Court of Parliament. Besides its normal appellate jurisdication in civil cases and its extraordinary appellate jurisdiction in criminal cases, the House of Lords has also jurisdiction as a court of first instance. It tried those impeached by the House of Commons, and it tries peers accused of treason or felony or misprision of either. The sittings of the House of Lords for appellate business are in theory ordinary sittings of the House at which any business may be transacted, but

[1] Appointed by the Crown on the recommendation of the Prime Minister.

in practice since *O'Connell's Case* in 1844 only the Law Lords have taken part. These are now the Lord Chancellor, the seven Lords of Appeal in Ordinary,[1] ex-Lord Chancellors and other peers who have held high judicial office.[2] The Lords of Appeal receive salaries and are bound to sit; the other Lords serve voluntarily. There is a convention, but no more than a convention, that ex-Lord Chancellors in receipt of pensions should serve when requested to do so by the Lord Chancellor. On the hearing of appeals there must be present three Law Lords. The House usually sits in divisions of five or three. Before 1876 there were frequently only one or two peers with judicial experience, and the Lords frequently summoned the judges of the High Court[3] to advise them on questions of law, but since the creation in that year of the Lords of Appeal in Ordinary this practice has tended to fall into disuse. The judges were last summoned in 1898 in a civil case and in 1901 on the occasion of the trial of a peer for felony; *Rex* v. *Earl Russell* [1901], A.C. 446. Appeals may be heard when Parliament is prorogued.

It is interesting to compare the procedure of the House of Lords with that of the Judicial Committee of the Privy Council, the final Court of Appeal from the Courts of the Empire.[4] In the House of Lords dissenting opinions are expressed. In the Judicial Committee one speech only is delivered, expressing the opinion of the majority of the judges, should there be any difference of opinion. The House of Lords is moved that an appeal be allowed or dismissed and the order made is entered in the Journals of the House. The Judicial Committee humbly advises His Majesty and the decision is formally embodied in a subsequent Order in Council.[5] The House of Lords is bound by its own decisions. The Judicial Committee is in theory and, to a modified degree, in practice free from

Comparison with Judicial Committee of the Privy Council.

---

[1] See Part III., Chap. I.

[2] *E.g.*, who have been Lords of Appeal, Judges of the Supreme Court or of the Court of Session in Scotland.

[3] See Part III., Chap. I.   [4] Part IX., Chap. V.

[5] For specimen, see Appendix C.

precedent. In 1929 the Judicial Committee examined the validity of one of their own decisions given two years previously ; *Wigg and Cochrane* v. *Attorney-General of Irish Free State* [1927], A.C. 694 ; *Re Transferred Civil Servants, (Ireland) Compensation* [1929], A.C. 242.

Impeachment. When the House of Lords is sitting as a court of first instance lay peers may and do take part in the business. A barrister who is a peer may practice before the House of Lords in appeals, when the House is a court in which there only sit peers with judicial qualifications, but he may not practice before the House when it is trying criminal charges ; *In re Lord Kinross* [1905], A.C. 468. The Commons may impeach any person before the Lords for any crime or political misdemeanour. Before the full development of ministerial responsibility impeachment was a useful weapon enabling the Commons to call to account Ministers appointed by and responsible to the Crown. There has, however, been no impeachment since 1805. The Commons now have direct control over Ministers and so do not need to employ the cumbrous weapon of impeachment. By the Act of Settlement of 1701 a pardon from the Crown cannot be pleaded in bar of an impeachment.

Trial of Peers. The trial of peers for treason, felony or misprision of either takes place, when the House is sitting, in the House of Lords ; when Parliament is dissolved or prorogued, in the Court of the Lord High Steward who is appointed for the trial and is usually the Lord Chancellor. The privilege of trial by their peers does not extend to the bishops, but does extend to peeresses in their own right and the wives and unmarried widows of peers. Indictments are found in an ordinary court and removed by Certiorari into the House of Lords. Bishops may sit, but not vote, in trials before the House of Lords, but may not even sit in the Court of the Lord High Steward. In the House of Lords all the peers, though presided over by the Lord High Steward, are judges alike of law and fact. In the Court of the Lord High Steward that officer is the sole judge on questions of law, while the judges of fact are the other members of the Court, who are such temporal peers—not less than twenty-three—as the

Lord High Steward may summon. For trials for treason or misprision of treason all the temporal peers who have seats in the House of Lords must be summoned.

It was at one time doubtful whether the House of Lords could try civil cases as a court of first instance. The exercise of such jurisdiction in the case of *Skinner* v. *East India Company* (1666), 6 St. Tr. 710, in the reign of Charles II., led to a prolonged dispute between Lords and Commons. Since that time no attempt has been made to exercise it. About the same time the case of *Shirley* v. *Fagg* (1675), 6 St. Tr. 1122, established the right of the Lords to hear appeals from the Chancery Court. *No Civil Jurisdiction in First Instance.*

Scotland has preserved her own law and her own system of courts. The chief inferior courts are the Court of the Sheriff and the Court of the Sheriff Substitute. The Court of Session corresponds to the Supreme Court in England. The Outer House of the Court of Session consists of five judges sitting singly. The Inner House sits in two divisions of four judges. The judges are the Lord President, the Lord Justice Clerk, and eleven Lords Ordinary. From the Inner House of the Court of Session an appeal lies to the House of Lords. *The Courts of Scotland.*

CHAPTER II.

THE INDEPENDENCE OF THE JUDGES.

Judicial Independence.

IT is clearly desirable that judges should not only be independent of the Executive, but also free from liability to vexatious actions for acts done in the exercise of their duty. It is better that private persons should suffer injuries than that judges should be influenced, to however slight a degree, in the dispensing of justice by fear of the consequences. These considerations apply to the judges of any country, but they apply with still greater force to the judges of a country in which individual rights and constitutional liberties depend upon the decisions of the ordinary courts.

Appointment and Dismissal of Judges.

In the exercise of such powers as that of issuing writs of Habeas Corpus [1] the judges are sometimes in the position of controlling the Executive in the interest of the liberty of the subject. It is essential that they should be free from any fear of dismissal by the persons whom they must be prepared to control. Judges are appointed by the Crown to hold office during good behaviour, but they can by the provisions of the Act of Settlement be dismissed by the Crown on the presentation of an address praying for their removal by both Houses of Parliament.

Judical Immunity from Civil Actions.

It is a general proposition of the Common Law that no action will lie against a judge for any acts done or words spoken in his judicial capacity in a court of justice. " It is essential in all courts that the judges who are appointed to administer the law should be permitted to administer it under the protection of the law independently and freely, without favour and without fear. This provision of the law

---

[1] Part VII., Chap. I.

is not for the protection or benefit of a malicious or corrupt judge, but for the benefit of the public, whose interest it is that the judges shall be at liberty to exercise their functions with independence and without fear of consequences"; *Scott* v. *Stansfield* (1868), L.R. 3 Ex. 220, per Kelly, C.B. at p. 223. It can be argued from the authorities that the judge of a superior court of record is not liable for anything done or said in the exercise of his judicial functions, even if he exceeds his jurisdiction, but it is the better opinion that the judges of both superior and inferior courts of record are in the same position in that they are liable if they act outside their jurisdiction, but not for any error or irregularity within their jurisdiction. In the case, however, of an inferior court, the judge must prove that he had jurisdiction; in the case of a superior court the plaintiff must prove want of jurisdiction.

In the case of acts done within the jurisdiction the im-munity exists, however malicious, corrupt or oppressive be the words complained of; *Anderson* v. *Gorrie* [1895], 1 Q.B. 668; K. & L. 168. Immunity does not attach to a minis-terial, as opposed to a judicial, act. Thus an action lies for a wrongful refusal to hear a case, but not for a wrongful decision; *Ferguson* v. *Earl of Kinnoull* (1842), 9 Cl. and F. 251; K. & L. 185. A judge of an inferior court is not liable where he exceeds his jurisdiction owing to a mistake of fact, unless he ought to have known the facts ousting his juris-diction. A similar immunity to that of judges attaches to the verdicts of juries; *Bushell's Case* (1670), 6 St. Tr. 999; K. & L. 170; and to words spoken by parties, counsel and witnesses in the course of judicial proceedings. It is prob-able that exactly the same immunity exists in the case of inferior courts not of record, *e.g.*, Petty Sessional Courts. It can, however, be argued that justices of the peace are liable for the malicious exercise of their powers even within their jurisdiction. This argument rests on the terms of the Justices' Protection Act, 1848, which enacts that " every action against a justice of the peace for any act done in execution of his duty as a justice with respect to any matter within his jurisdiction shall be an action on the case alleging and proving that the defendant acted maliciously and without

Scope of Immunity.

15

reasonable and probable cause." It is, however, clear law that no action lies against a justice of the peace in respect of defamatory words spoken by him when exercising judicial functions ; *Law* v. *Llewellyn* [1906], 1 K.B. 487. There seems no distinction in principle between actions for defamation and other actions. If this view be accepted, the words of the Justices' Protection Act, quoted above, must be explained as applying to irregularities which, though depriving a magistrate of full immunity, do not amount to acting wholly without jurisdiction.[1] Where a magistrate acts outside his jurisdiction, he has certain minor protections afforded by the Justices' Protection Act and other statutes, of which the most important is that no action may be brought in respect of anything done under a conviction, until the conviction has been quashed.

The over-riding importance of the protection of the liberty of the subject is shown by the fact that a High Court judge who unlawfully refuses to issue a writ of Habeas Corpus during vacation is liable to a fine of £500 to be paid to the person detained.

---

[1] See full discussion, *Halsbury's Laws of England*, Vol. XXIII., para. 680, note j.

CHAPTER III.

THE CROWN AND THE COURTS.

THE courts are the King's courts, " all jurisdictions of The King as Judge. courts are either indirectly or immediately derived from the Crown. Their proceedings are generally in the King's name, they pass under his seal, and are executed by his office," it is " impossible as well as improper that the King personally should carry into execution this great and extensive trust," [1] and further, as has been seen,[2] the English understanding of the separation of powers demands that the Judiciary should be independent of the Executive. The early Kings delivered justice in their own courts. The delegation of this duty to judges was an early and inevitable result of the growth of the business of government and the development of a system of law requiring specialised knowledge. The delegation of a power does not, however, necessarily involve the abandonment of the right to exercise it, should the occasion arise. In 1607 James I. claimed the right to determine judicially a dispute between the Common Law courts and the ecclesiastical courts. That the right of the King to administer justice himself no longer existed was decided by all the judges headed by Coke ; *Prohibitions del Roy* (1607), 12 Co. Rep. 63 ; K. & L. 276 :

> " The King in his own person cannot adjudge any case, either criminal, or treason, felony, etc., or betwixt party and party, concerning his inheritance, chattels or goods, etc., but this ought to be determined and adjudged in some court of justice according to the law and custom of England. God had endowed His Majesty with excellent science and great endowments of nature, but His Majesty was not learned in

[1] *Blackstone's Commentaries*, Book I., Chap. VII.
[2] Part II., Chap. II.

the laws of his realm of England, and causes which concern the life, or inheritance, or goods or fortunes of his subjects, are not to be decided by natural reason, but by the artificial reason and judgment of law, which law is an art which requires long study and experience, before that a man can attain to the cognizance of it. The law is the golden met-wand and measure to try the causes of the subjects ; and which protected His Majesty in safety and peace."

Of this case Dicey wrote : [1] " Nothing can be more pedantic, nothing more artificial, nothing more unhistorical, than the reasoning by which Coke induced or compelled James to forego the attempt to withdraw cases from the courts for His Majesty's personal determination. But no achievement of sound argument, or stroke of enlightened statemanship, ever established a rule more essential to the very existence of the Constitution than the principle enforced by the obstinacy and the fallacies of the great Chief Justice."

The Creation of New Courts. A similar limitation of the Prerogative is found in the rule that the Crown can no longer by the Prerogative create courts to administer any system of law other than the Common Law. The common lawyers were the allies of Parliament in the struggle with the Stuarts, and the victory of Parliament meant the disappearance of the prerogative courts of the Star Chamber and the High Commission. Even the Court of Chancery barely escaped the destructive ardour of the Commonwealth.

In the case of *In re Lord Bishop of Natal* (1864), 3 Moo. P.C. (N.S.) 115 ; K. & L. 278, the Judicial Committee held that the Crown had no power to create by Letters Patent a metropolitan see of Cape Town with coercive authority and jurisdiction over a suffragan bishop.

" It is a settled constitutional principle or rule of law, that although the Crown may by its Prerogative establish courts to proceed according to the Common Law, yet that it cannot create any new court to administer any other law."

Thus the creation of a court of equity in a settled colony [2] would require an Act either of the Imperial Parliament or the Colonial Legislature.

---

[1] *Law of the Constitution*, 8th edition, p. 18,
[2] Part IX., Chap. I,

There may appear to be an interference by the Executive with the courts in the right of the Attorney-General to stop a criminal prosecution by entering a *nolle prosequi*. This power of the Attorney-General is subject to no appeal. It is used to prevent vexatious prosecutions. Its exercise is, however, open to criticism by the Legislature, and any abuse of it is prevented by the ordinary principle of ministerial responsibility ; *Regina* v. *Allen* (1862), 1 B. & S. 850 ; K. & L. 274. Criminal proceedings may similarly be prevented by the exercise of the Royal Prerogative of pardon. This power is ordinarily used after sentence on the advice of the Home Secretary, when there is some special reason why a sentence should not be carried out. By the provisions of the Act of Settlement a pardon may not be employed to prevent an impeachment by the House of Commons.[1]

[1] Part IV., Chap. V.

CHAPTER IV.

REMEDIES AGAINST THE CROWN.

Immunity of the Crown. THE King cannot be sued in his own courts. Actions can neither be brought against the King in respect of his personal actions, nor against the Crown as the Executive in respect of contracts made by Government Departments on behalf of the Crown, or in respect of wrongs committed by servants of the Crown in the course of their employment. The immunity of the Crown extends, except in special cases where statutes provide otherwise, to all Government Departments and is not taken away by the modern practice of imposing powers and imposing duties upon Departments and Ministers in their own name in so far as they act as agents of the Crown. In considering the immunity of the Crown from civil actions it is convenient to deal separately with actions in respect of contracts and actions in respect of torts or civil wrongs.

Contracts— Petitions of Right. Although no action will lie against the Crown for breach of contract, a Petition of Right may be brought to recover damages for breach of a contract made on behalf of the Crown or to recover property which has fallen into the hands of the Crown; *Thomas* v. *The Queen* (1874), L.R. 10 Q.B. 31; K. & L. 231. The procedure is now statutory; Petitions of Right Act, 1860.[1] It is a condition precedent to such a proceeding that there should be obtained the fiat of the Attorney-General. There is no appeal against the refusal of the fiat, which is granted on showing a *primâ facie* cause of action. A judgment in favour of a suppliant in a Petition of Right takes the form of a declaration of the rights to which the suppliant is entitled and, being always observed by the Crown, is as effective as a judgment in an ordinary action.

---

[1] The text is summarised in K. & L. at pp. 229-31. The Petition must be brought against the King, not the Department concerned.

Just as in disputes between subjects an agent cannot ordinarily be sued in respect of a contract made by him on behalf of his principal, so a servant of the Crown cannot be made liable upon a contract made by him on behalf of the Crown ; *Macbeath v. Haldimand* (1786), 1 T.R. 172 ; K. & L. 260. It is a rule of law that the Crown cannot by contract hamper its future executive action, and it was held by Rowlatt, J., in *Rederiaktiebolaget Amphitrite* v. *The King* [1921], 3 K.B. 500 ; K. & L. 242, that no action would lie for breach of a contract by the Government promising freedom from detention to a Swedish ship trading with Great Britain during the Great War. It is because of this rule that no servant of the Crown can sue the Crown for damages for wrongful dismissal ; *Dunn* v. *The Queen* [1896], 1 Q.B. 116 ; K. & L. 241. The Crown cannot hamper its freedom to dismiss its servants at will in the public interest.

The maxim that " The King can do no wrong " leads to Torts. the rule that the Crown cannot be sued, even by Petition of Right, in respect either of civil wrongs expressly authorised by the Crown, or in respect of wrongs committed by servants of the Crown in the course of their employment ; *Viscount Canterbury* v. *Attorney-General* (1842), 1 Ph. 306 ; K. & L. 244. The only remedy open to an aggrieved party is to sue the actual wrong-doer, but in practice the Crown usually satisfies judgments so obtained. A superior servant of the Crown is not responsible for wrongs committed by his subordinates, unless he was himself a party to them. All the servants of the Crown are equally the servants of the Crown and not of one another ; *Raleigh* v. *Goschen* [1898], 1 Ch. 73 ; K. & L. 250 ; *Bainbridge* v. *Postmaster-General* [1906], 1 K.B. 178 ; K. & L. 252. A declaratory judgment may however be obtained in an action against the Attorney-General declaring illegal a contemplated action of the Crown ; but this procedure cannot be used to prejudge the issue of what may have to be adjudicated upon in a Petition of Right as to a money claim against the Treasury ; *Dyson* v. *Attorney-General* [1911], 1 K.B. 410 ; K. & L. 265 ; *Bombay and Persia S.N. Co.* v. *MacLay* [1920], 3 K.B. at p. 408.

Government
Depart-
ments.

The rule that the Crown may not be sued for torts protects also Government Departments whose executive acts are the acts of the Crown, but it has been laid down by statute that certain Government Departments may sue or be sued in their own name. It is necessary to look at the particular statute concerned to decide (1) whether such provision is merely procedural as, *e.g.*, under the Defence Act, 1842, s. 34, and designed to enable ordinary civil procedure to be used instead of procedure by Petition of Right (which does not lie for tort), or (2) whether such provision affects substantive rights and makes it possible to sue the Department or Minister in respect of a contract made on behalf of the Crown, or in respect of a tort committed by subordinates. It is clear that the Minister of Transport may be sued for torts arising out of his Department.[1] In *Graham* v. *Commissioners of Public Works* [1901], 2 K.B. 781, it was held that the Commissioners could be sued in respect of a contract made on behalf of the Crown. In *Rowland* v. *Air Council* (1923), 39 T.L.R. 228, it was held that the Air Council could not be sued on a contract made on the Crown's behalf, though the Act (Air Force (Constitution) Act, 1917, provided that the Council might sue and be sued by that name (s. 10 (1)); see also *Rowland and Mackenzie-Kennedy* v. *Air Council* (1927), 96 L.J. Ch. 470 (contract made on behalf of Crown), and *Mackenzie-Kennedy* v. *Air Council* [1927], 2 K.B. 517 (action in tort will not lie against the Air Council).

Procedural
Advantages.

In all suits to which the Crown is a party the subject has also to contend with the resources of the public purse, *i.e.*, the ability of the Crown to appeal to the House of Lords against a litigant who has succeeded at the trial. He has, too, to contend with certain procedural advantages enjoyed by the Crown. Except where expressly provided by statute, *e.g.*, revenue cases and Petitions of Right, the Crown neither pays nor receives costs.[2] Actions brought by the

---

[1] Ministry of Transport Act, 1919, S. 26 ; the section expressly provides for liability in contract, tort, or otherwise.

[2] The recent practice is to award costs to the successful party in proceedings where writs of Prohibition and Certiorari are sought in order to restrain Government Departments from exceeding statutory

Crown are brought not by the ordinary procedure, but by Latin or English Informations, archaic and unfamiliar forms which involve a defendant in extra legal expense. The Crown cannot be compelled to disclose documents by the process known as discovery, which is employed in the case of private individuals.

The Crown Proceedings Committee which reported in 1927,[1] recommended (*a*) that the Crown should be liable in tort, (*b*) that the Crown should enjoy the protection of the Public Authorities Protection Act, 1893,[2] (*c*) that Petitions of Right should be abolished, and that proceedings by and against the Crown should be assimilated, as far as is possible, to ordinary civil proceedings, (*d*) that costs should be awarded to and against the Crown, (*e*) that discovery should be given against the Crown with safeguards to prevent the disclosure of documents which it would be contrary to the public interest to disclose.[3] The Report has the support of lawyers, but it is possible that the opposition of Government Departments may prevent its adoption. This opposition is not based so much on the principle of liability as the fear that the taxpayer would be called upon in many cases to bear the costs of the Crown which would be irrecoverable from many unsuccessful claimants, and also to the extreme complexity of adjusting existing Crown procedure to a standard form.

Proposed Changes.

powers. Costs in these cases are awarded without argument, and it is more than doubtful whether there is any jurisdiction to award them, as there is no statutory provision abrogating in such cases the Common Law rule.

[1] Crown Proceedings Committee Report, 1927, Cmd. 2842 (9d.).

[2] Part II. Chap. V.

[3] It is difficult to secure fair treatment for the subject in actions against the Crown as far as discovery is concerned, because there are certain documents the contents of which must be concealed in the interest of the public. Unless, as in Scotland, the practice is adopted of showing all documents to the judge, it must be impossible to go behind an official certificate that there are documents the contents of which must not be disclosed.

CHAPTER V.

THE JUDICIARY AND THE PUBLIC.

THAT justice in England is administered fairly and freely no one could deny, and no one would dispute the impartiality of the judges. Political services are frequently taken into account in making appointments to the bench, but appointments which have been criticised as being due to the desire to reward a supporter of the Government have often proved justified. All, however, is not well with our legal system, and there are widespread complaints as to the expense of litigation. That the dissatisfaction felt is serious is shown by the growing tendency to submit disputes to arbitration before lay tribunals and the fall in the volume of litigation.

Arbitrations. Arbitrations are now governed by the provisions of the Arbitration Act, 1889. Since 1854 the courts have been empowered by statute to refuse to decide a dispute brought before them in breach of an agreement to refer disputes to arbitration. This power to stay proceedings is discretionary. Parties cannot by contract oust the jurisdiction of the courts, but they can do what in practice has that effect by agreeing that a reference to arbitration shall be a condition precedent to an action ; *Scott* v. *Avery* (1856), 5 H.L.C. 811.[1]

Costs. Court fees are high and in many cases bear no relation to the amount claimed or the importance of the case. The system by which a successful litigant normally recovers from his opponent only a certain portion—known as party and party costs—of the total costs incurred by him produces much dissatisfaction.[2] There should be some form of taxation to

[1] See Part II., Chap. V., for further discussion of arbitrations.
[2] See article " The Cost of Litigation," by E. S. Roscoe in the *Nineteenth Century*, January, 1930.

protect the defeated party from the payment of costs incurred unreasonably, but many items which are not recoverable as taxed costs are incurred of necessity by litigants. It seems unreasonable that a successful litigant should not recover from his opponent the cost of his preliminary consultations with his solicitors and the letters which lead up to the issue of a writ. A radical revision of the system of taxation of costs is urgently needed.

Much time, too, is wasted owing to the fact that ordinarily Fixing of no date is fixed for the hearing of a case. Judges dislike Cases. fixed lists which might result in wasted judicial time owing to last moment settlements. It would, however, both from the point of view of economy and of public satisfaction with the law, be better that judges (who are paid fixed salaries) should occasionally have nothing to do than that—as at present—both parties and witnesses should be kept at the courts losing money and time while waiting for their case to come on.

Another cause of reasonable annoyance on the part of Law of laymen is the technicality of the law of evidence. Expense Evidence. is caused by the unnecessary production of original documents, and cases are sometimes wrongly decided because of the neglect of a party to observe the requisite technicalities as to strict proof. Even the time-honoured rule which excludes hearsay evidence sometimes results in the exclusion of the best available evidence of the truth. It is largely owing to dissatisfaction with the procedure of the courts that the public are accepting without protest the growing tendency to transfer the decision of disputes to administrative tribunals from which there is no appeal.

Another deterrent to litigation is the risk that an un- Appeals. successful opponent may appeal from court to court, until the proceeds of victory are dissipated in costs which are not fully recovered on taxation. A strong body of opinion, both lay and judicial, advocated the abolition of the House of Lords as the final court of appeal at the time of the passing of the Judicature Act, 1873. It may be contended that one appeal is sufficient and that the valuable judgments delivered by the House of Lords do little to compensate the layman for the risk of expensive appeals from tribunal to tribunal. It has been ingeniously suggested that the salaries that would be saved by the abolition of the Lords of Appeal might be used to form a fund to insure litigants against the costs incurred by the reversal on appeal of the decision of a judge of first instance.[1] · Litigants should not have to pay costs which are due to a judge's mistake. In a recent group of cases concerning the de-rating of industry it was pointed out by Scrutton L.J.[2] that, whereas in Scotland there is only one appeal possible against a decision of an Assessment Committee that premises are entitled or not to the benefit of de-rating, in England there are four possible appeals—from the Assessment Committee to Quarter Sessions, from Quarter Sessions to the King's Bench Division and thence to the Court of Appeal and House of Lords.

[1] " Legal Expenses and the House of Lords," by Cyril Pearce, *English Review*, June, 1930.
[2] (1930) 46 T.L.R. at p. 604.

PART VI.

LOCAL GOVERNMENT.

An Outline of English Local Government (7th edition), by E. Jenks (Methuen).

Local Government and Local Taxation (7th edition), Wright and Hobhouse (Sweet & Maxwell).

Local Government in England, by J. Redlich and F. W. Hirst (2 vols.), 1903 (Macmillans).

The Ministry of Health, Whitehall Series (Putnams).

CHAPTER I.

GENERAL FEATURES.

A.

Introductory.

" England is pre-eminently a country of local government."—Jenks, *Outline of English Local Government.*

HITHERTO little has been said to justify this assertion. But Constitutional History reminds us that local administration preceded central government by several centuries. Whereas the origins of central government are traceable from the post-Conquest era only, Shire and Hundred, as well as Township, take us back to pre-Norman days. The central government of England was to a large extent super-imposed upon existing local organisation. In some matters it overwhelmed the local bodies, as to a large extent in the administration of justice. But nowhere did local authority entirely disappear. The more drastic innovations introduced by modern legislation have recognised local government as an established fact and have reflected old conditions, *e.g.*, in choice of areas.

It is, therefore, not surprising to find that a description of the organs and functions of internal government is entirely inadequate without some account of local government, without which the bulk of the internal government of the country could not be conducted to-day. Moreover, the check which local government brings to bear on the central power is a leading feature of constitutional development since the later years of the last century, a check which, of late, Whitehall has shown signs of resisting. But just as the chapters on the Central Government Departments have dealt only with a few of the more important functions, so only a broad outline of local government can be attempted in a book of these dimensions. Local government differs from central government mainly by reason of the scope of authority exercised by local bodies. Their authority is delimited by statutes, under which powers are defined, no less than geographical boundaries ; the former are defined directly, the latter usually by administrative action. In contrast the powers of the Central Government through its command of Parliament are limited only by political considerations.

The Twentieth Century. Local organs in the twentieth century are the creation of, but not subordinate to, the Central Government. If we cannot say of England to-day that its local government is independent of the central power, we can certainly say that its units are not, as yet, Sub-Departments of Whitehall. Local government services are not as a rule State services ; education may be regarded as a partial exception. They are not administered by officials appointed by the Central Government, though such officials exercise a large measure of control through supervision. Local government officers are appointed by and are responsible, with some exceptions, to the local authorities. These authorities are elected by the localities they serve. It is mainly in the judicial function of government that the centralising tendency has so far prevailed. Both for the local administration of civil and criminal justice the Central Government is responsible, though not for the police services.[1] But indirectly through finance Whitehall is to-day controlling local services more and more. During the latter part of the nineteenth and the beginning of the present century the tendency of Parliament was to decentralise control. The last twenty years have seen a reversal of this tendency, due to the recognition by Whitehall that by the earlier policy they were losing control. The Local Government Act, 1929, is a strong indication of

[1] Part IV., Chap. V. It is not proposed to deal with the police in the present Part.

this ; it lessens the number of local authorities and imposes financial provisions which give Whitehall a strong hold upon expenditure by local authorities. Whitehall even tends to bring pressure on local authorities in advance of legislation, such as requiring the enlargement of schools and the training of teachers before the introduction of a Bill raising the school-leaving age. At present this new tendency is an undercurrent, but sooner or later it will come to the surface. The resulting clash between the local authorities and the Central Government will probably result in the formation of larger local government areas than that of the County Council. Such a step would assist the problem of local government from Whitehall's point of view in an important respect, since that problem is largely the reconciliation of the comparative inefficiency and penury of a poor agricultural county with the efficiency and wealth of a prosperous and autonomous urban area within its geographical boundaries.

In one respect Local Government Law differs from Constitutional Law as related to the Central Government. The doctrine of the Prerogative plays no part. The powers are strictly legal, being derived by statutory bodies from statutes and exercised subject to the *ultra vires* rule. Within its legal limits each organ is free to act as it pleases ; its powers are at its own discretion, subject, however, to the pressure that the Central Government can bring to bear through (1) supervision, (2) finance, and (3) occasionally, in the last resort, supersession.

No further excuse is needed to explain why an important part of this book is devoted to local government organisation and law. The organisation is modelled on that of the Central Government. The functions of internal government cannot be clearly divided between the central and the local authority. Modern services like National Health and Unemployment Insurance, Widows', Orphans' and Old Age Pensions are State services centrally administered. Old services such as Public Assistance (Poor Law Relief), Sanitary and Highway are administered by locally elected bodies. The relationship of the subject with the State is actively concerned in these

Arrangement of Internal Government.

16

matters, irrespective of the centre of administration, since they impose upon him legal duties or give him legal rights. Moreover, it is in local government chiefly that the citizen in general, and particularly members of the legal profession, are afforded an opportunity of taking an active part in the work of government. Local government has its administration and legislatures, its executive and its judiciary. The elected bodies, such as the County Council, or the Council of a municipal borough are mainly administrative but partly legislative. They determine questions of policy and have power to enact by-laws, subject to the sanction of the Government Department concerned, and other regulations. The active work of these bodies is largely conducted by committees, which recall the Committees of the Privy Council, the fore-runners of Cabinet Government. To these committees falls the larger portion of a local authority's work, exercising the powers conferred by the Public Health and Local Government Acts. Nearly all work is started in committee. The general policy of a council arises on a committee report rather than by resolutions of the council at the outset. Most communications addressed to a council are sent to the appropriate committee and may never be seen or heard of by the council as a whole. It would be impossible to carry on the work of a local authority if the committee principle had not been adopted. The bulk of the members of councils are elected on a franchise which gives a full representation to the local tax-payers (ratepayers), bodies corporate excepted.[1] Herein, may be remarked a feature which the system of local representation possesses in contrast to that of parliamentary representation, where the direct taxpayers are outnumbered on the electoral roll by nearly twelve to one since the introduction in 1928 of universal adult franchise. No payment is as yet made generally to members of elected local bodies for their services, in contrast to the payment of salaries to all members of the House of Commons.

Administration and Legislation.

---

[1] A tenant who is a qualified local government elector may not always pay rates directly, but the rates will be reflected in the rent he pays his landlord.

The executive work is mainly in the hands of paid experts. Executive
They are not members of the Civil Service, and at present Work of
the system of recruitment falls short of the carefully con- Government.
trived system of that service. They are normally responsible
to the elected bodies by which they are appointed, though
in some cases the appointing authority is anomalously not
liable for the acts of its servants; *Stanbury* v. *Exeter
Corporation* [1905], 2 K.B. 838; cf. *Fisher* v. *Oldham Corporation* [1930], 2 K.B. 364. Direction of policy lies with
the unpaid layman, execution thereof with the paid official,
as in the case of the Central Government. But in the administration of justice there is a departure from the prin- Adminis-
ciple of local control. Geographically, in the organisation tration of
Justice.
for the purposes of Petty and Quarter Sessions, and less
closely for the County Court jurisdiction, areas akin to the
County or Hundred have been retained or reproduced, but
the judges—the justices of the peace and the judges of
County Courts—are appointed and are removable by the
Lord Chancellor. Others, Recorders of Borough Quarter
Sessions, are appointed by the Home Secretary. Formerly,
the justices of the peace used to perform the bulk of the
administrative work of local government in addition to
their then less extensive judicial powers. But nineteenth
century legislation left them with few of the former functions,
though regulation of licensed premises, the visitation of
prisons and mental hospitals may be mentioned among the
remaining administrative duties of the present-day justices.

B.

The Central Government in relation to Local Authorities.

The Ministry of Health was established by the Ministry Ministry
of Health Act, 1919, in order to centralise under one Depart- of Health.
ment the control of matters affecting public health. The
Department took over the work of the old Local Government
Board (which title would aptly describe its present most
important function), of the National Insurance Commission

16 *

and some functions of other Departments, *e.g.*, the Board of Control, supervising the care of mental patients, which was formerly under the Home Office, is now part of the Ministry of Health.

While Education comes under its own Board, the upkeep of roads chiefly under the Ministry of Transport and the Police and Elections under the Home Office, the Ministry of Health in most other matters is the State Department which supervises local government services. Other services, such as Unemployment and Health Insurance, Agriculture, War Pensions, though highly important matters of internal government, are not local services. Much of their administration is local, but the officials or committees administering them are responsible directly to the Minister concerned, who usually appoints them. The Ministry of Health is largely a supervising department; its duties in relation to local services are censorial rather than executive.

The old Local Government Board had as its chief functions (1) the control of poor relief; (2) powers in relation to public vaccination; (3) registration of births and deaths; and (4) supervision, with some control, of the administration of public health and local government in general, chiefly through supervising the work of local authorities, inspection by medical officers and by giving of grants in aid of local work. These and other functions have been transferred to the Ministry of Health; its purpose is, broadly, to co-ordinate measures conducive to the health of the people. It is the State Department which, above all others, has taken parliamentary powers of the widest description, enabling it to perform legislative and judicial functions. As such it has attracted the criticisms of constitutional critics brought up in the tradition of Dicey's Rule of Law. Without such powers it is doubtful whether it could have achieved the work it has by administering novel schemes of social welfare, such as Health Insurance. The headship of the Department is already one of the most sought-after political appointments a Prime Minister has to fill; it carries with it a seat in the Cabinet as a matter of course.

" The future structure of our local health organisation "

sums up the task that confronted the new Ministry in 1919. The Local Government Act, 1929, marks the end of a stage in the process of co-ordination of unco-ordinated services, preceded as that measure was by the Rating and Valuation Acts, 1925 and 1928, and the Poor Law Act, 1927 (now Poor Law Act, 1930). The policy of the Department is to reduce the number of local authorities and to widen the area of administration of local services. The local authorities selected as the chief administrative units for the future are the councils of counties and of county boroughs.[1]

The Board of Education administers in conjunction with the local education authorities the national system of education. The work of the Board includes some medical services which are still separate from the Ministry of Health. *Board of Education.*

The Ministry of Transport—and in particular the Roads Department—controls the local highway authorities, largely through the advances it makes towards the construction and upkeep of roads. It is also the Department concerned with traffic regulation and the licensing of public transport. *Ministry of Transport.*

The above are the principal Departments concerned with local government.

C.

Representative Principle in Local Government.

The nineteenth century saw the establishment of central control over local administration by Parliament. It is natural to find that the representative principle was extended to local authorities. But the system differs considerably from the parliamentary system in its application to local bodies. As a rule, though there are important exceptions to-day, there is no marked cleavage in the elected councils due to party politics. Politics, undoubtedly, play their part in the more important local elections, but the policy of a council is less susceptible to changes due to political influence. There is more continuity of personnel; members

---

[1] In 1929-30 the services administered by the Ministry of Health involved financial responsibility for the administration of £117,000,000.

are elected for fixed periods, and normally are re-elected from time to time if they offer themselves to the electors. County and municipal councils elect aldermen, who hold office for a longer period than elected councillors and consequently may have considerable sway in the direction of policy. The chairmen of all local bodies tend to be men with long experience of the work. Against this must be set the part-time nature of the services rendered by councillors and the absence of remuneration. It is not easy for a busy professional man, much less for a skilled employee, to serve on local bodies, while they are actively occupied in their professions or trades, and the days of leisured country gentlemen ready to devote ample time to local government are rapidly passing away. Accordingly the permanent officials, who are in the higher posts normally whole-time servants in receipt of fairly adequate remuneration, exercise a great measure of influence in their contact with the elected representatives. The work of a County or Borough Council is dependent very largely upon its Clerk (Clerk to the County Council or Town Clerk). County or Borough Accountants or Treasurers, Surveyors, Directors of Education, Managers of municipal owned public utility services, such as omnibuses, tramways, gas, water and electricity undertakings, are often in a position to reduce the Council's control to a minimum by reason of the specialised nature of the service they render.[1] But the presence of capable chairmen of committees who can devote time to council work is a safeguard against the danger of the permanent official directing the work and policy of his council.

Local Government Officers.

[1] See Port, *Administrative Law*, 87.

CHAPTER II.

LOCAL GOVERNMENT : ORGANISATION AND GENERAL DUTIES OF LOCAL AUTHORITIES.

PRINCIPAL Local Authorities in England and Wales.[1]

1. Councils of the Administrative Counties (County Councils).
2. Councils of Boroughs which are County Boroughs (County Borough Councils).
3. Councils of non-County Boroughs (Borough Councils).
4. Urban District Councils.
5. Rural District Councils.
6. Parish Councils.[2]

Boards of Guardians (Poor Law or Public Assistance Authorities) ceased to exist on March 31st, 1930, their duties and powers being transferred to the Councils of Counties and County Boroughs and carried out by the Public Assistance Committees of those bodies.

It is one of the most confusing features of that chaos of rules and regulations which pass under the name of local government law that different institutions are called by the same name. The English County affords an excellent example of this feature. For parliamentary purposes, for local administration and taxation, and for military organisation, the term " county " is used to describe areas which are only more or less co-terminous. The term is also used of the

Termin-ology.

---

[1] The Standing Joint Committee of the County Council and Quarter Sessions is the local police authority, except in boroughs possessing a separate police force. For Police see under Home Office, Part IV., Chap. V. ; the subject is purposely omitted from the present Part.

[2] In small rural parishes the parish meeting has some powers.

local civil court, the County Court, though here the divisions make no pretensions of corresponding with the county as depicted on the map of England.   Again, the term is used to distinguish those boroughs which, by virtue of possessing a population of a certain size, are regarded for administrative and parliamentary purposes as outside the area of the county in which they are situated.   The County Borough of Salford is in the County Palatine of Lancaster, the County Borough of Swindon in the County of Wiltshire ; yet for local government administration these places are, practically speaking, separate units from their respective counties.

Professor Jenks [1] has suggested that the old names of Township (now known by the ecclesiastical name of Parish), Hundred and Shire (County) afford the key to all aspects of English Local Government outside the Borough.   We propose to deal chiefly with the administrative organs, but it may be helpful to the reader to have before him the complete field of local government.   His key-plan is as follows :—

GROUP A : THE PARISH.

The Urban Parish.
The Rural Parish.

Parish is here used of the parish for civil purposes.   For ecclesiastical purposes the word is also applicable, though the boundaries of civil and ecclesiastical parishes do not necessarily coincide.

GROUP B : THE HUNDRED AND ITS ANALOGUES.

The hundred is to-day for most purposes extinct, but a number of institutions occupy a position midway between the parish and the shire, as did the old hundred.   It only survives in certain counties for the Divisions of Petty Sessions, and Income Tax areas.
The Hundred.
The Petty Sessional Division.
The County Court District.
The Public Health or Sanitary District (now Urban and
    Rural Councils).
The Poor Law Union (up till 1930 Boards of Guardians).
The Highway District (now Urban and Rural Councils).
    (In 1930 the County Council became the effective
    highway authority.)

---

[1] See Jenks, *English Local Government*, pp. 5 and 6.

GROUP C : THE COUNTY.

The Parliamentary County.
The Military County.
The Judicial County.
The Administrative County (including, since 1930, the Poor Law and Highways) (County Council).
The Standing Joint Committee (County Council and Quarter Sessions).

GROUP D : THE BOROUGH.

1. The Parliamentary Borough.
2. The County Municipal Borough.
3. Non-County Municipal Borough.

The term " city " is less important. Every city is also a municipal borough. Certain towns have, at various times, been called " cities " by royal charter or letters patent, usually the cathedral towns of ecclesiastical dioceses, or very large towns, such as Leeds and Bradford. There also are a few Counties of Cities, or Counties of Towns, formerly regarded as counties by themselves. At the present day these have separate Sheriffs, and in some cases separate Commissions of Assize. Otherwise the differences are unimportant. They usually rank as county boroughs on account of their population.

From this key-plan we may eliminate further discussion of the judicial bodies, namely, Petty Sessions and County Court under Group B, Assizes and Quarter Sessions under Group C (Part V., Chap. I.), as well as the Standing Joint Committee, the County Police Authority (Part IV., Chap. V.).

The Parliamentary County and Borough have also been dealt with in Part III. This leaves only the Military County, before the way is clear to discuss the administrative units. The part played by the old County Militia and the modern Territorial Army is described in Part VIII., Chap. I.

A.

Organisation of Counties.

The County is organized, apart from local government or administrative purposes, as follows :—

Formerly a military representative of the King and, as The Lord-such, commander of the local militia, yeomanry and volun- Lieutenant. teer forces, the Lord-Lieutenant is appointed by commission. He is usually the President of the County Territorial Army Association. Otherwise little remains of his official military duties, except the power to recommend appointments to first commissions in the Territorial Army. He may appoint not more than twenty Deputy-Lieutenants, subject to the Crown's power to decline approval. The office of Deputy-Lieutenant is to-day purely ornamental. The Lord-Lieutenant is the Head of the County Commission of the Peace, and Custos Rotulorum (Keeper of the Records). He recommends, with the assistance of an advisory committee, suitable persons in the county for appointment by the Lord Chancellor as justices of the peace, except in such boroughs as have a separate Commission of the Peace.

The
Sheriff.

　　The Sheriff is also a royal representative, who in former times played a far more important part in county affairs than to-day. He is still, however, the Crown's agent for the execution of processes of law. He summons juries and executes the judgments of the superior civil and criminal courts. As a revenue official he collects the Crown debts, such as fines and forfeited recognisances and bonds. He acts as returning officer in the county parliamentary elections; writs for the election of county members of Parliament are addressed to him. He is in attendance on the judges of the Assize, and has a general responsibility for the maintenance of order in the county. Some traces remain of the Sheriff's greater importance in former times. The office is compulsory. Selection is by the Crown from among three persons for each county " pricked " by a special Court which meets annually on November 12th. This Court is a kind of reproduction under a modern statute of the old Exchequer. Those entitled to sit are the Lord Chancellor, the Chancellor of the Exchequer, the Lord President of the Council, and other Privy Councillors, the Lord Chief Justice and two other High Court judges. The qualification for the office is the holding of sufficient land within the county to answer for any damages that may be awarded against the Sheriff for neglect of duty. Various persons are exempted from the office, such as members of Parliament and officers on the active list of the Regular Forces. The expenses of a Sheriff are such that in these days many qualified persons seek to be excused. No remuneration is payable, though the Sheriff is entitled to certain fines and a percentage of the Crown debts collected.

The Sheriff must appoint an Under-Sheriff and a Deputy-Sheriff. In practice he performs none but the ceremonial duties of his office in person. His legal representative for local business is the Under-Sheriff, usually a solicitor, whose firm practices in the county town. The Deputy-Sheriff is the Sheriff's London agent, who must have an office within three miles of the Temple. The purely ministerial work, such as levying executions, is carried out by bailiffs. *The Under-Sheriff. The Deputy-Sheriff.*

The Coroner is appointed by the County Council. It is his duty to hold enquiries into cases of sudden death and discovery of treasure trove.[1] His salary is paid out of county funds. Larger counties appoint more than one coroner, the county being divided for this purpose into districts. Coroners, both in counties and boroughs having the power to appoint separate coroners, must be barristers, solicitors, or legally qualified medical practitioners of five years' standing (Coroners (Amendment) Act, 1926). *The Coroner.*

Justices of the peace for the county are appointed by the Lord Chancellor on the recommendation of the Lord-Lieutenant, assisted by an advisory committee. The Court of Quarter Sessions is held by all the justices of the county, and sometimes sits in two courts. The Court of Petty Sessions is formed by at least two justices, sitting together in a regular Court House. *Justices of the Peace.*

The county is divided into separate divisions for Petty Sessional purposes, and there is a paid clerk to advise the justices in each division. We are not concerned here with the judicial duties of the Quarter and Petty Sessions.[2] Since the Local Government Acts of 1888 and 1894, only a few administrative powers remain vested in justices of the peace. They have, however, certain powers in connection with licensing and visiting mental hospitals, visiting prisons and the administration of the licensing law.

The Clerk of the Peace, to which office appointment is made by the Standing Joint Committee of the County Council *Clerk of the Peace.*

---

[1] Treasure trove, which consists of objects of gold or silver which have been hidden and of which the original owner cannot be traced, is the property of the Crown. The finder receives back the objects or their market value, provided he reports his discovery promptly to the Coroner of the district.

[2] Part V., Chap. I.

and Quarter Sessions, is also the Clerk of the Council of
the administrative county, holding the latter more important
office by virtue of tenure of the former. As Clerk of the
Peace he is an officer of the judicial county and acts as Clerk
of Quarter Sessions. He is also the registration officer of
the parliamentary county, excepting the separate parliamentary boroughs within the county. He acts, in place
of the Sheriff, as returning officer at parliamentary elections.

The
County
Council.

The Administrative County came into existence in 1888.
The Local Government Act of that year had for its principal
object the transfer of county administrative business from
the justices of the peace sitting in Quarter Sessions to
elected bodies. The same Act created the County Borough
which, for most administrative purposes, is a separate
county, while remaining for other purposes, *e.g.*, judicial,
within the geographical county in which it is situated.
Including London, which is a separate unit, there are sixty-
two administrative counties in England and Wales, and
eighty-three county boroughs. It is not proposed to give
separate treatment to the county borough. The trend of
development is to centralise local services under the administrative county and county borough to the exclusion of the
lesser local authorities, some of which (Boards of Guardians)
have been superseded, and others (Rural District Councils)
deprived of some of their important powers.

In each administrative county there is an elected County
Council, and in each county borough there is an elected
Borough Council, as also in the case of non-county boroughs.

Composition
of County
Council.

The County Council consists of a Chairman, Aldermen,
and Councillors, in the proportion of one alderman for every
three councillors. Councillors are elected by single member
electoral divisions for a term of three years. The electors
are the persons on the local government register.[1] The
aldermen are chosen by the councillors, one-half at every
third statutory meeting. A County Council must hold four
meetings in a year, including the statutory annual meeting,
but in practice it meets monthly.

[1] Chap. III.

The chief executive officers are the Clerk of the Council, Executive the Chief Constable, the County Accountant, the Medical Officers. Officer of Health, the Surveyor, the Director of Education, and other officials, technical experts or inspectors with qualifications suitable to their specialised sphere.   It may be remarked that the Clerk of the Council is the officer upon whom largely depends the efficiency of county administration.   He is usually a solicitor with special training in local government work, but a barrister may hold the office.

As we have seen, the work of the County Council is largely Work of the performed by committees.   A Council is bound, by statute, County to appoint committees for the following purposes :— Council.

Finance, Education, Public Assistance (the old Poor Law), Public Health, Housing, Agriculture, Child Welfare, Mental Defectives, and for Rating purposes.   To these committees may be delegated executive power, except the levying of local rates or the raising of loans.   There is, however, no general power of delegation of the functions of the County Council. In practice, other committees are also appointed, *e.g.*, Highways and Town Planning.   For some purposes persons not members of the Council may be appointed to serve on committees, *e.g.*, Public Assistance Committees.

The principal powers and duties of the County Council Powers relate to Highways, including county bridges, main and and Duties. classified roads and all roads in rural districts ; Town Planning, Health Services, including the power to enforce performance of their duties by the smaller authorities ; Elementary Education, except in boroughs with a population of over ten thousand and other urban districts with a population of over twenty thousand ; Higher Education ; Public Assistance ; and Pauper Mental Hospitals.   There are certain differences in the powers of County Borough Councils, *e.g.*, they are urban sanitary authorities.   In addition there are a large number of minor administrative services provided by and regulative duties performed by a County Council.   The important question of finance will be discussed in the next chapter.

B.

Organisation of Boroughs.

Boroughs, including the eighty-three county boroughs, are corporations consisting of a mayor, aldermen and burgesses. They are governed by a Council, to which the burgesses elect councillors to represent them for triennial periods. The Borough Council thus consists of the mayor, aldermen and councillors. The mayor and aldermen are elected by the Council, the mayor annually, the aldermen for six years ; one-half retiring every third year.

The borough is, and always has been, created by royal charter, but the three hundred and thirty-nine boroughs in England and Wales, including the county boroughs, which, although they have additional powers as administrative counties, are, so far as their status as municipalities is concerned, on the same footing as the non-county borough, are all subject to the Municipal Corporations Act, 1882, which also applies to new creations by charter. A charter of incorporation is sought by an Urban District Council wishing to become a borough by petition to the King. The petition is considered by a Committee of the Privy Council ; notice of the petition must first be given to the County Council concerned and to the Ministry of Health. The effect of the charter when granted is, apart from temporary arrangements, to extend the provisions of the Municipal Corporations Act, 1882, to the town.

Justices.   The majority of boroughs have a separate Commission of the Peace, justices being appointed by the Lord Chancellor on the recommendation of the borough advisory committee. The Crown may grant such boroughs a separate Court of Quarter Sessions, which involves a salaried Recorder appointed by the Crown.[1] The Mayor and his immediate predecessor are justices of the peace (the latter for one year), representing the borough, while the Mayor is also a justice for the county, except in the case of county boroughs. The grant of a separate Commission of the Peace enables the borough justices to act as a separate Petty Sessional Division,

[1] Also a Clerk of the Peace for the borough.

and in practice the county justices do not sit as a rule at the Borough Petty Sessions.[1] Borough justices have their own clerk, sometimes the Town Clerk, sometimes a separate officer. A Borough Council may apply to the Crown for the appointment of a Stipendiary Magistrate.

The most important official of the Borough Council is the Town Clerk, who, like the Clerk of the County Council, is the head of the borough staff. He is its legal adviser, and countersigns all orders for payments made out of borough funds. His office is essential for the due performance by the council of its duties. The other officials are the Borough Treasurer, the Medical Officer of Health, the Surveyor, the Chief Constable (if the borough possesses a separate police force), and other officials such as technical experts and inspectors. These officials perform executive or ministerial duties. Discretionary or administrative duties are delegated to committees of the councils. The full meetings of a council are largely for the purposes of confirming the recommendations of the committees. In this way alone the many-sided activities of a council are capable of being performed by an elected body, which only serves in a part-time capacity. *Executive Officers.*

The purposes of the borough organisation are various. The Council, in its capacity of Urban District Council, is the local sanitary authority under the Public Health Acts. It has also the housing and highway authority for the district. The corporate lands and buildings are vested in it with powers of management. It is the local education authority in the case of all but the smaller boroughs. Many boroughs possess a separate police force managed by the Watch Committee of the Council. There is no complete uniformity of function. In some matters a borough may be a separate unit of administration, while in others the County Council is the local authority. Many of the most important powers of the larger boroughs are derived from local or private Acts of Parliament, or from charters. Powers acquired in this *Work of the Borough Council.*

---

[1] County justices probably have no jurisdiction where a borough possesses a separate Court of Quarter Sessions and cannot sit at Borough Petty Sessions where the borough was exempt before the Municipal Corporations Act, 1835.

way relate to public utility undertakings, such as gas, water, electricity services, the running of omnibuses and tramways, the provision of local docks, harbours and markets, and many other amenities for the public good.

C.

Organisation of Urban and Rural Districts.

Urban and Rural District Councils.

The Administrative County, excluding County Boroughs, is divided into urban and rural areas. The former may be municipal boroughs, or urban areas not forming part of a borough (urban districts). Each of these areas has its elected council. As regards administrative local government powers the two types of urban areas do not greatly differ, but there are important differences between the powers of Urban and Rural District Councils. For example, an urban district of over 20,000 inhabitants is entitled to its own local education authority for elementary education. In rural districts the County Council is the education authority. (Higher education comes exclusively under County and County Borough Councils.) Both Rural and Urban District Councils were established by the Local Government Act, 1894. They replaced a confusing variety of public bodies which sprang up during the nineteenth century, such as Local Boards of Health and Rural Sanitary Authorities. Their powers are exclusively statutory and are derived mainly from the Public Health Acts, 1875 and 1925, the Housing Act, 1925, and similar Acts. They are accordingly the local sanitary, highway and housing authorities, subject in the case of highways to important powers vested in the County Council. Urban Councils have powers to regulate buildings and streets, to provide gas and electricity, public parks, libraries and allotments. Many powers can be obtained by the adoption of Acts empowering the provision of public amenities or conferring increased regulative powers on the council.

Both Urban and Rural District Councils have been the rating authorities since 1925. County Councils have to address their demands for rates (precepts) to them, though the

County Councils provide County Valuation Committees to assist the committees of each assessment area towards securing uniformity of rating throughout the county.

The chief official of both Urban and Rural District Councils is the Clerk, usually, like the Town Clerk and the Clerk to the County Council, a solicitor or a barrister.

In rural areas only there is a further unit—the Parish Council—elected by the local government voters of the civil, not the ecclesiastical, parish. The Parish Council is entrusted with the management of parish property, the custody of parish papers and limited sanitary powers. More extensive powers may be obtained under certain adoptive Acts, *e.g.*, the provision of street lighting, recreation grounds, public baths and washhouses, and libraries (the latter in default only of provision of library facilities by the County Council). *Parish Councils.*

In smaller parishes the Parish Council is replaced by the Parish Meeting, which has still more restricted powers. The Parish Meeting appears to be the only example of direct, as opposed to representative, government in the English Constitution. *Parish Meeting.*

D.

Metropolitan Local Government.

Neither the Public Health Act, 1875, the great general local government powers Act, nor the Municipal Corporations Act, 1882, apply to London. The Administrative County of London was created, like other administrative counties and county boroughs, by the Local Government Act, 1888, and the Metropolitan Boroughs, which cover the same area by the London Government Act, 1899. *Administrative County of London.*

The City of London stands apart. It is unaffected by the Municipal Corporations Act and is still governed partly under its old charters. The City enjoys practically the status of a county borough, except that the London County Council is the local education authority. The Lord Mayor, Aldermen and Common Councillors form the Court of Common Council. The last named are elected by the liverymen of *City of London.*

17

the City Companies.   For some purposes the Court of Aldermen forms a separate Council.

London County Council and Metropolitan Borough Councils.   The Metropolitan Borough Councils, though acting as the sanitary authorities for their areas, do not stand in the same relation to the London County Council, as do the councils of non-county boroughs to their county councils.   The London County Council is the education authority for the whole area.   It is also the housing authority, though the borough councils may take power to erect artisan dwellings. It resembles other county councils in that it became the public assistance (poor law) authority under the Local Government Act, 1929.   The subject of local government in the Metropolis is too specialised for further treatment in a work of this description.   It may, however, be noted that certain local services for London are provided by separate authorities, *e.g.*, the Metropolitan Police controlled by the Home Office, the water supply by the Metropolitan Water Board, traffic control by the London Traffic Committee, while the river Thames, up to a point beyond the metropolitan area, its docks and wharves come under the Port of London Authority.   The size of the greatest urban centre in the world is sufficient to justify the existence of distinctive organisation for local government purposes.

No attempt has been made to discuss in detail in this brief outline of local government organisation the powers and duties of the various authorities in relation to the services rendered by them.   The reader is referred to Wright and Hobhouse, *Local Government and Local Taxation*, for a concise account of such topics as the Poor Law, Highways, Education, Public Health, Housing, Pauper Lunatics and Licensing.

CHAPTER III.

LOCAL GOVERNMENT ELECTIONS, LEGISLATION AND FINANCE.

WHILE it is impossible to treat of the various units of local government and their numerous administrative and regulative powers under a common head, there are certain topics which may be discussed together.

These topics are :—

(1) Local Government Franchise.

(2) Qualifications and Disqualifications for Membership of Elected Bodies.

(3) Elections.

(4) Legislation affecting Local Authorities.

(5) Local Government Finance.

A.

Local Government Franchise.

The Representation of the People Acts, 1918 and 1928, have created a uniform local government franchise for elections of County Councils, Borough Councils, Urban and Rural District and Parish Councils. Any person, male or female, is, since 1929, entitled to be registered as a local government elector who (a) is the owner or tenant of any land or premises in the local government area for three months prior to June 1 in any year, (b) has attained the age of 21, and (c) is not subject to legal incapacity, such as alienage or lunacy. The wives or husbands of such persons residing with them on the premises, in respect of which the qualification arises, are also entitled to be registered as electors.

Tenant includes occupier of unfurnished lodgings and service occupiers of dwelling houses. Residence by itself does not qualify, as in the case of the parliamentary franchise. Thus the franchise corresponds broadly with liability to pay rates, though recent legislation has shifted the burden of rating in relief of productive industry, including agriculture.

B.

Qualifications and Disqualifications for Membership of Elected Bodies.

Qualifications.

There are three universal qualifications, and some others applicable to particular offices :—

(i) Registration as a local government elector within the particular area ;

(ii) Possession of freehold or leasehold property within the area ;

(iii) Residence for twelve full months before the election.

There is no such uniformity as in the franchise in the disqualifications for membership of the representative bodies, but the details of these can be more appropriately studied in a work on local government.

Disqualifications.

The chief disqualifications are :—

(i) The holding of paid office under the council concerned ;

(ii) An interest in a contract placed by the council ;

(iii) Conviction for breaches of election law ;

(iv) Bankruptcy, unless certified not to be attributable to the debtor's misconduct.

In connection with the second ground of disqualifications, a borough councillor, who is also a salaried managing director of a limited liability company having a contract with the council of which he is a member, has been held not to be disqualified, though a partner in a private firm in similar circumstances is disqualified ; *Lapish* v. *Braithwaite* [1926], A.C. 275 ; *cf. In re Sir Stuart Samuel* [1913], A.C. 514.

C.

Elections.

Councillors are elected to County Councils triennially. County
Elections are held for each administrative county as a whole Councils.
every third March. County aldermen are elected by the
councillors for six years, one-half retiring by rotation at
every triennial election of the Council.

Councillors of Borough Councils, whether County or non- Borough
County Boroughs, are elected every year for three years, one Councils.
third retiring by rotation each November ; Aldermen for six
years, one half retiring triennially.

The Councillors of these bodies likewise hold office for Urban and
three years and retire by thirds each year, but in both cases Rural
the County Council may, on the application of the District Councils.
Council, provide for simultaneous retirement every third
year. The elections for these Councils are held in April.

D.

Legislation affecting Local Authorities.

A local government authority is normally a body corporate, Constituent
constituted by Act of Parliament and endowed with statutory Acts.
powers. Municipal corporations form an exception in that
they are created by royal charter, but the charter can only
confer upon the corporation the status permitted by the
Municipal Corporations Act, 1882, and cannot enlarge the
statutory powers. County Councils, Urban and Rural District Councils, Parish Councils and Meetings, likewise the
recently defunct Boards of Guardians, have all been created
by statute. The Acts which constitute these bodies are not
usually exclusively constituent, but may also be properly
classed under the next heading, General Acts, so far as they
also confer powers on the bodies they create by transfer of
the powers of existing bodies, or otherwise, *e.g.*, Local Government Act, 1888 ; or the Education Act, 1921, which both
constituted local education authorities (first created by the

Education Act, 1902) and endowed them with powers of management. The Municipal Corporations Act, 1882, is an example of a constituent Act, dealing with the status of municipal corporations, though not creating them.

General Acts.

General Acts relate to the functions of local authorities and confer the powers necessary for their performance; they are capable of a twofold division; General Acts, strictly so-called, and Adoptive Acts.

By the first type of statute a local authority is given many compulsory powers and duties which it is both empowered and compelled to perform, as for example its chief powers and duties under the Public Health Acts, 1875 and 1925, as local sanitary authority, or under the Poor Law Act, 1930, as public assistance authority. Even in a General Act many of the powers are discretionary.

Adoptive (General) Acts.

An Adoptive Act confers powers which may be utilised by a local authority at its option; once adopted the powers must be exercised as rigidly in conformity with the terms of the statute as those conferred by a General Act strictly so-called. By way of example the Public Libraries Acts, 1892-1919, may be cited. The local authorities which are given the opportunity of adopting the Acts need not do so, unless they so elect, but having elected, the library facilities provided are limited by the terms of the Acts.

Private Acts.

The legislation discussed above is enacted by means of Public General Acts. We must now examine Private or Local Acts. The Private Act has been one of the means whereby Parliament has exercised control over local administration. The Constituent and General Acts for this purpose are a comparatively modern method, dating from the period succeeding the Reform Act, 1832. Private Bill legislation is much older; the process was utilised by local authorities most actively during the nineteenth century and is still freely resorted to for the purpose of acquiring additional powers peculiar to a local authority's own area.

A Private or Local Act of Parliament, though it passes at one stage through an essentially different type of procedure in Parliament resembling litigation between its promoters

and opponents,[1] is as much the law of the land as a Public
General Act. The difference lies in the local effect of the
law it enacts. Herein lies its utility for enabling a local
authority to obtain parliamentary sanction for powers not
exercisable under a General or Adoptive Act. The larger
municipalities and public utility undertakings generally, *e.g.*,
the Railway Companies, constantly enlarge their powers by
this method. Private Bills promoted by municipalities are
usually of the omnibus type and embrace a great diversity
of provisions. To take an example at random from the
Statutes, 1929, the Nottingham Corporation Act is entitled :

> An Act to authorise the Lord Mayor, Aldermen and
> Citizens of the City of Nottingham, and County of the
> same City,[2] to construct sewerage and sewage disposal
> works, street works and waterworks, to purchase lands com-
> pulsorily for various purposes, to extend the limits of the
> Corporation for the supply of water, to empower the Cor-
> poration to run trolley vehicles on further routes, to confer
> further powers upon the Corporation with regard to streets
> and buildings and the health and good government of the
> City and for other purposes.

The immense growth of local needs, coupled with the Provisional
expense to the local authority of the promotion of such legis-
Orders.
lation, and the dilatory and antiquated procedure in Parliament,[3] has led to the creation of another method—that of
legislation by Provisional Order. A Provisional Order is
an ordinance made by a Government Department, which
acquires the force of law, either automatically after a fixed
period, during which it may be contested by petition to
Parliament, or by the express confirmation of Parliament
itself—that is to say, by inclusion in a Provisional Order
Confirmation Act.

Some Government Departments have power conferred
by statute to make these Orders after local enquiry. The
Order authorises the execution of some work of public
utility and is not confined to the needs of municipalities

---

[1] Part III., Chap. IV.　　　　[2] See Chap. II. above.

[3] In 1930 the procedure was expedited by the process of " certification "
in the case of Private Bills promoting work for the relief of unemployment. The power to certify was conferred by Standing Orders of
Parliament on the Lord Privy Seal.

alone. These Orders are grouped together periodically and scheduled to a Confirmation Bill, which goes through Parliament as a Private Bill. Opposition to the Bill, as opposed to the Orders when first made, is rare. The method is both more expeditious and cheaper than the separate Private Bill.

Confirma-
tion Orders.   Provisional Orders adopt schemes as separate enactments, which, when enacted, cannot be questioned. Frequently a somewhat different procedure is provided. The local authority is empowered to prepare a scheme, which is to be submitted to a Government Department for approval. This is given, usually after public enquiry, in the form of an Order by the Minister concerned. Such Order is usually expressed to have effect, when made, as if enacted in the statute which authorises the Minister to make it.

By-Laws.   These are an important means whereby a local authority exercises its regulative functions. A County Council, or a Borough or Urban Council, possess power to make by-laws for the good rule and government of their areas and to prevent and suppress nuisances not already punishable. The Public Health Act, 1875, confers upon sanitary authorities power to make by-laws and regulations. There are various restrictions on the power to make by-laws, such as a limit on the penalty to be prescribed for breach. They normally require confirmation by the Minister of Health or by the Home Office, as the case may be. The courts may declare a by-law invalid, either on the ground of *ultra vires* or as being an unreasonable exercise of power ; *Kruse* v. *Johnson* [1898], 2 Q.B. 91 ; K. & L. 25.[1] The Town Police Clauses Acts, 1847 and 1889, consolidate the usual provisions which were formerly to be found in Acts for the regulation of police of towns. The Acts enable a variety of by-laws to be made for traffic control, public vehicles, street regulation, lighting and kindred subjects.

[1] Part II., Chap. I.

E.

Local Government Finance.

There are three principal sources of revenue available to Sources of meet the needs of a local authority ; Rates, Contributions Revenue. from the Central Government and other local authorities, and Loans. The smaller units of local government are restricted as to their expenditure to the proceeds of a fixed rate, *e.g.*, in the case of Parish Councils 8d. in the £ of rateable value, including debt charges.

Rates are a species of local taxation payable by the occu- 1. Rates. piers of land and buildings. The amount varies with the annual value of the property. There are certain total or partial exemptions. By recent legislation,[1] agricultural land no longer pays rates, while property used for productive, industrial or " freight-transport " purposes is rated at a quarter of the normal figure. The purpose of these exemptions is to shift the incidence of local finance from productive to distributive undertakings.

A rate is assessed upon the annual (rateable) value of land Rateable or buildings. This value represents the rent at which the Value. property might reasonably be expected to let from year to year, less the annual cost of repairs, insurance and other expenses. The law thus assumes the existence of a hypothetical tenant (where none exists), and calculates what sum he would be prepared to pay for a lease on such terms. Special methods are provided for calculating the value of large undertakings, such as railways, waterworks, harbours and mines.

The mode of assessment, changed by the Rating and Mode of Valuation Act, 1925, is as follows : The district councils are Assessment. the rating authorities for all purposes of local government. Rating is thus a principal function of the councils of all boroughs (including county boroughs), other urban districts and

---

[1] Local Government Act, 1929, and Rating and Valuation Act, 1928. The latter Act has given rise to a veritable torrent of litigation. The hearing of two cases by the House of Lords was expedited with a view to checking the flood (Dec., 1930). In his speech in the first of these cases, Lord Buckmaster remarked that 18,000 appeals were said to be pending to Quarter Sessions, and 800 to the Divisional Court ; *Moon* v. *L.C.C. ; Potteries Electric Traction Co. Ltd.* v. *Bailey* [1931], A.C. 151.

rural districts. County Councils address their demands for rates to meet county expenses to the rating authorities in their areas. In rural areas these expenses since 1930 constitute the major part of the total rate. A valuation list, containing particulars of all interests in land, including buildings, within the rating area and the names of the occupiers, is prepared by the officials of the rating authority. There is an Assessment Committee (usually for a combined district of rating areas) which receives the draft valuation list and hears objections raised by any occupier affected before finally approving the list. An objector may appeal from the Committee to Quarter Sessions and thence, on a case stated, to the Divisional Court of the King's Bench Division, and through the Court of Appeal up to the House of Lords. Subject to certain contingencies, the valuation list remains in force for five years. The rating authority levies the rate to meet the expenses of a fixed period, usually six months, on the current list. The rate is a uniform amount in the £ on the value of each unit (hereditament) of land and buildings. This is the general rate for the district and includes the expenses both of the rating authority itself and of the County Council. Special rates are leviable on the same basis on separate parishes in rural areas, *e.g.*, where a charge has been incurred under an Adoptive Act, such as for street lighting, which only benefits a particular part of the district. In urban areas such expenses other than water are included in the general rate, since the services are in theory available for all ratepayers.

Payment of Rates.   Payment is enforced by summary proceedings before justices of the peace. The amount received by the local authorities in England and Wales, prior to the recent de-rating legislation, was in the neighbourhood of £170,000,000 a year. By comparison it will be remembered that the National Budget has in recent years approached £800,000,000, of which more than three-eights is for the service of the National Debt. To compensate local authorities for loss of rates, provision is now made out of the Consolidated Fund.

Uniformity of Assessment.   An attempt has been made to secure greater uniformity in assessment by the Act of 1925. Under this Act every County Council must appoint a County Valuation Committee, containing representatives of each assessment area in the county, to promote uniformity in valuation and to assist the rating authority and assessment committee in each area. A Central Valuation Committee has been appointed by the Minister of Health to act in an advisory capacity, so as to secure co-ordination of rating throughout the country and to make recommendations for the valuation in cases of special difficulty. By the end of 1930 this body had issued five reports containing many valuable recommendations.

Hitherto certain national taxes and the produce of certain licences collected by County Councils have been granted to those bodies out of the Local Taxation Account of the Central Exchequer. Various grants for education, for modern health services and for the upkeep of the roads (from the proceeds of motor registration taxes and fines for motoring offences) have also been made. By the Local Government Act, 1929, there will be paid annually to the Councils of Counties and County Boroughs, in lieu of these sources of revenue and to compensate for losses from de-rating, contributions to local government expenses from funds provided by Parliament. These are called General Exchequer Contributions. The amount of the grant is fixed at intervals for a period of years. The method of calculation is by an ingenious and elaborate formula, into the details of which it is unnecessary to enter. The grant includes sums payable over by the County Council to other authorities in its area. The new system is designed to make a fair contribution from the Exchequer towards the cost of local services, adapted to the needs of each area. It leaves a large measure of freedom to local administration and initiative, but at the same time provides for adequate general control by the Central Government, which has the power to withhold grants, if the standard of efficiency is not maintained. The education grant from the Central Government has not been affected by the Local Government Act, 1929.

The inter-relation between rates and exchequer contributions may be appreciated from the following particulars taken from a demand note for general and special rates in a rural district in 1930 :—

2. Contributions from the Central Government.

General Exchequer Contributions.

SERVICES ADMINISTERED BY THE RURAL DISTRICT COUNCIL :—

(a) GENERAL EXPENSES :—

	d.	d.
*Housing (including ·5d. for assisted Scheme 1919 and 3·06d. for Financial Provisions Act, 1924) . . .	4·75	
Public Health	2·415	
Other Services and Expenses . .	3·245	
	10·41	
Deduct in respect of :— Other credits of Rural District Council (not being Government Grants) .	4·38	
		6·03
The equivalent in terms of a Rate in the Pound of—The Exchequer Grants under Local Government Act, 1929, other than that under Section 92		6·03

SERVICES ADMINISTERED BY THE COUNTY COUNCIL :—

(a) GENERAL COUNTY PURPOSES :—

*Education : Higher . . .	3·505	
Public Assistance	14·53	
*Highways and Bridges . . .	22·765	
Public Health . . .	3·365	
Mental Deficiency	1·235	
Other Services and Expenses . .	1·855	
	47·255	
Deduct in respect of credits of the County Council (not being Government Grants)	1·41	
		45·845†

(b) SPECIAL COUNTY PURPOSES :—

*Education : Elementary. . .	24·49	
*Police	7·585	
Public Health . . .	2·125	
Other Services . . .	6·655	
	40·855	
Deduct in respect of :— Credits of the County Council (not being Government Grants) . .	·105	
		40·75
		86·595
The equivalent in terms of a Rate in the Pound of—The Exchequer Grants under Local Government Act, 1929, other than under Section 92		17·845†
		68·75

* After allowing for Specific Government Grants towards expenses of these Services.

† The Rate in the Pound actually called for by the County Council for General County purposes is the difference between the two amounts marked †, namely 2s. 4d.

SERVICES ADMINISTERED BY PRECEPTING AUTHOR-
ITIES OTHER THAN THE COUNTY COUNCIL :—

	d.	*d.*
Assessment Committee . . .		·25
Parish Council	6·0	
Deduct the equivalent in terms of a rate in the Pound of—The Exchequer Grants under Section 92, Local Government Act, 1929 .	3·0	
		3·0
General rate in the Pound payable by Ratepayer		6s. od.

SPECIAL RATE (for particular Parish).

SERVICES ADMINISTERED BY THE RURAL DISTRICT
COUNCIL :—

	d.	
Sewerage	6·5	
Deduct—The equivalent in terms of a Rate in the Pound of the sum applicable in aid of the Special Rate (Section 92 of the Local Government Act, 1929)	1·5	
		5
Special Rate in the Pound payable by Ratepayer		5d.

Just as a trading company increases its capital by bor- 3. Loans.
rowing on the security of its assets to finance further developments, so a local authority, subject to strict statutory
regulation, may raise loans for the purpose of financing its
permitted activities. The security offered is normally that of
the fund formed by the produce of the rates and other sums
under the authority's control, and of its property.

The power to borrow may be conferred in three ways. Power
By the general law borrowing powers are given subject to the to raise
sanction of a Government Department, usually the Ministry Loans.
of Health. In the second place loans authorised by local
Acts are raised by the larger urban authorities ; in this way
powers may be obtained over and above those conferred by
the general law. Borrowing powers conferred by local Acts
may be made exercisable without the sanction of a Government Department, if the estimates are proved before the
Select Committee of Parliament which considers the Bill.
Thirdly, a Provisional Order may confer borrowing powers,

in which case the previous consent of a Government Department is required.

Other sources of revenue may be briefly noted : profits from productive undertakings (chiefly confined to urban authorities), *e.g.*, gas, water, electricity, omnibuses, and tramways ; income from other corporate property, fines imposed by courts of summary jurisdiction and miscellaneous fees.

Departmental control over local authorities in finance is not exclusively exercised through the payment of the General Exchequer contribution. District Auditors of the Ministry of Health conduct annual audits of the accounts of all local authorities, except extra-metropolitan municipal boroughs. Expenditure incurred without statutory authority must be disallowed by the auditors, as well as excessive expenditure upon lawful objects. Illegal payments are surcharged personally upon those who have authorised them—the elected representatives. In the case of boroughs outside the Metropolis, expenditure on education and housing, two of the largest items in the accounts, are subject to the audit of the Ministry of Health. Other municipal accounts are audited by the borough's own auditors. A surcharge of over £500 disqualifies the person surcharged from membership of the local authority concerned.

CHAPTER IV.

THE COURTS AND PUBLIC AUTHORITIES.

THE most interesting aspect of local government law to the student of the Constitution lies in the adjustment which it involves between the claims of the community and the private rights of individual citizens. This adjustment applies equally to the law of public administration so far as it is administered directly by the Departments of the Central Government. But there is this difference, that the Prerogative may be available to a Government Department, whereas there are no prerogative rights exercisable by local authorities, which derive their powers exclusively from statutes and charters. The difference is, however, not of great importance, in so far as the powers exercised by those Government Departments charged with the duty of administering the modern services are almost exclusively the creation of statute law.

It is an axiom of Constitutional Law that any interference with the personal liberty or private property of the citizen must be justifiable in law. Otherwise the interference constitutes a tortious, and sometimes a criminal, act. The Crown, by virtue of its immunity from process, has a special protection when sued by the subject, though this protection is occasionally removed by statute, *e.g.*, Ministry of Transport Act, 1919, s. 26 (1), which enables the Minister to sue and be sued in contract or tort or otherwise.[1] Apart from this, public servants, with certain important exceptions, and private citizens alike, interfere at their peril with their fellow-subject's person or property.

---

[1] See Part V., Chap. IV., and *cf.* Air Force (Constitution) Act, 1917, s. 10, discussed in *Rowland* v. *Air Council* (1923), 39 T.L.R. 228; and other cases cited at p. 232 above.

Discretion-
ary Powers.

So far the problem is simple. An act, it would seem, is either justifiable in law, or it is not. But the requirements of a modern state are such that those who govern and administer its complicated laws must be entrusted with a wide discretion. In the exercise of this discretion by a powerful bureaucracy the citizen may feel as aggrieved in the twentieth century as his ancestors, chafing under the tyranny of a personal tyrant, in the seventeenth. Yet it is no part of the courts' function to offer him any redress if the discretion is properly exercised. On the other hand, if the limits of authorised discretion be exceeded, an action

Principles
of Exercise.

will lie against the official or body concerned. Further, unless Parliament has expressly enacted to the contrary, a discretionary power must be exercised in accordance with two elementary principles : (1) That a fair hearing be afforded to the parties affected by the contemplated action, and (2) that the official (or body) exercising the power shall not be a judge in his (or its) own cause.[1]

In the well-known *Arlidge Case* [2] Parliament had provided a special procedure. The citizen's grounds of complaint could not be upheld by the court, since the interference with his property had been carried out in accordance with the statutory procedure. But had Parliament not provided this machinery for adjudicating demolition and closing orders, Arlidge might have succeeded on the grounds that he was denied a hearing by the actual authority which made the order against him, and that he was not made acquainted with that authority's reasons for its decision.

It is a fundamental rule that a man shall not be a judge in his own cause ; no man may have a pecuniary interest in the suit he is called upon to adjudicate ; nor may he be biased. Recent decisions go very far and indicate that, even if no actual bias be proved, the appearance of bias is sufficient to invalidate a decision. In *The King* v. *Sussex Justices, ex parte McCarthy* (1924), 93 L.J.-K.B., 129 ;

---

[1] See Part II., Chap. I., for general discussion of powers and duties ; in particular a discretionary power may be *absolute*, as it is called, and cannot be questioned by any means.
[2] Part II., Chap. I.

The acting clerk to the justices was a member of a firm of solicitors who represented a proposed plaintiff in civil proceedings pending as a result of the same collision in connection with which the applicant was summoned for a motoring offence. The acting clerk did not in fact advise the justices in the decision they arrived at to convict the applicant, but as usual retired with the bench. Held that the clerk was so connected with the case in the civil matter that he was unfit to advise the justices in the criminal matter and therefore could not, had he been required to do so, properly have discharged his duties as clerk.

The conviction was accordingly quashed, despite the fact that the clerk had actually taken no part in the decision to convict, the bench not asking for his opinion or advice. It is of importance that justice should not only be done, but manifestly and undoubtedly seem to be done.

Public bodies acting in the course of their lawful powers might be thought to have an interest therein to the extent that they are anxious to achieve by the exercise of their powers the good government of the area entrusted to them, even if they are brought into conflict with private rights. If they are called upon to exercise a discretionary power, such discretion cannot be set aside merely because the decision has been made by them, and not by an independent tribunal or other authority. If, in every case of dispute between a public body and a private citizen or corporation, a third party had to adjudicate, administration would be gravely impeded. But it is usual, though not the invariable practice, to provide a method of " appeal " from the decision of the public body, *e.g.*, to a Government Department, as in *Arlidge's Case*, or to an independent tribunal. The appeal may not be in strictly judicial form ; it may take the form of requiring the order to be confirmed by a higher authority with provisions for the party aggrieved to make representations to that authority in the interval before confirmation. The appeal, or protest, cannot be based on the plea that the body exercising the discretion, even though in a judicial or quasi-judicial capacity, has an interest in the result, if Parliament has expressly conferred the discretion. But, in the absence of such procedure, as was prescribed in *Arlidge's Case*, which ousted their jurisdiction, the courts

Interest of Adjudicating Body in Dispute.

18

will see that a discretion is exercised in compliance with the rules of natural justice.

In *Cooper* v. *Wandsworth Board of Works* (1863), 14 C.B. (N.S.), 180 ; K. & L. 194.[1]

> Under a now repealed metropolitan Act dealing with housing (*inter alia*), the District Board was empowered to demolish buildings, if notice of intention to erect them had not been given by the owner. The plaintiff started to erect a house without giving notice, whereupon the Board summarily ordered its demolition without any previous communication with the plaintiff. *Held*, that the Board should have given the plaintiff some opportunity of excusing, if he could, his non-compliance with the provision as to giving notice of building, whether it purported to act judicially or ministerially in ordering the demolition.

Surcharge.   Another example of the check which the courts can impose upon the exercise of discretionary power is to be found in the surcharge of excessive or illegal expenditure by public bodies upon the individual members responsible. It has been pointed out that the power of disallowance and surcharge is vested, with some exceptions, in District Auditors appointed by the Ministry of Health. A right of appeal from a surcharge ordered by an auditor lies to the High Court. In *Roberts* v. *Hopwood* [1925], A.C. 578 ; cited K. & L. at p. 140, where it was held *ultra vires* for a poor law authority to pay its servants wages in excess of the standard rate, having regard to the cost of living, Lord Atkinson said at p. 595 :

> " A body charged with the administration for definite purposes of funds contributed in whole or in part by persons other than the members of that body owes, in my view, a duty to these latter persons to conduct that administration in a fairly business-like manner with reasonable care, skill, and caution, and with due regard to the interests of those contributors who are not members of the body."

Because local bodies have discretionary powers to fix wages for their employees, they must not, since they are handling other people's money, abandon reasonableness from their decisions. Similar rulings have been given, as we have seen, in relation to the power of local authorities to

---

[1] Also cited, Part II., Chap. I.

enact by-laws; *Kruse* v. *Johnson* [1898], 2 Q.B. 91 ; K. & L.
25. A by-law must be not merely *intra vires*, but also
reasonable.

The independence enjoyed by the bench from executive Control of
control and the immunity from process which protects Administrative Organs.
judges and magistrates in the exercise of their jurisdiction
are safeguards of the utmost importance to the ordinary
citizen. The line of demarcation, however, between judicial
or quasi-judicial and ministerial acts is confused, and under
cover of the exercise of a discretion much legislation is in
fact enacted. Not merely are the acts themselves difficult
to classify under one head or the other, but purely judicial
matters tend more and more to be entrusted to administrative bodies or officials. Such bodies or officials are not
trained to act judicially. By this means the Government
Departments are obtaining for themselves powers of determining matters which would otherwise have had to be settled
in the civil or magisterial courts. It is necessary to examine
the machinery whereby decisions of administrative organs
may be brought under review of the courts. The grounds
upon which such decisions can be reviewed, particularly the
application of the *ultra vires* rule, have already been discussed.[1]

The machinery of review is provided by the Prerogative Prerogative Writs.
Writs. These writs are being applied progressively to the
control of public authorities in matters of government.
They do not, however, provide a means of appealing against
the exercise of a lawful discretionary power, except to the
extent of ensuring that the discretion has in fact been
exercised in such a way as not to offend elementary ideas of
justice.

The writ of Habeas Corpus can be dismissed briefly, Writ of Habeas Corpus.
because its application and the procedure appropriate thereto
will be discussed under Personal Freedom.[2] The *Case of
Art O'Brien*, there cited, shows that even in the twentieth
century, the personal liberty of the subject may need to be
defended against the arbitrary conduct of the Executive,

----

[1] Part II., Chap. I.   [2] Part VII., Chap. I.

18 *

but these cases are, nowadays, rare. On the other hand, protection of the property of the subject from administrative acts is frequently afforded by the other writs. The procedure applicable to Habeas Corpus closely resembles that governing the writs now to be discussed.

Writ of Mandamus.

Mandamus is a peremptory order, issuing out of the King's Bench Division of the High Court, commanding a body, or person, to do that which it is its, or his, duty to do. The writ does not lie against the Crown. If a Department is acting as agent of the Crown and is responsible only to the Crown, having no duty to the subject in the matter, it is not amenable to the orders of the court in the exercise of its prerogative jurisdiction in granting or refusing the writ; *The Queen* v. *Lords of the Treasury* (1872), L.R. 7 Q.B. 387. But it will lie to enforce the performance of some purely statutory duty allotted to the Department as such; *The Queen* v. *Special Commissioners for Income Tax* (1888), 21 Q.B.D. 313, at p. 317. The distinction turns upon the rule that no third party (the Courts) can compel an agent (the Department) to do its duty to its principal (the Crown). Against other bodies or persons the writ will only be granted where the applicant has a right to the performance of a legal duty and has no other specific or adequate means of compelling its performance. He must have demanded its performance and been refused. The duty must be an imperative, and not a discretionary one, but there may be an imperative duty to exercise a discretion one way or another. The exercise of such discretion is enforceable by the writ. The issue of the writ is entirely a matter for the court's discretion.

As an illustration of the operation of the writ it was held in *The King* v. *Housing Tribunal* [1920], 3 K.B. 334, that Mandamus lay against the Tribunal to compel it to hear and determine an appeal. Its previous decision had been given without hearing the appellants and was accordingly brought up and quashed by a writ of Certiorari (see below).

At one time the operation of the writ of Mandamus was confined to a limited class of cases affecting the administration of public affairs, and in particular it was invoked to compel inferior courts to proceed in matters within their jurisdiction, or public officers to perform their legal duties. But the many Acts of Parliament, largely Private or Local Acts, which confer powers and obligations upon public utility undertakings of all descriptions, normally require the execution of certain works for the benefit of private persons, *e.g.*, landowners who may have been dispossessed of their property or some of its amenities by the undertaking. An Act may impose the duty of erecting a bridge over a new railway, or of constructing a road in place of one which has been stopped up. The execution of works of this description is enforceable at the instance of persons aggrieved by the writ of Mandamus.

The writ of Prohibition issues out of a higher court (King's Writ of Bench Division) primarily to prevent a lower court from Prohibition. exceeding its jurisdiction, or acting contrary to the rules of natural justice, *e.g.*, to restrain the judge from hearing a case in which he is personally interested. But for many years past it has also been granted against Ministers of the Crown and public or semi-public bodies of a non-judicial character to control the exercise of judicial or quasi-judicial functions. It does not lie against private bodies, such as a social club, *e.g.*, in relation to the expulsion of a member.

It is not clear what are the precise limitations of the writ; but it is certain that it will only lie against a body exercising public functions and cannot be used to restrain legislative powers. An attempt to invoke the writ (together with Certiorari) against the National Assembly of the Church of England and its Legislative Committee to restrain that body from proceeding with the Prayer Book Measure, 1928, was unsuccessful, on the ground that neither the Assembly nor the Committee was empowered to act, or did in fact attempt to act, judicially in matters affecting the interests of the subject; *The King* v. *The Legislative Committee of the Church Assembly, ex parte Haynes-Smith* [1927], 1 K.B. 491. Nevertheless, the tendency is to enlarge the scope of the writ's effectiveness. The courts ought to exercise the power of controlling any body of persons to whom has been entrusted by statute the power of imposing obligations upon others. The case of *The King* v. *Electricity Commissioners, ex parte London Electricity Joint Committee* [1924], 1 K.B. 171 ; K. & L. 187, is of particular interest in this connection :

> The Commissioners possessed statutory powers enabling them to draw up schemes for improving the existing organisation for the supply of electricity in districts. A scheme was not to become operative, until a public enquiry had been held and other conditions fulfilled. A writ of Prohibition was granted to prevent the holding of an enquiry on the ground that the scheme to be presented at the enquiry was *ultra vires*.

A public body, which could not be regarded as a court of law, was attempting to exercise powers which affected the rights of private companies responsible for the existing supply of electric current. It could not be regarded as exercising legislative, but judicial, functions in proposing to arrive at a decision on a scheme which would affect the rights of the electricity undertakings. Clearly in this sense judicial has a wide meaning not referable exclusively to what is done within the jurisdiction of a court of justice. The judgment of Atkin, L.J., as he then was, deserves careful study as affording many illustrations of the circumstances in which the courts have granted the writ in the past. It is also made clear that the common requirement of confirmation by a higher authority does not put an order of a local authority outside the category of a judicial proceeding which can be restrained by means of the writ of Prohibition. The case should also be studied in connection with the writ of Certiorari.

Writ of Certiorari.   Certiorari issues to remove a suit from an inferior court into the High Court (King's Bench Division). It may be used before a trial is completed (*a*) to secure a fairer trial than can be obtained before an inferior court ; (*b*) to prevent an excess of jurisdiction. It is invoked also after trial to quash an order which has been made without jurisdiction or in defiance of the rules of natural justice. While it is only applicable to review a judicial act, " judicial " is again used in the widest sense and must not be confined to acts of bodies which would ordinarily be considered courts.

The rule lies against a County Council for giving an applicant authority to do that which he is expressly forbidden to do by statute, *i.e.*, to open a cinema on a Sunday ; *The King* v. *London County Council, ex parte The Entertainments Protection Association Ltd., The Times*, January 28, 1931. It is accordingly frequently sought along with the writ of Prohibition, so that not merely may an *ultra vires* act be reviewed (Certiorari), but its operation also restrained (Prohibition). The operation of the writs not infrequently overlaps ; there may be a record to remove into the higher court and also an excess of jurisdiction left to prevent.

The Crown has an absolute right to the writ of Certiorari, since it is a prerogative one. If in a criminal case the Attorney-General makes application, the writ is granted as a matter of course. A private prosecutor must show sufficient grounds, such as the impossibility or improbability of obtaining a fair trial in the local court. In the type of civil case in which it is commonly invoked against a public body the applicant must show a special grievance over and above that suffered by the public at large.

Two recent decisions of the Court of Appeal illustrate the working of these writs (Certiorari and Prohibition). They both arose out of housing schemes prepared in terms not authorised by the Housing Act, 1925. In *The King* v. *Minister of Health, ex parte Davis* [1929], 1 K.B. 619, a property owner in the area affected by the proposed scheme successfully applied for a writ of Prohibition to prevent the Minister proceeding to consider the scheme with a view to confirmation. The scheme contained provisions *ultra vires* the Housing Act, and, therefore, it was not within the iurisdiction of the Minister to confirm it. The Act only contemplated the submission to the Minister of *intra vires* schemes for confirmation. *[margin: Illustrations of Operation of Certiorari. and Prohibition.]*

In the second case ; *The King* v. *Minister of Health, ex parte Yaffé* [1930], 2 K.B. 98),[1] the scheme, which was admitted to be *ultra vires* the local housing authority, had actually been confirmed by the Minister. The writ of

[1] The decision of the Court of Appeal was reversed by the House of Lords ([1931] W.N. 90) on the facts of the case, but the principle that the courts could quash a scheme which was not one contemplated or provided for by the Act was approved.

Prohibition was, therefore, of no avail. But the applicant applied for a writ of Certiorari to review the Minister's decision. In this he was successful. Although the Housing Act provided that the Minister's order, *when made*, should have statutory effect, *as if enacted in the Act*, the Court of Appeal held that this did not prevent the fact of making the order being enquired into by the court. The Act only contemplated orders having statutory effect, if the scheme presented had been drawn up in strict compliance with its terms. The enquiry showed that the Minister had purported to make an order which it was not within his power to make, since it related to an *ultra vires* scheme *quâ* the local authority.

Importance of Writs.

Thus the importance of these writs, despite parliamentary formulas to prevent executive acts being questioned in the courts, lies in the fact that they provide means of questioning the legality, but not the discretion, of judicial or quasi-judicial acts (in the broadest sense) of public bodies, including Government Departments, as well as of courts of justice, other than the High Court itself. In this connection the High Court includes the Assize Courts and the Central Criminal Court, though an order in the nature of Certiorari may be used to remove an indictment from the criminal side of an Assize to the Central Criminal Court.

Information in Nature of Writ of Quo Warranto.

A remedy for deciding disputes between private persons or bodies of persons as to the authority by which an office is held is provided by an Information in the nature of a writ of Quo Warranto. By this process those who have improperly assumed to exercise an office may be removed. In *The King* v. *Speyer, The King* v. *Cassel* [1916], 1 K.B. 595 ; [1916], 2 K.B. 858, this process was used to question the legality of appointments to the Privy Council. It lies " for usurping any office, whether created by charter alone, or by the Crown with the consent of Parliament, provided the office be of a public nature and a substantive office, not merely the function or employment of a deputy or servant at the will and pleasure of others " ; *Darley* v. *The Queen* (1845), 12 Cl. & F. 520—office of City Treasurer of Dublin.

Relator Actions.

An action lies at the writ of the Attorney-General, with or without a relator, either in the Chancery or King's Bench

Divisions of the High Court, to restrain a public nuisance or to prevent an individual or a corporation from contravening or exceeding the powers conferred on them by statute or by charter. A relator need have no personal interest in the subject-matter of the writ, except his interest as a member of the public. This remedy is utilised both by and against local authorities. If a public body is doing an illegal act which tends to injure the public, it is the right of the Attorney-General to intervene, and he will be successful, even though it cannot be proved that injury would actually result from the act. A relator's action lies to restrain *ultra vires* acts, even though a special mode exists of testing the validity of the act by Certiorari ; *Attorney-General* v. *Tynemouth Corporation* [1899], A.C. 293 ; or though the infringement of public rights can be visited with other penalties ; *Attorney-General* v. *Sharp* [1931], 1 Ch. 121.

There are two cases where a person can sue without joining the Attorney-General ; *Boyce* v. *Paddington Borough Council* [1903], 1 Ch. 109 ; (1) if interference with the public right also constitutes an interference with the plaintiff's private right, *e.g.*, special loss suffered by a householder from an obstruction which also constitutes a public nuisance ; *Lyon* v. *Fishmongers Co.* (1876), 1 App. Cas. 662 ; (2) where no private right of the plaintiff is interfered with, but he, in respect of his public right, suffers special damage peculiar to himself from the interference with the public right, *e.g.*, where as a result of a public nuisance a plaintiff's premises have been rendered unhealthy and incommodious ; *Benjamin* v. *Storr* (1874), L.R. 9 C.P. 400.

PART VII.

THE CITIZEN AND THE STATE.

Law of the Constitution, by A. V. Dicey, Part II. (The Rule of Law), Chaps. V., VI. and VII.

CHAPTER I.

FREEDOM OF PERSON AND PROPERTY.

A.

Introductory.

ALLEGIANCE is owed by every subject of the King. Resident Allegiance.
aliens, other than enemy aliens as such, owe temporary
allegiance. We have already discussed the law of Nationality and Naturalisation and the legal position of resident
aliens.[1] No oath of allegiance is exacted, except on appointment to certain offices, *e.g.*, judgeships, and from naturalised
aliens, as a condition of the grant of letters of naturalisation.

In discussing the Rule of Law it has been seen that the Functions of
modern State with its increasing social and economic Modern State.
activities calls upon the citizen to sacrifice his individualism
for the common weal. It imposes on him duties compelling
contribution to insurance schemes and compliance with
sanitary and sumptuary laws. These inevitably detract from
his liberty to do what he likes with his own. This is the
discipline of social inter-dependence. Much of the law of
public administration in its constitutional aspects which
have been discussed in Part II., Chap. VI., has a bearing on
this topic. It is now time to discuss what may be called the
constructive side of the Rule of Law, and examine how
thoroughly the rights of the subject are safeguarded against
interference both from the State and from his fellow-
citizens; but at the same time it must be borne in mind
that the State is no longer mainly concerned with the
enforcement of rights and the protection of its citizens from
internal and external aggression.

[1] Part IV., Chap. V.

No Special
Protection
under
English
Constitution.
Our so-called rights of personal freedom and liberty of speech, including the kindred right of public meeting, are not rights which are granted by any provision in the Constitution. The Constitution of the Irish Free State, like the continental State with its code of guarantees, promises its subjects the enjoyment of their liberty. But such a code usually provides circumstances in which the executive government can suspend those liberties and assume autocratic power. Under the English Constitution a guarantee finds no place. Instead the law provides adequate remedies against wrongdoers, including those who trespass against the personal property of their fellow-citizens and those who defame their reputations. It is then in the law of crimes and of torts, part of the Common Law of the land, the ordinary law and not the fundamental Constitutional Law, that the Englishman finds protection for his liberty. Nor has the Executive power, as under many continental constitutions, to suspend the operation of the remedies which the Common Law affords. It is true that the Emergency Powers Act, 1920 (as to a greater extent did the temporary Defence of the Realm Acts, 1914-15), entrusts the Executive under strict parliamentary control with the enactment and enforcement of emergency regulations in times of disorder, but this falls very far short of giving the Executive, as under the continental system, power to suspend the operation of the Constitution and declare a state of siege, which virtually amounts to arbitrary rule by the Executive.

B.

Personal Freedom.

In spite of such documents as Magna Charta, Clause 39 :

> Nullus liber homo capiatur, vel imprisonetur, aut dissaisiatur, aut utlagetur, aut exuletur, aut aliquo modo destruatur, nec super eum ibimus, nec super eum mittemus, nisi per legale judicium parium suorum vel per legem terrae ;

a British subject cannot claim that freedom is his special privilege, but he can, nevertheless, protect himself against all who interfere with his liberty by an ordinary action in the courts. A privilege is of little use, unless it is protected and enforced. Under English Law interference with freedom, *i.e.*, physical coercion and restraint, can only be justified on five grounds. If none of these be present, the person detained has a cause of action against his gaoler, or he can prosecute him for assault. The grounds are : *[margin: Justification for Imprisonment.]*

(1) Arrest and detention, when permissible, on a criminal charge, including a remand for further enquiry.

(2) Sentence of imprisonment or detention after conviction on a criminal charge.

(3) Imprisonment for civil debt and for contempt of court.[1]

(4) Detention under the law relating to lunacy and mental deficiency.

(5) The exercise of parental authority over an infant. This does not extend to the authority of a husband over his wife ; *Regina* v. *Jackson* [1891], 1 Q.B. 671.

The police have rather wider powers of arrest on suspicions than the ordinary citizen.[2] The Executive, however, has no power to interfere, through the police or otherwise, with the personal freedom of the subject by means of arbitrary arrest. This is a consequence of the rule that the only justification for interference with the private rights of the subject is a defence recognised by law. Although the law, to the great inconvenience of the subject, allows limited immunity from process to the Crown, it does not protect the actual official who commits an illegality, even though he be acting under the orders of a superior. We have seen that the plea of an Act of State is no defence to an action brought by a subject.[3] A public officer cannot defend himself by alleging the public interest, except perhaps in times of grave emergency. It was in connection with the arrest of the subject and the invasion of his property that this principle was established in the eighteenth century cases, known as the *General Warrant Cases*. *[margin: Powers of Arrest.]*

---

[1] Since Debtors Act, 1869, imprisonment for debt normally is confined to the case of persons of proved capacity to pay who decline to obey the order of the court to satisfy the debt.

[2] Chap. III. below. [3] Part II., Chap. IV.

The General Warrant Cases.   The practice of issuing a general warrant to arrest unspecified persons is said to have originated with the Court of Star Chamber.   It is obviously a powerful weapon to assist an embarrassed Executive.   At a later stage it was authorised by the Licensing Act of 1662 for use by a Secretary of State.   It continued to be issued after the repeal of that Act in 1694.   The cases arose out of the attempt of George III.'s Government to stifle the political activities of John Wilkes and the publication known as the North Briton. Even at a later date the severity of the law against seditious publications was maintained largely by executive action, but the cases decided once and for all the illegality of warrants of this type and thus deprived the Executive of a formidable instrument of oppression.

Leach v. *Money* (1765), 19 St. Tr. 1002, decided that a general warrant to arrest an unnamed person was illegal ; *Wilkes* v. *Wood* (1763), 19 St. Tr. 1153, that the papers of an unnamed person cannot be seized on a warrant of this description ; *Entick* v. *Carrington* (1765), 19 St. Tr. 1030 ; K. & L. 145, that a general warrant as to papers of a named person is illegal.   The sequel to these cases was a successful action against Lord Halifax as the Secretary of State who had issued the warrants.

Search Warrants.   There are a number of cases where search warrants may lawfully be issued.   These in effect form exceptions to the rule that General Warrants are illegal.   The oldest, and, indeed, one which was admitted in *Entick* v. *Carrington* (above) to exist at Common Law, relates to search for missing property on premises which are suspected of being made a receptacle for stolen goods ; *Jones* v. *German* [1896], 2 Q.B. 418 [1] ; the more important from the constitutional point of view is that conferred by the Official Secrets Act, 1911, s. 9 :

> (1) If a justice of the peace is satisfied by information on oath that there is reasonable ground for suspecting that an offence under this Act has been, or is about to be committed, he may grant a search warrant authorising any con-

---

[1] Extended to goods subject to other fraudulent practices by the Larceny Act, 1916, s. 42 (1).

stable named therein to enter at any time any premises or place named in the warrant, if necessary, by force, and to search the premises or place and every person found therein and to seize . . . anything which is evidence of an offence under this Act having been or being about to be committed. . . .

(2) Where it appears to a superintendent of police that the case is one of great emergency and that in the interests of the State immediate action is necessary, he may by a written order . . . give to any constable the like authority. . . .

Under the authority of various statutes search warrants may be issued, *e.g.*, for explosive substances intended to be used for felonious purposes; for forged documents and instruments of forgery; for counterfeit coins and coinage tools; for goods which infringe the provisions of the Merchandise Marks Act, 1887; for obscene books and pictures; for blasphemous and obscene libels. Search for a woman or girl detained for immoral purposes or for ill-treated or neglected children may be authorised by warrant. In certain special cases under the Larceny Act, 1916, s. 42 (2), any constable may be authorised in writing by a chief police officer without a justice's warrant to search premises for stolen property.

For interference with freedom of action on any grounds Remedies other than the above, the subject has four types of remedies, for Infringe-ment of if the first may properly be called a remedy at all. These Freedom. are: Self-defence, a prosecution for assault, an action in respect of wrongful arrest, and the prerogative writ of Habeas Corpus. These remedies are available equally against an executive official as against a private fellow-citizen.

Self-defence [1] is an extra-judicial remedy and is of little Self-use against officials of the executive government. In parti- Defence. cular it is inexpedient to resort to self-defence to resist arrest by a police-officer, because, if the resistance cannot be justified on this ground, the consequential assault of the officer is aggravated by reason of his position. Self-defence must, however, be examined in brief. Although the subject is by no means clear, it does not appear to mean that the use of any amount of necessary force is lawful. The amount of force used must not merely be necessary for the protection

[1] See Dicey, *op. cit.*, Appendix, Note IV.

19

of liberty, which includes freedom from interference both for one's person and property, but also proportionate to the harm it is intended to avert. For example, if a person, walking along the coast alone, is compelled to turn aside from his path by the aggression of three men who accost him, he is not at liberty to shoot them dead, merely because they threaten to assault him if he does not turn back. But if the same person is surrounded by the trio on the top of Beachy Head and they gradually force him to the cliff's edge, thereby imperilling his life, it is both necessary for the protection of his person and also proportionate to the harm which he desires to avert, namely death, that he should shoot his aggressors. There is some authority for saying that a man who is set upon in his own house may shoot to kill anyone who seeks forcibly to evict him, because he cannot reasonably be expected to retreat further. In *Rex* v. *Hussey* (1925), 41 T.L.R. 205, a conviction for attempted manslaughter was quashed, the circumstances being that the tenant shot his landlord through the keyhole, while the latter and some friends were seeking forcibly to evict him.

Prosecution for Assault and Action in respect of Wrongful Arrest.

A civil action for damages lies for assault and false imprisonment; further, an action for malicious prosecution may be maintained by any person who is prosecuted for an offence in the criminal courts maliciously and without reasonable and probable cause. These remedies are properly described in text-books on the law of torts. They may be brought against anyone including officers of State, police officials and keepers of asylums. In addition, criminal proceedings may be brought for an assault and it is perhaps in the criminal law that the greater safeguard of the subject is provided against his fellow citizen's interference with personal liberty. From a constitutional point of view it should again be noted that, while the Crown under its prerogative immunity cannot be made liable for the tortious acts of its servants, this immunity does not protect the servant who actually commits the wrongful act.

Prerogative Writ of Habeas Corpus.

It is not sufficient that the subject should be able to defend himself or pursue his remedy under the ordinary law in the courts. What if he is detained by the State, or, for that matter, by an individual, and so is not in a position to institute legal proceedings ? Accordingly the Law of England provides means by which a person who is confined without legal justification may secure release from his confinement. These means do not punish the wrongdoer; they release the person imprisoned who is then at liberty to pursue his remedies against the wrongdoer in the ordinary way. The following passage from Blackstone describes the nature of the process, namely, the prerogative writ of Habeas Corpus : Blackstone on Habeas Corpus.

> The great and efficacious writ, in all manner of illegal confinement, is that of *habeas corpus ad subjiciendum ;* directed to the person detaining another, and commanding him to produce the body of the prisoner, with the day and cause of his caption and detention, *ad faciendum, subjiciendum et recipiendum,* to do, submit to and receive whatsoever the judge or court awarding such writ shall consider in that behalf. This is a high prerogative writ, and therefore by the common law issuing out of the Court of King's Bench not only in term time, but also during the vacation by a *fiat* from the chief justice or any other of the judges and running into all parts of the King's dominions ; for the King is at all times entitled to have an account, why the liberty of any of his subjects is restrained, wherever that restraint may be inflicted.

The writ of Habeas Corpus is obtainable by any person on behalf of the prisoner as well as by the prisoner himself. This is an important safeguard, though in practice every facility is granted to a person in prison to make application for the writ, if he so wishes. Though the writ is strictly a prerogative one, its issue will be granted as a matter of course on showing *primâ facie* ground. The procedure is as follows[1] : application is made, usually to a judge in chambers, for a rule *nisi* addressed to the person who detains the prisoner, ordering him to appear and show cause before a Divisional Court of the King's Bench Division (or, in vacation time, before any judge of the High Court), why the issue of the writ against him should not be made. Appearance has to be made on the day named in the rule *nisi*. Argument on the merits of the application then takes place and, if the court decides that the application is justified, the rule is made absolute by ordering the

Procedure.

---

[1] This procedure is also applicable to the other prerogative writs which have been discussed in detail in Part VI., Chap. IV.

19 *

respondent to produce the prisoner on an appointed day, whereupon he is released. This procedure may be illustrated by the following documents taken from *Secretary of State for Home Affairs* v. *O'Brien* [1923], A.C. 603; K. & L. 178.

IN THE COURT OF APPEAL [1]

ON APPEAL FROM THE HIGH COURT OF JUSTICE

KING'S BENCH DIVISION

Friday the 13th day of April 1923.

ENGLAND.—Upon reading the affidavit of Art O'Brien and the several exhibits therein referred to it is ordered that Monday the 23rd day of April instant be given to His Majesty's Secretary of State for Home Affairs to show cause why a writ of Habeas Corpus should not issue directed to him to have the body of Art O'Brien immediately before this Court at the Royal Courts of Justice London to undergo and receive all and singular such matters and things as this Court shall then and there consider of concerning him in this behalf.

Upon notice of this order to be given to His Majesty's Secretary of State for Home Affairs in the meantime.

IN THE COURT OF APPEAL

ON APPEAL FROM THE HIGH COURT OF JUSTICE

KING'S BENCH DIVISION (ENGLAND)

Wednesday the 9th day of May 1923.

Upon reading the affidavit of the Right Honourable William Clive Bridgeman and upon hearing Mr. Attorney-General of Counsel for His Majesty's Secretary of State for Home Affairs and Mr. Hastings of Counsel for Art O'Brien it is ordered that a writ of Habeas Corpus do issue directed to His Majesty's Secretary of State for Home Affairs commanding him to have the body of Art O'Brien immediately before this Court at the Royal Courts of Justice London to undergo and receive all and singular such matters and things as this Court shall then and there consider of concerning him in this behalf And it is ordered that the said Secretary of State for Home Affairs be allowed until the 16th day of May instant within which to make his return to the said writ.

With liberty to apply,

BY THE COURT.

[1] The Divisional Court refused the writ ; hence the appeal, which was not treated as being in a criminal cause or matter (see below).

It has recently been decided in a curious case which came Successive Applications for Writ. before the Judicial Committee of the Privy Council from the West Coast of Africa, *Eshugbayi Eleko* v. *Government of Nigeria* [1928], A.C. 459, that successive applications for the writ to be issued may be made by an applicant to every court or judge having jurisdiction to hear applications. In this case a tribal chieftain whose deportation had been ordered, sought to apply for the writ to one judge after another of the High Court of Nigeria, and the Privy Council upheld his contention ; moreover, on each application, the case has to be decided on its merits. This illustrates the important constitutional safeguard that the writ of Habeas Corpus affords. An applicant may thus, by way of renewed application, take his case before every judge of the High Court of Justice, until he has exhausted all the available judges, but not, except by way of appeal, to the Court of Appeal ; *In re Carroll* [1931], 1 K.B. 104. He may appeal from a decision of the High Court or of a judge thereof refusing the issue of the writ, or discharge under the writ, to the Court of Appeal and thence to the House of Lords, provided that the application is not in a criminal cause or matter ; *ex parte Woodhall* (1888), 20 Q.B.D. 832 ; *cf. Re Clifford and O'Sullivan* [1921], 2 A.C. 570. It has been held that no appeal lies to the Court of Appeal in the case of a person for whose deportation application has been made under the Fugitive Offenders Act, 1881, and who applies unsuccessfully for the issue of the writ in the King's Bench Division ; *The King* v. *Governor of Brixton Prison, ex parte Savarkar* [1910], 2 K.B. 1056. If any court has ordered the release of the applicant after hearing the merits of the case, there is no appeal from the decision of that court available to the respondent, *i.e.*, the person who is ordered to obey the writ by discharging the prisoner. Disobedience to the writ is punishable by fine or imprison- Effect of disobeying Writ. ment for contempt of court, and the offender may be exposed to heavy penalties recoverable by the person injured. Not merely is it used against governors of prisons to prevent a prisoner being detained without trial, but by its means a wife may question the legality of her husband's detention of herself, or parents may urge that a child is detained in an institution, such as an orphanage or rescue home, contrary to their wishes; *Barnardo* v. *Ford* [1892], A.C. 326.

Habeas Corpus Acts. The writ of Habeas Corpus, like other prerogative writs, is of Common Law origin, but the Habeas Corpus Acts, 1679, 1816 and 1862, made the writ more effective by improving procedure and checking devices for evasion. Severe penalties were imposed for sending a prisoner outside the realm for the purpose of evading the writ. At one time a common practice of evasion was the transfer of a prisoner from one prison to another. The Act of 1679 made the writ peremptory, thus rendering transfers more difficult. It made the writ issuable in vacation, and imposed a severe penalty of £500 recoverable by the party injured on any judge who refuses the writ during vacation. It did not, however, check the evil of a judge or magistrate requiring excessive bail as a condition of release ; hence the somewhat vague clause in the Bill of Rights, 1689, which declared that " excessive bail ought not to be required." The Habeas Corpus Act of 1816 extended the statutory procedure to civil imprisonment, the 1679 Act only relating to imprisonment on alleged criminal charges. It also prevented the respondent from assigning a false cause of detention behind which the court could not go. The Habeas Corpus Act, 1862, precludes the writ from issuing to any Colony [1] in which there is a court with authority to grant and issue the writ and with power to ensure its execution in the Colony ; otherwise the writ may be enforced in any part of the overseas possessions of the Crown.

Double Purpose of Writ. The writ of Habeas Corpus protects the citizen in two ways from an arbitrary Executive. If the cause of detention shown to the court is insufficient, the prisoner must be discharged forthwith; but suppose that the cause is sufficient, by means of the writ the prisoner can secure a speedy trial and so prevent detention by the Executive for as long as is considered expedient. A prisoner charged with a misdemeanour can in general insist upon being bailed ; in the case of treason or felony a prisoner must be released on bail,

[1] Including the Self-Governing Dominions.

if he is not indicted at the next Assizes after his committal, unless the witnesses for the Crown cannot appear. If he is not indicted and tried at the next subsequent Assizes, he must be discharged.

Dicey sums up the net result of the Habeas Corpus procedure by saying that " while the Habeas Corpus Act is in force, no person committed to prison on a charge of crime can be kept long in confinement, for he has the legal means of insisting upon either being let out upon bail, or else of being brought to speedy trial." He claims that the existence of the writ has greatly strengthened the position of the judges by investing them with the means of hampering and supervising the whole administrative action of the Government. He is speaking of the effect of the writ in preventing arbitrary arrest and imprisonment in time of emergency, and as has been seen (Part VI., Chap. IV.), the prerogative writs in general are powerful weapons in the hands of the subject against the encroachments of the Executive in the law of public administration. There is no question but that in times of emergency the judicial control of the Executive may be not merely disadvantageous, but positively dangerous to the community as a whole. But arbitrary arrest and imprisonment in such times can only be made legal by the intervention of Parliament, which takes the form of the suspension of the Habeas Corpus Acts. *Dicey; Views on Habeas Corpus.*

Such a suspension makes it impossible for persons arrested by the Executive to insist on discharge or being brought to a speedy trial. Dicey gives several illustrations of cases where the suspension was in relation to persons suspected of particular offences, such as treason. The practice was that this suspension should be for a short period only, and the Acts merely prevented the use of the writ for the purpose of insisting on a speedy trial or the right to bail. So soon then as the period of suspension was passed, the person who, for the time being, had been denied the assistance of the writ could seek his remedy in the courts by establishing the fact of malicious prosecution or wrongful arrest. Accordingly, it was the practice to ask Parliament at the close of the period of suspension to pass an Indemnity Act, whereunder the *Suspension of Habeas Corpus Acts.* *Indemnity Acts.*

officials concerned were protected from the consequences of any incidentally illegal act which they might have committed under cover of the suspension of the prerogative remedy. Suspension, then, of the Habeas Corpus Acts does not, *ipso facto*, legalise illegal arrest. It merely suspends a particular remedy. During a period of suspension many illegalities may well be committed by the Executive in their efforts to cope with a critical situation. The unavowed object of suspending the Acts is to enable the Government to take steps which, though politically expedient, are, or may be, not strictly legal. An Indemnity Act can legalise all such illegalities and so supplement the Suspending Act which may not have given the Executive all the power that it required.

C.

Defence of the Realm Acts, 1914-15.[1]

By these Acts for the first time the writ of Habeas Corpus was suspended by Parliament delegating the power of suspension to the Executive. In effect, practically all powers, other than that of taxation, were concentrated in the Executive, and even as regards supplies of money the Executive knew that Parliament would not refuse their demands, however extravagant. The Executive by Order in Council was empowered to issue regulations for securing public safety and the defence of the realm in general.

The regulations could authorise trial by court-martial, thereby ousting the jurisdiction of the ordinary courts. That imprisonment without trial was authorised is shown by *The King* v. *Halliday, ex parte Zadig* [1917], A.C. 260; K.& L. 13.

> The House of Lords held that a regulation was valid which authorised the Secretary of State to intern a British subject on the grounds of his hostile origin or association. It was contended on behalf of Zadig, who was a nationalised British subject, that some limitation must be put upon the general words of the statute delegating power to the Executive; that there was no provision for imprisonment without trial, and indeed the Defence of the Realm Act, 1915, had ex-

[1] And see p. 339 below.

pressly provided for the trial of British subjects in a civil
court by a jury; that general words in a statute could not
take away the vested rights of a subject or alter the fundamental law of the Constitution; that the statute being
penal in nature must be strictly construed and that no construction should be adopted which was repugnant to the
constitutional tradition of the country. The majority of
the court swept aside these arguments and held that on the
construction of the Act the Executive had unrestricted
powers. Lord Shaw of Dunfermline delivered a dissenting
judgment which has been preferred by some; he declined
to infer from the delegation of a power to make regulations
for public safety and defence that Zadig could be interned
without a trial and indeed without being accused of any
offence, save that he was of hostile origin or associations
as defined by the regulation; Parliament had not expressly
said in words any one of these things.

The cases which came before the courts arising out of the
regulations made under these Acts were numerous, but it is
only necessary to mention one more in detail.

In *Chester* v. *Bateson* [1920], 1 K.B. 829; K. & L. 21, a
regulation was before the court which was so framed as to
prohibit the owner of property from access to all legal tribunals. The regulation empowered the Minister of Munitions
to declare an area in which munitions were manufactured,
stored or transported a special area. The effect of such declaration was to prevent any person without the consent of
the Minister taking proceedings for the recovery of possession
of, or for the ejectment of a tenant of, any dwelling-house
in the area, if a munition worker was living in it and duly
paying rent. Chester took proceedings to recover possession
of a house which he had let to the respondent, a munitions
manufacturer, but he omitted to obtain the consent of the
Minister. The court held that Parliament had not deliberately deprived the citizen of resort to the courts and accordingly that a regulation framed to forbid the owner of
property access to legal tribunals, though such a result
might be achieved by Act of Parliament, was invalid, unless
it could be shown to be a necessary or even reasonable way
of securing public safety or the defence of the realm.

The Indemnity Act which followed the emergency period Indemnity
of 1914-20 is the most sweeping example of its kind. Despite Act, 1920.
very wide powers conferred on the Executive by the Defence
of the Realm Acts, thousands of technical illegalities were
committed during the period in which the regulations were
in force, including attempts to tax the subject by *ultra vires*

regulations ; *Attorney-General* v. *Wilts United Dairies* [1921], 37 T.L.R. 884 ; K. & L. 119.

The War Charges Validity Act, 1925, was a special Indemnity Act, relating to illegal charges.   The Indemnity Act itself legalised retrospectively illegalities other than money charges.

D.

Emergency Powers Act.

The Defence of the Realm Acts, 1914-15, have expired, but Parliament has sanctioned, by the Emergency Powers Act, 1920, a modified form of rule by regulation in the event of emergency.   The power is surrounded by the safeguard of parliamentary control, which may be said to distinguish it from the old claims to legislate independently of Parliament by virtue of necessity.   The power is only exercisable when a state of emergency prevails.   It is for the Executive to declare such a state, but the circumstances in which they can do so require careful consideration.[1]

State of Emergency.

Before it is lawful to declare a state of emergency, action must have been taken or threatened, which is calculated to deprive the community, or any substantial portion of it, of the essentials of life by interfering with the supply and distribution of food, water, fuel or light, or with the means of locomotion.   The state of emergency is declared by proclamation, which can only remain in force for one month, though in practice the period may be continued indefinitely by the issue of a new proclamation.   The proclamation must be forthwith communicated to Parliament ; even if Parliament is not sitting, it must be summoned within five days. So long as the proclamation is in force, regulations may be made by Order in Council for securing the essentials of life to the community.   Such powers may be conferred on Government Departments or others as may be deemed necessary for the purpose of preserving peace or for securing and regulating the supply and distribution of necessities and

Regulations under Act.

---

[1] The text of the Act is given in Keir and Lawson, *Cases in Constitutional Law*, pp. 365-7.

maintaining the means of transport. But the regulations must stop short of imposing compulsory military service or industrial conscription, and no regulation may make it an offence for anyone to take part in a strike or peacefully to persuade others to do. so. This latter provision must be read subject to the Trade Disputes and Trade Unions Act, 1927, ss. 1 and 3, which respectively define a legal strike and restrict the right of peaceful picketing. There is no power to alter the existing procedure in criminal cases or to punish by fine or imprisonment without trial, but the regulations may provide for the trial by courts of summary jurisdiction of persons guilty of offences against the regulations, subject to maximum penalties. The regulations must be laid before Parliament and expire after seven days, unless a resolution is passed by both Houses providing for their continuance.

So far there has only been one opportunity of considering Comment on the effectiveness of this measure, but the occasion was so Act. important a one, namely, the General Strike and the Coal Strike, 1926, that it may be regarded as having provided an effective means of suppressing internal disorder on a large scale. The Act does not appear to permit the suspension of the writ of Habeas Corpus in criminal matters, so far as it expressly prohibits the alteration of any existing procedure in criminal cases or the conferring of any right to punish by fine or imprisonment without trial. The Trade Disputes and Trade Unions Act, 1927, which was passed as a direct result of the General Strike, aimed at preventing a repetition of such an event by making illegal sympathetic strikes or lockouts by persons in trades not effected by any existing dispute. It also, as a result of the experience gained in the 1926 Strike, modified the provision of s. 2 of the Trade Disputes Act, 1906, in relation to peaceful picketing.

E.

Freedom of Property.

The subject enjoys his property free from disturbance or Ordinary invasion, because, as with his personal liberty, trespass to Remedies protect his property is a civil wrong and, if malicious injury be Property.

inflicted, also a criminal offence. Under the Prerogative there is power to deprive the subject of his property for the defence of the realm in time of danger. This was recognised by the House of Lords in *Attorney-General* v. *De Keyser's Royal Hotel, Ltd.* [1920], A.C. at pp. 524, 525. The various records point to a usage of payment, but Lord Dunedin, in the case cited, did not consider that such usage imposed a customary obligation upon the Crown to pay. As regards land, the prerogative power is now governed by the Defence Act, 1842. Apart from emergency, there are two ways in which Parliament from time to time authorises the Crown to take the property of the subject.

Taxation.

The first of these is by way of taxation and the necessity for parliamentary consent in this respect has already been fully discussed. The second may be described as compulsory

Compulsory Acquisition of Land with Compensation.

acquisition of land and, although it is not of such general application as taxation, it is nevertheless a process which is resorted to in the public interest day by day. Apart from legislation neither the Central Government nor a local authority has the power to acquire land, except by agreement with the owner. The Air Ministry may use statutory powers for the purpose of acquiring the site of a new aerodrome ; the Corporation of a municipal borough may compel private owners to grant them rights for the purpose of developing their water undertaking, or for a street widening scheme ; and indeed a public utility undertaking, not identified with either the central or local government, such as a railway company, may similarly acquire land by compulsion by this method. But in each case compensation is payable. The need for these statutory powers, which interfere with private rights, really depends on the principle that only Parliament can alter the law of the land. Private rights are protected under the law and, save in the case of grave necessity, those private rights cannot be transgressed. Public utility purposes can hardly be regarded as a ground of such necessity.

Lands Clauses Acts.

In 1845-47 there were passed a series of Acts which provided a code for regulating the giving of compensation whenever powers of compulsory acquisition are conferred. The practice is to incorporate the code into any Act, whether

Public or Private, which confers powers of taking the subject's land. The various Acts forming the code are the Lands Clauses Consolidation Act, 1845; the Railways Clauses Consolidation Act, 1845; the Water-Works Clauses Act, 1847; and the Towns Improvement Act, 1847. The statutory provisions for compulsory acquisition do not exclude the purchase of the land by agreement. If compulsory powers are exercised under the conditions laid down in the Acts, which are comprehensively described as the Lands Clauses Acts, there are several methods of assessing compensation. The usual method where the claim exceeds £50 is by arbitration. Later legislation is less favourable to the subject. Under the Housing Acts, 1925 and 1930, the owner of property which is acquired by a local authority in connection with " slum clearance schemes " is only to be compensated to the extent of the site value of the property, and not the extent of any loss that he may suffer from demolition of the houses thereon.

The *General Warrant Cases* have shown that the Executive has no power, apart from statute, arbitrarily to invade the property of the subject for the purpose of arrest, search or other interference.

Before leaving the subject of enjoyment of property, it is important to note that the above limitations on the right of free enjoyment are confined to cases of deprivation of ownership in the public interest. But the law does not allow a private owner unlimited and unlicensed use of his property. He may not use his land so as to constitute a nuisance either to the public at large or to his neighbour in particular. Adjoining owners are liable to support adjacent land, but not buildings thereon, in the absence of a right of support being acquired. There is a liability accruing from the escape of dangerous things. Both as to land and other forms of property there are numbers of statutory restrictions on use, enjoyment and sometimes even on disposition. No building can be erected without approval of the plans by the appropriate authorities. Many modes of transfer are prescribed by statute. The use of many articles, except under licence from the State, is prohibited. Freedom of contract in other

General Restrictions on Use of Property and Freedom of Contract.

spheres than property law is often restricted ; masters are obliged to insure their servants ; landlords to compensate their tenants for improvements. These are not topics for Constitutional Law ; they are mentioned merely to indicate that the citizen of modern England is not permitted either to be king of his castle or master of his affairs.

CHAPTER II.

FREEDOM OF DISCUSSION.

THE attitude of English Law towards freedom of discussion is that a speaker or writer has no special protection to enable him to give free expression to his opinions, but that there is no restriction which can interfere with this freedom, unless he oversteps the bounds set by law, and, in particular, by the law of defamation.

The law of defamation is capable of a twofold division Law of into slander, *i.e.*, defamation in a transitory form, such as the Defamation. spoken word, and libel, *i.e.*, defamation in a permanent form, such as the printed word. Without embarking on a technical discussion of this branch of law it may be said that there can be no defamation, so far as liability for damages in a civil action is concerned, unless the defamatory matter be published to a third person, but there may be criminal liability, even if the words are only published to the person defamed, since the basis of liability here rests on the probability of a breach of the peace. Generally speaking, there is no remedy to restrain in advance the publication of alleged defamatory matter. The ordinary remedy is an action for damages, coupled with an injunction to restrain further publication if necessary. The law, then, throws the risk on the speaker or writer.

The Press may be said to be in much the same position as The Press. the ordinary individual. At one time under the Licensing Act printing was a monopoly and had to be under licence. But since 1695, when the Act was not renewed, the liberty of the Press has consisted in printing without licence, subject to the consequences of ordinary law. It is not surprising that the Press figures largely in the cases relating to the law of defamation. There are, however, a number of enactments which give the Press some not unimportant privileges which are not enjoyed by the ordinary citizen.

Special Defence open to Press.

The defence of apology is only available in an action for libel contained in a public newspaper or other periodical publication ; the defendant must prove (1) that the libel was published without actual malice and without gross negligence, and (2) that before the commencement of the action, or at the earliest opportunity afterwards, he inserted in such newspaper or publication a full apology for the libel. (3) Moreover, there must be a payment made into court by way of amends, which precludes any other defence denying liability being pleaded ; Libel Act, 1843.

Privilege.

Privilege attaches to reports of parliamentary debates, judicial proceedings and public meetings. Reports of proceedings in courts of justice must be fair and accurate, not prohibited by order of the court, and not blasphemous, seditious or immoral ; such reports are also subject to the provisions of the Judicial Proceedings (Regulations of Reports) Act, 1926, which prohibits the publication of indecent matter, and in the case of reports of matrimonial cases, restricts what may lawfully be published to a bare summary of the names of the parties, their legal advisers, the witnesses and the judgment.[1] Newspaper reports of parliamentary proceedings are only privileged if they are fair and accurate, and without malice,[2] which is a ground for rebutting privilege generally, except in those cases where it is absolute, *e.g.*, publications made by authority of Parliament, actual proceedings in Parliament or a court of law. The reports of proceedings of a public meeting must also be fair, accurate, and contemporaneous, containing no blasphemous or indecent matter, and the publication must be for the public benefit or relate to a matter of public concern. This privilege may again be rebutted on proof that the report was published maliciously, or on the ground that the defendant has refused to insert in the newspaper a reasonable letter or statement

---

[1] In addition to a statement of the matter at issue and submissions, together with the decision thereon, of points of law.

[2] Part III., Chap. III. A.

by way of contradiction or explanation. In connection with criminal libels the Press enjoys some protection, and in particular an order of a judge of the High Court is required before a newspaper can be prosecuted for criminal libel. *Criminal Libels in Newspaper.*

But it cannot be pretended that these minor variations in the ordinary law amount to a special law for the Press. In the old days printing was a monopoly, and breach of the monopoly was punished in the Court of Star Chamber. Nowadays offences by the Press are tried in the ordinary civil and criminal courts, and the State is content to leave the public expression of opinion to the working of the ordinary law, subject only to the censorship of stage plays [1] and the regulation of certain types of judicial reports. *No Special Law of Press.*

The criminal law of blasphemy and obscenity is a further restriction, in the interests of the public, on a person's liberty to say what he likes, and unlicensed speech and criticism of the conduct of the Government is punishable under the law of sedition. It is a misdemeanour to publish words or documents with seditious intention. Though the definition of sedition is wide enough to cover almost any act of disaffection or disloyalty whether to State or Church, in practice prosecutions for seditious offences are rare, largely on account of the difficulty of obtaining from a jury the conviction of a man for his expression of opinion relating to public affairs. Moreover, the political inexpediency of prosecuting weakens the administration of the law in this respect and correspondingly increases the licence of expression of opinion. *Sedition and other Offences.*

[1] By the Lord Chamberlain.

CHAPTER III.

FREEDOM OF PUBLIC MEETING.

As a result of the view taken by the courts of the liberty of the individual with regard to freedom of person and of speech, the right of public meeting in English Law consists of nothing more than the exercise by a number of individuals acting in unison of their liberty to go where they like and say what they like. This statement is subject, however, to the law of conspiracy. Conspiracy is a criminal offence, but it may also be a cause of a civil action ; *Sorrell* v. *Smith* [1925], A.C. 700. Like the single individual, those present at a meeting take upon themselves the risk of infringing the law. They may trespass, commit a nuisance, or utter defamatory words. On any of these acts occurring the meeting becomes an unlawful assembly, if a breach of the peace is apprehended. In this connection it should be observed that there is no right to hold a meeting on the highway—at all events if obstruction or other injury is thereby caused ; the normal use of the highway which the citizen is entitled to enjoy is merely that of passing and repassing ; *Harrison* v. *Duke of Rutland* [1893], 1 Q.B. 142 ; *Hickman* v. *Maisey* [1900], 1 Q.B. 752.

Unlawful Assembly : how created.   In addition to the commission of a tort or of a crime, there is another circumstance in which it has been held that a meeting is unlawful. It seems that if the assembly of three or more persons inspires peaceable citizens in the locality with reasonable fear that a breach of the peace is threatened, an unlawful assembly is thereby constituted, and those who take part therein are guilty of a misdemeanour. To constitute the assembly unlawful the meeting must actually be held, and, moreover, it is not unlawful merely because it is expected to excite unlawful opposition. The police have no power (apart from any regulation that may be made

306

under the Emergency Powers Act, 1920), to order that an advertised meeting be abandoned. But if the meeting assembles and in the course of its proceedings a breach of the peace is committed, then the meeting can be dispersed. Further, where the meeting assembles for a lawful purpose and no illegality is committed, if the authority on the spot forms the opinion that the peace can only be preserved by dispersing the meeting, it may be dispersed.

This statement of the law may be illustrated by reference to the following cases : *Beatty* v. *Gillbanks* (1882), 9 Q.B.D. 308 ; K. & L. 354.

> The Salvation Army processions in Weston-super-Mare had provoked organised opposition, in consequence of which disorder had taken place. After several disturbances a notice signed by two justices of the peace was served on the leader and other members of the Salvation Army requiring all persons to abstain from assembling to the disturbance of the public peace in the streets of the town. Despite the notice the Salvation Army again met, and the leader, when requested by a police sergeant to desist, declined to do so, whereupon he was arrested, and his followers continued the procession. Neither the leader nor his other followers who were subsequently arrested were guilty of any act of violence. On the other hand, there was sufficient reason to suppose that a continuance of the procession would, as on former occasions, have led to a collision with the organised opposition, whereby a breach of the peace would have ensued. The magistrates bound the Salvationists over on a charge of unlawful assembly. The Divisional Court reversed this decision on the ground that the finding of the justices amounted to convicting a man for doing a lawful act, because he knew that his doing so might cause another to do an unlawful act. It was pointed out that it was an unlawful organisation which had assumed to itself the right to prevent the Salvationists from lawfully assembling.

It seems, then, that a meeting assembling for a lawful object cannot be prohibited in advance. But actually the Salvationists' meeting had assembled and on the authority of the case now to be cited it would seem that, if there was no other way in which the breach of the peace could have been avoided except by dispersing the Salvationists' meeting, then the authorities would be justified in taking that step.

In *O'Kelly* v. *Harvey* (1883), 14 L.R. Ir. at pp. 109-12.

A magistrate dispersed a meeting upon the ground that he believed upon reasonable and probable grounds that the meeting was held with unlawful intent ; he proved that he had grounds for his belief, though he could not prove that the meeting was in fact unlawful. Held that his reasonable belief was a sufficient defence to an action for assault brought against him by one of the persons whom he laid hands on in the act of dispersing the assembled crowd. The judgment of Law, C., at p. 109, is :—

Assuming the plaintiff and others assembled with him to be doing nothing unlawful, but yet that there were reasonable grounds for the defendant believing, as he did, that there would be a breach of the peace if they continued so assembled, and that there was no other way in which the breach of the peace could be avoided but by stopping and dispersing the plaintiff's meeting . . . in my opinion the plaintiff was justified in taking the necessary steps to stop and disperse it. Under such circumstances the defendant was not to defer action until a breach of the peace had actually been committed. His paramount duty was to *preserve the peace unbroken,* and that by whatever means were available for the purpose.

In *Wise* v. *Dunning* [1902], 1 K.B. 167 ; K. & L. 357.

A Protestant lecturer conducted a vigorous campaign of open-air meetings in the Roman Catholic quarter of Liverpool. On previous occasions his conduct had caused disturbance, largely on account of the lecturer's offensive utterances regarding Roman Catholics. Wise was summoned under an information which stated that breaches of the peace had taken place in consequence of his meetings, and that there was reason to believe that he intended to hold similar meetings whereby serious breaches of the peace would follow. The summons asked that he be ordered to find sureties to keep the peace. There was a local Act in force in Liverpool prohibiting under a penalty the use of threatening, abusive, or insulting words and behaviour in the streets whereby a breach of the peace might be occasioned. *Held,* that the magistrate had jurisdiction to bind Wise over in recognisances to be of good behaviour.

This case is distinguishable from *Beatty* v. *Gillbanks* in that the person summoned had actually been guilty of a breach of law, whereas in the latter case the Salvationists had committed no illegal act.

Definition of Unlawful Assembly.   Thus the offence of unlawful assembly is constituted by the meeting of three or more persons for the accomplishment of some common, unlawful design. The act of assemblage is sufficient, and the design need not be put into execution, but it must be shown that there is reasonable apprehension of a breach of the peace. If a number of persons meet together to commit a fraud, the meeting is not an unlawful assembly, but the persons may be guilty of a criminal offence of conspiracy. But if the meeting is for the purpose of participating in a prize-fight, which is illegal and also involves a danger to the peace, then all the participants may be charged with the offence. Moreover, instant fear of a breach of peace occurring (and thus creating the assembly unlawful), may justify those charged with the duty of maintaining order, as magistrates or police officers, requiring the dispersal of a meeting actually assembled for a lawful object, if their fear of disorder is based upon reasonable apprehensions.

There are two other offences in connection with unlawful Rout. meetings. If the members of an unlawful assembly take some step towards achieving their object, a rout is constituted. A procession of strikers on their way to attack the premises of their workplace would constitute a rout.

As soon as the unlawful purpose is put into actual execution Riot. by three or more persons the rout becomes a riot at Common Law. This, like a riot, is a misdemeanour punishable with imprisonment. But if the unlawful common purpose which the rioters are engaged in committing is itself felonious, *e.g.*, arson, then the riot is at Common Law a felony. The distinction is of some importance, because although there is a Common Law duty on both magistrates and citizens to use necessary force to disperse any unlawful assembly, the amount of force necessary to suppress a felony may be greater than in the case of a misdemeanour. The elements essential to constitute a Common Law riot are five in number :

(1) A number of persons, three or more.

(2) An unlawful common purpose. These elements are essential to any unlawful assembly.

(3) The execution, or attempted execution, of the common purpose.

(4) Intention to help one another by force if necessary.

(5) Display of force sufficient to alarm at least one person of reasonable stability.

Statutory
Riot also a
Felony.

A riot may also become felonious under the provisions of the Riot Act, 1714, quite apart from the actual commission of an independent felony which, as has been seen above, is sufficient to constitute the riot felonious.   By the provisions of this Act a magistrate is empowered to order any twelve or more persons who are assembled together to the disturbance of the public peace to disperse within one hour after the reading of the proclamation in the Act.   Failure to comply with the proclamation within the hour renders the rioters liable to be adjudged felons and punished with the maximum penalty of penal servitude for life.

Damage done
by Rioters.

Formerly compensation for damage done to property by rioters was payable by the Hundred.   The Riot (Damages) Act, 1886, enables property owners to recover compensation out of the county or borough funds (police expenses), thus throwing the burden on to the general body of the rate-payers.   In a claim for compensation under this Act it has been held that acts which constitute a riot when committed by civilians equally constitute a riot when committed by soldiers, notwithstanding that the acts took place at a military camp in England during the war of 1914-19 ; *Pitchers* v. *Surrey County Council* [1923], 2 K.B. 57.

Reference should be made to the *Charge to the Bristol Grand Jury* in the case of *Rex* v. *Pinney* (1832), 5 C. & P. 254 ; K. & L. 359, for a statement of the law regarding the duty of magistrates and ordinary citizens to assist in the suppression of any acts calculated to cause a breach of the peace. It is not merely a magistrate or other person in authority who may be required to take active steps to suppress disorder. Any passer-by may be called upon by a constable to assist him, provided that the constable actually saw a breach of the peace committed by more than one person (or has been assaulted or obstructed in the arrest of a felon), and that there was a reasonable necessity for his calling upon others to assist him.   To refuse aid to constables in such circumstances is a misdemeanour at Common Law ; *Regina* v. *Brown* (1841), Car and M. 314 ; K. & L. 364.[1]   At Common Law a private

[1] It is stated in 2 Hawkins, Pleas of the Crown, c. 12, s. 1, that all present when a felony is committed are bound to arrest the felon on pain

person has power to arrest (1) for treason, felony or dangerous wounding actually committed in his presence.

(2) For any breach of the peace so committed, but only during its actual continuance.

(3) On any reasonable suspicion of treason, felony or dangerous wounding.

In the third case he acts, unlike a constable, at his peril, and will be liable to an action for false imprisonment at the suit of the person arrested, if it happens that the alleged felony was not in fact committed. In *Walters* v. *W. H. Smith and Son, Ltd.* [1914], 1 K.B. 595, it was held that, when a private person makes or causes an arrest, he must prove that the same felony has been committed for which the plaintiff who is suing him for false imprisonment has been given into custody. By statute further powers have been conferred on private persons, *e.g.*, the arrest for any indictable offence whatever committed by a man in his presence. The powers of a constable are wider. If he arrests on suspicion of treason, felony or dangerous wounding, he will be protected from the consequences of his own act. By statute he may arrest anyone whom he finds loitering at night and whom he suspects of offences under such Acts as the Larceny Act, 1916, or the Offences Against the Person Act, 1861. In London a constable may arrest anyone whom he may find loitering at night unable to give a satisfactory account of himself.

This short account relates to the power of arrest without warrant. In the majority of cases the police act on a written warrant for arrest granted by a justice of the peace or other judicial authority empowered to issue warrants after application (an information) supported by oath. It will be remembered that the warrant must indicate specifically the person whose arrest is to be affected, and that there is no power to issue a general warrant for the apprehension of all persons suspected of a crime.

of being fined and imprisoned for neglect. *Sed quaere* whether this is still law.

PART VIII.

A. THE FORCES OF THE CROWN AND THE DISCIPLINE THEREOF.

B. MARTIAL LAW.

Law of the Constitution, by A. V. Dicey, Part II. (The Rule of Law), Chaps. IX. and X. ; and Appendix, Notes VI. and X.
Manual of Military Law (for reference).

CHAPTER I.

THE FORCES OF THE CROWN.

Army : Regular Forces.

(1) The British Army, subject to Army Act, 1881, wherever employed.

(2) The Indian Army, subject to Military Law enacted by the Governor-General of India in Council.

(3) The Dominion Military Forces, subject to Dominion legislation.

Reserve Forces.

(1) Army Reserve, subject to Army Act, when under training or " called out."

(2) Militia (late Special Reserve), subject to Army Act, when under training or " called out."

(3) Supplementary Reserve, subject to Army Act, when under training or " called out."

Territorial Army, subject to Army Act during training and " embodiment."

Royal Marines.

Regular Force and Reserves, subject, when on active list, to Army Act, unless employed on board a warship in commission, when under Naval Discipline Acts.

Navy : Regular Forces.

(1) Royal Navy, subject to Naval Discipline Acts, 1866 and 1884.

(2) Dominion Navies, subject to Dominion legislation.

(3) Royal Indian Navy (in formation), subject to disciplinary code enacted by Governor-General of India in Council.

315

Reserve Forces.

(1) Royal Naval Reserve, subject to Naval Discipline Acts, when on board warship in commission, or otherwise actually serving.

(2) Royal Naval Volunteer Reserve, subject to Naval Discipline Acts, when on board warship in commission, or otherwise actually serving.

Air Force : Regular Force.

Royal Air Force.   Discipline as for Army.

Reserve Force.

Air Force Reserve.   Discipline as for Army Reserve.

Territorial Force.

Auxiliary Air Force.   Discipline as for Territorial Army.

A.

Introductory.

Hitherto the reader has been introduced to the legal aspect of government in time of peace, if we except the brief account of emergency powers available in time of civil disturbance given in Part VII., Chapter I. above.   When the State is engaged in war with another Power, or Powers, it is highly probable that " a state of emergency " as defined by the Emergency Powers Act, 1920, s. 1, would be deemed to exist, but it is equally probable that, should hostilities take place in the British Isles, on the Continent of Europe, or on the seas within several thousands of miles from this country, further powers would be required by the Government of the day to deal with the internal situation.   We must accordingly consider, after discussing in detail the Armed Forces and their constitutional position, what such powers are.   This will be attempted under Chapter III. (Martial Law).

The subject of the Forces falls into three sections :—

(1) The mode in which the Forces are composed and disciplined ;

(2) The executive control by which the Forces are governed ;

(3) The status of their members.

B.

Composition and Discipline of the Army.

Before the Commonwealth there had been two distinct Feudal national forces. The Feudal Levy had, since in 1159 actual Levy. service was commuted for a money payment (scutage), ceased to be of importance. The payment of scutage constituted a burdensome incident of land tenure, until the Act for the Abolition of Military Tenures at the Restoration. The National Levy was a defensive force, organised by counties, National with no liability, save in case of invasion, to serve outside the Levy. county. This force was subject to much statutory regulation, and at its head the Sheriff was replaced by the official now known as the Lord-Lieutenant. There was a general liability to military service in this force, though the actual forces of the Crown for war came to be raised by commissions of array, whereby each county supplied a compulsory quota for the King's Army. Strictly speaking, forces so raised could not, apart from invasion, be compelled to serve outside their own counties. These commissions were a frequent ground of complaint in the time of the three Edwards ; by them and by other means the Crown strove to acquire a third force (a standing army), which could be employed, as the need for a permanent force began to be recognised, irrespective of the limitations as to time and place which attached to the Feudal and National Levies. The King provided himself with such an army either by voluntary enrolment, by im- Standing pressment, or by contract, if he could afford to pay it, or if Army. Parliament granted him the necessary funds. How far such a force had a lawful basis in time of peace is doubtful. The Petition of Right, 1628, moreover, furnished a difficulty in maintaining army discipline, because no departure from the ordinary law was henceforth permissible, except on actual service, commissions of martial law (the law of the Marshal) being thereby expressly declared illegal ; they were probably illegal apart from this declaration.

The Militia. The National Levy, by this time known as the Militia, was reorganised after the Restoration by the Militia Act, 1662. The command of this force was indisputably made the King's.

The King was not, however, henceforth permitted to keep a standing army beyond " Guards and Garrisons " of unspecified numbers. On this footing, with constant disputes between King and Parliament, the matter continued *Bill of Rights.* until the Revolution of 1688. The Bill of Rights provided that :

> The raising or keeping of a standing army within the Kingdom in time of peace, unless it be with the consent of Parliament, is against the law.

This provision was not due so much to the objection to military service as to the realisation that the army might be dangerous to the liberty of the subject in the hands of an unwise ruler.

Regular Army. A standing army in peace time is thus (1) unlawful, (2) its discipline cannot be enforced by rules differing from the ordinary law, and (3) the supplies necessary for its maintenance (since the King has no private revenue to meet the expenditure) are lacking. All three objections can only be overcome by legislation, which must first affect the provision in the Bill of Rights. There was, and is, no doubt that a permanent army is required for national security. For a long while the first two legal objections were overcome by a *Mutiny Acts.* succession of Mutiny Acts, the first of which was passed some time previous to the Bill of Rights in 1689. These Acts served the double purpose of legalising for a fixed period, by convention one year only, the keeping of permanent land forces by the Crown and of providing codes of rules, over and above the ordinary law, for enforcing discipline in their ranks. From 1713 to 1879 there was no break in these Acts. In 1879 military law was codified in a single

enactment, subsequently replaced by the Army Act, 1881. Army Act,
This code is continued in force from year to year by an Army and
annual Act, known as the Army (Annual) Act, instead of the Air Force
Mutiny Act, the necessity for which still remains, in order to Acts.
suspend for the time being the unrepealed provision of the
Bill of Rights. The Preamble to this annual Act expressly
fixes the maximum numbers of the land forces, other than
the Marines. Since the constitution of a separate Air Force
in 1917 the Act has been entitled the Army and Air Force
(Annual) Act, its application to the new force bringing it
under the same parliamentary control as the Army.[1] The
Annual Act from time to time effects amendments to military
law in the Army Act, 1881, which since 1917 also applies
with variations to the Air Force. The Royal Marines, a
force of infantry and artillery, are enrolled and maintained
by the Admiralty and only come under the Army Act when
not serving on board ship ; hence their number is not fixed
by the Annual Act.

The Preamble of the Annual Act is as follows :—

> Whereas the raising or keeping of a standing army within
> the United Kingdom in time of peace, unless it be with the
> consent of Parliament, is against law :
>
> And whereas it is adjudged necessary by His Majesty and
> this present Parliament that a body of land forces should be
> continued for the safety of the United Kingdom and the
> defence of the possessions of His Majesty's Crown, and that
> the whole number of such forces should consist of one
> hundred and forty-eight thousand nine hundred, including
> those to be employed at the depots in the United Kingdom
> for the training of recruits for service at home and abroad,
> but exclusive of the numbers actually serving within His
> Majesty's Indian possessions, other than Aden :
>
> And whereas under the Air Force (Constitution) Act, 1917, 7 & 8
> His Majesty is entitled to raise and maintain the air force, Geo. 5,
> and it is judged necessary that the whole number of such force c. 51.
> should consist of thirty-two thousand, including those em-
> ployed as aforesaid, but exclusive of the numbers serving as
> aforesaid :
>
> And whereas it is also judged necessary for the safety of
> the United Kingdom, and the defence of the possessions of

---

[1] For 1929-30 the numbers of the Regular Army were fixed at
150,050, excluding troops serving within His Majesty's Indian possessions ; the Air Force figure was 32,000.

this realm, that a body of Royal Marine forces should be employed in His Majesty's fleet and naval service, under the direction of the Lord High Admiral of the United Kingdom, or the Commissioners for executing the office of Lord High Admiral aforesaid :

And whereas the said marine forces may frequently be quartered or be on shore, or sent to do duty or be on board transport ships or vessels, merchant ships or vessels, or other ships or vessels, or they may be under other circumstances in which they will not be subject to the laws relating to the government of His Majesty's forces by sea :

And whereas no man can be forejudged of life or limb, or subjected in time of peace to any kind of punishment within this realm, by martial law, or in any other manner than by the judgment of his peers and according to the known and established laws of this realm ; yet, nevertheless, it being requisite, for the retaining all the before-mentioned forces, and other persons subject to military law or to the Air Force Act, in their duty, that an exact discipline be observed and that persons belonging to the said forces who mutiny, or stir up sedition, or desert His Majesty's service, or are guilty of crimes and offences to the prejudice of good order and military or air force discipline, be brought to a more exemplary and speedy punishment than the usual forms of the law will allow :

And whereas the Army Act and the Air Force Act will expire in the year one thousand nine hundred and thirty on the following days :—

(*a*) In Great Britain and Ireland, the Channel Islands, and the Isle of Man, on the thirtieth day of April ; and

(*b*) Elsewhere, whether within or without His Majesty's dominions, on the thirty-first day of July :

Be it therefore enacted by the King's most Excellent Majesty, by and with the advice and consent of the Lords Spiritual and Temporal, and Commons, in this present Parliament assembled, and by the authority of the same, as follows :—

The operative sections (1) specify the period during which the Army Act, 1881, and the Air Force Act, 1917, are to remain in force, (2) apply the Acts to persons subject to Military and Air Force law, (3) fix billeting rates, (4) make any amendments to the Acts.

Since the cost of the Forces is met exclusively out of public funds, Parliament has a further control through scrutiny of the estimates and the consequent votes of supply each year.

Terms of Service : (*a*) Rank and File. So far as the rank and file are concerned, the troops are recruited by voluntary enlistment for varying fixed periods of service, with liability to serve anywhere within or without the realm. Compulsory service, which until recently was probably enforceable for home service only in the now extinct Militia,[1] the successor of the National Levy, can only be legalised by Parliament. Conscription for general military service was, however, imposed at a somewhat advanced stage of the War of 1914-18 by the Military Service Acts, 1916. The Acts have now expired. Enlistment, which is accompanied by attestation before a justice of the peace, is on stated terms, which may be varied afterwards by the Crown, but can never be enforced by the soldier in a court of law. Service in the Forces is a species of unilateral agreement; in this respect it resembles all government service, which is liable to be terminated at pleasure by the Crown. Payment for military service can never be enforced either by action or Petition of Right; *Leaman* v. *The King* [1920], 3 K.B. 663.

Officers, in all branches of the Forces, are appointed by (*b*) Officers. the King's Commission. They cannot resign or retire without leave, though they are usually in peace time permitted to retire at their own request; *The Queen* v. *Cuming, ex parte Hall* (1887), 19 Q.B.D. 13. They, too, are liable to be discharged at the pleasure of the Crown.

All ranks of the Regular Army, whilst actively employed, are subject to military law; it is somewhat unfortunate that the Preamble to the annual Act still speaks of this as " martial law." This liability applies to the soldier whether he is serving at home or overseas, including service in India.

A large part of the British Regular Army is employed in British India; the number of these troops is excluded from the total Army in India. authorised by the Preamble to the Army and Air Force (Annual) Act. The control of these troops is vested in the Government of India. The Commander-in-Chief in India is always a member of the Governor-General's Council.

The Indian Army is recruited from native sources. The Indian officers are partly non-Indian British subjects, partly natives Army. of India. Until recently an Indian could not attain any but

---

[1] This force was disbanded in 1908, its place being taken by the Special Reserve, which in 1921 was renamed the Militia (see below).

distinctive subordinate rank, but the policy of Indianisation of all government services is being extended to the Army. Indian military law is promulgated by the Governor-General in Council ; it applies to all natives of India who are members of the Indian Army. The non-Indian British officers come under the Army Act. Both the Indian Army and the British Army in India are maintained out of Indian revenue. It is doubtful, having regard to the exclusion from the numbers fixed by the Army and Air Force (Annual) Act of both these forces, whether without parliamentary sanction they could be employed outside India in time of peace. In this connection it must be observed that persons subject to military law are not exempt therefrom by reason of the statutory maximum being exceeded, while the Government of India Act, 1915, provides that, except in cases of invasion, the expenses of any expedition carried on outside the frontiers of India cannot be defrayed out of Indian revenues without the consent of both Houses of the British Parliament.

Dominion Military Forces.
Each of the Self-Governing Dominions has its own Military and Air Forces, and they should in part be classified as Regular Forces, though none of them can be regarded as standing armies. Their permanent organisation is, broadly speaking, on a skeleton footing, providing for rapid expansion in time of war or other emergency. They are part of the Forces of the Crown, but their organisation, discipline, and employment are exclusively under the control of their respective governments. All legislation affecting them is enacted by the Dominion Parliaments. During 1914-19 all the Self-Governing Dominions, as well as India, contributed their own armies or smaller units for service in the various arenas of war.

Reserve Forces. Army Reserve.
The Army Reserve consists of ex-Regular soldiers who are liable, for a fixed number of years after their period of service has expired, to be called up for annual training and for general service in the Regular Army in the event of war or other emergency. Officers are also normally liable to recall until they attain a given age, which varies with their rank.

Militia.
The Militia has no direct connection with the old county force which existed from the seventeenth century and

before that in the form of the National Levy, until 1908, when it was disbanded. The new force was from its creation by the Territorial and Reserve Forces Act, 1907, entitled the Special Reserve. But in 1921 it was re-named the Militia by the Territorial Army and Militia Act of that year. (The same Act repealed the various statutory provisions empowering the raising of Militia, the old force disbanded in 1908.) It is at present in a state of suspended animation, but the organisation still exists on paper. The infantry units of this new Militia are stationed at the regimental depots. In 1924 Supplementary a new force, designated the Supplementary Reserve, was Reserve. formed under the Reserve Forces Act, 1882, and the 1907 Act. This force in law ranks as Militia.

Although one class of the Army Reserve proper (Class A) is liable to be called up without Royal Proclamation, the issue of such Proclamation calling up the Reserves is one of the first steps taken to indicate that in the opinion of the Government a national crisis has arisen. All branches are liable for general service at home or abroad, and, when called to the colours, become subject to military law.

The Territorial Army forms the second line of defence and, Territorial in the event of the Regular Army being sent abroad as an Army. Expeditionary Force, it is the only defence force available. Until 1907 its place was filled by the Volunteers, which as the name implies were an unpaid body of troops (as is the Territorial Army) ; various statutes dating from 1863, which remain unrepealed, governed their service. Their organisation was purely local. Mounted volunteer troops, known as Yeomanry, were recognised by statute in 1804. The Territorial and Reserve Forces Act, 1907, embodied an important part of the Army reforms associated with the name of one of the greatest War Ministers, Lord Haldane. By this Act the Volunteers and Yeomanry became units in the Territorial Force (re-named the Territorial Army in 1921), organised by counties and comprising an establishment (of fourteen infantry divisions, besides other arms) far larger than that of the Regular Army of six or seven divisions. Originally there was no liability to serve outside the United Kingdom, unless such service had been voluntarily undertaken. But since

1920 all members of the Territorial Army are required to accept liability to serve overseas, so that the Territorial Army is liable for general service, provided that an Act of Parliament is passed expressly authorising its despatch overseas. Every member of this force is required to undergo annual training. This force is put on active service footing by " embodiment " ; this may take place on the Army Reserve being called out by Royal Proclamation. During training and embodiment, as well as on certain other occasions, the Territorial soldier is subject to military law and receives the pay and allowances appropriate to his rank.

C.

Composition and Discipline of the Other Forces.

Royal Marines.
This force of infantry and artillery forms part of the Regular Forces and is liable for general service on board ship and on shore. Although it is raised and maintained by the Admiralty for naval service, its discipline and regulation when employed on shore is provided for by the Army Act with some modifications. When on board one of H.M. ships a marine comes under the Naval Discipline Acts. The Army and Air Force (Annual) Act sanctions the Marines as a standing land force, but does not restrict their number.

The Royal Navy.
The Navy is the senior branch of the Forces, but its constitutional interest is less. Unlike the Army, the Navy did not in former times come under the suspicion of Parliament. There is no reason to suppose that naval service was regarded as less burdensome than service in the Army, nor that naval discipline could be enforced without interfering with the common law rights of the sailor as citizen. But the Navy had never been used by the King to coerce Parliament and so was not included in the prohibition against a standing armed force in the Bill of Rights. It has remained a prerogative force maintained on a standing footing. So much is this so that the recruitment of the Navy by impressment has never been declared illegal, though the press-gang has, of course, long fallen into disuse.

Enlistment is governed by the Naval Enlistment Acts, 1853 to 1884, discipline by the Naval Discipline Acts, 1866 and 1884. Both types of enactment are permanent and do not come under review annually by Parliament for renewal. Conditions of service and regulations for discipline so closely resemble those applicable to the Army and Air Force that they do not call for separate discussion. Despite its prerogative nature it must not be supposed that the Navy is not under the control of Parliament, since its requirements come under annual review in the estimates presented to Parliament and the consequential votes in Committee of Supply afford full opportunity for discussion of naval administration and expenditure, which on account of constructional requirements is highly controversial.

This force consists of two main divisions : the Royal Naval Reserve, recruited from members of the Mercantile Marine ; and the Royal Naval Volunteer Reserve. Seamen of the Navy in receipt of pensions are liable to recall in certain circumstances for a further period of not more than five years' service. *Naval Reserve.*

Naval forces, under the control of their own Parliaments for all purposes, including discipline, except when lent to the Royal Navy, are maintained by three of the Dominions, Australia, Canada, and New Zealand. *Dominion Navies.*

This is a comparatively small force, in course of formation, largely for the purpose of replacing the Royal Indian Marine for survey and police purposes. It is subject to the Governor-General of India in Council. *Royal Indian Navy.*

The Royal Air Force is the Regular part of this arm. It was constituted a separate force by the Air Force (Constitution) Act, 1917, which applies the Army Act, 1881, and like that Act requires annual renewal by Parliament. Except as regards executive control the Air Force does not call for separate notice. *Royal Air Force.*

The Air Force Reserve and the Auxiliary Air Force, created by an Act of 1924, correspond respectively to the Army Reserve and the Territorial Army.

D.

Executive Control of the Forces.

Royal Pre-
rogative. The Royal Prerogative in relation to the command of the Forces is still largely uncontrolled by statute. Even in relation to the Army (and the Air Force), to which the Army Act applies, the Prerogative is all important as regards administration and the movement of troops. This branch of the Prerogative is exercised through civilian Cabinet Ministers at the head of Government Departments, composed partly of service members and partly of civilians. The First Lord of the Admiralty is responsible to Parliament and to the King for the Navy and is the political chief of the Board of Admiralty. The Army is administered by the Secretary of State for War at the head of the War Office. Another Secretary of State is at the head of the Air Ministry. The King is, however, technically the Commander-in-Chief of all the Forces of the Crown.

Admiralty. The Board of Admiralty represents an office, that of the Lord High Admiral, entrusted by Letters Patent to Commissioners. The composition of the Board, which has varied from time to time since the office was permanently put into commission in 1713, is now fixed by Order in Council. It consists of the following members, styled Lords of the Admiralty, or Lords Commissioners :—

> The First Lord of the Admiralty (President),
> The Four Sea Lords, each responsible for separate branches of naval organisation,
> The Civil Lord,

assisted by the Parliamentary and Financial Secretaries, who, like the First Lord and the Civil Lord, sit in Parliament, and the Permanent Secretary, who is the chief civil servant in the Department. Nominally the First Lord is on an equality with his colleagues, but Orders in Council have made him directly responsible to both the King and Parliament, the other members of the Board being responsible to him for matters assigned to them. Moreover, as a member of the Cabinet, the First Lord has an advantage over his colleagues in the event of disagreement.

No Government Department has had a more chequered War Office. career than the War Office. The present organisation, in substance, dates from 1904, when the Army Council was established by Letters Patent. The composition of the Council follows closely that of the Board of Admiralty, and since 1924 has consisted of :—

> The Secretary of State for War (President),
> The Four Military Members, each responsible for technical business relating to the Army,
> The Under-Secretary of State and the Financial Secretary (ministerial appointments),

together with a Permanent Secretary, who is also the Secretary to the War Office.

There is a separate system of administration for the Territorial Army, whereby certain, but not all, duties of administration and organisation are transferred or assigned, in conformity with Army Council plans, by the Secretary of State to county associations. By this means the county basis of the Territorial Army is maintained. The President of each county association is the Lord-Lieutenant.

Territorial Army Associations.

The Air Council is modelled on similar lines to the Army Council :—

Air Ministry.

> The Secretary of State for Air (President),
> The Three Air Force Members,
> The Under-Secretary of State,

together with the Permanent Secretary.

The co-ordination of defence problems through the Committee of Imperial Defence, on which the Ministers and the Chief of Staff of each branch of the Forces sit, has been dealt with in Part IV., Chap. III. There is no Ministry of Defence combining all services, as in many countries.

Certain civilian matters are allotted to the Service Departments : Civil Aviation and the Meteorological Office under the Air Ministry ; the Coastguard Service, however, is under the Board of Trade, and not the Admiralty.

CHAPTER II.

MILITARY LAW AND COURTS-MARTIAL.

A.

Military Law.

MILITARY law is contained in the Army Act, 1881, and the Acts relating to the Auxiliary and Reserve Forces (subject to subsequent amendment), supplemented by rules of procedure, by King's Regulations and other regulations, by Royal Warrant, *e.g.*, as to pay and promotion and by Army Orders. An Army cannot be disciplined by the ordinary law applicable to civilians. Any association of individuals organised for the achievement of a particular object is bound to lay down certain rules by which the members agree to be bound on joining. In the case of a " members' " club these rules are purely contractual and in no way conflict with the ordinary law of the land, to which, of course, all the members remain subject. In the case of the learned professions, particularly the law and medicine, the special rules are to a large extent impressed with the authority of the State, being sanctioned by Parliament and enforceable in courts of justice. With the Armed Forces of the Crown the position is similar in that the sanction of Parliament is required for the more stringent provisions, supplementing common law duties and essential for preserving military discipline ; but the courts through the prerogative writs only play the part of supervisors of the special military tribunals which are established by the Army Act for adjudication upon offences against military law. Prior to 1879 military law in time of peace consisted of those rules sanctioned each year by the Mutiny Act. From 1715 the form of the statute was to implement the prerogative right, exercisable in time of war only, to make articles of war, by extending the right to time of peace. By the provision of a code of rules, governing both peace and war, in the Army Act, 1881, all important changes are now brought under review by Parliament annually when it reviews the code for another twelve months with necessary amendments by the Army and Air Force (Annual) Act. But there is still power for the Crown to promulgate articles of war. Such regulations must be judicially noticed, but may not inflict capital punishment or penal servitude, except with regard to crimes made so punishable by the Army Act, nor punish any crimes made offences by the Act, save as therein prescribed.[1] There is also power to make rules of procedure for the administration of military law. These latter rules must be laid before Parliament.

It is unnecessary to give a detailed account of military law. A few illustrations will serve to explain how its substantive provisions differ from the Common Law.

(1) Desertion is a serious offence, whenever committed. At Common Law desertion would normally be equivalent to a breach of a contract of employment redressable by an action for damages. This remedy would be of little use for the purpose of keeping a reluctant soldier in the service against his will.

(2) Conduct prejudicial to good order and military discipline is a specific offence. There is no equivalent in Common Law.

(3) The relation between the various ranks of the Army is governed by military law. Otherwise no commanding officer could compel his officers or men to perform any duty, since there is no contract of employment between him and those under his command.

The Army Act regulates the constitution and proceedings Military of tribunals for the enforcement of military law. These Tribunals. tribunals are called Courts-Martial. Their jurisdiction is exclusively over persons subject to military law.

---

[1] Army Act, 1881, s. 69. No articles of war are at present in force.

Forms of Court-Martial. The following are the usual forms of Court-Martial : [1]

A *General Court-Martial* can try any offence under the Army Act, whether committed by an officer or a member of the rank and file.

A *District Court-Martial* cannot try an officer or award the punishments of death or penal servitude ; otherwise any offence under the Act is within its jurisdiction.

A *Field-General Court-Martial* is for the trial of offences committed by troops on active service, or when overseas for offences committed against the local inhabitants, where a General Court-Martial is not practicable.

Summary Jurisdiction. A Commanding Officer has a statutory jurisdiction to deal with minor offences in a summary way, subject to the offender's right to elect to be tried by court-martial, if the award involves forfeiture of pay or any punishment other than a minor regimental one.[2]

No Right of Appeal. A person sentenced by a court-martial may complain by petition to a higher authority, but there is no right of appeal to a higher military tribunal before which the case can be argued on its merits. Independently of petitions the proceedings of courts-martial are reviewed in the office of the Judge Advocate-General in order to detect any miscarriage of justice. Sentences must be confirmed by a competent higher military authority ; there is no power to increase the sentence recommended by the court.

Relation of Courts-Martial to Civil Courts. Courts-martial, are, however, limited to the powers conferred on them by statute, and an excess of jurisdiction may be questioned by an application to the Divisional Court of the King's Bench Division for one of the prerogative writs of Habeas Corpus, Certiorari or Prohibition. There is no doubt that the writ of Certiorari lies, at the discretion of the High Court, to inferior courts which are shown, not merely to have exceeded their jurisdiction, but to have failed to observe the principles of natural justice. Yet the High

---

[1] The Tribunals, also called Courts-Martial, for the trial of offences by members of the Royal Navy and Royal Air Force do not call for separate treatment.

[2] The Army Act, 1881, also provided for Regimental Courts-Martial, these were abolished by the Army and Air Force (Annual) Act, 1920, s. 5.

Court has shown itself disinclined to interfere with the decision of military tribunals solely on the ground that matters properly cognisable by such tribunals in the ordinary course of military discipline have been decided against the accused person maliciously or without reasonable and probable cause. This reluctance has been exhibited when the prejudicial act of military discipline complained of resulted in civil proceedings for libel being brought by a subordinate officer against his commanding officer; *Dawkins* v. *Paulet* (1869), L.R. 5 Q.B.D. 94; K. & L. 341. But if the military court has exceeded its jurisdiction by applying military law to persons not subject to that law, as in *Wolfe Tone's Case* (1798), 27 St. Tr. 614, or, in the case of persons so subject, misapplying military law by punishing without regular trial or inflicting a punishment in excess of its jurisdiction, the prerogative writs afford a means of reviewing the case, and the officers concerned will be liable to an action for damages, or criminal proceedings for assault, manslaughter or even murder. These conclusions are stated with some hesitation as on the authorities [1] no clear distinction can be drawn between acts done in abuse of military authority (malice or lack of reasonable and probable cause), and acts done in excess of jurisdiction.

B.

Status of Members of the Forces.

A person subject to military law does not cease to be subject to the ordinary law. The position of a member of the Royal Navy or Air Force is similar. Except so far as the statutes creating military law provide, he enjoys all the rights of the ordinary citizen and his obligations as a soldier imposed by the Army Act and King's Regulations are in addition to his duties as a citizen. In practice all serious crimes of soldiers are dealt with in peace time by the civil courts, but offences against the ordinary law committed by a person subject to

[1] See K. & L., pp. 336-340.

Ordinary
Offences
triable by
Court-
Martial.

military law are triable by court-martial, with the exception of certain serious felonies, such as murder, which must, if committed in the United Kingdom, be tried by the competent civil court (the Assizes or the Central Criminal Court); if such felonies are committed outside the United Kingdom, they are not triable by court-martial, unless committed on active service or more than one hundred miles from a competent civil court. The Jurisdiction in Homicides Act, 1862, provides for the removal of the trial of a person subject to military law who is accused of murder or manslaughter to the Central Criminal Court. Application is made to the King's Bench Division by the Secretary of State (for War or Air), if he considers that in the interests of good order and military discipline the trial should be expedited by the removal to London. Thus the criminal law reaches persons subject to military law in places beyond the ordinary jurisdiction of the courts and it may be administered by court-martial in places within and without the jurisdiction of the ordinary courts.

Persons
subject to
Military
Law triable
by Ordinary
Courts.

Equally, a person subject to military law may be tried by any competent civil court for the offences for which he would be liable if he were not subject to military law. He enjoys, however, the benefit of certain privileges and exemptions from the ordinary civil law and its processes. He is entitled to vote at parliamentary elections by post as an " absent voter." When on active service he can make a will in nuncupatory form without complying with the formalities of the Wills Act, 1837, even if he be a minor. Unless he is charged with a felony or misdemeanour, or a civil claim against him exceeds £30, he cannot be taken out of the service of the Crown by being compelled to attend the civil court, nor can his person be put under restraint by any form of execution.

Dual
liability.

A person subject to military law, though sentenced or acquitted by court-martial, may afterwards be tried by a civil court, if the offence is one triable under the ordinary law. The sentence of the court-martial must be taken into consideration by the civil court in awarding punishment.

A person acquitted by a civil court is not liable to be tried by court-martial in respect of the same offence.

It is sometimes alleged that obedience to military law may be in conflict with a soldier's duty as an ordinary citizen. Military law is, however, part of the statute law and obedience to it cannot be unlawful. On the other hand a soldier is required by military law to obey the commands of his superior officer. This obligation only extends to lawful commands and a soldier is not liable in military law for disobeying an unlawful order. But how is the soldier to judge the lawful character of the order? He has not the time to weigh up its merits, even if he had the inclination. His training makes compliance instinctive. Unlawful injury inflicted as a result of such compliance renders him liable to criminal and civil proceedings. He cannot plead obedience to the orders of his military superior, because no such defence is accepted by a civil court. If the order of the superior is in the soldier's opinion unlawful, he disobeys it at the peril of being court-martialled for a serious military offence and runs the risk of the court-martial not accepting his view of the orders' unlawful character. Moreover, unless the order is wholly unreasonable, it would prejudice military discipline if strict compliance were not enforced by military law. A soldier, therefore, ought to obey orders at the peril of civil proceedings being instituted against him for the resulting act. If such proceedings result from obedience to the order, there is some authority for saying that, if the order was not necessarily or manifestly illegal, he cannot be made criminally liable. In *Keighley* v. *Bell* (1866), 4 F. & F. at p. 790, this opinion is expressed *obiter* by no less authority than Willes, J.; it has been followed by a special tribunal in South Africa.[1] It is argued that this defence, if it be available, is not a serious danger to civil liberty, but the employment of troops in time of civil disorder might lead to criminal proceedings in which a jury would take a different view and convict a soldier who had obeyed an order resulting in injury to a civilian, but not

Conflict of Duty.

[1] See K. & L., p. 348.

appearing to the accused necessarily or manifestly illegal. The question is, perhaps, somewhat academic, since the Court of Criminal Appeal would be open to the defendant ; from the sentence of a court-martial' which would result from disobeying the order there is no right of appeal to a higher tribunal, other than by way of petition.

CHAPTER III.

MARTIAL LAW.[1]

MARTIAL LAW must be carefully distinguished from military law, which is statutory. The term, Martial Law, describes (i) a certain state of relations between the military and the civil authorities in time of serious emergency; and (ii) it is also used of the powers exercised by military commanders in the field. We are not immediately concerned with the second meaning. What is done by a commander-in-chief in occupation of foreign territory is not a matter for the civil courts of his own country; it is governed by the International Law rules of warfare to a large extent.

It is exclusively in the first sense of the term that martial law will be discussed in this chapter. Its nature cannot be defined with accuracy. The particular state of relations between military and civil authorities has not arisen in this country since the Civil War of the seventeenth century, and there is only one decision on martial law which is directly binding on an English court. The House of Lords in *Re Clifford and O'Sullivan* [1921], 2 A.C. 570 (a case from Ireland before the establishment of the Irish Free State), discussed an application for the prerogative writ of Prohibition to stay proceedings of a military tribunal set up after a proclamation of martial law. The decision turned upon the technical scope of the writ, which is only available against persons or bodies in the nature of inferior courts exercising a jurisdiction. It was held that the military tribunal in question was not such a body, but only an

---

[1] The reader is referred to the passage dealing with the Maintenance of Order (Emergency Powers Act, 1920) in Part VII., Chap. I. D., above).

advisory committee of officers to assist the commander-in-chief, against which the writ could not lie. The Law Lords expressly refrained from discussing the merits of an application under a writ of Habeas Corpus or other process than Prohibition.

Effect of an Emergency.   It is not easy to state the precise legal effect of an emergency. Measures like the Defence of the Realm Acts, 1914-15, and the Emergency Powers Act, 1920,[1] are enacted so as to remove as far as possible the actions of the Executive at such a time from the scrutiny of the courts. But at Common Law, apart from statute, just as the plea of necessity is accepted as justifying an injurious act done in self-defence of person or property, so necessity justifies acts of the Executive, provided they are shown to be required in the interests of the public safety. Every subject has the right to repel force by force in certain circumstances; every subject is under a duty to assist in preserving the peace if called upon to do so ; *Regina* v. *Brown* (1841), Car & M., 314 ; K. & L. 364 ; so the Executive with organised and powerful military forces at its disposal may, even at Common Law, take the law into its own hands. When such a state of affairs has arisen, there is probably a state of martial law, irrespective of a proclamation to that effect. If this be so, it is not the proclamation which makes martial law, but the events which have created the emergency. Subjects have the right to question any act of the Executive in the courts, which can decide whether or not a state of martial law exists. A proclamation may be evidence of such a state being already in existence, but it cannot change existing conditions from a peace-time footing to one of war within the realm. The Prerogative of declaring war does not enable the Crown to declare war on the people. But the Executive has a common law duty, which it shares with every subject, to assist in the maintenance of order. If it is compelled in the exercise of this duty to hand over control to the military forces, it acts at its own risk as regards legal responsibility, and there is a state of martial law, not law in the sense of a code of rules, but a condition of affairs.

[1] Part VII., Chap. I. D.

The next question is to determine what degree of emer- When does an Emergency constitute Martial Law. gency constitutes a state of martial law ? Clearly in any true emergency the authorities may have to act without regard to their strict legal powers, since perils to the public safety cannot always be suppressed by prosecuting under the criminal law or applying for an injunction in the civil courts. If the civil courts have on account of hostilities ceased to sit for the time being, the maintenance of order passes from the civil power to the military. The military can, it may safely be asserted, then take control. What is necessary in such a situation is clearly more a matter of discretion for the commander-in-chief and his advisers, though even so, when the courts are again able to sit, the acts of the military may be shown to be illegal as having been in excess of necessity. Much has been written as to whether the test in such cases would be strict necessity or *bonâ fide* belief in the necessity of the action, and as to whether it would be for the defendant to show that the test had been complied with or for the complainant to show that it had not been complied with. There is no authority which makes it possible to answer these questions. Supposing that the courts have not ceased entirely to operate, as where the insurrection is confined to part of the country, there is authority for the legality of military government. Martial law is thus a state of fact not to be decided by the simple test : Were the civil courts sitting at the time ? The test would seem to be : Is the insurrection still of a kind that military rule is justified ? It falls to the civil courts alone to determine this difficult question of fact.

This leads to a further problem. In so far as the civil Control of Military by Civil Courts. courts may be sitting, what control, if any, have they over the acts of the military ? In *Marais* v. *General Officer Commanding* [1902], A.C. 109; K. & L. 383, the Privy Council held that such acts are not justiciable by the ordinary courts sitting in a martial law area where " war is still raging." Once a state of war is recognised by the courts, and such recognition in the nature of things must be *ex post facto*, the Executive, with the aid of its military forces, may conduct warlike operations with impunity. They may deal with the inhabitants of a martial law area on the same footing as with the population of hostile invaded territory in time of war, subject only, it may be presumed, to such rules of warfare as International Law prescribes. It is difficult to say how far the military authorities could be called to account in the civil courts after hostilities, because an Act of Indemnity in the ordinary course would be passed by Parliament to protect them from legal proceedings. Probably such an Act would not indemnify them for acts done otherwise than in the course of *bonâ fide* operations for the suppression of the insurrection.

The *Marais Case* was followed by the Irish Courts in 1920-21. At that time the Restoration of Order in Ireland Act, 1920, was in force. That Act gave exceptional powers to the Executive, and the military were employed to execute those powers. In *Rex* v. *Allen* [1921], 2 I.R. 241 ; K. & L. 389, the King's Bench Division of Ireland accepted the statement of the military authority that the statutory powers were insufficient and declined to interfere with a sentence passed by a military tribunal (not being a statutory court-martial) sitting in an area where the rebellion was raging. In one case the statutory powers were exceeded and the prisoner released as the result of Habeas Corpus proceedings ; *Egan* v. *Macready* [1921], 1 I.R. 265. The decision of the Irish Chancery Division in the last-named case is difficult to reconcile with *Rex* v. *Allen* and has been criticised on the ground that the exceptional statutory powers were not, like the prerogative statutory powers in the *De Keyser Case*, exclusive of the common law powers, and that the Common Law gives the Executive the right to conduct operations without interference from the courts, if a state of war is raging.

Conclusion. Thus the law, if it be correctly stated above, affords little protection to persons in a martial law area who have, at all events, been convicted of " capital offences " under the military régime. If the courts are not sitting, they have no remedy. If the courts are in session, the writ of Prohibition, according to the decision in the *Clifford and O'Sullivan Case*, will not lie ; while the writ of Habeas

Corpus is only available provided that the courts hold that war was not raging at the time of the commission of the offence (*Rex* v. *Allen*, above).

Although the military obtained, under the Defence of the The United Realm Acts, 1914-15, a large measure of control in the Kingdom in United Kingdom and in Ireland, it cannot be claimed, apart 1914-18. from the Irish disturbances, that at any time a state of war was raging, despite hostilities by way of occasional enemy air-raids and bombardments from the sea. The control exercised during that period over the civilian population was strictly legal, while the courts were exercising, under certain statutory restrictions, their full functions. Both civil and military authorities exceeded their legal powers from time to time, and there are many illustrations of the courts intervening at the instance of persons aggrieved. It is of interest to reproduce here the main operative section of the Indemnity Act, 1920, which, subject to certain provisos, expressly restricts the indemnity afforded to the authorities to acts done in good faith and in the public interest.

No action or other legal proceeding whatsoever, whether Indemnity civil or criminal, shall be instituted in any court of law for Act, 1920, or on account of or in respect of any act, matter or thing done, s. 1 (1). whether within or without His Majesty's dominions, during the war before the passing of this Act, if done in good faith, and done or purported to be done in the execution of his duty or for the defence of the realm or the public safety, or for the enforcement of discipline, or otherwise in the public interest, by a person holding office under or employed in the service of the Crown in any capacity, whether naval, military, air force, or civil, or by any other person acting under the authority of a person so holding office or so employed : and, if any such proceeding has been instituted whether before or after the passing of this Act, it shall be discharged and made void . . . .

The *Law Quarterly Review*, Vol. XVIII., contains four articles on this difficult subject at pp. 117, 133, 143 and 152.

PART IX.

THE BRITISH COMMONWEALTH.

The Sovereignty of the British Dominions, by A. Berriedale Keith (Macmillans).

The Colonial Service, by Sir Anton Bertram (Cambridge University Pess).

Constitutional Laws of the British Empire, by L. le M. Minty (Sweet & Maxwell).

Responsible Government in the Dominions, by A. Berriedale Keith (Clarendon Press)—for reference.

Imperial Conference, 1926.   Summary of Proceedings (Stationery Office, 1926, Cmd. 2768).

Imperial Conference, 1930.   Summary of Proceedings (Stationery Office, 1930, Cmd. 3717).

Report of Conference on the Operation of Dominion Legislation and Merchant Shipping Legislation (Stationery Office, 1930, Cmd. 3479).

CHAPTER I.

THE BRITISH COMMONWEALTH.

A.

The British Isles.

ENGLAND and Wales, Scotland and Northern Ireland form the United Kingdom of Great Britain and Northern Ireland. Scotland possesses her own system of law, her own courts and her own established church, but is united with England and Wales for purposes of government (other than local government) and legislation. The position of Northern Ireland is unique. In 1921 Southern Ireland separated by agreement from the United Kingdom and became a Dominion, the Irish Free State. It was originally intended that Ireland should gain a wide measure of Home Rule, while remaining part of the United Kingdom. Though abandoned as far as Southern Ireland was concerned, the Constitution framed with this intention came into force in Northern Ireland (Ulster).[1] Northern Ireland possesses her own Executive, a Governor-General, appointed by the Crown, and a Cabinet, and a Legislature consisting of a Senate and House of Commons. She has also retained representation in the Parliament of the United Kingdom. Certain subjects, e.g., defence, foreign trade, coinage, are reserved for the United Kingdom Government and Parliament. From the Courts of Northern Ireland an appeal lies to the House of Lords.

The Channel Islands and the Isle of Man are included among the British Isles, but do not form part of the United Kingdom. The law of the Channel Islands is based on the ancient customs of the Duchy of Normandy, of which

[1] Government of Ireland Act, 1920.

they formed part until 1205. The sovereignty of His Majesty to the present day is only admitted in his right as Duke of Normandy. They are subject to the legislative supremacy of the United Kingdom Parliament, which is exercised for them in relation to such subjects as defence and customs. The legislative assemblies of Jersey and Guernsey, known as the States, have power to pass Acts which require the approval of the Crown in Council. The States of Guernsey legislate for the adjoining islands, Alderney, Sark, Herm and Jethou. The Channel Islands possess their own courts from which an appeal lies to the Judicial Committee of the Privy Council. The Crown claims the right to legislate for the Islands by Order in Council, but it is doubtful how far such Orders in Council, which are registered in the Royal Courts of the Islands, are effectual until so registered. The States and Royal Courts of Jersey and Guernsey are presided over by a Bailiff appointed by the Crown.

Isle of Man. The Isle of Man has its own Parliament, known as the Tynwald Court ; it consists of the Governor and Council and the House of Keys. There is a general power to legislate, subject to the approval of the Crown in Council. The Isle of Man also has its own courts, from which an appeal lies to the Judicial Committee of the Privy Council.

B.

The Commonwealth Overseas.

Classification.

The Parliament of the United Kingdom is the Imperial Parliament and possesses legal supremacy over all parts of the British Commonwealth. An Act of Parliament is never presumed to extend beyond the United Kingdom, unless apt words are expressly inserted. A Colony is defined by the **Definition** Interpretation Act, 1889, as " Any part of Her Majesty's **of Colony.** dominions exclusive of the British Isles and of British India." Omitting consideration of India and Protectorates and Mandated Territories, the dominions of the Crown fall naturally into two groups, the Self-Governing Dominions [1] and the Colonies. At the present time it is impossible, in strict theory of law, to draw a distinction between these two groups. In political reality there is, however, an immense distinction. The Self-Governing Dominions possess, while the Colonies do not possess, responsible government. Responsible government means government by an Executive; a Cabinet, which is, as in the United Kingdom, responsible to, and dismissible by, an elected legislature, which alone can impose taxes and without whose authority laws cannot be made. Moreover, by constitutional convention the Dominions are, while the Colonies are not, free in practice from all control by the Imperial Parliament and Government. [2]

Responsible Government in the Dominions rests, with one exception, as in the United Kingdom, not upon express law, but upon constitutional conventions. Though the Constitutions of Australia and South Africa provide that the Governor-General shall act on the advice of an Executive Council, there are no provisions requiring the Councils to consist of those commanding the confidence of the Legislature. In the Constitution of the Irish Free State it is expressly enacted that the Executive Council shall be responsible to the Dail Eireann, the Free State House of Commons. Responsible Government does not necessarily coincide with the possession of a wholly-elected legislature, for three Colonies, the Bahamas, Barbados and Bermudas have since the seventeenth century possessed wholly elected legislatures, but do not enjoy responsible government. Apart from these three Colonies, the grant of a representative legislature has usually marked the final stage in progress towards responsible government. A representative legislature, which means an assembly with a majority of elected

Responsible Government.

---

[1] Except where the context otherwise requires the word, Dominion, in the pages which follow, means Self-Governing Dominion.

[2] The distinction between the Dominions and Colonies will be given a legal basis should the recommendations of the Imperial Conference of 1930 be adopted, see Chap. II. The existing convention of non-interference is so established as to amount already almost to a distinction in law, in a wide sense of the word.

members, does not easily work in harmony with a nominated executive. Accordingly it soon becomes necessary either to grant responsible government or to abolish the representative legislature as being prematurely granted.

Settled and
Conquered
or Ceded
Colonies.

A distinction, legally valid and important in the sphere of private law, but politically and in the sphere of public law unimportant, is drawn between settled colonies and conquered or ceded colonies. Settlers carry with them the law of England, both the Common Law and, in so far as it is applicable, enacted law existing at the time of the settlement. The Crown cannot by virtue of the Prerogative legislate for or raise taxes in a settled colony by Order in Council. Either the powers of the Imperial Parliament must be invoked or the Crown may by the Prerogative establish a legislature within the colony. Conquered or ceded colonies preserve their own system of law, *e.g.*, Roman-Dutch law in South Africa, French law in Quebec, until the laws are changed or repealed. For such colonies the Crown may legislate by Order in Council. Once the Crown has granted a representative legislature to such a colony, the power to legislate and raise taxes by Order in Council has been irrevocably abandoned, unless, as is the almost invariable practice, the Order in Council which grants a legislature reserves the power to legislate by Order in Council and revoke the Constitution, if need should arise ; *Campbell* v. *Hall* (1774), Lofft 655 ; K. & L. 420. The distinction between these two types of colonies is of little political importance to-day ; for many conquered colonies have received grants of representative legislatures, while the Crown has been empowered by the British Settlements Act, 1887, to legislate for newly settled colonies.[1]

---

[1] In many cases too colonies have voluntarily surrendered their constitutions in order to obtain more efficient government. As recently as 1928 an Act of the Imperial Parliament empowered the Crown to create a new constitution for British Guiana by Order in Council.

C.

Colonial Constitutions.

Space does not permit a description of the various colonial constitutions. Variety and local individuality are chief features in our colonial system. The Colonies are in fact, as well as in theory, subject to the legislative supremacy of the Imperial Parliament, and to the right of the Crown acting on the advice of the Imperial Government to disallow their legislation. " The government of a Crown Colony consists of the direct personal rule of the Governor." The constitutions are derived from Letters Patent issued by the Crown in Council constituting the office of Governor and Instructions to the Governor. The Governor is responsible to the Imperial Parliament, and acts on instructions received from the Secretary of State for the Colonies through the Colonial Office. Though assisted by an Executive Council, the Governor may disregard its advice. The most important officers of a Colony under the Governor are the Colonial Secretary and the Attorney-General. The daily work of administration is performed by District Officers who, under varying names and forms, appear in almost all the regions ruled by the Colonial Office.

The Bahamas, Barbados and Bermuda are, by virtue of Legislatures. possessing representative (though not responsible) government, exempt from legislation by Order in Council, but other colonies are subject to such legislation. Gibraltar and St. Helena and some of the smallest colonies, have no legislative assembly. Some legislatures are nominated by the Crown, *e.g.*, in the Gold Coast and British Honduras ; in most colonies the legislature is partly elected, but has a nominated element with an official majority. There is infinite variety in the proportion of elected to nominated members, and official to unofficial nominated members. " The official majority is the very kernel and essence of Crown Colony Government." [1] By its means the Governor

---

[1] *The Colonial Service*, by Sir Anton Bertram, a book of absorbing interest, upon which the author has drawn.

controls his legislative assembly. The common feature of the constitutions is the Executive responsible to the Imperial Parliament, not to the local legislatures.

Indirect Rule.

The most interesting movement now proceeding in the Colonial Empire is the development of Indirect Rule. Indirect Rule means government through Native Chiefs. The District Officer acts, not as a direct administrator, but as an adviser. He may be compared with the Political Officers resident in the Native States of India. The theory and practice of Indirect Rule was first worked out in Nigeria by Lord Lugard.

Ceylon Report.

An entirely novel constitution is shortly to be introduced in Ceylon as the result of the Report of a Commission known as the Donoughmore Commission.[1] It is proposed that the government shall be in the hands not of the Governor, but of committees of the legislative assembly. The Governor's functions will be limited to veto and suspension. There will be no Colonial Secretary. The model which has provided inspiration for this proposed constitution is the London County Council. Its purpose is to avoid the divorce of executive from legislative responsibility.

East Africa.

It is in the Colonies that the constitutional experiments of the future will be made. The problem of East Africa, where native interests must be reconciled with the legitimate claims by white settlers to progressive self-government, must inevitably be productive of developments of first importance and interest. It is impossible in this book to do more than indicate a field for study and the practical applications of the principles of Constitutional Law.[2]

Malta and Southern Rhodesia.

Malta and Southern Rhodesia stand alone. They possess self-government, save for the reservation of certain subjects for the Imperial Government. Southern Rhodesia is under the Dominions, and not the Colonial, Office. Their constitu-

---

[1] Ceylon. Report of the Special Commission on the Constitution (1928, Cmd. 3131).

[2] Report of the Commission on Closer Union of the Dependencies in Eastern and Central Africa (Cmd. 3234, Jan. 1929) ; see also Report of Sir S. Wilson (Cmd. 3378, Oct. 1929) ; Memorandum on Native Policy in East Africa (Cmd. 3573) and White Paper on Closer Union in East Africa (Cmd. 3574, June 1930).

tions contain only limited powers of revocation and legislation by Order in Council. A recent constitutional crisis in Malta has necessitated the suspending of the Constitution. An ordinance to this effect was made by the Governor under a wide general power contained in Letters Patent of 1921, enabling the Governor to legislate on *inter alia* all matters " touching the public safety and defence of Our Empire and the general interests of Our Subjects not resident in Malta." The Maltese Courts expressed the view that this power did not enable the Governor to suspend the Constitution. To remove doubts Letters Patent were issued by the Crown in Council amending the already wide powers given by the original Letters Patent, under which the Governor purported to act.

A colonial Governor, though representing the King, is not immune from suits in the courts of his colony ; *Musgrave* v. *Pulido* (1879), 5 App. Cas. 102 ; K. & L. 457. He must justify his acts of State as being both within the general powers of the Crown in relation to subjects, and also within the special powers of his own Commission. It would seem that the Viceroy of India is immune from suits as being in a special sense the King's representative. Criminal prosecutions against colonial Governors are tried in the King's Bench Division. *(margin: Legal Liability of Governors.)*

In Appendix C there are reproduced in full the Letters Patent, Instructions and Governor's Commission for a colony (Fiji) with a partly elected legislature and the Kenya (Annexation) Order in Council, 1920. *(margin: Documents providing for Government of a Colony.)*

D.

Dominion Constitutions and Federalism.

The Self-governing Dominions are Canada, Australia, New Zealand, South Africa and the Irish Free State.[1] *(margin: Federalism.)*

[1] The Colony of Newfoundland possesses Dominion status in that it enjoys responsible government and non-interference by the Imperial Government. It is represented at Imperial Conferences on an equality with the Dominions, but is not, as the other Dominions, a separate member of the League of Nations. It will not be a " Dominion "

In order to understand the relations between the Dominions and the United Kingdom it is necessary to know something of the Dominion constitutions, and especially of the problems arising in federations.   In 1867 the Dominion of Canada was formed by a federation of the self-governing Provinces of Canada ; in 1900 there was formed the Commonwealth of Australia by a federation of the Australian States ; and in 1909 the four South African Colonies were united as the Union of South Africa.   Federation presupposes a desire for unity among independent states, which, though desiring unity for military, economic, or other purposes, nevertheless wish to preserve their identity and some measure of independence.   The constitution of a federation must be to a large degree a rigid constitution.   If it could be changed without the consent of the States forming the federation, there would be no safeguard for the preservation of State rights.   Powers must be distributed between the federal government and the governments of the several States forming the federation.   Some authority, normally the courts, must be able to prevent the federal government from usurping the powers of the States and the States from usurping the powers of the federal government.

Federalism and Sovereignty.   It follows that the legislature of a federal government cannot be supreme in the sense that the Imperial Parliament possesses supremacy.[1]   There must be constitutional laws which cannot be changed at the will of the federal legislature. There must be courts which can declare legislation void. In the British Dominions the great safeguards of the rights of the component parts of federations are the supremacy of the Imperial Parliament,[2] and in some cases the right of appeal on the *ultra vires* rule to the Judicial Committee of the Imperial Privy Council.   The Constitutions of the Dominions

The Courts in Federations.   depend upon Acts of the Imperial Parliament, and any violation of such Constitutions would be held invalid by the courts —either the courts of the Dominions or the Judicial Com-

within the meaning of the legislative changes proposed in the Statute of Westminster, 1931, by the Imperial Conference of 1930, but it is well understood that the Statute may be applied to it, see Chap. II.
    [1] Chap. II.   [2] *Ibid.*

mittee [1] on an appeal—as being repugnant to an Act of the Imperial Parliament. The most important constitutional function of the Supreme Court of Canada and the High Court of Australia is to declare invalid laws passed by either the Federal or Member State Legislatures which are *ultra vires* their constitutional powers. Just as the Supreme Court is the great safeguard of the Constitution in the United States, so are the Supreme Court of Canada and the High Court of Australia the great safeguards of federalism in these two Dominions. The legislative supremacy of the Imperial Parliament ensures that federal constitutions shall only be amended in accordance with the procedure for amendment laid down in such constitutions, but it is only through the courts that this legislative supremacy can be enforced. From the Supreme Court of Canada an appeal lies to the Privy Council, but no appeal lies from the High Court of Australia on constitutional matters.

(margin: Imperial Parliament and Federations.)

This safeguard of the legal supremacy of the Imperial Parliament is not merely the safeguard of a written constitution which, as in the United States, can only be amended with the consent of the States; for there is no available process, save an Act of the Imperial Parliament to enable the amendment of Sections 1 to 8 of the Commonwealth of Australia Act, 1900, which established federation in Australia, and there is no constitutional provision enabling Canada to amend the British North America Act, 1867, which established the Canadian Constitution.[2]

In the United States of America it has been laid down as a general principle that there may be no interference by the Federal Government with State Instrumentalities—the organs of State government—and no interference by the States with Federal Instrumentalities, *e.g.*, that a State may not tax the salary of a Federal Officer. No such general principle is recognised by the courts of the British Empire.

(margin: Federal Instrumentalities.)

[1] Chap. V.
[2] Thus during the Great War when the Dominion Government wished to prolong the duration of the Canadian Parliament, the necessary legislation was passed by the Imperial Parliament; British North America Act, 1916.

The point to be decided in each case is whether or not the power claimed is granted by the Act of Parliament in question.

Constitution of Canada.   The Dominion of Canada is a Federation of ten Provinces. Executive power is vested in the Governor-General, advised by a Privy Council nominated by him. The Governor-General acts on the advice of those members of the Privy Council who form the Cabinet and enjoy the confidence of the House of Commons. There is the same distinction between the formal Privy Council and the Cabinet as in England.[1] Legislative power is vested in the Governor-General, a Senate nominated by the Governor-General for life and an elected House of Commons. In both the Senate and the House of Commons the Provinces are represented, not by an equal number of members, but in proportion to their population, so that it cannot be said that either Chamber of the Legislature is constituted on a federal basis. There is, however, a certain concession to federalism in the provisions which enable the Governor-General, in the event of a deadlock between the two Chambers, to add to the Senate four or eight members corresponding to the four divisions of Canada. Each Province enjoys responsible government,

Provincial Government. and the Executive of each Province is vested in a Lieutenant-Governor, appointed by the Governor-General, and an Executive Council. Provincial Legislatures may, provided that they do not disturb the distribution of powers between the Dominion and the Provinces, alter their own Constitutions, except as regards the office of Lieutenant-Governor. The Governor-General has the right to veto provincial legislation, and such veto is exercised on the advice of Federal ministers. The Dominion Parliament has power over all matters not exclusively assigned to the Provinces. The Provincial Courts administer both dominion and provincial law, but general criminal law, as opposed to the passing of a law containing penal provisions to enforce provincial legislation, is reserved to the Dominion.

Constitution of Australia.   The Commonwealth of Australia is a federation of six States and possesses a more truly federal constitution than

---

[1] Part IV., Chaps. II. and III.

that of Canada. Executive power is vested in the Governor-General and an Executive Council (the Cabinet), which is responsible to a Legislature, consisting of an elected Senate and an elected House of Representatives. The House of Representatives is elected on a population basis, but the Senate consists of six members for each State, irrespective of population. In contrast to Canada, all powers not exclusively assigned to the Commonwealth Government are vested in the States. The Governors of the States have hitherto been appointed by the Crown on the advice of the Imperial Government. The High Court of Australia and the State Courts have separate jurisdictions, but the State Courts may by Act of the Commonwealth Parliament be compelled to administer Commonwealth law. There is a direct relation between the States and the Imperial Government in regard to the disallowance and reservation [1] of State legislation, and the Governor-General has no right to veto such legislation on the advice of the Federal Government. In the event of a deadlock between the two Chambers of the Legislature, the Governor-General may convene a joint sitting of the Senate and the House of Representatives.

The Union of South Africa is a federation only in name. Union of The Provinces possess certain powers of local government, South Africa. but the Union Parliament may over-ride any provincial legislation. New Zealand and the Irish Free State possess unitary constitutions.

[1] Chap. II.

CHAPTER II.

THE DOMINIONS AND THE UNITED KINGDOM.

Dominions and United Kingdom Parliament. THE relationship between the Dominions and the Crown and the Imperial Parliament presents questions of great difficulty. At the present time the Dominions are, just as the Colonies, subject to the legal—though not to the political—supremacy of the Imperial Parliament, the Parliament of the United Kingdom. Though this supremacy has for many years not been exercised positively, *i.e.*, by the passing of Acts affecting a Dominion, except at the request of such Dominion, *e.g.*, at the request of Canada to amend the British North America Act, 1867, yet it still exists, in as much as there are in force Acts of the Imperial Parliament (especially the Acts creating the Dominion constitutions) which apply to the Dominions, and the courts would be compelled to hold any Dominion legislation conflicting with such Acts to be inoperative.

Dominions and the Crown. Also the rights of the Crown in relation to the Dominions, *e.g.*, the appointment of Governors-General and the conclusion of treaties have until very recently been exercised on advice given by the Imperial Government, the Government of the United Kingdom, though such advice has been given only after consultation with the Dominion concerned and with its concurrence.

Responsible Government and Dominion Status. While, however, the strict legal status of the Dominions has remained unchanged, their political status has altered with extreme rapidity, largely owing to their participation in the War of 1914-1919 and the subsequent negotiations for a world settlement. Responsible government in the Dominions dates from the Durham Report of 1839, which was followed by instructions to the Governors of Upper and Lower Canada that they should act on the advice of Ministers acceptable to the representative legislatures. There followed the grant of responsible government to the other great Colonies, Newfoundland, New South Wales, Victoria, South Australia, New Zealand, Queensland, the other Provinces of Canada and the South African Colonies. In each case a relaxation of Imperial control followed the grant of responsible government. But just as responsible government was granted without being formally embodied in the several colonial constitutions, so the formal legal supremacy of the Imperial Parliament has remained unfettered, although in practice the Self-Governing Dominions have for long exercised complete internal sovereignty.

Since 1887 there have been periodic conferences for the purpose of consultation between the Governments of the Empire. *Imperial Conferences.* The Imperial Conference of 1926 realised that the disparity between the legal status of the Dominions and political reality was too great to last. The Dominions had obtained the right to make separate treaties with foreign powers in the name of the Crown without the participation of the Imperial Government or Parliament, except in regard to the issue of full powers and to instruments of ratification. It had been recognised that the Canadian Government could appoint a separate Minister to represent them diplomatically at Washington,[1] and in 1924 the Irish Free State appointed an Irish Minister to the United States.[2] The Dominions are independent members of the League of Nations. It was abundantly clear that the old forms did not correspond to existing facts. The Imperial Conference of 1926 made the following declaration. The United Kingdom and the Dominions are " autonomous communities within the British Empire, equal in status, in no way subordinate one to another in any aspect of their domestic or external affairs, though united by common allegiance to the Crown, and freely associated as members of the British Commonwealth *Imperial Conference of 1926.*

---

[1] Such an appointment has since been made.
[2] Other Dominion diplomatic representatives have since been appointed.

23 *

Insoluble difficulties re defence & Foreign relations

of Nations." The declaration added this rider : " But the principles of equality and similarity appropriate to status do not universally extend to function. Here we require something more than immutable dogmas."

Report of 1929.

A Conference was set up to consider how far legal forms should be changed and brought into line with this declaration. That Conference reported in 1929.[1] This Report has been adopted with minor alterations by the Imperial Conference of 1930, and if the resolutions of that Conference are put into effect there will be a radical change in the formal legal status of the Dominions.

Imperial Conference of 1930.

Existing Limitations and Proposed Changes.

It will be convenient to examine the existing limitations upon Dominion autonomy and to consider how each in turn is affected by the proposals of the Imperial Conference.

Legislative Supremacy of Imperial Parliament.

Colonial Laws Validity Act.

The Imperial Parliament possesses the right to legislate for all parts of the King's dominions. By Section 2 of the Colonial Laws Validity Act, 1865, any colonial law (and colony includes the Self-Governing Dominions) which is repugnant to an Imperial Act is to that extent inoperative. It was at one time thought that the Acts of Colonial Legislatures were void if repugnant to English Common Law, but this doctrine was shown to be incorrect ; *Phillips* v. *Eyre* (1870), L.R. 6 Q.B. 1 ; K. & L. 426. To remove any doubts it was expressly enacted by Section 3 of the Colonial Laws Validity Act that no colonial law shall be deemed to have been void or inoperative on the ground of repugnancy to the Law of England, unless the same shall be repugnant to the provisions of some Act of Parliament extending to the colony. The Imperial Conference of 1930 did not propose to abolish the legal supremacy of the Imperial Parliament, but it did propose changes in the law which, with certain exceptions which will be discussed later, will render it inoperative. In law the Imperial Parliament cannot abolish its own legal supremacy, but by convention it can restrict the power to exercise it to a vanishing point. It is proposed :

[1] Report of the Conference on the operation of Dominion Legislation and Merchant Shipping Legislation, 1929 (1930, Cmd. 3479).

(1) That the Colonial Laws Validity Act, 1865, shall cease to apply to any law made by the Parliament of a Dominion.

(2) That no Dominion law shall be void or inoperative on the ground of repugnancy to an Act of the Imperial Parliament. The doctrine of repugnancy will still apply to Provincial legislation in Canada and State legislation in Australia.

(3) That Dominions shall have power to repeal or amend Acts of the Imperial Parliament, in so far as they are part of the law of the Dominion.

(4) That it should be placed on record by Statute of the Imperial Parliament that no Act of Parliament of the United Kingdom passed hereafter shall extend to a Dominion as part of the law in force in that Dominion, unless it is expressly declared that the Dominion has requested and consented to the enactment thereof.

(5) That the term, Colony, shall no longer include Dominion. The expression, Dominion, means Canada, Australia, New Zealand, the Union of South Africa and the Irish Free State.[1]

It is suggested that the Statute to be passed to embody these changes shall be called " The Statute of Westminster." [2] Statute of Westminster.

The Imperial Conference realised that, unless and until general opinion in the Dominions desired its abolition, it was important to preserve the legal supremacy of the Imperial Parliament, in so far as it safeguards State and Provincial rights in Australia and Canada. Before considering the proposals of the Conference on this question, there must be considered the existing powers of Dominions to alter their Constitutions. Such powers depend upon the terms of the Imperial Act creating the Constitution. The Safeguarding of Federalism State Right.

Powers of Constitutional Amendment.

---

[1] It appears that the proposed changes will not immediately apply to Newfoundland, see Chap. I. Newfoundland possesses a Legislature founded on Letters Patent of great antiquity. It is not possible to state precisely the constitutional basis of the relations between Newfoundland and the Imperial Parliament.

[2] It is proposed that such Statute shall become operative on Dec. 1st, 1931, for such Dominions as approve the proposed changes.

Constitution of Canada depends upon the British North America Act, 1867, and can only be amended by Act of the Imperial Parliament, though any such Act would be passed on the request of the Dominion Parliament, provided that no Province objected. The unalterable form of the Canadian Constitution is due to its early date and the strong local feeling of the Province of Quebec. The Commonwealth of Australia Act, 1900, provides an elaborate machinery by which the Constitution may be changed. There is needed the assent of both Houses of the Commonwealth Parliament and of the electorate. State rights cannot be diminished without the consent of a majority of the voters in the State concerned. In the case of the Union of South Africa, where the Provinces are of relatively small importance, there are very wide powers of change, though Bills effecting certain constitutional changes must at present be reserved for the pleasure of the Crown to be expressed. The Constitution of New Zealand can be amended freely with certain limitations which do not call for special discussion. The Constitution of the Irish Free State was enacted as the result of an Agreement between the United Kingdom and the Irish Free State in 1921. It can be freely amended, provided that such amendment does not conflict with the Articles of the Agreement, as subsequently enacted.[1] The Imperial Conference of 1930 proposed that the projected Statute of Westminster and the repeal of the Colonial Laws Validity Act should not be deemed to confer any power to repeal or alter the Constitutions of Australia or New Zealand, otherwise than in accordance with the existing law. No decision has been taken as to whether or not it should be made easier to amend the Canadian Constitution, and no decision will be taken until the Provinces have been consulted. The first eight sections of the Commonwealth of Australia Act, 1900, which form a preface to the Constitution and make it clear that the basis of the Constitution is federal, cannot be amended or altered, except by Act of the Imperial Parliament. The basis of this view is that the

[1] See p. 362 below.

Constitution itself, which can be amended by the machinery described above, is scheduled to these eight Sections of the Act, and that the machinery for change only applies to the scheduled Constitution. Just as the machinery for amendment of that Constitution can only be altered by an Act of the Imperial Parliament, so such an Act is requisite to repeal ss. 1-8 from which the Constitution itself draws its force. It is not proposed to make it possible to repeal these sections, unless, and until, the Federal and State Governments in Australia request it. If, and when, Canada and Australia desire further powers to amend the Constitution, it would seem that such powers can only be conferred by Act of the Imperial Parliament.

Further limitations upon Dominion autonomy have been : Disallowance (1) the power of the Governor-General of the Dominion, as and the representative of the Crown, to refuse his assent to legislation, or to reserve legislation for the assent of the King, which assent has hitherto been given or withheld on the advice of the United Kingdom Government, and (2) the power of the Crown to disallow legislation, even after it has received the Governor-General's assent. These powers have received statutory expression and vary from Dominion to Dominion. Reservation of certain Bills is in some cases compulsory by statute. These powers have been seldom exercised. Their main purpose was to make it possible for the United Kingdom Government to intervene where grave Imperial interests were concerned. The Imperial Conference of 1930 has laid it down that advice can only be given to the Crown on Dominion matters by the Ministers of the Dominions concerned, and that it would be improper for the United Kingdom Government to advise the Crown on reserved Bills. It is proposed that legislation should be introduced to abolish the powers of disallowance and reservation, if any Dominion requests such legislation. These proposed changes will not affect the right of the Crown to disallow Provincial or State legislation in Canada and Australia respectively, and there will be no interference with the direct relationship between the States of Australia and the Imperial Government in respect of disallowance and reservation.

Extra-
territorial
Legislation.

Yet a further limitation upon Dominion legislation has been the rule that, though supreme within the spheres allotted to them, Dominion Legislatures are confined to legislating for the peace, order and good government of their own territories. Dominion legislatures cannot legislate with extra-territorial effect. In *Macleod* v. *Attorney-General of New South Wales* [1891], A.C. 455, it was held by the Judicial Committee of the Privy Council that the appellant could not be punished under a Colonial Act for bigamy committed in the United States of America. It was indicated in *Nadan* v. *The King* [1926], A.C. 482 ; K. & L. 437, that a provision of the Canadian Criminal Code attempting to limit the right of the Crown in Council to grant special leave to appeal in criminal cases was void, among other reasons, as being an attempt to legislate extra-territorially.[1] The Imperial Conference of 1930 proposed that an Act of the Imperial Parliament should be passed giving power to the Dominions to legislate extra-territorially.

Governors-
General.

The position of the Governor-General of a Dominion is of considerable importance in inter-Imperial relations. The assent of the Governor-General is required for all legislation, just as the Royal Assent is required for the legislation of the Imperial Parliament. The Governor-General in the past received his instructions from the Crown acting on the advice of the Imperial Government,[2] but now these instructions are prepared on the advice of Dominion Ministers. The Governor-General was formerly the channel of communication between the Dominions and the Imperial Government. The Imperial Conference of 1926 expressed the view that the Governor-General must be regarded solely as the King's representative, and not in any way as the representative of the Imperial Government. There is now direct communication between Dominion Governments and the Government of the United Kingdom, and the

Communica-
tion between
Dominions
and Imperial
Government.

[1] Though these cases are commonly cited in support of the general proposition of the limited power of Dominion legislatures, they were both decided on narrower grounds. The limitation depends upon the express or implied words of the Imperial Statutes creating the Dominion Legislatures, and not upon any general principle.

[2] Through the Dominion Office.

Dominions are represented in London by High Commis-
sioners. Similarly the British Government may (and in
Canada and South Africa has done so) appoint High
Commissioners in the Dominions. The Imperial Conference
of 1930 recommended that a High Commissioner of the
Dominions should have precedence in England after
Secretaries of State. The High Commissioner recently
appointed by the Imperial Government to represent it in
South Africa has been made High Commissioner of South
Africa responsible for the supervision of Basutoland and
the native Protectorates of Bechuanaland and Swaziland.
This office had hitherto been held by the Governor-General
of South Africa.

The Governor-General is expected to act in relation to Appoint-
the administration of public affairs on the constitutional ment of
practice regulating the exercise of the powers of the Crown Governors-
General.
in the United Kingdom. He should be kept informed of all
political affairs. The Governor-General is appointed by
the Crown. The Imperial Conference of 1930 has placed
on record the view that, in making such appointments, the
Crown should in the future act solely on the advice of the
Ministers of the Dominion concerned. Whether or not the
existing practice of appointing distinguished Englishmen
to the post of Governor-General will in general be continued
will depend upon the sentiments of the people of the
Dominions. Since the Imperial Conference of 1930 an
Australian has been appointed Governor-General of Australia
on the recommendation of the Commonwealth Govern-
ment, apparently without previous formal consultation with
the United Kingdom Government, while a member of the
United Kingdom peerage has been appointed to the Canadian
Governor-Generalship on the advice of the Dominion
Premier.

The adoption of the recommendations of the Imperial Effect of Pro-
Conference of 1930 will make even more difficult than at posed
Changes on
present the task of defining the legal status of the British Dominion
Commonwealth. The Dominions and the rest of the Status.
Commonwealth will still be united by the tie of common
allegiance to the Crown. It is agreed that no change should

be made in the Royal Title without the consent of the
whole Commonwealth. It has been seen that the legal
supremacy of the Imperial Parliament is still operative.
The very fact that its legislative power is to be invoked to
give effect to the recommendations pre-supposes its reality.
Apart, however, from the limitations imposed on constitutional amendment in the interest of State rights in
Canada and Australia, there will remain no practical limitations upon Dominion autonomy in inter-Imperial relations.
It is manifest that the position might give rise to insuperable
difficulties, if legal rights were pressed to their logical
conclusion. The unity of the Commonwealth under the
Crown is not, and never has been, a mere personal union
under one King, as was the union between Great Britain
and Hanover. The Crown is one and indivisible throughout the Commonwealth ; *Williams* v. *Howarth* [1905], A.C.
551. It may be that the Crown, which in affairs concerning
a Dominion will in future be advised only by Dominion
Ministers, will be advised to take contrary actions by the
Ministers of different parts of the Commonwealth.

Right to Secede. Have Dominions the legal right to secede from the
Commonwealth ? The Irish Free State, though possessing
almost complete power of constitutional amendment, is
bound by the agreement known as the " Articles of Agreement
for a Treaty between Great Britain and Ireland " which
received statutory effect in the Irish Free State (Agreement)
and (Constitution) Acts, 1922, passed by the Parliament of
the United Kingdom, and the Constitution of the Irish Free
State (Saorstat Eireann) Act, 1922, passed by the Free State
Assembly. It cannot, therefore, secede without a breach
of these obligations. No power will at present be given to
Canada to amend the British North America Act, 1867, or
to Australia to amend the preamble to the Commonwealth of
Australia Act.[1] Complete powers of constitutional amendment will, however, clearly be given as soon as general opinion
in the Dominions concerned demands them. The legal
supremacy of the Imperial Parliament is preserved to safeguard Provincial or State rights and as a measure of ultimate co-ordination, and not to maintain authority over the

[1] Ss. 1-8.

Dominions. The Parliaments of the Dominions must in future be regarded not as subordinate law-making bodies, but, as in practice, co-ordinate with the Imperial Parliament. Secession, however, involves more than constitutional amendment. It can only be said that secession is altogether outside the law. It could be effected only by a declaration of independence followed by a treaty or some form of recognition. In practice, no Dominion could be kept by force within the Commonwealth. The altering of legal forms to correspond with present usage will not give to the Dominions a legal right to secede, inasmuch as secession would be an extra-legal act. Equally, secession could certainly not be prevented by any attempt to preserve the legal supremacy of the Imperial Parliament, as it used to exist.

Even less capable of definition is the status of the Dominions in International Law, with which is closely connected the problem of reconciling autonomy with the general conduct of foreign affairs by the Imperial Government. Although normally employing the British Ambassadors as their diplomatic representatives, the Dominions may appoint their own Ministers to foreign countries. The Imperial Conference of 1930 has expressed the hope that, except where such separate appointments are made, the existing diplomatic channels, *i.e.*, communication through the Imperial Government, will continue to be used. Where Dominion Governments, in cases of urgency, address communications direct to a British ambassador on matters of general concern, it is desired that there shall be a simultaneous communication made to the United Kingdom Government. It is realised that at present the United Kingdom Government must still remain primarily responsible for general foreign affairs ; this is an instance of equality of status, but dissimilarity of function.[1] On matters of purely Dominion concern there will be direct communication between Dominions and British ambassadors with no obligation to inform the United Kingdom Government. Dominion Governments may in relation to their own Dominion make agreements with foreign

International Relations.

[1] See p. 356 above.

Governments, and, further, may advise the exercise of the Crown's treaty-making prerogative powers. Where treaties are made in the name of the Crown on behalf of the whole Commonwealth, a United Kingdom plenipotentiary will sign on behalf of Great Britain and Northern Ireland, and all parts of the British Empire which are not separate members of the League of Nations : separate plenipotentiaries will sign for each separate Dominion. While recognising the special functions of the United Kingdom Government in foreign affairs, stress is laid on the vital importance of frequent consultation on matters of common interest. As far as inter-Imperial obligations are concerned, it is clearly understood that no Dominion will be bound by a treaty made in the name of the Crown to which it has not assented, and which it has not ratified.

Dominion Status in International Law. It will be seen that, as between the United Kingdom and the Dominions, full equality and practical independence in international relations are freely recognised. Inter-Imperial declarations do not, however, in themselves alter International Law or bind foreign States. The Dominions are independent members of the League of Nations and have independent relations with the Permanent Court of International Justice. The crux of the matter, however, lies in War and Neutrality. War is declared by the Crown. It is improbable that foreign States would recognise the neutrality of a British Dominion, when the Crown declared war.[1]

The Future. Enough has been said to show how difficult are the problems created by an attempt to combine legal autonomy with union under one Crown in one Commonwealth. It is clear, however, that there will still be room for conventions and gradual development in the sphere of inter-Imperial relations. The abolition of legal forms will render still more necessary, if real unity is to be preserved, the building up of machinery for frequent consultation and co-operation on all questions of general concern, whether imperial or foreign. A useful recommendation made by the Imperial Conference of 1930 is the formation of a Commonwealth

Commonwealth Tribunal.

---

[1] *Cf.* Oppenheim's *International Law* (Longmans), 4th edition, by A. D. McNair, Vol. I., at p. 194.

Tribunal for the settlement of justiciable disputes between members of the Commonwealth. It is not intended to establish a permanent court, but that there shall be standing panels of eminent jurists of the Commonwealth, from which, in the event of a dispute, an *ad hoc* arbitration tribunal can be selected.

NOTE.

While the author hopes that the two foregoing chapters give an accurate account of the legal aspect of Dominion status, he is conscious that there is much that is controversial in the subject. His colleague and others have suggested that the strictly legal view taken appears to give insufficient recognition to the changes which are taking place as the result of recent Imperial Conferences and the recognition of the Dominions as members of the League of Nations. There is a large body of informed opinion in this country which welcomes the changes and is impatient of the legal intricacies with which their interpretation and achievement inevitably are involved. Such opinion regards the full measure of autonomy, in practice already achieved, as the surest basis for retaining the bonds of Empire. These considerations appear to the author to lie beyond the scope of a work on Constitutional Law. The author fully recognises the practical autonomy of the Dominions, but feels it impossible to reconcile legal autonomy with a direct relationship, as in Australia, between the Imperial Government and component parts of the Dominion.—G. G. P.

CHAPTER III.

INDIA.

Native
States. The Indian Empire is divided into the Native States and British India. The Native States are protected territories which stand in a peculiar relationship to the British Crown as Paramount Power in India. The paramountcy of the British Crown is based partly on treaties, partly on usage and the political practice adopted by the Political Department, which is responsible for the relations between the Crown and the States. The Crown possesses paramountcy independently of treaties, though treaties may, and do, regulate the exercise of the Crown's rights. Paramountcy is not identical with sovereignty, which is shared between the Crown and the Native Rulers, and it is probably confined to the express rights conferred by treaties and the general right of interference in the interest of India as a whole. In a sense this general paramountcy may be said to be based on consent, and it is urged that the paramountcy to which the States have consented is the paramountcy of the Crown acting on the advice of the British Government, responsible to the British Parliament, and that, therefore, any handing over of the Crown's relations with the States to a Government responsible to an Indian Legislature would release the States from their obligations. Any satisfactory project for the self-government of British India must involve some federal relationship between British India and the States. The legal rights of the States are, therefore, of the first importance. Acts of the Crown in the exercise of paramountcy are Acts of State not cognizable in any British court.[1]

[1] The author has attempted to summarise briefly the views expressed by Sir W. S. Holdsworth, K.C., D.C.L., in an article in the *Law Quarterly Review*, Oct., 1930 : " The Indian States and India," *cf. Sovereignty and Paramountcy in India*, by Julian Palmer (Stevens & Sons, 1930).

366

British India is governed by a Governor-General, or British
Viceroy, with an Executive Council and Legislature, but the India
Central
Government of India is under the supervision of the Secretary Government.
of State for India, who is responsible to the Imperial
Parliament. The Secretary of State for India is assisted
by a Council consisting of from ten to fourteen salaried
members. The Secretary of State may disregard the advice
of the Council, except as to expenditure of Indian revenue,
which must be sanctioned by the Secretary of State and a
majority of his Council. The Viceroy is appointed for five
years, but his term of office may be prolonged. Members
of the Viceroy's Executive Council are placed in charge of
various departments of the Central Government, but they are
not responsible to the Indian Legislature. The Legislature
consists of a Council of State of sixty members with a
majority of elected members, and a Legislative Assembly
of 140 members, 100 of whom are members elected on a
more democratic franchise than that used for the election of
the Council of State. Certain subjects are withdrawn from
the cognizance of the Legislature, and, when interests of State
demand it, the Viceroy may authorise expenditure and
put into force legislation without the consent of the
Legislature. There is no High Court for the whole of
British India. The various High Courts are the supreme
judicial tribunals of the Provinces, whence an appeal lies
direct to the Privy Council.

British India is divided into nine Provinces. Subjects Provincial
of government not exclusively assigned to the Central Government
Dyarchy.
Government are assigned to Provincial Legislatures. Each
Province has a Governor, assisted by an Executive Council
and a Legislative Council. As a prelude to the gradual
introduction of self-government in India, there was introduced by the Government of India Act, 1919, the system of
dyarchy. The business of government in each Province
was divided into reserved and transferred subjects. Reserved
subjects, including justice and police, are administered by
the Governor and the Executive Council, who are responsible to the Viceroy and through him to the Secretary of
State for India. Transferred subjects are administered by

the Governor and Ministers who are responsible to the Legislative Assembly. The Legislative Assembly has cognizance of both reserved and transferred subjects, but only in respect of transferred subjects is there any measure of responsible government.

Simon Commission.

The Government of India Act, 1919, provided for the setting up of a Commission in 1929 to enquire into the working of responsible government in India. That Commission, the appointment of which was ante-dated, has under the chairmanship of Sir John Simon issued its report,[1] but the future development of the Indian Constitution is so uncertain that any forecast of possible changes would be out of place in this book. A Round Table Conference has met, at which the problems of the future constitutional development of India have been discussed by representatives of India and of the Imperial Parliament. The function of the Conference was advisory only. Legislative changes can only be made by the Imperial Parliament. The Conference accepted the necessity of a federation, a decision which has only been made practicable by the unexpectedly favourable attitude of the Native States Delegation to such a solution.

[1] Report of the Indian Statutory Commission, Vol. I., Survey ; Vol. II., Recommendations (Cmd. 3568, 3569, 1930).

CHAPTER IV.

PROTECTORATES AND MANDATED TERRITORIES.

PROTECTORATES are not part of the British Empire. They are territories not yet fully settled, or territories in which by treaty or the consent (sometimes enforced) of native rulers the inhabitants have accepted British protection and whose foreign relations are guided by Great Britain. The inhabitants of a Protectorate do not become British subjects. Among Protectorates the degree and the extent of the exercise by the protecting State of those sovereign powers which have been described as " a bundle or collection of powers which may be separated one from another," may, and in practice do, vary considerably. Although both may be described as protected States, there is a vast gulf between the practical extent of the exercise of the powers of the Crown in the Native States of India and their exercise in the African Protectorates of Bechuanaland and Swaziland or the Federated Malay States.[1] Protectorates are foreign countries and the Crown legislates for these under the Foreign Jurisdiction Acts, 1890 and 1913, just as though the protected territory had been acquired by conquest or cession as part of the dominions of the Crown. The principal African Protectorates are governed as Colonies with constitutions established by Orders in Council.

Even apart from the Foreign Jurisdiction Act, 1890, any act of the Crown in a Protectorate would be an Act of State,[2] and therefore not to be questioned in a British

---

[1] It is argued that, as in the case of the Native States of India, so in the African Protectorates the element of consent in the paramountcy of the Crown should prevent any transfer of jurisdiction to the Union of South Africa.

[2] Part II., Chap. IV. C.

24

court. In *The King* v. *Crewe, ex parte Sekgome* [1910], 2 K.B. 576, an application for a writ of Habeas Corpus by the chief of a native tribe in Bechuanaland was refused; it was held that an Order in Council conferring power on the High Commissioner for South Africa to do all such things as are lawful for the preserving of peace justified the detention of the chief and could not be questioned. It can thus be seen that there are practically no legal safeguards for the inhabitants of protected territories against the exercise of arbitrary power. In the case under discussion, Vaughan Williams, L.J., said: " The idea that there may be an established system of law to which a man owes obedience, and that at any moment he may be deprived of the protection of that law, is an idea not easily accepted by English lawyers. It is made less difficult if one remembers that the Protectorate is over a country in which a few dominant civilised men have to control a great multitude of the semi-barbarous." It was argued in that case that the Foreign Jurisdiction Act of 1890 applied only to the exercise of jurisdiction over British subjects in foreign countries, but in spite of the terms of the Act itself, which lend support to the argument, the court rejected it, largely owing to the fact that in practice it had never been so interpreted. On similar principles it was held in *Cook* v. *Sprigg* [1899], A.C. 572, that obligations assumed under a treaty of annexation are not obligations which can be enforced in the courts. The Crown cannot, except by statute, deprive itself of freedom to make Orders in Council, even such as are inconsistent with previous Orders; *Sobhuza II.* v. *Miller* [1926], A.C. 518. The Crown cannot fetter its own supreme legislative authority and the issue of an Order in Council under the Foreign Jurisdiction Act is a legislative act. It cannot therefore be argued that the Crown cannot subsequently deal with territory which it has previously granted to an inhabitant of a Protectorate; *North Charterland Exploration Co.* v. *The King* [1931], 1 Ch. 169.

Jurisdiction in Foreign Countries.   The Foreign Jurisdiction Act, 1890, provides also for the exercise by the Crown of jurisdiction in foreign countries acquired through treaty or grant. Such jurisdiction is exercised in civilised countries through consular or similar courts.

Mandated Territories are not part of the British Dominions. Mandated They are former enemy colonies, the administration of Territories. which is entrusted to the British Crown by the League of Nations, which supervises the carrying out of the mandates by means of a Permanent Mandates Commission.

Mandated Territories are divided into three classes. Class A, *e.g.*, Palestine, future independent kingdoms to which the mandatory power must give advice and assistance ; Class B, *e.g.*, Tanganyika, in which the mandatory power is responsible for internal administration ; and Class C, territories which are to be administered as integral parts of the territory of the mandatory power, *e.g.*, Samoa, over which the mandate has been assigned to New Zealand. In the case of *Rex* v. *Christian* [1924], S.A.A.D. 101, the Supreme Court of South Africa decided that, although Mandated Territories are not part of the British dominions, yet the mandatory power has sufficient internal sovereignty over such territory to permit of the conviction for treason of an inhabitant of such territory. The Crown legislates for Mandated Territories under the Foreign Jurisdiction Acts.

The entrusting of mandates to Dominions raised a difficult Dominion question of Constitutional Law. The mandate over the Mandates. former German South-West Africa was entrusted to the Union of South Africa, and it was assumed that the Union Parliament had power to legislate for such territory. In New Zealand, on the other hand, it was assumed that the territorial limitation upon Dominion legislation made it necessary to obtain an Imperial Order in Council under the Foreign Jurisdiction Act, empowering the Dominion Parliament to legislate for mandated territory. The latter was more probably the correct view. The British Crown accepts a mandate from the League of Nations on behalf of a Dominion Government, but only the Imperial Parliament can increase the constitutional power of a Dominion Legislature.

CHAPTER V.

THE JUDICIAL COMMITTEE OF THE PRIVY COUNCIL.

THE Judicial Committee of the Privy Council is one of the most important links of the Empire. It acts as a Supreme Court of Appeal for the Empire from the Courts of India and every Dominion, Colony or Protectorate, where the Crown exercises jurisdiction. Though not attempting to introduce the Common Law, where other systems of law prevail, e.g., French Law in Quebec, it preserves the uniformity of the Common Law in those parts of the Empire which are ruled by English Law. It may be called upon to enforce the legal limitations upon Dominion autonomy which result from the supremacy of Imperial legislation in matters concerning the relations of Federal and State or

Jurisdiction of Judicial Committee. Provincial legislatures. Its jurisdiction is the ancient jurisdiction of the King in Council to hear appeals from the Overseas Dependencies. This jurisdiction of the Council, which was in practice exercised by its legal members, was in 1833 made statutory by the Judicial Committee Act of that year (amended by the Judicial Committee Act, 1844 and subsequent Acts) which set up a Judicial Committee to hear appeals, either in virtue of that Act itself, or in virtue of the customary jurisdiction of the Privy Council.[1]

Composition of Judicial Committee. The Judicial Committee of the Privy Council is composed of all members of the Privy Council who have held high judicial office (including the seven Lords of Appeal in Ordinary), two salaried members with Indian legal experience, to whose salary India contributes, and any judges of the

[1] An Order in Council approving a Report of the Judicial Committee is reproduced in Appendix C.

superior courts of the Dominions or of any Colony who are Privy Councillors. The latter are determined by Order in Council. The King may also appoint two other Privy Councillors with no restrictions as to their qualifications. Any judge of a Colony from which an appeal is being heard may be summoned to sit as an assessor.

The right to appeal varies from Colony to Colony, and is Right to regulated according to the amount at stake, either by Orders Appeal. in Council made under the authority of the Judicial Committee Act, 1844, or by local Acts. The Judicial Committee may always give special leave to appeal, except when prevented from so doing by Imperial statute or a statute made under the authority of an Imperial statute. Appeals are not allowed in criminal matters, unless there has been a flagrant violation of justice. In *Knowles* v. *The King* [1930], A.C. 366, an appeal was allowed from the decision of a judge in Ashanti, who, sitting without a jury, convicted and sentenced a man to death for murder without considering the possibility of manslaughter. Appeals from the Provincial Courts of Canada lie, either to the Supreme Court of Canada, or direct to the Judicial Committee. From the Supreme Court of Canada an appeal only lies by special leave of the Privy Council. From the High Court of Australia and from the State Courts there is an appeal to the Judicial Committee, except where constitutional rights between States, or between States and the Commonwealth are in question. In such cases there is only an appeal when a certificate is given by the High Court itself, and in such cases the Privy Council may not give special leave to appeal. The Commonwealth of Australia Act gave power to Australia to limit the right to obtain special leave from the Privy Council to appeal, subject to the reservation of any such measure for his Majesty's Pleasure. This right was exercised in 1907, when the right to appeal from State Courts in cases involving constitutional rights was abolished.

From the Union of South Africa appeals only lie when special leave is given to appeal from the Appellate Division of the Supreme Court. From New Zealand, Newfoundland, India and the Colonies, Protectorates and Mandated

Territories appeals lie as of right, subject to limitations as to the nature of the suit or amount at stake. In the Irish Free State Constitution appeals as of right are abolished, but the right to petition the Privy Council for special leave to appeal is expressly preserved.

Future of
Dominion
Appeals.

There is a body of opinion in the Dominions, and especially in the Irish Free State, which regards the appeal to a court sitting in the United Kingdom, and composed predominantly of United Kingdom judges, as a limitation upon Dominion autonomy, and as casting an aspersion upon the competency of Dominion courts. The Imperial Conference of 1926 stated that : /" it was no part of the policy of His Majesty's Government in Great Britain that questions affecting judicial appeals should be determined otherwise than in accordance with the wishes of the part of the Empire primarily affected."/ It has, however, been agreed, and the argument has found favour with the Judicial Committee itself,[1] that the abolition by the Irish Free State of the right to petition for special leave to appeal would be a breach of the Agreement of 1921, inasmuch as the Agreement provides that " the position of the Irish Free State in relation to the Imperial Parliament and Government and otherwise shall be (subject to the provisions of the treaty) that of the Dominion of Canada, and the law, practice and constitutional usage governing the relationship of the Crown, or the representative of the Crown, and of the Imperial Parliament to the Dominion of Canada shall govern their relationship to the Irish Free State."

Appeals also lie to the Judicial Committee from the Ecclesiastical Courts of England and the Prize Courts throughout the Empire, and from the Channel Islands and Isle of Man.

References.

Non-judicial matters can be referred by the Crown to the Judicial Committee for advice, *e.g.*, the dispute between Canada and Newfoundland as to the Labrador Boundary ; *In re Labrador Boundary* (1927), 43 T.L.R. 289. This type of Commonwealth dispute would in future possibly be referred to the proposed Commonwealth Tribunal, which

---

[1] *Performing Right Society* v. *Bray U.D.C.* [1930], A.C. 377.

would otherwise in no way take the place of the Judicial Committee.

The following is a judicial pronouncement by Viscount Haldane of Cloan, delivered on the occasion of the hearing of the first appeals to the Judicial Committee from the Irish Free State. It is of great interest as illustrating the functions of the Committee when hearing appeals from both federal and unitary States, as understood by one of the greatest statesmen and most profound thinkers of the twentieth century :—

We are not Ministers in any sense ; we are a Committee of Privy Councillors who are acting in the capacity of judges, but the peculiarity of the situation is this : it is a long-standing constitutional anomaly that we are really a Committee of the Privy Council giving advice to His Majesty, but in a judicial spirit. We have nothing to do with policies, or party considerations ; we are really judges, but in form and in name we are the Committee of the Privy Council. The Sovereign gives the judgment himself, and always acts upon the report which we make. Our report is made public before it is sent up to the Sovereign in Council. It is delivered here in a printed form. It is a report as to what is proper to be done on the principles of justice ; and it is acted on by the Sovereign in full Privy Council ; so that you see, in substance, what takes place is a strictly judicial proceeding. That being so, the next question is : what is the position of the Sovereign sitting in Council in giving formal effect to our advice, and what are our functions in advising him ? The Judicial Committee of the Privy Council is not an English body in any exclusive sense. It is no more an English body than it is an Indian body, or a Canadian body, or a South African body, or, for the future, an Irish Free State body. There sit among our numbers Privy Councillors who may be learned judges of Canada—there was one sitting with us last week—or from India, or we may have the Chief Justice, and very often have had others, from the other Dominions, Australia and South Africa. I mention that for the purpose of bringing out the fact that the Judicial Committee of the Privy Council is not a body, strictly speaking, with any location. The Sovereign is everywhere throughout the Empire in the contemplation of the law. He may as well sit in Dublin, or at Ottawa, or in South Africa, or in Australia, or in India as he may sit here, and it is only for convenience, and because we have a court, and because the members of the Privy Council are conveniently here that we do sit here ; but the Privy Councillors from the Dominions may be summoned to sit with us, and then we sit as an Imperial court which represents the Empire, and not any particular part of it. It is necessary to observe what effect that has upon the present situation. The Sovereign, as the Sovereign of the Empire, has retained the prerogative of justice, but by an Imperial Statute to which he assented, that was modified as regards constitutional questions in the case of Australia. That is the only case that I need refer to where there has been any modification.

In Ireland, under the Constitution Act, by Art. 66, the Prerogative is saved, and the Prerogative therefore exists in Ireland, just as it does in Canada, South Africa, India, and right through the Empire with the single exception that I have mentioned—that it is modified in the case of the Commonwealth of Australia in reference to, but only in reference to, constitutional disputes in Australia. That being so, the Sovereign retains the ancient Prerogative of being the supreme tribunal of justice ; I need not observe that the growth of the Empire and the growth particularly of the Dominions, has led to a very substantial restriction of the exercise of the Prerogative by the Sovereign on the advice of the Judicial Committee. It is obviously proper that the Dominions should more and more dispose of their own cases, and in criminal cases it has been laid down so strictly that it is only in most exceptional cases that the Sovereign is advised to intervene. In other cases the practice which has grown up, or the unwritten usage which has grown up, is that the Judicial Committee is to look closely into the nature of the case, and, if, in their Lordships' opinion, the question is one that can best be determined on the spot, then the Sovereign is not, as a rule, advised to intervene, nor is he advised to intervene normally—I am not laying down precise rules now, but I am laying down the general principles —unless the case is one involving some great principle or is of some very wide public interest. It is also necessary to keep a certain discretion, because when you are dealing with the Dominions you find that they differ very much. For instance, in States that are not unitary States—that is to say, States within themselves—questions may arise between the central Government and the State, which, when an appeal is admitted, give rise very readily to questions which are apparently very small, but which may involve serious considerations, and there leave to appeal is given rather freely. In Canada there are a number of cases in which leave to appeal is granted because Canada is not a unitary State, and because it is the desire of Canada itself that the Sovereign should retain the power of exercising his Prerogative ; but that does not apply to internal disputes not concerned with constitutional questions, but relating to matters of fact. There the rule against giving leave to appeal from the Supreme Court of Canada is strictly observed where no great constitutional question, or question of law, emerges. In the case of South Africa, which is a unitary State, counsel will observe that the practice has become very strict. We are not at all disposed to advise the Sovereign, unless there is some exceptional question, such as the magnitude of the question of law involved, or it is a question of public interest in the Dominion to give leave to appeal. It is obvious that the Dominions may differ in a certain sense among themselves. For instance, in India leave to appeal is more freely given than elsewhere, but the genesis of that is the requirements of India, and the desire of the people of India. In South Africa, we take the general sense of that Dominion into account, and restrict the cases in which we advise His Majesty to give leave to appeal. It becomes with the Dominions more and more or less and less as they please. We go upon the principles of autonomy on the question of exercising the discretion as to granting leave to appeal. It is within the Sovereign's power, but the Sovereign, looking at the matter, exercises this discretion.—Extract from the Speech of Lord Haldane in *Hull* v. *M'Kenna and others* [1926], I.R. 402.

PART X.

CHURCH AND STATE.

Constitutional History, by F. W. Maitland (Cambridge University Press). Period V., Section J.

Law Relating to the Church and Clergy, by H. W. Cripps, 7th edition (Sweet & Maxwell)—for reference.

CHAPTER I.

RELIGIOUS BODIES.

THERE are to-day no restrictions upon freedom of worship, Religious Freedom.
and with but few exceptions there are to-day no disabilities
attached to membership of any particular religious community.
The Sovereign must join in communion with the Church of
England, and Roman Catholics and those who marry Roman
Catholics are expressly excluded from the Throne by the
provisions of the Act of Settlement; nor may a Roman
Catholic hold the office of Lord Chancellor or High Commissioner of the Church of Scotland. There are, too, certain
statutory restrictions upon the entry into Great Britain of
members of religious orders. There are other statutory
exceptions to the general principle that membership of a
religious body can no longer affect civic rights, but they are
of minor importance and do not concern the student of
Constitutional Law.

The recognition by the State of religious bodies necesarily Effects of
involves contact between these bodies and the State. The Recognition.
position of the Church of England as an established church
is peculiar and requires separate treatment, but all other
religious bodies can be regarded as being upon the same
footing as far as their relations with the State are concerned.
The Roman Catholic Church, though an international Roman
organisation, is to the constitutional lawyer a non-con- Catholic
formist religious body distinguished from other non- Church.
conformist bodies only by the survival of certain special
statutory restrictions. Religious bodies may hold property, Property.
but the law of property requires that such property should
be held upon trusts which conform to the rules of law
relating to charitable trusts. It is solely by this means that

381

The Courts and Non-Conformist Bodies.

property can be bequeathed to the perpetual use of a religious body. The courts are therefore called upon to decide whether bequests to religious bodies constitute good charitable trusts, and also to enforce the provisions of such trusts. The courts, too, may be required to enforce and pronounce upon the validity of the rules by which religious communities are governed. Members of a religious body may bind themselves to observe rules, and tribunals may be created to enforce such rules. Such tribunals, like other quasi-judicial bodies, may be restrained by the courts from violating their own rules or the rules of natural justice. It may be necessary for the courts to determine as a question of fact the nature of the doctrines of a religious community. Thus, in the famous case of *Free Church of Scotland* v. *Lord Overtoun* [1904], A.C. 515, the House of Lords held that a majority of the members of a religious community might not without committing a breach of trust, disentitling them to hold the property of the community, change the doctrines on which the identity of the community was based.

Church of Scotland.

The Established Church of Scotland is a Presbyterian Church with only a limited connection with the State. Church government in Scotland is based upon the Presbytery, or assembly of ministers of a district. The supreme legislative and judicial body of the Scottish Church is the General Assembly. Though presided over by the Moderator—an officer of the Church—there is present at its meetings the High Commissioner, appointed by the Crown, who takes no part in discussions, but represents the connection between Church and State.

In Ireland and Wales there are now no established churches.

CHAPTER II.

THE CHURCH OF ENGLAND.

THE Church of England is in a different position to other religious bodies. As an established church it has peculiar privileges which involve a close relationship with the State. Its chief officers, the Archbishops and Bishops, sit in the House of Lords as spiritual peers [1] and are appointed by the Crown. In dioceses where there is a Dean and Chapter, the Crown sends to the Dean and Chapter a *congé d'élire* with letters missive containing the name of the person who is to be elected as Bishop. This permission to elect is a form only. If the election is not made, the Crown appoints by Letters Patent, as is the practice in recently created dioceses with no Dean and Chapter. The law of the Church is part of the law of the land of which the civil courts take judicial notice. The ecclesiastical courts are courts in the full sense of the word. Their decrees are enforced by the State, and they are subject to the control of the ordinary courts by means of prerogative writs.[2] The establishment involves the royal supremacy. The Church may legislate for itself, but its legislation requires the consent of the State. Its forms of worship cannot be altered without the consent of Parliament.

The Church of England is divided into two provinces, the province of Canterbury and the province of York. Each province is governed by an Archbishop. The Archbishop of Canterbury is not only the ruler of his own diocese and province, but is also Primate of all England and the President of the Church Assembly. Each province is divided into dioceses governed by Bishops. Dioceses are divided into archdeaconries, and archdeaconries into rural deaneries.

The Established Church.

Appointment of Bishops.

Ecclesiastical Law.

Church Organisation.

[1] Part III., Chap. I.   [2] Part VI., Chap. IV.

383

A rural deanery is composed of parishes, each with its church and parish priest.

Convocation.   The ancient legislative assemblies of the Church are the Convocations of the two provinces of Canterbury and York. In each Convocation the Bishops of the province form the Upper House, and the clerical representatives of the Clergy form the Lower House. Convocation can meet only when summoned by the Crown. Its legislation takes the form of canons, which are of no effect without the Royal Assent. Such canons bind the clergy alone, unless they subsequently receive the authorisation of Parliament.

National Assembly of the Church of England.   The difficulty of obtaining proper discussion in Parliament of proposed measures affecting the Church, and the pressure of ordinary business upon parliamentary time, led in 1919 to the passing of the Church of England Assembly (Powers) Act and the setting up of a new legislative assembly for the Church under the name of the National Assembly of the Church of England. The Assembly consists of three houses, the House of Bishops, the House of Clergy consisting of the members for the time being of the Upper and Lower Houses respectively of the Convocations of Canterbury and York, and the House of Laity consisting of representatives elected by a system of indirect representation, the foundation of which is the Parochial Church Council elected by parishioners on the electoral roll of each parish.[1] The Assembly may pass measures to be submitted by its Legislative Committee to the Ecclesiastical Committee of Parliament, which consists of fifteen members of the House of Lords and fifteen members of the House of Commons, nominated at the beginning of each Parliament by the Lord Chancellor and the Speaker. The Ecclesiastical Committee reports to Parliament upon the expediency of measures submitted to it, especially with relation to the constitutional rights of His Majesty's subjects. The report and the proposed Measure are laid before both Houses of Parliament, and, upon the passing by both Houses of resolutions to that effect, the Measure is presented for the

---

[1] Any member of the Church of England is entitled to be placed on the electoral roll, not as is often supposed communicants only. Those elected must be communicants.

Royal Assent. On the receipt of such Assent a Measure has all the force and effect of an Act of Parliament. This procedure preserves the control of the State while enabling the Church to prepare its own Measures with full deliberation. The formation of the Church Assembly gave to the laity for the first time an official voice in the counsels of the Church. The National Assembly is a deliberative, and not a judicial, body, and Prohibition does not lie to it from the High Court;[1] *The King* v. *The Legislative Committee of the Church Assembly, ex parte Haynes-Smith* [1927], 1 K.B. 491.

There had for a long time been a growing feeling that the House of Commons comprising not only many non-churchmen, but even professed non-Christians, was not a fit body to legislate for the spiritual needs of the Church of England. The forms of worship of the Church of England, though not a result of parliamentary authorship, are sanctioned by parliamentary authorisation, and without such authorisation cannot be changed. The Prayer Book of the Church was given statutory force by the Act of Uniformity of 1558, and subsequent changes were authorised by Parliament in 1662 and again in 1872. The need of the sanction of King and Parliament for an alteration to the services of the Church is an essential part of the Royal Supremacy and the Establishment as regulated by the Elizabethan settlement. The dissatisfaction felt with the existing position was due to the change in conditions since the sixteenth century. In Elizabethan England there was no antithesis between Church and State. Every member of the State was a member of the Church. A conflict between Church and State meant only a conflict between the laity of the Church and the Clergy. "The amalgamation of Church and State had been brought about less by the Act of Supremacy than by the admission of the laity to the churchman's privileges and of the clergy to the layman's."[2] It was expected by many that the creation of the National Assembly would avert a conflict between the Church and the State; that the House of Commons would

Church and State.

---

[1] Part VI., Chap. IV.

[2] A. F. Pollard, *Political History of England*, Vol. VI. (Longmans).

not resist the demands of a body representing the lay as well as the clerical element in the Church of England ; that spiritual freedom could thus be obtained without the need of disestablishment. These expectations were not fulfilled when there was rejected in 1927, and again in 1928, a revised Prayer Book carried by a large majority in both Convocations and in the National Assembly. It may well be that the outcome of this rejection will be the disestablishment of the Church of England. A large body in the Church insists upon the need of complete freedom to legislate upon spiritual matters, while the fear of " Romish " tendencies in a section of the Church combined with the ancient Non-Conformist hostility to Church privileges makes it unlikely that Parliament will consent to the maintenance of the privileges of the Establishment, together with the abandonment of State control. A solution might possibly be found in Elizabeth's view of the Royal Supremacy. The Royal Supremacy to her meant, not the supremacy of Parliament, but the supremacy of the Crown. It was not for Parliament to meddle with ecclesiastical matters. She, the Queen, was the Supreme Governor of the Church of England. It might satisfy both Parliament and the Church if there was maintained the control of the Crown acting on the advice of its Ministers. State control would still be a reality, but no Government would be very ready to advise the Crown to reject a measure representing the considered desires of the National Church.

The Law of the Church.   The law of the Church consists of (*a*) statute law, (*b*) such canons and ancient customs as were in force in England before the Reformation and have been continuously acted upon since, and are not in conflict with the laws of the land, and (*c*) post-Reformation canons which have received the Royal Assent.

The Ecclesiastical Courts.   These laws are enforced by the Ecclesiastical Courts. These courts constitute a graduated hierarchy, the Court of the Archdeacon, the Consistory Court of the Bishop of each diocese and the Provincial Court of the Archbishop of each of the two provinces. The Archdeacon's Court is to-day practically obsolete, though the Archdeacon still possesses minor rights of jurisdiction. The judge of the Consistory Court is the Chancellor of the Diocese, usually a barrister, appointed by the Bishop from whom he derives his authority. In appointing the Chancellor the Bishop may reserve the right to exercise jurisdiction himself in matters where statutes do not prescribe a lay judge. Since the transfer in 1857 of the testamentary and matrimonial jurisdiction of the Ecclesiastical Courts to the Probate and Divorce Courts, the Consistory Courts deal mainly with moral offences by the clergy and applications for faculties for additions to and alterations in consecrated buildings. The Clergy Discipline Act, 1892, provides for the assistance of the Chancellor by five assessors in the case of moral offences. An appeal always lies from the Consistory Court to the Provincial Court, in the province of Canterbury the Court of Arches, in the province of York the Chancery Court of York. The Dean of Arches is judge of both these Courts. The authority of diocesan courts has been weakened by statutes setting up special tribunals and procedure for special classes of offences. Thus doctrinal and non-moral offences by clergy against ecclesiastical law are heard, under the provisions of the Clergy Discipline Act, 1840, not in the Consistory Court, but by Commissioners appointed by the Bishop of whom the Chancellor may or may not be one. Offences in respect of ritual and ceremony under the Public Worship Regulations Act, 1874, are either sent direct to the Provincial Court by letters of request from the Bishop, or are heard by consent by the Bishop himself. By the Benefices (Ecclesiastical Duties) Measure, 1926, the court for the determination of cases concerning negligence in the performance of ecclesiastical duties is the Archbishop of the province and a judge of the Supreme Court, appointed by the Lord Chancellor. A recent Commission of the Church Assembly set up to consider the working of the Ecclesiastical Courts has made recommendations with a view to restoring the authority of the diocesan courts and the Chancellor, while emphasising the fact that the authority of the Chancellor is derived from the Bishop and is of a spritual nature. Prohibition lies to the Ecclesiastical Courts from the King's Bench Division when

25 *

they act in excess of their jurisdiction or contrary to the rules of natural justice ; *The King* v. *North, ex parte Oakey* [1927], 1 K.B. 491.

Appeals to the Crown.

The Royal Supremacy involves the right of appeal to the Crown from the Provincial Courts in all cases. In 1832 the hearing of ecclesiastical appeals was transferred from the Court of Delegates to the Judicial Committee of the Privy Council [1] sitting with ecclesiastical assessors. Much dissatisfaction has been expressed with the Judicial Committee as a final court of appeal for the Church, and it has been said that disobedience and disregard of the authority of the Church courts has been due to the fact that a lay court has been the supreme tribunal for declaring the doctrines of the Church. The system " entrusts the interpretation of the formularies, the exposition of the traditions, and the infliction of the spiritual censures of the Church to persons of no theological education ; it grants no representation to the voice of the Church except in the utterances of episcopal assessors which may be totally disregarded by the lay tribunal alone acquainted with their purport." [2] These criticisms are largely based upon a misconception. The decision as to whether or not a given opinion is or is not in accordance with the received doctrines of the Church involves no claim to make or unmake those doctrines. It is, however, widely felt that the supreme tribunal of the Church should have some spiritual authority, and that pronouncements as to doctrine should be made by the Church and not by a lay court. The Commission of the Assembly referred to above recommends the constitution of a new court to be called the " Court of Appeal to the Crown," consisting of a permanent body of lay judges and other persons learned in ecclesiastical law, all of whom should be members of the Church of England. The Commission recommends also that in all cases in which it is necessary to determine what is the doctrine of the Church of England such question should be referred to an Assembly of the Archbishops and Bishops of both provinces.

[1] Part IX., Chap. V.
[2] *Report of Ecclesiastical Courts Commission*, 1883.

The clergy, like soldiers, are subject not only to their The Clergy. own special laws, but also to the ordinary laws of the land. They have certain privileges and also certain disabilities. The most important civic disability is that no clergyman of the Established Church or the Church of Scotland (as no Roman Catholic priest) can be elected to the House of Commons. It has been seen that the clergy are still summoned to Parliament by the *præmunientes* clause.[1] The Church of England is not a corporate body, and church property is Property the property of various corporations, sole and aggregate, which exist within the Church, *e.g.*, the Dean and Chapter of a Cathedral or the Rector or Vicar of a Parish. There must be especially mentioned the ancient liability on all landowners to pay tithe for the benefit of the Church. Tithe, originally Tithe. a tenth of the fruits of the land, became commuted in 1836 for a charge upon land varying with the price of corn, and must now be paid to Queen Anne's Bounty, which provides a sinking fund for the ultimate redemption of all Tithe ; Tithe Act, 1925. Queen Anne's Bounty, a corporation set up to administer the property restored to the Church by the Crown in the reign of Queen Anne, holds these payments in trust for tithe-owners. The largest holders of Church property are the Ecclesiastical Commissioners. In the reign Ecclesiastical of William IV. there was a redistribution and fixing of the Commis-sioners. incomes of many Bishops and Cathedral Chapters. The surplus income was handed over to the Ecclesiastical Commissioners, a corporation appointed by Act of Parliament, to be administered for the general benefit of the Church. Much other Church property has since been acquired by the Commissioners.

Advowsons—an advowson is the right to appoint a Advowsons. clergyman to a benefice—are a species of property. They may be transferred, but may not be separately sold or transferred for valuable consideration after two vacancies have occurred subsequently to July 4th, 1924.[2] Advowsons are held by laymen as well as by Bishops, Chapters, Clerical Trusts, and Colleges in the older Universities.

[1] Part III., Chap. I.
[2] Benefices Act, 1898 (Amendment) Measure, 1923.

APPENDICES.

INDEX TO APPENDICES.

APPENDIX A. LEGISLATIVE FORMS.

APPENDIX B. NOTE ON EXECUTIVE DOCUMENTS.

APPENDIX C. FORMS OF EXECUTIVE DOCUMENTS.

APPENDIX A.

Legislative Forms.[1]

HOUSING ACT, 1930.

CHAPTER 39.

AN Act to make further and better provision with respect to the clearance or improvement of unhealthy areas, the repair or demolition of insanitary houses and the housing of persons of the working classes ; to amend the Housing Act, 1925, the Housing, etc., Act, 1923, the Housing (Financial Provisions) Act, 1924, and the other enactments relating to housing subsidies ; and for purposes connected with the matters aforesaid. Example of Full Title.

[1st August, 1930] Date of Royal
Assent.

BE it enacted by the King's most Excellent Majesty, by and with the advice and consent of the Lords Spiritual and Temporal, and Commons, in this present Parliament assembled, and by the authority of the same as follows : Example of Enacting Clause.

TREATY OF PEACE ACT, 1919.

CHAPTER 33.

AN Act for carrying into effect the Treaty of Peace between His Majesty and certain other Powers.

[31st July, 1919]

WHEREAS at Versailles, on the twenty-eighth day of June, nineteen hundred and nineteen, a Treaty of Peace (including Example of Recital.

---

[1] Excluding Orders in Council and Departmental Regulations.

a protocol annexed thereto), a copy of which has been laid before each House of Parliament, was signed on behalf of His Majesty, and it is expedient that His Majesty should have power to do all such things as may be proper and expedient for giving effect to the said Treaty :

Be it therefore enacted, etc. :

Examples of Delegated Powers.

1. (1) His Majesty may make such appointments, establish such offices, make such Orders in Council, and do such things as appear to him to be necessary for carrying out the said Treaty, and for giving effect to any of the provisions of the said Treaty.

(2) Any Order in Council made under this Act may provide for the imposition, by summary process or otherwise, of penalties in respect of breaches of the provisions thereof, and shall be laid before Parliament as soon as may be after it is made, and shall have effect as if enacted in this Act, but may be varied or revoked by a subsequent Order in Council and shall not be deemed to be a statutory rule within the meaning of section one of the Rules Publication Act, 1893 :

Example of one method of Parliamentary Control of Delegated Power.

Provided that, if an address is presented to His Majesty by either House of Parliament within the next twenty-one days on which that House has sat after any Order in Council made under this Act has been laid before it praying that the Order or any part thereof may be annulled, His Majesty in Council may annul the Order or such part thereof, and it shall thenceforth be void, but without prejudice to the validity of anything previously done thereunder.

(3) Any expenses incurred in carrying out the said Treaty shall be defrayed out of moneys provided by Parliament.

Short Title.

2. This Act may be cited as the Treaty of Peace Act, 1919.

FINANCE ACT, 1930.

CHAPTER 28.

AN Act to grant certain duties of Customs and Inland Revenue (including Excise), to alter other duties, and to amend the law relating to Customs and Inland Revenue (including Excise) and National Debt, and to make further provision in connection with finance.

[*1st August,* 1930]

MOST GRACIOUS SOVEREIGN,

We, Your Majesty's most dutiful and loyal subjects, the Commons of the United Kingdom in Parliament assembled, towards raising the necessary supplies to defray Your Majesty's public expenses, and making an addition to the public revenue, have freely and voluntarily resolved to give and grant unto Your Majesty the several duties hereinafter mentioned ; and do therefore most humbly beseech Your Majesty that it may be enacted, and be it enacted by the King's most Excellent Majesty, by and with the advice and consent of the Lords Spiritual and Temporal, and Commons, in this present Parliament assembled, and by the authority of the same, as follows :

Example of Enacting Clause (Supply Bill).

APPROPRIATION ACT, 1930.

Schedule (B), *Part* 9.

Civil—Class II.

Specimen of Vote for Supply Services.

Schedule of sums granted and of the sums which may be applied as appropriations in aid in addition thereto, to defray the charges of the several Civil Services herein particularly mentioned, which will come in course of payment during the year ending on the 31st day of March, 1931, viz. :

	Sums not Exceeding	
	Supply Grants.	Appropriation in Aid.
No.	£	£
1. For the salaries and expenses of the department of His Majesty's Secretary of State for Foreign Affairs . . .	195,930	117,090
2. For the expenses in connection with His Majesty's embassies, missions, and consular establishments abroad, and other expenditure chargeable to the Consular Vote, relief of refugees from the Near East, certain special grants, including a grant in aid, sundry services arising out of the war and a loan to the European Commission of the Danube . .	1,076,679	504,307
3. For a contribution towards the expenses of the League of Nations and for others expenses in connection therewith, including British Representation before the Permanent Court of International Justice	92,000	—
4. For the salaries and expenses of the Department of His Majesty's Secretary of State for Dominion Affairs (including a supplementary sum of £7,450) . .	65,610	43,511
5. For sundry Dominion services, including certain grants in aid and for expenditure in connection with ex-service men in the Irish Free State and for a grant in aid to the Irish Free State in respect of compensation to transferred officers .	81,309	42,817

	Sums not Exceeding	
	Supply Grants.	Appropria- tion in Aid.
	£	£
No. 6. For a grant in aid of the Empire Marketing Fund (including a supplementary sum of £62,500)	612,500	—
7. For the expenses connected with Oversea settlement, and expenses arising out of the Empire Settlement Act, 1922 .	833,250	72,500
8. For the salaries and expenses of the department of His Majesty's Secretary of State for the Colonies (including a supplementary sum of £4,000) . .	151,306	4,783
9. For sundry Colonial and Middle Eastern services under His Majesty's Secretary of State for the Colonies (including certain non-effective services and grants in aid)	1,218,565	48,100
10. For a grant in aid of the Colonial Development Fund and for grants towards Interest on certain Oversea Loan .	812,200	— ·
11. For a contribution towards the cost of the department of His Majesty's Secretary of State for India in Council, including a grant in aid (including a supplementary sum of £35,000)	207,500	—
12. For certain salaries and expenses of the Imperial War Grave Commission, including purchase of land in the United Kingdom, and a grant in aid of the Imperial War Graves Commission Fund, formed under Royal Charter, 21st May, 1917, and a contribution towards an endowment fund	652,295	—
Total, Civil, Class II. . £	5,999,144	833,108

MEASURES (20 GEO. 5)—NO. 1.

Specimen Title of Measure of National Assembly.

A Measure passed by the National Assembly of the Church of England.

To consolidate and amend the Law relating to the sale, purchase and improvement of Parsonage Houses.

[*20th March*, 1930]

9 and 10 GEO. 5. P. LXXV.

Specimen Title of Provisional Order Confirmation Act (Private and Local Act).

An Act to confirm certain Provisional Orders of the Local Government Board [1] relating to Birkenhead, Blackburn, Godalming, Hyde and the District of the Heywood and Middleton Water Board (Local Government Board's Provisional Orders Confirmation No. 1).

[1] Now Ministry of Health.

APPENDIX B.[1]

Note on Executive Documents.

SOME appreciation of the wide activities of executive government may best be gathered from a consideration of documents issued by the Executive. These fall into two main classes : (1) Documents executed by, or in the name of the King, many of which bear His Majesty's signature, and (2) Departmental Orders. The latter category is so vast that, beyond a reproduction in Appendix C of some specimen orders, no attempt can be made to enumerate the documents which issue from the Departments in the course of their administrative activities. We have, however, given some figures of Statutory Rules and Orders published in recent years, which include the more important documents of this class.[2]

Executive (as opposed to purely departmental) documents fall under three heads :

(1) Orders in Council.

(2) Warrants, Commissions and Orders under the Sign Manual.

(3) Proclamations, Writs, Letters Patent, Charters, Grants and other documents under the Great Seal.

(1) By means of Orders made by the King, by and with the advice of His Privy Council, are exercised the prerogative and statutory powers of the Crown. As an example of a prerogative Order in Council may be cited Colonial legislation such as the Nigeria (Legislative Council) Order, 1928, reconstituting the Legislative Council of the Colony, or the Order in Council commanding the issue of writs for the calling of a new Parliament, which accompanies the Proclamation dissolving Parliament. The statutory powers of the Crown are normally

Orders in Council.

---

[1] Halsbury, *Laws of England*, Vol. VII., pp. 8 ff., may be consulted on this subject.

[2] Part II., Chap. VI., *Delegated Legislation*, by C. T. Carr (Cambridge University Press) is a valuable little work which should be consulted.

exercised in this way if they are conferred upon the Crown, as under the Foreign Jurisdiction Act, 1890, and not upon a specified Minister or Department, as such. The results attendant on appeals to the Judicial Committee are promulgated in this manner, the King in Council making an Order on the advice tendered by the Committee. While legal responsibility for Orders in Council rests upon the members of the Privy Council in attendance at the meeting (usually not more than four or five), other than the Sovereign, if he be present, political responsibility rests with the Minister in whose Department the draft Order is framed.

Warrants, Commissions and Orders under the Sign Manual.

(2) These again relate both to prerogative and statutory powers. They are used to authorise the performance of executive acts and to make appointments to office or to commissioned ranks in the Forces. Instructions to Colonial Governors, as well as their Commissions of Appointment, are examples of documents so executed. Either the Seal of the Secretary of State concerned or the counter-signature of such Secretary or responsible Minister is required.

The Great Seal.

(3) The Great Seal is employed for the issue of writs for parliamentary elections and to summon peers to sit in Parliament; for treaties; for all public instruments and orders of State which relate to the whole kingdom. It is brought into use by a Warrant under the Sign Manual, signed by the King's own hand and counter-signed either by the Lord Chancellor, a Secretary of State, or two Lords Commissioners of the Treasury, but in some cases it may be employed by order of the Lord Chancellor without previous authorisation by Sign Manual Warrant; Great Seal Act, 1884. Proclamations may only be issued by authority of the Crown under the Great Seal; no private person may issue a proclamation. Proclamations are valid in law on publication in the *London Gazette ;* they receive judicial notice and are of the same validity as Acts of Parliament, though their lawful use is restricted to prerogative acts and calling attention to existing provisions of law; *Case of Proclamations,* (1611).

Letters Patent are used (*inter alia*) to constitute an office; to confer a title; to appoint a Royal Commission enquiring into an important problem of the day; to provide for the government of a colony. They must be distinguished from a Patent conferred by statutory authority under the seal of the Patent Office, granting a monopoly of making, using and selling an article of manufacture new within the realm on the first and true inventor, a purely departmental matter.

Grants and Charters confer franchises, create corporations, and grant prerogative privileges, many of which are now regulated by statute.

APPOINTMENTS TO OFFICE.

The following are a few examples of the various ways in which appointments to office are effected :—

Office.	*Mode of Appointment.*
Important Posts in Ministry.	Delivery of Seals of Office.
Governor-General of India.	Warrant under Sign Manual.
Colonial Governor.	Commission under Sign Manual and Signet.
Lord President of the Council.	Declaration by the Sovereign.
Army Officer.	Commission from the Sovereign.
Naval Officer.	Commission from Lords Commissioners of the Admiralty.
Civil Service Commissioners.	Order in Council.

APPENDIX C.

Forms of Executive Documents.

THE object of this Appendix is to present the reader with specimens of some of the executive documents to which reference has been made from time to time. Both documents issued in the name of the King and specimens of departmental rules and orders, which are a leading feature of present-day administration, are included. The authors desire to acknowledge the assistance of the Departments of State in facilitating the reproduction of certain documents and the courtesy of the Comptroller of H.M. Stationery Office in allowing the reproduction in an unofficial work of documents the copyright of which is vested in the Crown. For the accuracy of reproduction the authors alone are responsible. The Letters Patent, the Instructions and the Commission appointing the Governor of the Colony of Fiji are reproduced in full as affording an excellent example of the enactment in precise terms of a Constitution reflecting in many ways the rules of English Constitutional Law.

Royal
Proclama-
tion.

BY THE KING.

A PROCLAMATION.

For Dissolving the Present Parliament, and Declaring the Calling of another.

GEORGE R.I.

WHEREAS We have thought fit, by and with the advice of Our Privy Council, to dissolve this present Parliament which stands prorogued to Friday, the Twenty-fourth day of May instant; We do, for that End, publish this Our Royal Proclamation, and do hereby dissolve the said Parliament accordingly: And the

Lords Spiritual and Temporal, and the Knights, Citizens, and Burgesses, and the Commissioners for Shires and Burghs, of the House of Commons, are discharged from their Meeting and Attendance on the said Friday, the Twenty-fourth day of May instant : And We being desirous and resolved, as soon as may be, to meet Our People, and to have their Advice in Parliament, do hereby make known to all Our loving Subjects Our Royal Will and Pleasure to call a new Parliament : And do hereby further declare, that, by and with the advice of Our Privy Council, We have given Order that Our Chancellor of Great Britain and Our Governor of Northern Ireland do respectively, upon Notice thereof, forthwith issue out Writs, in due Form and according to Law, for calling a new Parliament : And we do hereby also, by this Our Royal Proclamation under Our Great Seal of Our Realm, require Writs forthwith to be issued accordingly by Our said Chancellor and Governor respectively, for causing the Lords Spiritual and Temporal and Commons who are to serve in the said Parliament to be duly returned to, and give their Attendance in, Our said Parliament on Tuesday, the Twenty-fifth day of June next, which Writs are to be returnable in due course of Law.

> Given at Our Court of Saint James, this Tenth day of May, in the year of our Lord One thousand nine hundred and Twenty-nine, and in the Twentieth year of Our Reign.
>
> GOD SAVE THE KING.

A Proclamation followed commanding all the peers of Scotland to meet at the Palace of Holyroodhouse, Edinburgh, at noon on Friday, May 31, to choose the 16 peers to sit and vote in the House of Lords in the next Parliament.

Orders in Council were also gazetted as follows :

The Lord High Chancellor of Great Britain and the Governor of Northern Ireland were ordered forthwith to cause writs to be issued for the calling of a new Parliament, to meet on Tuesday, June 25.

The Convocations of Canterbury and York were forthwith dissolved, and the Lord Chancellor was to cause writs to be issued for electing new members of the Convocations. The writs were to be returnable on Wednesday, July 10.

26 *

4. KENYA.

THE KENYA (ANNEXATION) ORDER IN COUNCIL, 1920.

1920, No. 2342.

At the Court at Buckingham Palace, the 11th day of June, 1920.

PRESENT,

The King's Most Excellent Majesty in Council.

WHEREAS the territories in East Africa situate within the limits of this Order and forming part of the Protectorate known as the East Africa Protectorate, are under the Protection of His Majesty the King :

And whereas British subjects have settled in large numbers in the said territories, and it is expedient, with a view to the further development and more convenient administration of the said territories, that they should be annexed to and should henceforth form part of His Majesty's Dominions :

Now, therefore, His Majesty is pleased, by and with the advice of His Privy Council, to order, and it is hereby ordered, as follows :—

I. This Order may be cited as the Kenya (Annexation) Order in Council, 1920.

II. Until further provision shall be made in respect thereof, the limits of this Order are the territories comprised in the East Africa Protectorate as specified in the East Africa Order in Council, 1902 (*a*), save and excepting only such territories therein included as form part of the Dominions of His Highness the Sultan of Zanzibar.

III. From and after the coming into operation of this Order the said territories shall be annexed to and form part of His Majesty's Dominions and shall be known as the Colony of Kenya, hereinafter called the Colony.

IV. Nothing in this Order shall effect the validity of any Commission or Instructions issued by His Majesty under the Royal Sign Manual and Signet to the Governor and Commander-in-Chief of the territories now included within the limits of this Order, or of any Order in Council affecting the said territories, or of any Ordinance, Proclamation or Regulations passed or issued under any such Instructions or Order, or of any act or thing done under such Instructions, Order,

Ordinance, Proclamation or Regulations, save in so far as any provision of any such Order in Council, Ordinance, Proclamation or Regulations may be repugnant to the provisions of any Act of Parliament which may, by reason of the annexation hereby declared, become extended to the Colony, or to any Order or regulation made under the authority of any such Act, or having in the Colony the force and effect of any such Act.

V. This Order shall be published in the Official Gazette of the East Africa Protectorate, and shall thereupon commence and come into operation (*a*), and the Governor shall give directions for the publication of this Order at such places and in such manner, and for such time or times, as he thinks proper for giving publicity thereto within the Colony.

VI. His Majesty may from time to time revoke, alter, add to, or amend this Order.

And the Right Honourable Viscount Milner, G.C.B., G.C.M.G., one of His Majesty's Principal Secretaries of State, is to give the necessary directions herein accordingly.

ALMERIC FITZ ROY.

STATUTORY RULES AND ORDERS, 1912.   No. 913.
COPYRIGHT.

INTERNATIONAL COPYRIGHT.

ORDER IN COUNCIL UNDER THE COPYRIGHT ACT, 1911 (1 & 2 GEO. 5, C. 46), REGULATING COPYRIGHT RELATIONS WITH THE FOREIGN COUNTRIES OF THE BERNE CONVENTION UNION.

At the Court at Buckingham Palace, the 24th day of June, 1912.

PRESENT,
The King's Most Excellent Majesty in Council

WHEREAS on the 9th day of September, 1886, a Convention with respect to the protection to be given by way of copyright to the authors of literary and artistic works (hereinafter called the Berne Convention) set out in the Second Schedule to this Order was concluded between Her late Majesty Queen Victoria and the foreign countries following, that is to say :—Belgium, France, Germany, Hayti, Italy, Spain, Switzerland and Tunis, and on

(marginal note:) Orders in Council. (2) Statutory Preamble.

the 5th day of September, 1887, the ratifications of the said Berne Convention were duly exchanged between Her late Majesty Queen Victoria and the aforesaid countries :

And whereas subsequently the foreign countries following, namely, Luxemburg, Monaco, Montenegro, Norway and Sweden, acceded to the said Berne Convention :

And whereas an additional Act to the said Berne Convention (hereinafter called the Additional Act) set out in the Third Schedule to this Order was agreed upon between Her late Majesty Queen Victoria and the foreign countries following, namely, Belgium, France, Germany, Italy, Luxemburg, Monaco, Montenegro, Spain, Switzerland and Tunis, for the purpose of varying the provisions of the said Berne Convention and the ratifications of the said Additional Act were, on the 9th day of September, 1897, exchanged between Her late Majesty Queen Victoria and the aforesaid countries :

And whereas subsequently the Republic of Hayti acceded to the said Additional Act, and the foreign countries following, namely, Denmark and the Faröe Islands, the German Protectorates, Japan and Liberia, acceded to the said Berne Convention and the said Additional Act, and the Principality of Montenegro duly denounced the said Berne Convention and the said Additional Act :

And whereas by the Orders in Council mentioned in the Fifth Schedule to this Order and made under the authority of the International Copyright Acts, 1844 to 1886, effect is now given throughout His Majesty's dominions to the said Berne Convention and the said Additional Act :

And whereas a Convention (hereinafter called the Berlin Convention) set out in the First Schedule to this Order was on the 13th day of November, 1908, agreed upon between His late Majesty King Edward VII. and the foreign countries following, namely : Belgium, Denmark, France, Germany, Italy, Japan, Liberia, Luxemburg, Monaco, Norway, Spain, Sweden, Switzerland and Tunis, for the purpose of replacing the said Berne Convention and the said Additional Act :

And whereas it is provided by the said Berlin Convention that the contracting States may make reservations by declaring at the exchange of ratifications that they desire to remain bound, as regards any specific point, by the provisions of the said Berne Convention and the said Additional Act, and it is further provided by the said Berlin Convention that the said Berne

Convention and the said Additional Act shall remain in force in regard to relations with contracting States which do not ratify the said Berlin Convention :

And whereas the said Berlin Convention was ratified by His Majesty on the 14th day of June, 1912, subject to the reservation mentioned in Part I. of the Fourth Schedule to this Order :

And whereas the said Berlin Convention has also been ratified by the foreign countries following, namely, Belgium, France, Germany, Hayti, Japan, Liberia, Luxemburg, Monaco, Norway, Spain, Switzerland and Tunis, subject to the reservations mentioned in Part II. of the Fourth Schedule to this Order :

And whereas the Republic of Portugal has acceded to the said Berlin Convention :

And whereas by the Copyright Act, 1911, the aforesaid International Copyright Acts, 1844 to 1886, are repealed, as from the commencement of the said Copyright Act, 1911, in the parts of His Majesty's dominions to which the said Act extends :

And whereas by the said Copyright Act, 1911, authority is conferred upon His Majesty to extend by Order in Council the protection of the said Act to certain classes of foreign works within any part of His Majesty's dominions, other than self-governing dominions, to which the said Act extends :

Now, therefore, His Majesty, by and with the advice of His Enactment. Privy Council, and by virtue of the authority conferred upon Him by the Copyright Act, 1911, is pleased to order, and it is hereby ordered as follows :—

(1) This Order shall extend to the foreign countries following, namely, Belgium, Denmark and the Faröe Islands, France, Germany, and the German Protectorates, Hayti, Italy, Japan, Liberia, Luxemburg, Monaco, Norway, Portugal, Spain, Sweden, Switzerland and Tunis. And the above countries are in this Order referred to as the foreign countries of the Copyright Union.

(2) The Copyright Act, 1911, including the provisions as to Application existing works, shall subject to the provisions of the said Act of Principal and of this Order apply— Act.

    (*a*) to works **first** published in a foreign country of the Copyright Union, in like manner as if they had been first published within the parts of His Majesty's dominions to which the said Act extends :

(*b*) to literary, dramatic, musical and artistic works, the authors whereof were at the time of the making of the works subjects or citizens of a foreign country of the Copyright Union, in like manner as if the authors had been British subjects.

(*c*) in respect of residence in a foreign country of the Copyright Union, in like manner as if such residence had been residence in the parts of His Majesty's dominions to which the said Acts extends.

Provided that—

(i.) Sections 1 (2) (*d*) and 19 of the Copyright Act, 1911, and such other part or parts thereof as confer upon the owner of the copyright in a literary, dramatic or musical work the exclusive right of making any record perforated roll cinematograph film or other contrivance by means of which the work may be mechanically performed and such other part or parts thereof as confer copyright in any record or perforated roll shall not apply in the case of any work of which the country of origin is Denmark, Italy, or Sweden.

(ii.) The term of copyright within the parts of His Majesty's dominions to which this Order applies shall not exceed that conferred by the law of the country of origin of the work.

(iii.) The enjoyment of the rights conferred by the Copyright Act, 1911, shall be subject to the accomplishment of the following conditions and formalities, that is to say :—

(Here follow five special cases.)

(iv.) Nothing in the provisions of the Copyright Act, 1911, as applied to existing works, shall be construed as reviving any right of preventing the production or importation of any translation in any case where the right has ceased by virtue of Section 5 of the International Copyright Act, 1886.

(3) Subject to the provisions of Article (2) proviso (i) of this Order where any musical work to which this Order applies has been published before the commencement of the Copyright Act, 1911, but no contrivances by means of which the work may be mechanically performed have before the commencement of this Order been lawfully made, or placed on sale, within the parts of His Majesty's dominions to which this Order applies, copy-

right in the work shall include all rights conferred by the said Act with respect to the making of records, perforated rolls and other contrivances by means of which the work may be mechanically performed.

(4) In this Order the expression " the country of origin " as applied to a work has the same meaning as in the third paragraph of Article 4 of the Berlin Convention.

(5) (*a*) This Order shall apply to all His Majesty's dominions, colonies, and possessions, excepting to those hereinafter named, that is to say, except to the— *Order not to apply to Dominions.*

> Dominion of Canada,
> The Commonwealth of Australia,
> The Dominion of New Zealand,
> The Union of South Africa,
> Newfoundland.

(*b*) This Order shall also apply to Cyprus, and to the following territories under His Majesty's protection, that is to say—the Bechuanaland Protectorate, East Africa Protectorate, Gambia Protectorate, Gilbert and Ellice Islands Protectorate, Northern Nigeria Protectorate, Northern Territories of the Gold Coast, Nyasaland Protectorate, Northern Rhodesia, Southern Rhodesia, Sierra Leone Protectorate, Somaliland Protectorate, Southern Nigeria Protectorate, Solomon Islands Protectorate, Swaziland, Uganda Protectorate, and Weihaiwei.

(6) The Orders mentioned in the Fifth Schedule to this Order are hereby revoked, as from the date of the commencement of this Order, so far as regards the parts of His Majesty's dominions to which this Order applies :

Provided that neither such revocation nor anything else in this Order shall prejudicially affect any right acquired or accrued before the commencement of this Order by virtue of any Order hereby revoked, and any person entitled to such right shall continue entitled thereto, and to the remedies for the same, in like manner as if this Order had not been made.

(7) This Order shall be construed as if it formed part of the Copyright Act, 1911. *Order to be construed as part of the Act.*

(8) This Order shall come into operation in the United Kingdom on the 1st day of July, 1912, and in any other part of His Majesty's dominions to which this Order applies, on the day on which the Copyright Act, 1911, comes into operation in such part ; which day is in this Order referred to as the commencement of this Order.

And the Lords Commissioners of His Majesty's Treasury are to give the necessary orders accordingly.

ALMERIC FITZ ROY.

First Schedule—Berlin Convention.
Second Schedule—Berne Convention.
Third Schedule—Additional Act of Paris.
Fourth Schedule—Reservations to Berlin Convention.
Fifth Schedule—Orders in Council.

JUDICIAL ORDER IN COUNCIL.

(L.S.)

Orders in Council. (3) Order on Report of Judicial Committee of Privy Council.

At the Court at Buckingham Palace, the 26th day of June, 1930.

PRESENT,

The King's Most Excellent Majesty.

Lord President.   Lord Colebrooke.
Lord Passfield.   Lord Blanesburgh.

WHEREAS there was this day read at the Board a Report from the Judicial Committee of the Privy Council dated the 23rd day of June, 1930, in the words following, viz. :

WHEREAS by virtue of His late Majesty King Edward the Seventh's Order in Council of the 18th day of October 1909 there was referred unto this Committee the matter of an Appeal from the Supreme Court of Canada between the Trustees of St. Luke's Presbyterian Congregation of Saltsprings a body Corporate Alex. C. Macdonald William Fraser William H. Mackay D. Hedley Ross Munro Gunn Robert A. Robertson George Gray Roderick Mackay and John R. Young Appellants and Alexander Cameron Gordon Proudfoot C.A. Maxwell K. A. Murray John Bishop W. C. Proudfoot Robert Johnston John McN. Campbell and Alexander Halliday Respondents (Privy Council Appeal No. 98 of 1929) and likewise a humble Petition of the Appellants setting forth that on the 1st September 1925 the Respondents brought an Action in the Supreme Court of Nova Scotia alleging that in accordance with the United Church of Canada Act (Statutes of Canada 14-15 Geo. 5, c. 100) the St. Luke's Presbyterian Congregation of Saltsprings at a meeting regularly called and held decided by a majority of votes not to enter the Union of Churches provided for by the Act ; that under the Act and the Nova Scotia Act c. 122 of the Acts of

1924 the congregation became and was a non-concurring congregation and that an alleged subsequent meeting of the congregation held on or about the 27th July 1925 and all proceedings thereat were null and void and of no effect and the Respondents' claimed declarations injunctions and other relief : that on the 2nd February 1926 the Supreme Court delivered judgment dismissing the Respondents' Action : that the Respondents having appealed to the Supreme Court of Novia Scotia *in banco* the Court by a majority (Mellish J. dissenting) on the 9th April 1927 delivered judgment allowing the Appeal : that the Appellants having appealed and the Respondents having cross-appealed to the Supreme Court of Canada the Court on the 5th February 1929 delivered judgment by a majority (Duff J. dissenting) varying the Judgment of the Supreme Court of Nova Scotia *in banco* by striking out the fourth paragraph thereof containing the declaration that the congregation might still enter into the Union and suspending the enforcement of the Judgment and subject to such variation affirming the Judgment : that by Your Majesty's Order in Council dated the 15th August 1929 the Appellants were granted special leave to appeal upon depositing in the Registry of the Privy Council the sum of £400 as security for costs which condition has since been complied with : And humbly praying Your Majesty in Council to take their Appeal into consideration and that the Judgment of the Supreme Court of Canada dated the 5th February 1929 may be reversed altered or varied or for further or other relief :

THE LORDS OF THE COMMITTEE in obedience to His late Majesty's said Order in Council have taken the Appeal and humble Petition into consideration and having heard Counsel on behalf of the Parties on both sides Their Lordships do this day agree humbly to report to Your Majesty as their opinion (1) that the Judgment of the Supreme Court of Nova Scotia *in banco* dated the 9th day of April 1927 as varied by the Judgment of the Supreme Court of Canada dated the 5th day of February 1929 ought to be further varied by deleting from the second paragraph thereof sub-paragraph ' (2) that the Reverend Robert Johnston was at all material times and is Moderator *pro tempore* or Interim Moderator of the said congregation ' and also by deleting from the third paragraph thereof the following words with which that paragraph concludes : ' and from interfering with the exercise by the Plaintiff Robert Johnston of the rights powers and privileges of the office of

Moderator *pro tempore* or *interim* Moderator of the said congregation ' ; (2) that in all other respects this Appeal ought to be dismissed and the Judgment of the Supreme Court of Canada dated the 5th day of February 1929 affirmed ; and (3) that there ought to be paid by the Appellants to the Respondents their costs of this Appeal incurred in the Supreme Court of Canada and that out of the said sum of £400 so deposited as aforesaid the Registrar of the Privy Council ought to be directed to pay out to the Solicitors for the Respondents in England the sum of £361 12s. 10d. (being the amount of the Respondents' taxed costs of this Appeal incurred in England) and to repay to the Solicitors for the Appellants in England the sum of £38 7s. 2d. (being the balance of the said sum of £400 after payment thereout of the said taxed costs of the Respondents).

HIS MAJESTY having taken the said Report into consideration was pleased by and with the advice of His Privy Council to approve thereof and to order as it is hereby ordered that the same be punctually observed obeyed and carried into execution.

Whereof the Governor-General or Officer Administering the Government of the Dominion of Canada for the time being and all other persons whom it may concern are to take notice and govern themselves accordingly.

M. P. A. HANKEY

DEPARTMENTAL REGULATIONS.

UNEMPLOYMENT.

RELIEF WORKS.

THE MINISTRY OF TRANSPORT (UNEMPLOYMENT RELIEF WORKS PROCEDURE) ORDER, 1920. DATED DECEMBER 18, 1920.

1920, No. 2350.

(1) Administrative Order.

To the several Local Authorities in Great Britain for those purposes of the Unemployment (Relief Works) Act, 1920, in respect of which the Ministry of Transport is the appropriate Government Department within the meaning of the Act :

And to all others whom it may concern :
WHEREAS under and by virtue of the Unemployment (Relief Works) Act, 1920 (hereinafter referred to as " the Act "), and

the enactments applied thereby, and subject to and in accordance with the provisions of those enactments as adapted and modified in pursuance of the Act, the Ministry of Transport (hereinafter referred to as " the Minister ") is empowered to prescribe the form of order (hereinafter referred to as " Compulsory Order ") to be made by a Local Authority for the compulsory acquisition of land for the purpose of works of public utility as defined in that Act for which the Ministry of Transport is the appropriate Government Department within the meaning of the Act ; the manner of publication of a Compulsory Order ; the notice to be given in the locality and to the owners, lessees and occupiers of the land proposed to be acquired ; and the periods within which objections to a Compulsory Order shall be presented.

The Minister of Transport hereby in pursuance of such powers orders as follows :—

1. A Compulsory Order shall be in the form set forth in the First Schedule hereto, or in a form to the like effect.

2. (1) Before they submit a Compulsory Order to the Minister for confirmation the Local Authority shall cause the same to be published by advertisement in one or more of the local newspapers circulating in the district of the Local Authority and in the parish or parishes in which the land to which the Compulsory Order relates is situated.

(2) The advertisement shall contain, in addition to a copy of the Compulsory Order, a notice setting out the following particulars :

(*a*) a statement that any objection to the Compulsory Order must be presented to the Minister within the period of fourteen days after the date of the publication of the advertisement : and

(*b*) a statement of the period, times and place or places during and at which the plan referred to in the Schedule to the Compulsory Order may be inspected by or on behalf of any person interested in the land to which the Compulsory Order relates.

(3) The plan referred to in the Schedule to the Compulsory Order shall be deposited by the Local Authority on or before the date of the advertisement at a place convenient for the purposes of inspection by persons interested in the land shown thereon, and shall be kept deposited thereat for a period not being less than fourteen days from the date of the publication

of the advertisement; and the said plan shall be open for inspection by any person interested or affected, without payment of any fee at all reasonable hours on any week-day during the said period. The Local Authority shall also make suitable provision for affording to any such person inspecting the said plan any necessary explanation or information in regard thereto.

3. (1) The Local Authority shall, not later than the seventh day after the making of the Compulsory Order, cause notice thereof to be served in manner hereinafter prescribed upon every owner, lessee and occupier of the land to which the Compulsory Order relates, and every such notice shall include a printed copy of the Compulsory Order to which shall be appended a notice containing the particulars mentioned in Article 2 (2) of this Order.

(2) The Local Authority shall furnish a printed copy of the Compulsory Order, free of charge, to any person interested in the land to which the Compulsory Order relates upon his applying for the same.

4. The period within which an objection to a Compulsory Order may be presented to the Minister by a person interested in the land to which the Compulsory Order relates shall be the period of fourteen days from and after the date of the publication of the advertisement of the Compulsory Order.

5. (1) The Local Authority shall, as soon as practicable after the confirmation of a Compulsory Order, cause a printed copy of the Compulsory Order as confirmed to be served on every owner, lessee and occupier of the land to which the Compulsory Order relates.

(2) A printed copy of a Compulsory Order as confirmed shall be furnished free of charge by the Local Authority to any person interested in the land authorised to be purchased upon his applying for the same, and a copy of any plan to which reference is made in the Compulsory Order as confirmed shall also be furnished by the Local Authority to any such person in so far as such plan relates to his land upon his applying for such copy and paying the reasonable cost of preparing the same.

6. Every notice or other document which, in pursuance of Article 3 (1) or 5 of this Order, is required to be given or served by the Local Authority to or on an owner, lessee or occupier shall be served :

    (*a*) by delivery of the same personally to the person required to be served, or, if such person is absent abroad or cannot be found, to his agent ; or (*b*) by leaving the same at the usual or last known place of abode of such person as aforsesaid ; or

(*c*) by post as a registered letter addressed to the usual or last known place of abode of such person ; or

(*d*) in the case of a notice required to be served on a Local Authority or corporate body or company, by delivering the same to their clerk or secretary or leaving the same at his office with some person employed there, or by post as a registered letter addressed to such clerk or secretary at his office.

Provided that in the case of any such owner, lessee or occupier who cannot be found, a notice sent by registered post to his last known place of abode shall be sufficient service of notice.

Provided also that if the owner, lessee or occupier of any such land cannot be ascertained, a notice exhibited in some conspicuous position or positions on the land shall be sufficient service of notice upon such owner, lessee or occupier.

7. For the purpose of the application of this Order to Scotland a reference to the Second Schedule to this Order shall be substituted for the reference to the First Schedule in Article 1 of this Order.

8. This Order may be cited as the Ministry of Transport (Unemployment Relief Works Procedure) Order, 1920.

[Schedules.]

ROAD VEHICLES.

(2) Statutory Regulations.

THE MOTOR VEHICLES (DRIVING LICENCES) REGULATIONS, 1930, DATED 17TH NOVEMBER, 1930, MADE BY THE MINISTER OF TRANSPORT.

The Minister of Transport under and by virtue of the powers conferred upon him by Section 30 of the Road Traffic Act, 1930 (hereinafter referred to as " the Act "), hereby makes the following Regulations :—

1. These Regulations may be cited as " The Motor Vehicles (Driving Licences) Regulations, 1930," and shall come into force on the first day of December, 1930.

2. The Motor Car (Registration and Licensing) Order, 1903, and the Motor Car Registration and Licensing (Scotland) Order, 1903, are hereby revoked.

3. Except where the context otherwise requires, the term " licence " in these Regulations shall include a provisional licence granted under sub-section (3) of Section 5 of the Act and a licence granted under Section 3 of the Motor Car Act, 1903.

4. (1) Any person who desires to obtain the grant of a licence to drive a motor vehicle shall apply to the Council of the County or County Borough in which he resides or, if he has no residence in Great Britain, to any such Council (hereinafter in either case referred to as " the Licensing Authority ") and shall furnish all relevant particulars and make any relevant declaration specified in the form set out in the First Schedule to these Regulations.

(2) Applications for the grant of a licence may be received and dealt with at any time within one month before the date on which the grant of the licence is to take effect.

(3) The fee of five shillings prescribed by the Act shall be paid before the applicant is entitled to receive a licence.

5. (i.) The diseases and disabilities in the case of which the applicant for a licence shall not be entitled to claim to be subjected to a test as to his fitness or ability to drive a motor vehicle under sub-section (2) of Section 5 of the Act shall be the following :—

> Epilepsy ; liability to sudden attacks of disabling giddiness or fainting ; inability to read at a distance of 25 yards in good daylight (with the aid of glasses, if worn) a series of six letters and figures in white on a black ground of the same size and arrangement as those prescribed for the identification mark of a motor car.

(ii.) The fee to be paid by an applicant who claims under that sub-section to be subjected to such test shall be ten shillings.

(iii.) In order to pass such test the applicant for a licence shall prove to an examiner approved by the Licensing Authority his ability unaided to :

(*a*) Start the vehicle from rest, to move away in a reasonably quick time and to maintain an accurate course.

(*b*) Turn right and left hand corners correctly.

(*c*) Stop the vehicle within a reasonable distance when travelling at various speeds. (In this respect he must satisfy the examiner that in an emergency he will be able to apply the brakes promptly and effectively.)

(*d*) Operate all controls with safety and without moving from the driving seat.

(*e*) Give all recognised signals to other persons using the road and to traffic controllers in a clear and unmistakable manner. (If, owing to his disability, it is impracticable or undesirable that he should give such signals by hand, the vehicle must be fitted with a device or devices which in the opinion of the examiner will be satisfactory for this purpose.)

(*f*) Except in the case of a motor-cycle, make the vehicle proceed backwards for a reasonable distance, make a left and right hand turn in reverse gear, and back the vehicle into an indicated position.

(*g*) Turn the vehicle round so as to proceed in the opposite direction in a roadway 30 feet in width.

(*h*) Stop, hold and start the vehicle on a gradient of at least 1 in 15, but not steeper than 1 in 10.

Generally, the applicant shall satisfy the examiner that he is capable of driving a motor vehicle or a motor vehicle of the particular construction or design to which the application relates without danger to other users of the road.

.   .   .   .

FORM OF ORDER FOR DEMOLITION OF A DWELLING-HOUSE.

HOUSING ACT, 1930.

Whereas the
(hereinafter referred to as " the Council ") after complying with the requirements of Section 19 of the Housing Act, 1930, are satisfied that the dwelling-house.
being occupied or of a type suitable for occupation by persons of the working classes is unfit for human habitation and is not capable at a reasonable expense of being rendered so fit and have accepted no undertaking from an owner or mortgagee with respect to the carrying out of works or the future user of the house ;

Now therefore the Council, in pursuance of Sub-section (3) of Section 19 of the Housing Act, 1930, order as follows :

(1) The said dwelling-house be vacated within
days from the date on which this Order becomes operative ·

(3) Demolition Order, Form of, under Housing Act, 1930, s. 57. Scheduled to Provisional Rules and Orders, 1930, Housing, England.

(2) the said dwelling-house be demolished within six weeks after the expiration of the last-mentioned period, or if the house is not vacated by that date within six weeks after the date on which it is vacated.

Dated this   day of   19   .

(To be sealed with the Common Seal of the Local Authority.)

PATENT FOR CREATION OF A PEER.

Letters Patent. Form for creation of Baron.

GEORGE THE FIFTH by the Grace of God of Great Britain Ireland and the British Dominions beyond the Seas King Defender of the Faith To all Lords Spiritual and Temporal and all other Our Subjects whatsoever to whom these Presents shall come Greeting Know Ye that We of Our especial grace certain knowledge and mere motion do by these Presents advance create and prefer Our   to the state degree style dignity title and honour of Baron   of in Our County of   And for Us Our heirs and successors do appoint give and grant unto him the said name state degree style dignity title and honour of Baron to have and to hold unto him and the heirs male of his body lawfully begotten and to be begotten Willing and by these Presents granting for Us Our heirs and successors that he and his heirs male aforesaid and every of them successively may have hold and possess a seat place and voice in the Parliaments and Public Assemblies and Councils of Us Our heirs and successors within Our United Kingdom amongst other Barons And also that he and his heirs male aforesaid successively may enjoy and use all the rights privileges pre-eminences immunities and advantages to the degree of a Baron duly and of right belonging which other Barons of Our United Kingdom have heretofore used and enjoyed or as they do at present use and enjoy.

In Witness, &c.

APPOINTMENT OF AMBASSADOR.

GEORGE R.I.

GEORGE, by the Grace of God, of Great Britain, Ireland and the British Dominions beyond the Seas King, Defender of the Faith, Emperor of India, etc., etc., etc.

To All and Singular to whom these Presents shall come, Greeting !

Whereas it appears to Us expedient to nominate some Person of approved Wisdom, Loyalty, Diligence, and Circumspection to represent Us in the character of Our Ambassador Extraordinary and Plenipotentiary to

Now Know Ye that We, reposing especial trust and confidence in the discretion and faithfulness of Our (Right) Trusty and Well-beloved (Counsellor) (Sir)........................... have nominated, constituted and appointed, as We do by these Presents nominate, constitute and appoint him the said

to be Our Ambassador Extraordinary and Plenipotentiary to

as aforesaid.   Giving and Granting to him in that character

all Power and Authority to do and perform all proper acts, matters and things which may be desirable or necessary for the promotion of relations of friendship, good understanding and harmonious intercourse between Our Realm and

and for the protection and furtherance of the interests confided to his care ; by the diligent and discreet accomplishment of which acts, matters and things aforementioned he shall gain Our approval and show himself worthy of Our high confidence.
    And We therefore request all those whom it may concern to receive and acknowledge Our said

as such Ambassador Extraordinary and Plenipotentiary as aforesaid and freely to communicate with him upon all matters which may appertain to the objects of the high Mission whereto he is hereby appointed.
    Given at Our Court of Saint James, the   day of
                        in the Year of Our Lord One Thousand Nine Hundred and Thirty   , and in the
Year of Our Reign.

By His Majesty's Command.

(Countersigned by One of His Majesty's Principal Secretaries of State.)

27

FORM OF FREE PARDON.

GEORGE THE FIFTH, by the Grace of God, of Great Britain, Ireland and the British Dominions beyond the Seas King, Defender of the Faith. To all to whom these Presents shall come, Greeting !

WHEREAS A.B.   convicted of
and was thereupon sentenced to
Now KNOW YE that We in consideration of some circumstances humbly represented to Us are graciously pleased to extend Our Grace and Mercy to the said A.B.
and to grant him Our Free Pardon in respect of the said conviction, thereby pardoning, remitting and releasing unto him all pains penalties and punishments whatsoever that from the said conviction may ensue ; and We do hereby command all Judges, Justices and others whom it may concern that they take due notice hereof ; and We do require and direct our Prison Commissioners and the Governor of any Prison in which the said A.B.
may be detained in respect of the said conviction to cause him to be forthwith discharged therefrom ;
And for so doing this shall be a sufficient Warrant.
Given at Our Court at St. James's the   day of
19   in the   year of Our reign.
By His Majesty's Command.

DOCUMENTS PROVIDING FOR GOVERNMENT OF A COLONY WITH A PARTLY ELECTED LEGIS- LATURE.

LETTERS PATENT passed under the Great Seal of the United Kingdom, constituting the Office of Governor and Commander-in-Chief of the Colony of Fiji, and providing for the Government thereof.

Letters Patent, dated 9th February, 1929.

George the Fifth by the Grace of God of Great Britain, Ireland and the British Dominions beyond the Seas King, Defender of the Faith, Emperor of India : To all to whom these Presents shall come, Greeting !

WHEREAS by certain Letters Patent passed under the Great Seal of the United Kingdom, bearing date at Westminster the Thirty-first day of January 1914, provision was made for the administration of the government of Our Colony of Fiji : *Recites Letters Patent, 31st January, 1914.*

And whereas by certain further Letters Patent, bearing date the Twentieth day of July 1916, the aforesaid Letters Patent of the Thirty-first day of January 1914 have been amended : *Recites Letters Patent of 20th July, 1916.*

And whereas We are minded to make fresh provision for the administration of the government of Our Colony of Fiji :

Now know ye that We do by these Presents revoke the above recited Letters Patent of the Thirty-first day of January 1914, and the Twentieth day of July 1916, but without prejudice to anything lawfully done thereunder, and We do by these Our Letters Patent declare Our Will and Pleasure as follows :— *Revokes Letters Patent of 31st January, 1914, and 20th July, 1916.*

1. There shall be a Governor and Commander-in-Chief (hereinafter called the Governor) in and over Our Colony of Fiji (hereinafter called the Colony), and appointments to the said Office shall be made by Commission under the Royal Sign Manual and Signet. *Office of Governor constituted.*

2. The Governor shall do and execute, in due manner, all things that belong to his said office, according to the several powers and authorities granted or appointed him by virtue of these Our Letters Patent and of such Commission as may be issued to him under the Royal Sign Manual and Signet, and to such other powers and authorities, being still in force, as may have been heretofore given to any of his predecessors in his said office, and according to such Instructions as may from time to time be given to him, under Our Sign Manual and Signet, or by Our Order in Our Privy Council, or by Us through a Secretary of State, and according to such Laws as are now or shall hereafter be in force in the Colony. *Governor's powers and authorities.*

3. Every person appointed to fill the office of Governor shall with all due solemnity, before entering on any of the duties of his office, cause the Commission appointing him to be Governor to be read and published at the seat of Government, in the presence of the Chief Justice of the Colony, and of such Members of the Executive Council thereof as can conveniently attend, which being done, he shall then and there take before them the Oath of Allegiance, in the form provided by an Act passed in the Session holden in the Thirty-first and Thirty-second years of the Reign of Her Majesty Queen Victoria, intituled an Act to amend the Law relating to Promissory Oaths ; and likewise *Publication of Governor's Commission.* *Oaths to be taken by Governor. Imperial Act, 31 & 32 Vict. c. 72.*

the usual Oath for the due execution of the office of Governor and for the due and impartial administration of justice ; which Oaths the said Chief Justice, or, if he be unavoidably absent, the senior Member of the Executive Council then present, is hereby required to administer.

Public Seal. 4. The Governor shall keep and use the Public Seal of the Colony for sealing all things whatsoever that shall pass the said Public Seal.

Executive Council. 5. For the purpose of advising the Governor, there shall be an Executive Council for the Colony, and the said Council shall consist of such persons and shall be constituted in such manner as may be directed by any Instructions which may from time to time be addressed to the Governor under the Royal Sign Manual and Signet, or through a Secretary of State, and all such persons shall hold their places in the said Council at Our pleasure.

Legislative Council. 6. On and after a date to be fixed by the Governor by Proclamation the Legislative Council constituted in accordance with the above recited Letters Patent of the Thirty-first day of January 1914, and the Twentieth day of July 1916, shall cease to exist, and in place thereof there shall be in and for the Colony a Legislative Council constituted as hereinafter provided.

Until the date to be fixed by the Governor as aforesaid but no longer, the constitution, appointment and powers of the Legislative Council constituted in accordance with the said Letters Patent of the Thirty-first day of January 1914, and the Twentieth day of July 1916, shall continue in force notwithstanding the revocation of the said Letters Patent under the provisions of these Our Letters Patent.

Composition of Legislative Council. 7. The Legislative Council shall consist of the Governor as President, not more than thirteen Nominated Members, six European Elected Members, three Native Members, and three Indian Elected Members.

Nominated Members. Qualifications. 8. The Nominated Members of the Legislative Council shall be such persons holding public office in the Colony as the Governor may from time to time by instrument under the Public Seal of the Colony appoint, subject to Our disallowance or confirmation through a Secretary of State. The Nominated Members of the Council shall hold their places therein during Our Pleasure, and **Vacation of Seats.** shall in any case vacate their seats at the next dissolution of the Council after their appointment. If any Nominated Member cease to hold public office in the Colony his seat upon the Council shall thereupon become vacant.

The Governor shall without delay report to Us for Our confirmation or disallowance, to be signified through a Secretary of State, every appointment of any person as a Nominated Member of the Council. Appointments of Nominated Members to be immediately reported.

9. The European Elected Members of the Council shall be elected as follows :—

> (1) Two Members by persons duly qualified as European electors as hereinafter provided. (Here follow electoral areas.)

.   .   .   .

10. The Native Members shall be appointed as follows :— Native Members.

> (1) The Great Council of Native Chiefs in the Colony shall at the Meeting held by the said Great Council next following a dissolution of the Legislative Council, or when required so to do, submit to the Governor the names of not less than four, nor more than six persons, being aboriginal natives of the Colony, who are able to speak and understand the English language, and from the persons submitted the Governor shall select three persons who shall upon such selection be and become Members of the Legislative Council.
>
> Provided that the Governor may, without assigning any reason, require the said Great Council to submit the names of other persons qualified as aforesaid in addition to the persons first submitted.
>
> Provided further that the names submitted by the Great Council of Chiefs at a Meeting held in November 1928 shall be deemed to be names submitted under this sub-clause for the purpose of the constitution of the first Legislative Council to be held under the provisions of these Our Letters Patent.
>
> (2) The Provisions of Article 23 of these Letters Patent with regard to the resignation of and vacation of seats by Elected Members (except in so far as they impose disqualifications by reason of the receipt of salary payable out of the Public Revenue of the Colony) shall apply to Native Members and if a Native Member resign his seat, or his seat become vacant, the Governor may, from the names already submitted as provided in sub-clause (1) hereof, select another person to fill the vacant seat. If the Legislative Council be dissolved, the Governor may upon the constitution of a

new Council select from the names so submitted, any three persons to be Members of the Legislative Council. The persons selected shall be to all intents and purposes Native Members of the said Council, but only until the next meeting of the Great Council of Chiefs following a dissolution of the Legislative Couneil.

Election of Indian Elected Members. 11. The Indian Elected Members shall be elected by persons duly qualified as Indian electors as hereinafter provided.

Indian Electoral Divisions. 12. For the purpose of the election of Indian Elected Members the Colony shall be divided into the following three Electoral Divisions :—

. . . .

Precedence of Members. One Member shall be elected for each of the said divisions.

13. The Members of the Legislative Council shall take precedence as follows :—

(1) Firstly, the Nominated Members according to their seniority in the Executive Council, or, if they are not Members thereof, according to the priority of their respective appointments, or, if appointed by the same instrument, according to the order in which they are named therein.

(2) Secondly, the European Elected Members according to the length of time during which they have been continuously Members of the Legislative Council, Members elected at the same general election, being deemed to have become Members of the Council at the same time and taking precedence amongst themselves according to the alphabetical order of their names.

(3) Thirdly, the Native Members according to the length of time during which they have been continuously Members of the Legislative Council, Members appointed for the first time at the same general election being deemed to have become Members of the Council at the same time and taking precedence according to the alphabetical order of their names.

(4) Fourthly, the Indian Elected Members according to the length of time during which they have been continuously Members of the Legislative Council, Members elected at the same general election being deemed

to have become Members of the Council at the same time and taking precedence according to such order as the Governor shall appoint.

14. No Member of the Council shall sit or vote therein until he shall have taken and subscribed the following oath before the Governor, or some person authorised by the Governor to administer such oath :— Oath to be taken by Members of Council.

" I, A.B., do swear that I will be faithful and bear true
" allegiance to His Majesty King George, his heirs and
" successors, according to law.
" So help me God."

Provided that every person authorised by law to make an affirmation instead of taking an oath may make such affirmation instead of taking the said oath.

15. Whenever any Nominated Member of the Legislative Council shall die or shall, with the permission of the Governor, by writing under his hand addressed to the Governor, resign his seat in the Council, or shall be suspended, or shall be declared by the Governor by an instrument under the Public Seal to be incapable of exercising his functions as such Member, or shall be temporarily absent from the Colony, or whenever the seat of a Nominated Member shall become vacant from any cause other than a dissolution of the Council, the Governor may by an instrument under the said Seal appoint some other person holding a public office in the Colony to be provisionally a Nominated Member of the Legislative Council in the place of the Member so dying, resigning, or being suspended, or declared incapable, or absent, or whose seat has become vacant as aforesaid. Provisional Appointment of Nominated Members.

The Governor shall without delay report to Us for Our confirmation or disallowance to be signified through a Secretary of State every provisional appointment of any person as a Nominated Member of the Council. Every such person shall hold his place in the Council during Our pleasure and every such provisional appointment may be disallowed by Us through a Secretary of State, or may be revoked by the Governor by any such instrument as aforesaid.

Every person so provisionally appointed shall be to all intents and purposes a Nominated Member of the Council until his appointment shall be disallowed, or revoked, or superseded by the permanent appointment in his place of a Nominated Member of the Legislative Council, or until the person in whose place he has been appointed shall be relieved from suspension, or declared by the Governor by an instrument under the Public Seal to be capable of exercising the functions of a Member of the Legislative Council or shall have returned to the Colony.

Suspension of Nominated Members.

16. The Governor may by an instrument under the Public Seal of the Colony suspend any Nominated Member of the Legislative Council from the exercise of his functions as a Member of the Council. Every such suspension shall be forthwith reported by the Governor to a Secretary of State, and shall remain in force unless and until it shall be either removed by the Governor by an instrument under the said Seal, or disallowed by Us through a Secretary of State.

Qualifications of European Elected Members.

17. No person shall be qualified to be elected as a European Elected Member of the Council, or, having been so elected, to sit or vote in the Council unless he—

(1) Is qualified to be registered as a European elector ; and

(2) Has been continuously resident for two years in the Colony ; and either

(3) (Here follow alternative property qualifications.)

. . . .

Qualifications of Indian Elected Members.

18. No person shall be qualified to be elected as an Indian Elected Member of the Council, or having been so elected, to sit or vote in the Council unless he—

(1) Is qualified to be registered as an Indian Elector ; and

(2) Has been continuously resident for two years in the Colony ; and

(3) Is able to speak and understand the English language to the satisfaction of the Registration Officer subject to an appeal from the decision of the Registration Officer to the Supreme Court ; and either

(4) (Property qualifications.)

. . . .

Disqualification of Elected Members.

19. No person shall be capable of being elected a Member of the Council, or, having been elected, shall sit or vote in the Council, who—

(1) Has been sentenced by any competent British Court, whether of the Colony or not, for any crime punishable by death, hard labour for any period, or imprisonment for a period exceeding one year, and has not received a free pardon from Us for the crime for which he has been so sentenced ; or

(2) Is an undischarged bankrupt, whether he has been declared a bankrupt by a Court in the Colony or by any other British Court ; or

(3) Has within five years before the election received charitable relief in the Colony from any public source ; or

(4) Is of unsound mind ; or

(5) Is in receipt of salary payable out of the public revenue of the Colony.

20. (1) Every candidate nominated at any election of a Member of the Council, or someone on his behalf, shall, as soon as his nomination has been accepted by the returning officer or registration officer, or within forty-eight hours thereafter, deposit, or cause to be deposited, with the returning officer or registration officer the sum of twenty-five pounds sterling, and if he fails to do so, he shall be deemed to have withdrawn from his candidature. *Deposit by Candidate.*

(2) If after the deposit is made, but before the poll is commenced, the candidate dies, the deposit, if made by him, shall be returned to his legal personal representative, or, if not made by him, shall be returned to the person by whom the deposit was made.

21. If a candidate who has made the required deposit is not elected, and the number of votes polled by him does not exceed, in the case of an electoral division returning one Member, ten per cent. of the total number of votes polled, or in the case of an electoral division returning more than one Member, ten per cent. of the total number of votes polled divided by the number of Members to be elected for that electoral division, the amount deposited shall be forfeited to the Colonial Revenue ; but in any other case the amount shall be returned to the candidate, where the candidate is elected, as soon as he has taken the oath, affirmation or declaration as a Member, and where the candidate is not elected, as soon as practicable after the result of the election is declared. *Forfeiture of Deposit in certain cases.*

22. All questions which may arise as to the right of any person to be or remain an Elected Member of the Council shall be referred to and decided by the Supreme Court of the Colony. *Questions as to qualification of Members or vacating of seats to be determined by Supreme Court.*

23. If any Elected Member of the Council shall, by writing under his hand addressed to the Governor, resign his seat in the Council, or shall become subject to any of the disqualifications specified in Article 19 of these Letters Patent, or shall take any *Seat of Elected Member ; how vacated.*

oath or make any declaration of allegiance to any Foreign State or Power, his seat in the Council shall thereupon become vacant.

Absence of Elected Member. An Elected Member of the Council may, with the permission of the Governor, be absent from the sittings of the Council or from the Colony for a period or periods not exceeding twelve calendar months at any one time ; but if any Elected Member shall for any reason be so absent for more than twelve consecutive calendar months, or shall be absent, except on the ground of illness, from the sittings of the Council for a period of two calendar months during the session of the Council, without the leave of the Governor, his seat in the Council shall thereupon become vacant.

Writ for Election to Supply Vacancy. Whenever the seat of an Elected Member has become vacant, the Governor shall, as soon as possible, issue a writ for the election of a new Member in the place of the Member whose seat has become vacant.

Penalty for Unqualified Persons Sitting or Voting as Members of Council. 24. Every person who, having been returned as a Member of the Council, but not having been at the time of his election qualified to be elected, shall sit or vote in the Council, shall for every day on which he shall sit or vote in the Council, and every person who shall sit or vote in the Council after his seat shall have become vacant shall for every day on which he shall sit or vote after his seat shall have become vacant, be liable to a penalty not exceeding Fifty Pounds, to be recovered by action in the Supreme Court of the Colony by any person who shall sue for the same.

25, 26. (Qualifications of European and Indian Electors.)

. . . .

Governor to make Regulations for Registration, etc. 27. The Governor of the Colony shall, as soon as possible after the promulgation of these Letters Patent, establish by proclamation such regulations, not inconsistent with these Letters Patent, as he may think necessary for regulating the registration of electors, and generally in regard to the election of Members of the Legislative Council, and such regulations shall take effect and have the force of law in the Colony immediately on the proclamation thereof ; and the provisions of any Letters Patent, Orders in Council, or Ordinances repugnant to the provisions of any such regulations shall be read subject to those regulations, and shall to the extent of such repugnancy be void and inoperative ; but any regulations so made may be repealed or altered by any Ordinance or Ordinances hereafter to be enacted by the Governor, with the advice and consent of the Legislative Council, or by any Letters Patent, or Orders in Council which may hereafter be issued or passed.

Until any such regulations shall be made and subject to any regulations to be so made, the regulations now in force shall remain in force and apply, so far as the same are applicable, to the election of Members of the Legislative Council established by these Letters Patent.

28. It shall be lawful for the Governor, with the advice and consent of the Legislative Council, to make laws for the peace, order, and good government of the Colony. Such laws shall be styled "Ordinances enacted by the Governor of Fiji, with the advice and consent of the Legislative Council thereof." *Power to make Laws. Style of Ordinances.*

29. We do hereby reserve to Ourselves, Our heirs and successors, power to disallow any such Ordinance, either in whole or in part, such disallowance to be signified to the Governor through a Secretary of State. Every such disallowance shall take effect from the time when the Governor shall have signified the same by proclamation in the *Fiji Royal Gazette*. *Power of Disallowance reserved to the Crown.*

30. We do also hereby reserve to Ourselves, Our heirs and successors, Our and their undoubted right, power, and authority to make, by and with the advice of Our or their Privy Council, all such laws for the peace, order, and good government of the Colony as to Us or them may seem necessary, and all such laws shall be of the same force and effect in the Colony as if these Letters Patent had not been made. *Reservation of power to legislate by Order in Council.*

31. When a Bill passed by the Legislative Council is presented to the Governor for his assent he shall, according to his discretion, but subject to the provisions contained in these Our Letters Patent, and to any Instructions addressed to him under the Royal Sign Manual and Signet or through a Secretary of State, declare that he assents thereto, or refuses his assent to the same, or that he reserves the same for the signification of Our pleasure. *Presentation of Bills to the Governor for his assent.*

32. No law shall take effect until either the Governor shall have assented thereto in Our name and on Our behalf, and shall have signed the same in token of such assent, or until We shall have given Our assent thereto by Our Order in Our Privy Council or through a Secretary of State. *Laws not to take effect until assented to.*

Bills assented to by the Governor shall take effect, and come into operation as law, from and after the date on which such assent shall be given, or on which it shall be enacted that they are to take effect and come into operation as law. *Time from which Bills assented to by the Governor are to take effect.*

Reserved Bills.

33. The Governor may reserve for the signification of Our pleasure thereon any Bill passed by the Legislative Council, and shall so reserve any such Bill by which any provision of these Our Letters Patent is repealed, altered, or amended, or which is in any way repugnant to or inconsistent with any of the provisions of these Our Letters Patent. A Bill so reserved shall take effect so soon as We shall have given Our assent thereto, either by Our Order in Our Privy Council, or through a Secretary of State, and the Governor shall have signified such assent by Proclamation in the *Fiji Royal Gazette*.

Enrolment of Ordinances.

34. The Governor shall transmit to the Chief Justice of the Colony, to be enrolled in the Supreme Court, a transcript, authenticated under the Public Seal of the Colony, and by his own signature, of every Ordinance passed by the Governor, with the advice and consent of the Legislative Council, and of every Bill reserved by him for the signification of Our pleasure. He shall also from time to time transmit to the Chief Justice, to be enrolled in the said Court, a certificate under his hand and seal, of the effect of every Order or other direction which he may have received from Us for confirming or disallowing, in the whole or in part, the provisions of any such Ordinance or Bill, which certificate shall in like manner be enrolled in the said Court, and there remain on record to the intent that the Judges of the said Court may without further or other proof take cognisance of all Ordinances made and promulgated for the peace, order, and good government of the Colony : Provided always, and We do hereby declare, that the Judges of the said Court have not, and shall not have, any right or authority to prevent or delay the enrolment of any such Ordinance or Bill, and that the validity thereof doth not, and shall not, depend upon such enrolment.

Power to make Standing Orders.

35. Subject to the provisions of these Our Letters Patent and such Instructions as aforesaid, the Legislative Council may from time to time make Standing Rules and Orders for the regulation of its own proceedings, and until any such Rules and Orders shall be made, and subject to any Rules and Orders to be so made, the Standing Rules and Orders of the Legislative Council now in force shall remain in force and apply, so far as the same are applicable thereto, to the Council established by these Letters Patent.

Governor or Member to be appointed by Governor to preside.

36. The Governor, if present, or, in the absence of the Governor, such Member of the Legislative Council as the Governor shall from time to time appoint, or in default of such

appointment the Member present who stands first in order of precedence, shall preside at the meetings of the Council. The Governor, or any Member for the time being presiding at a meeting of the Council, shall have a casting vote, but not an original vote. President to have a Casting Vote but not an Original Vote.

37. The Legislative Council may require the aid of any Judge of the Colony in the discussion of any law. Council may require the aid of the Judges.

38. All questions arising at meetings of the Legislative Council shall be determined by a majority of the votes of all the Members present, except the Governor or other presiding Member, and in case of an equality of votes the question shall be determined by the casting vote of the Governor or other presiding Member. Provided that the Governor may disallow any vote or resolution of the Council, and any vote or resolution so disallowed shall have no force or effect. Voting. Governor may disallow any Vote or Resolution.

39. Every Member of the Legislative Council may, upon due notice being given, propose any Ordinance or resolution which does not impose any tax or dispose of or charge any part of the public revenue. Initiation of Ordinances, etc., other than Money Votes.

40. No Member of the Legislative Council may propose any Ordinance, vote or resolution, the object or effect of which is to impose any tax or to dispose of or charge any part of the public revenue, unless such Ordinance, vote, or resolution shall have been proposed by the direction or with the express sanction of the Governor. Initiation of Money Votes.

41. The Legislative Council shall not be disqualified for the transaction of business by reason of any vacancy or vacancies among the Members, but no business except that of adjournment shall be transacted unless there shall be present at least six Members besides the Governor or other presiding Member. Legislative Council may transact business notwithstanding vacancies. Quorum.

42. Subject to the provisions of these Letters Patent the Governor and the Legislative Council shall, in the transaction of the business of the Council, and the passing of, assenting to, and enrolment of Bills or Ordinances, conform as nearly as may be to the directions contained in any Instructions under Our Sign Manual and Signet which may herewith or hereafter be addressed to the Governor in that behalf; but no Ordinance enacted by the Governor, with the advice and consent of the Legislative Council, shall be invalid by reason that in the enactment thereof any such Instructions were not duly observed. Governor and Legislative Council to conform to Royal Instructions.

43. The Sessions of the Legislative Council shall be held at such times and places as the Governor shall from time to time by proclamation appoint. There shall be at least one Session of Sessions of Legislative Council.

the Council in every year, and there shall not be an interval of twelve months between the last sitting of one Session and the first sitting of the next following Session. The first Session shall be held within six months from the promulgation of these Letters Patent.

Prorogation and Dissolution of Legislative Council.

44. The Governor may at any time, by proclamation, prorogue or dissolve the Legislative Council.

Duration of Legislative Council.

45. The Governor shall dissolve the Legislative Council at the expiration of three years from the date of the return of the first writs at the last preceding general election, if it shall not have been sooner dissolved.

General Elections.

46. A general election of members of the Legislative Council shall be held at such time not more than six months after the coming into operation of these Our Letters Patent, and unless We shall otherwise direct through a Secretary of State, a general eletcion shall be held at such time within three months after every dissolution of the Legislative Council, as the Governor shall by proclamation appoint.

Grant of Lands.

47. The Governor, in Our name and on Our behalf, may make and execute under the Public Seal of the Colony grants and dispositions of any lands or other immovable property which may be lawfully granted and disposed of by Us within the Colony, provided that every such grant or disposition be made in conformity with some law in force in the Colony, or with some Instructions addressed to the Governor under Our Sign Manual and Signet, or through a Secretary of State, or in conformity with such Regulations as are now in force or may be made by the Governor in that behalf and duly published in the Colony.

Proviso. Land Grants to be made in conformity with the Laws.

Governor authorised to appoint Judges, Commissioners, Justices of the Peace, etc.

48. The Governor may constitute and appoint all such Judges, Commissioners, Justices of the Peace, and other Officers as may lawfully be appointed by Us, all of whom, unless otherwise provided by law, shall hold their offices during Our pleasure.

Dismissal and suspension of Officers.

49. The Governor may, upon sufficient cause to him appearing, dismiss any public officer not appointed by virtue of a Warrant from Us, whose pensionable emoluments do not exceed one hundred pounds sterling a year in the case of an officer appointed to an office in the Colony before the date of the coming into operation of these Our Letters Patent, or two hundred pounds sterling a year in the case of an officer appointed to an office in the Colony on or after that date, provided that in every such case unless the officer has been convicted on a

criminal charge the grounds of intended dismissal are definitely stated in writing, and communicated to the officer in order that he may have full opportunity of exculpating himself, and that the matter is investigated by the Governor with the aid of the head for the time being of the department in which the officer is serving. If such an officer is convicted on a criminal charge, the Governor may call for the records of the trial and form his decision thereon, with the assistance, if necessary, of the officer who tried the case.

The Governor may, upon sufficient cause to him appearing, also suspend from the exercise of his office any person holding any office in the Colony whether appointed by virtue of any Commission or Warrant from Us, or in Our name, or by any other mode of appointment. Such suspension shall continue and have effect only until Our pleasure therein shall be signified to the Governor. If the suspension is confirmed by a Secretary of State, the Governor shall forthwith cause the officer to be so informed, and thereupon his office shall become vacant. In proceeding to any such suspension, the Governor is strictly to observe the directions in that behalf given to him by Our Instructions.

50. When any crime or offence has been committed within the Colony, or for which the offender may be tried therein, the Governor may, as he shall see occasion, in Our name and on Our behalf, grant a pardon to any accomplice in such crime or offence, who shall give such information and evidence as shall lead to the conviction of the principal offender or of any one of such offenders if more than one; and further, may grant to any offender convicted of any crime or offence in any Court, or before any Judge, Justice, or Magistrate, within the Colony, a pardon, either free or subject to lawful conditions, or any remission of the sentence passed on such offender, or any respite of the execution of such sentence, for such period as the Governor thinks fit, and may remit any fines, penalties, or forfeitures which may become due and payable to Us. *Grant of Pardons, etc.* *Remission of Fines.*

51. Whenever the office of Governor is vacant, or if the Governor becomes incapable or is absent from the limits of his Government, or is from any cause prevented from acting in the duties of his office, such person or persons as may be appointed under the Royal Sign Manual and Signet, and, in case there shall be no person or persons within the Colony so appointed, then the Senior Member of the Executive Council then resident *Succession to the Government.*

in the Colony, and capable of discharging the duties of administration, shall, during Our pleasure, administer the Government of the Colony, first taking the oaths hereinbefore directed to be taken by the Governor, and in the manner herein prescribed, which being done, We do hereby authorise, empower and command any such Administrator as aforesaid, to do and execute, during Our pleasure, all things that belong to the office of Governor and Commander-in-Chief, according to the tenour of these Our Letters Patent, and according to Our Instructions as aforesaid, and the laws of the Colony. Provided always, that the Governor during his passage from one Island of the Colony to another, or while visiting or residing at any place within any such Island, or during his absence from the Colony in the execution of any commission or other authority under the Pacific Order in Council, 1893, or any similar Order, shall not for any of the purposes aforesaid, be considered as being absent from the limits of his said Government.

Appointment of Deputies to Governor.

52. During his temporary absence for a short period from the seat of Government, but while he is within the limits of his said Government as aforesaid, or during his absence from the Colony in the execution of any Commission or other authority under the Pacific Order in Council, 1893, or any similar Order, the Governor may, by an instrument under the Public Seal of the Colony, appoint any person or persons to be his Deputy or Deputies within any part or parts of the Colony, and in that capacity to exercise, perform and execute, for and on behalf of the Governor during such absence, but no longer, all such powers and authorities vested in the Governor, as shall in and by such instrument be specified and limited, but no others. Every such Deputy shall conform to and observe all such Instructions as the Governor shall from time to time address to him for his guidance. Provided, nevertheless, that by the appointment of a Deputy or Deputies as aforesaid, the power and authority of the Governor shall not be abridged, altered, or in any way affected, otherwise than We may at any time hereafter think proper to direct.

All persons called upon to be obedient, aiding, and assisting to the Governor.

53. We do hereby require and command all officers, civil and military, and all other the inhabitants of the Colony, to be obedient, aiding, and assisting unto the Governor.

Publication of Letters Patent.

54. We do further direct and enjoin that these Our Letters Patent shall be read and proclaimed at such place or places within the Colony as the Governor shall think fit, and shall come into operation on a day to be fixed by the Governor by proclamation.

55. In these Letters Patent, unless inconsistent with the Interpreta-
context, " the Colony " means the Colony of Fiji, comprising tion.
all islands, rocks, reefs, and foreshores, lying between the
fifteenth and twenty-second degrees of south latitude and
between the one hundred and seventy-seventh degree of west
longitude and the one hundred and seventy-fifth degree of east
longitude from the meridian of Greenwich, and the Island of
Rotuma and its Dependencies, that is to say, all islands, rocks,
reefs, and foreshores lying between the twelfth degree and the
fifteenth degree of south latitude and between the one hundred
and seventy-fifth degree and the one hundred and eightieth
degree of east longitude from the meridian of Greenwich.

" Governor " includes the officer for the time being administering the Government of the Colony.

" Secretary of State " means one of Our Principal Secretaries
of State.

56. And We do hereby reserve to Us, Our heirs and suc- Power
cessors, full power and authority, from time to time, to revoke, reserved
alter, or amend these Our Letters Patent as to Us or them shall to His
Majesty to
seem meet. revoke,
In witness whereof We have caused these Our Letters to be alter or
made Patent. Witness Ourself at Westminster, the Ninth day amend the
of February, in the Nineteenth year of Our Reign. present
Letters
By Warrant under the hands of the Counsellors of State. Patent.

SCHUSTER.

INSTRUCTIONS TO GOVERNOR OF COLONY.

Dated 9th February, 1929.

Signed on behalf of His Majesty the King : [1]— Instructions
passed under
EDWARD P. the Royal
Sign Manual
ALBERT. and Signet to
STANLEY BALDWIN. the Governor
and Com-
INSTRUCTIONS to Our Governor and Commander-in-Chief in mander-in-
and over Our Colony of Fiji, or, in his absence, to the Chief of the
Colony of
Officer for the time being administering the Government of Fiji.
Our said Colony. Preamble.

WHEREAS by certain Letters Patent, bearing even date here- Recites
Letters
with, We have constituted, ordered and declared that there Patent
constituting
[1] Signed by three of the Counsellors of State appointed to act for the the office
King during illness (Part IV., Chap. I.). of Governor.

28 *

shall be a Governor and Commander-in-Chief (hereinafter called the Governor) in and over Our Colony of Fiji as defined in the said Letters Patent (hereinafter called the Colony), And We have thereby authorised the Governor to do and execute in due manner all things that belong to his said office according to the several powers and authorities granted or appointed him by virtue of Our said Letters Patent and of such Commission as may be issued to him under the Royal Sign Manual and Signet, and to such other powers and authorities, being still in force, as may have been heretofore given to any of his predecessors in his said office, and according to such Instructions as may from time to time be given to him, under Our Sign Manual and Signet, or by Our Order in Our Privy Council, or by Us through a Secretary of State, and according to such Laws as are now or shall hereafter be in force in the Colony :

And whereas We are minded to issue these Our Instructions under Our Sign Manual and Signet for the guidance of the Governor or other Officer administering the Government of the Colony :

Revokes Instructions of 31st January, 1914. We do hereby revoke, as from the date of the coming into force of Our above recited Letters Patent of even date, the Instructions under Our Sign Manual and Signet bearing date the Thirty-first day of January 1914, but without prejudice to anything lawfully done thereunder, and We do direct and enjoin and declare Our Will and Pleasure as follows :—

Administration of Oaths. 1. The Governor may, whenever he thinks fit, require any person in the public service of the Colony to take the Oath of Allegiance, in the form prescribed by the Act mentioned in Our said Letters Patent, together with such other Oath or Oaths as may from time to time be prescribed by any laws in force in the Colony. The Governor is to administer such Oaths or cause them to be administered by some public officer of the Colony.

Instructions to be observed by Deputies. 2. During the absence of the Governor from the Colony these Our Instructions, so far as they apply to any matter or thing to be done, or to any power or authority to be exercised by a Deputy acting for the Governor, shall be deemed to be addressed to and shall be observed by such Deputy.

Deputies may correspond direct with Secretary of State in urgent cases. 3. If in any emergency arising in the Colony during the absence of the Governor it is necessary that Instructions should be obtained from Us without delay, the Deputy (if any) acting for the Governor may apply to Us, through a Secretary of State, for instructions in the matter : but every such Deputy shall forthwith transmit to the Governor a copy of every despatch or communication which he has so addressed to Us.

4. The Executive Council of the Colony shall consist of the persons for the time being lawfully discharging the functions of the respective offices of Colonial Secretary, Attorney-General, and Colonial Treasurer of the Colony, who shall be styled *ex officio* Members of the Executive Council, and of such other persons as are now Members of the said Council, or as We may from time to time appoint by any Instructions or Warrant under Our Sign Manual and Signet, or as the Governor, in pursuance of Instructions from Us, through a Secretary of State, may from time to time appoint by an instrument under the Public Seal of the Colony. Constitu-
tion of
Executive
Council.

Whenever upon any special occasion the Governor desires to obtain the advice of any person within the Colony touching Our affairs therein, he may, by an instrument under the Public Seal of the Colony, summon for such special occasion any such person as an Extraordinary Member of the Executive Council. Extra-
ordinary
Members.

5. Every Member, other than an *ex officio* Member, of the Executive Council shall vacate his seat in the Council at the end of five years from the date of the instrument by which or in pursuance of which he is appointed, or at such earlier date or at the end of such shorter period as may be provided by that instrument. Vacation
of Seats.

Provided that if any such Member is provisionally appointed to fill a vacant seat in the Council, and his provisional appointment is immediately followed by his definitive appointment, the aforesaid period of five years shall be reckoned from the date of the instrument provisionally appointing him.

Every such Member shall be eligible to be re-appointed by the Governor by an instrument under the Public Seal of the Colony for a further term or terms, each not exceeding five years, subject to Our approval conveyed through a Secretary of State. Re-appoint-
ment of
Members.

6. The Members of the Executive Council shall have seniority and precedence among themselves as We may specially assign, and, in default thereof, first the *ex officio* Members in the order in which their offices are named in Clause 4 of these Our Instructions, then other Members in the order they now hold, and Members hereafter appointed by Us, or by the Governor in pursuance of Instructions from Us through a Secretary of State, or provisionally appointed by the Governor in pursuance of Precedence.

Clause 8 of these Our Instructions, according to the priority of their respective appointments, or if appointed by the same instrument according to the order in which they are named therein, and finally Extraordinary Members according to the like priority.

Suspension of Members.
7. The Governor may, by an instrument under the Public Seal of the Colony, suspend any person from the exercise of his functions as a Member of the Executive Council. Every such suspension shall be forthwith reported by the Governor to a Secretary of State and shall remain in force, unless and until it shall either be removed by the Governor by an instrument under the said Seal or disallowed by Us through a Secretary of State.

Provisional appointment of Members.
8. If any Member, other than an *ex officio* Member, of the Executive Council shall, by writing under his hand, with the permission of the Governor, resign his seat in the Council, or shall die, or become incapable, or be suspended or removed from his office, or if his office be abolished or amalgamated with another, or if he be absent from the Colony, or be temporarily absent from the Island in which the meetings of the Council are held, or be declared by the Governor, by an instrument under the Public Seal, to be incapable of exercising his functions as a Member of the Council, or shall be acting in an office the holder of which is an *ex officio* Member of the Council, or if his seat in the Council shall become vacant, the Governor may, by an instrument under the Public Seal of the Colony, provisionally appoint any person in the Colony to be temporarily a Member of the said Council in the place of such Member.

Such person shall forthwith cease to be a Member of the Council if his appointment is disallowed by Us, or if the Member in whose place he was appointed shall return, or be released from suspension, or be declared by the Governor, by any such instrument as aforesaid, capable of discharging his functions in the Council, or cease to sit as an *ex officio* Member of the Council, or if his appointment is superseded by the definitive appointment of a Member of the Council.

Provided that when any person shall be lawfully discharging the functions of more than one of the offices the holders of which are *ex officio* Members of the Council the Governor may by an instrument as aforesaid provisionally appoint any person to be a Member of the Council so long as the functions of the said offices shall continue to be discharged by one person as aforesaid.

9. The Governor shall without delay, report to Us, for Our Provisional approval or disallowance, through a Secretary of State, every appointments to be provisional appointment of any person to be a Member of the reported. Executive Council. Every such person shall hold his place in the Council during Our pleasure, and the Governor may, by an instrument under the Public Seal, revoke any such appointment.

10. The Governor shall forthwith communicate these Our Governor Instructions to the Executive Council, and likewise all such to communicate others, from time to time, as We may direct, or as he shall find Instructions convenient for Our service to impart to them. to Executive Council.

11. The Executive Council shall not proceed to the despatch Executive of business unless duly summoned by authority of the Governor, Council not nor unless two Members at the least (exclusive of the Governor to proceed to or of the Member presiding) be present and assisting throughout business the whole of the meetings at which any such business shall be moned despatched. by the Governor's authority.

12. The Governor shall attend and preside at all meetings of Quorum. the Executive Council, unless when prevented by illness or other Governor to grave cause, and in his absence such Member as the Governor attend and may appoint, or in the absence of such Member, or if no such preside. Member be appointed, the senior Member of the Council actually present shall preside.

13. A full and exact Journal or Minute shall be kept of all the Journals or proceedings of the Executive Council ; and at each meeting of Minutes the Council the Minutes of the last preceding meeting shall be Executive confirmed or amended, as the case may require, before proceed-Council to ing to the despatch of any other business. Twice in each year a be kept. full and exact copy of all Minutes for the preceding half year To be transshall be transmitted to Us through a Secretary of State. mitted home twice a year.

14. In the execution of the powers and authorities granted to Governor to the Governor by Us he shall in all cases consult with the Exe-consult cutive Council, excepting only in cases which are of such a Council nature that, in his judgment, Our service would sustain material except in prejudice by consulting the Council thereupon, or when the specified matters to be decided are too unimportant to require their advice, or too urgent to admit of their advice being given by the time within which it may be necessary for him to act in respect of any such matters. In all such urgent cases he shall, within Proviso : the earliest practicable period, communicate to the Executive Urgent Council the measures which he may so have adopted, with the cases. reasons thereof.

Governor alone entitled to submit questions.

15. The Governor shall alone be entitled to submit questions to the Executive Council for their advice or decision ; but if he decline to submit any question to the Council when requested in writing by any Member so to do, it shall be competent to such Member to require that there be recorded upon the Minutes his written application, together with the answer returned by the Governor to the same.

Governor may act in opposition to Executive Council. Reporting the grounds for so doing. Members may require to be recorded on Minutes their adverse opinions. Suspension of Officers.

16. The Governor may act in opposition to the advice given to him by the Members of the Executive Council, if he shall in any case deem it right to do so ; but in any such case he shall fully report the matter to Us, by the first convenient opportunity, with the grounds and reasons of his action. In every such case it shall be competent to any Member of the Council to require that there be recorded at length on the Minutes the grounds of any advice or opinion he may give upon the question.

17. Before suspending from the exercise of his office any public Officer, whose annual pensionable emoluments exceed £100 sterling in the case of an Officer appointed to an office in the Colony before the date of the coming into operation of Our above recited Letters Patent bearing even date herewith, or £200 sterling in the case of an Officer appointed to an office in the Colony on or after such date, the Governor shall signify to such Officer, by a statement in writing, the grounds of the intended suspension, and shall call upon him to state in writing the grounds upon which he desires to exculpate himself ; and if the Officer does not furnish such statement within the time fixed by the Governor, or fails to exculpate himself to the satisfaction of the Governor, the Governor shall appoint a Committee of the Executive Council to investigate the charges made and to make a full report to the Executive Council. The Governor shall forthwith cause such report to be considered by the Council, and shall cause to be recorded on the Minutes whether the Council or the majority thereof does or does not assent to the suspension ; and if the Governor thereupon proceed to such suspension he shall transmit the report of the Committee and the evidence taken by it, together with the Minutes of the proceedings of the Council, to Us through a Secretary of State, at the earliest opportunity. But if in any case the interests of Our service shall appear to the Governor to demand that a person shall cease to exercise the powers and functions of his office instantly, or before there shall be time to take the proceedings hereinbefore directed, he shall then interdict such person from the exercise of the powers and functions of his office.

18. In the making of Ordinances within the Colony the Governor and Legislative Council shall observe, as far as practicable, the following Rules :— Rules and Regulations under which Laws are to be enacted.

(1) All Ordinances shall be distinguished by titles, and shall be divided into successive clauses or paragraphs consecutively numbered, and to every such clause there shall be annexed in the margin a short summary of its contents. The Ordinances of each year shall be distinguished by consecutive numbers, commencing in each year with the number one. Ordinances to be numbered and methodically arranged.

Except in the case of Bills reserved for the signification of Our pleasure, all Ordinances passed by the Legislative Council in any one year shall, if assented to by the Governor, be assented to by him in that year, and shall be dated as of the day on which the assent of the Governor is given, and shall be numbered as of the year in which they are passed. Ordinances not so assented to by the Governor, but reserved by him for the signification of Our pleasure shall be dated as of the day and numbered as of the year on and in which they are brought into operation.

(2) Each different matter shall be provided for by a different Ordinance without intermixing in one and the same Ordinance such things as have no proper relation to each other ; and no clause is to be inserted in or annexed to any Ordinance which shall be foreign to what the title of such Ordinance imports, and no perpetual clause shall be part of any temporary Ordinance. Different subjects not to be mixed in the same Ordinance. No clause to be introduced foreign to what the title of the Ordinance imports. Temporary Ordinances.

19. The Governor shall not (except in the cases hereunder mentioned) assent in Our name to any Bill of any of the following classes :— Description of Bills not to be assented to.

(1) Any Bill for the divorce of persons joined together in holy Matrimony ;

(2) Any Bill whereby any grant of land or money, or other donation or gratuity, may be made to himself ;

(3) Any Bill affecting the Currency of the Colony, or relating to the issue of Bank Notes ;

(4) Any Bill establishing any Banking Association, or amending or altering the constitution, powers, or privileges of any Banking Association ;

(5) Any Bill imposing differential duties ;

(6) Any Bill, the provisions of which shall appear inconsistent with obligations imposed upon Us by Treaty ;

(7) Any Bill interfering with the discipline or control of Our forces by sea, land or air ;

(8) Any Bill of an extraordinary nature and importance, whereby Our prerogative or the rights and property of Our subjects not residing in the Colony, or the trade and shipping of Our dominions, may be prejudiced ;

(9) Any Bill whereby persons not of European birth or descent may be subjected or made liable to any disabilities or restrictions to which persons of European birth or descent are not also subjected or made liable ;

(10) Any Bill containing provisions to which Our assent has been once refused, or which have been disallowed by Us ;

Proviso in cases of emergency for immediate operation of a Bill.

unless the Governor shall previously have obtained Our Instructions upon such Bill through a Secretary of State, or unless such Bill shall contain a clause suspending the operation of such Bill until the signification in the Colony of Our pleasure thereupon, or unless the Governor shall have satisfied himself that an urgent necessity exists requiring that such Bill be brought into immediate operation, in which case he is authorised to assent in Our name to such Bill unless the same shall be inconsistent with any obligations imposed on Us by Treaty. But he is to transmit to Us by the earliest opportunity the Bill so assented to, together with his reasons for assenting thereto.

Private Bills.

20. Every Bill intended to affect or benefit some particular person, association, or corporate body shall contain a section saving the rights of Us, Our heirs and successors, all bodies, politic and corporate, and all others, except such as are mentioned in the Bill, and those claiming by, from, or under them. No such Bill, not being a Government measure, shall be introduced into the Legislative Council until due notice has been given by three successive publications of the Bill in the *Fiji Royal Gazette ;* and the Governor shall not assent thereto in Our name unless it has been so published. A certificate under the hand of the Governor shall be transmitted with the Bill signifying that such publication has been made.

21. When any Ordinance shall have been passed, or when any Bill shall have been reserved for the signification of Our pleasure, the Governor shall forthwith lay it before Us for Our approval, disallowance, or other direction thereupon, and shall transmit to Us through a Secretary of State a transcript in duplicate of the same, together with a marginal abstract thereof, duly authenticated under the Public Seal of the Colony, and by his own signature. Such transcript shall be accompanied by such explanatory observations as may be required to exhibit the reasons and occasion for passing such Ordinance or Bill. *Ordinances to be sent home duly authenticated.*

22. In the month of January, or within the earliest practicable period after the commencement of each year, the Governor shall cause a complete collection to be published, for general information, of all Ordinances enacted during the preceding year. *Collection of Ordinances to be published every year.*

23. Minutes shall be regularly kept of all the proceedings of the Legislative Council, and at each meeting of the said Council the Minutes of the last preceding meeting shall be confirmed or amended, as the case may require, before proceeding to the despatch of any other business. The Governor shall transmit to Us through a Secretary of State, as soon as possible after every meeting, a full and exact copy of the Minutes thereof. *Minutes of proceedings of Legislative Council to be kept and sent home after every meeting.*

24. Before disposing of any vacant or waste lands to Us belonging, the Governor shall cause the same to be surveyed, and such reservations to be made thereout as he may think necessary for roads or other public purposes. The Governor shall not, directly or indirectly, purchase for himself any of such lands without Our special permission given through a Secretary of State. *Surveys and reservations to be made before waste lands are disposed of. Governor not to purchase lands.*

25. All Commissions to be granted by the Governor to any person for exercising any office or employment shall, unless otherwise provided by law, be granted during pleasure only ; and whenever the Governor shall appoint to any vacant office or employment, the initial emoluments of which exceed £200 per annum, any person not by Us specially directed to be appointed thereto, he shall, at the same time, expressly apprise such person that such appointment is to be considered only as temporary and provisional until Our allowance or disallowance thereof be signified. *Appointments to be provisional and during pleasure.*

26. Whenever any offender shall have been condemned to suffer death by the sentence of any Court in the Colony, the Governor shall call upon the Judge who presided at the trial to make to him a written report of the case of such offender, and *Regulation of power of Pardon in Capital Cases.*

Judge's Report to be laid before the Executive Council. Governor to take the advice of the Executive Council in such cases. May exercise his own judgment. Entering his reasons on the Council Minutes.

shall cause such report to be taken into consideration at the first meeting of the Executive Council which may be conveniently held thereafter, and he may cause the said Judge to be specially summoned to attend at such meeting and to produce his notes thereat. The Governor shall not pardon or reprieve any such offender unless it shall appear to him expedient so to do, upon receiving the advice of the Executive Council thereon ; but in all such cases he is to decide either to extend or to withhold a pardon or reprieve, according to his own deliberate judgment, whether the Members of the Executive Council concur therein or otherwise ; entering, nevertheless, on the Minutes of the Executive Council a Minute of his reasons at length, in case he should decide any such question in opposition to the judgment of the majority of the Members thereof.

Governor to promote Religion and Education.

27. The Governor is, to the utmost of his power, to promote religion and education among the native inhabitants of the Colony ; and he is especially to take care to protect them in their persons and in the free enjoyment of their possessions, and by all lawful means to prevent and restrain all violence and injustice which may in any manner be practised or attempted against them ; and he is to adopt and support such measures as may appear to him conducive to their civilisation and as tend to the suppression of barbarous customs among such natives.

Blue Book.

28. The Governor shall punctually forward to Us from year to year, through a Secretary of State, the annual book of returns, commonly called the Blue Book, relating to the Revenue and Expenditure, Defence, Public Works, Legislation, Civil Establishments, Pensions, Population, Schools, Course of Exchange, Imports and Exports, Agricultural Produce, Manufactures, and other matter in the said Blue Book more particularly specified, with reference to the state and condition of the Colony.

Governor's absence.

29. Except during his passage to or from any Island included in his Government, or for some urgent reason which he shall without delay communicate to Us, the Governor shall not quit the Colony without having first obtained leave from Us for so doing under Our Sign Manual and Signet, or through a Secretary of State, unless for the purpose of visiting the Governor-General of the Commonwealth of Australia, the Governor-General of the Dominion of New Zealand, or the Governor of any Australian State, for periods not exceeding six weeks at any one time, nor exceeding in the aggregate one month for every year of his service in the Colony.

If, nevertheless, We appoint the Governor to be Our High Proviso. Commissioner of the Western Pacific, or if the said High May be absent Commissioner appoint him to any office under the Pacific Order without in Council, 1893, or any similar Order, the Governor may quit leave if the Colony without leave from Us, for the purpose of discharging High the duties of such appointment. Commis-

30. In these Our Instructions, unless inconsistent with the sioner, etc. context, the term " the Governor " shall include every person " Governor " for the time being administering the Government of the Colony, and " Secre- and the term " Secretary of State " means one of Our Principal tary of State " Secretaries of State. explained.

Given at Our Court at Saint James's this Ninth day of February, 1929, in the Nineteenth Year of Our Reign.

COMMISSION APPOINTING COLONIAL GOVERNOR.

Dated 28th June, 1929.   GEORGE R.I.

Commission passed under the Royal Sign Manual and Signet, appointing Sir Arthur George Murchison

George the Fifth, by the Grace of God of Great Britain, Ireland Fletcher, Kt., and the British Dominions beyond the Seas King, Defender C.M.G., of the Faith, Emperor of India : To Our Trusty and Well- C.B.E., to be beloved Sir Arthur George Murchison Fletcher, Knight, Governor Companion of Our Most Distinguished Order of Saint and Com- Michael and Saint George, Commander of Our Most mander-in- Excellent Order of the British Empire, Greeting. Chief of the Colony in

WE do, by this Our Commission under Our Sign Manual and Fiji. Signet, appoint you, the said Sir Arthur George Murchison Appoint- Fletcher, to be, during Our pleasure, Our Governor and A. G. M. Commander-in-Chief in and over Our Colony of Fiji, with all Fletcher, Kt., the powers, rights, privileges and advantages to the said Office C.M.G., belonging or appertaining. C.B.E., to be Governor.

II. And We do hereby authorise, empower, and command you to exercise and perform all and singular the powers and Powers, etc., directions contained in any Letters Patent for the time being in under force relating to Our said Colony, according to such Orders and Patent. Instructions as the Governor and Commander-in-Chief for the Instructions. time being of Our said Colony hath already received, or as you may hereafter receive from Us.

III. And further We do hereby appoint that, so soon as you Commission shall have taken the prescribed Oaths and have entered upon January, the duties of your Office, this Our present Commission shall 1925, super- seded.

supersede Our Commission under Our Sign Manual and Signet bearing date the Fifteenth day of January, 1925, appointing Our Trusty and Well-beloved Sir Eyre Hutson, Knight Commander of Our Most Distinguished Order of Saint Michael and Saint George, to be Our Governor and Commander-in-Chief in and over Our Colony of Fiji.

Officers, etc., to obey Governor. IV. And We do hereby command all and singular Our Officers, Ministers, and loving subjects in Our said Colony, and all others whom it may concern, to take due notice hereof and to give their ready obedience accordingly.

Given at Our Court at Saint James's, this Twenty-eighth day of June, 1929, in the Twentieth Year of our Reign.

By His Majesty's Command,

PASSFIELD.

GENERAL INDEX.

Note.—Where two or more references are given to the same subject, the principal reference (if any) is shown in **thicker type**.

A

29 *

M

30 *

PRINTED IN GREAT BRITAIN BY THE UNIVERSITY PRESS, ABERDEEN